The publisher gratefully acknowledges the generous support of the Sue Tsao Endowment Fund in Chinese Studies of the University of California Press Foundation.

The Missionary's Curse and Other
Tales from a Chinese Catholic Village

ASIA: LOCAL STUDIES/GLOBAL THEMES

Jeffrey N. Wasserstrom, Kären Wigen, and Hue-Tam Ho Tai, Editors

The Missionary's Curse and Other Tales from a Chinese Catholic Village

Henrietta Harrison

UNIVERSITY OF CALIFORNIA PRESS

Berkeley · Los Angeles · London

University of California Press, one of the most
distinguished university presses in the United States,
enriches lives around the world by advancing scholarship
in the humanities, social sciences, and natural sciences.
Its activities are supported by the UC Press Foundation
and by philanthropic contributions from individuals and
institutions. For more information, visit www.ucpress.
edu.

University of California Press
Berkeley and Los Angeles, California

University of California Press, Ltd.
London, England

Library of Congress Cataloging-in-Publication Data

Harrison, Henrietta.
    The missionary's curse and other tales from a Chinese
Catholic village / Henrietta Harrison.
        pages cm. — (Asia: local studies, global themes; 26)
    Includes bibliographical references and index.
    ISBN 978-0-520-27311-5 (cloth : alk. paper)—
    ISBN 978-0-520-27312-2 (pbk. : alk. paper)
    1. Catholic Church—China—Shanxi Sheng—
History.   2. Shanxi Sheng (China)—Religious life
and customs.   3. Shanxi Sheng (China)—
Folklore.   I. Title
    BX1666.S53H37 2013
    282'.5117—dc23

                                        2012051058

Manufactured in the United States of America

22 21 20 19 18 17 16 15 14 13
10 9 8 7 6 5 4 3 2 1

In keeping with a commitment to support
environmentally responsible and sustainable printing
practices, UC Press has printed this book on 50-pound
Enterprise, a 30% post-consumer-waste, recycled,
deinked fiber that is processed chlorine-free. It is
acid-free and meets all ANSI/NISO (Z 39.48) requirements.

World is crazier and more of it than we think,
Incorrigibly plural.

Louis MacNeice, "Snow"

Contents

Illustrations

Acknowledgments

Because this book covers three hundred years of history, has taken ten years to research and write, moves between China and Europe, and uses sources in five languages, I have needed a lot of help in writing it. I am deeply indebted to many people though I fear that, for the same reasons, there are probably still many mistakes.

For help with the research I would especially like to thank Augustine Lee for his support over the years and especially for making available to me the early twentieth-century archives of Taiyuan diocese. Liu Anrong not only accompanied me during interviews but also gave me her own interview notes tracing the origins of every family in Cave Gully. Liza Wang was an enthusiastic companion and assistant during other interviews. Roger Thompson, Alessandro dell'Orto, Richard Madsen, David Faure, and Feng Xiaocai all kindly gave me copies of documents I would not otherwise have found.

Professor Xing Long and the staff of the Shanxi University Social History Institute gave me access to their extraordinary collection of local history materials from the post-1949 period. I am also grateful to staff of the archives of the Propaganda Fide, the Franciscan General Curia, the Franciscan Province of Bologna, the Propagation de la Foi in Lyon, the Roman Jesuit Archives, and especially to Leonello Malvezzi of the Pontificia Opera dell'Infanzia Missionaria in Rome for his hospitality and kindness.

Early versions of chapters were presented as papers at the Fairbank Center at Harvard University, at Princeton University, and at the Columbia University Seminar on Modern China; I received many useful comments at all these events. I am grateful to Alessandro dell'Orto for arranging for me to give a paper at the Pontifical Urbaniana University in Rome where the audience's enthusiasm was deeply moving—the help I received as a result has made this a far deeper and richer book. I benefited from discussions with many students at Harvard, but especially Melissa Inouye whose ideas about the history of True Jesus church greatly influenced my thinking. Elizabeth McGuire kindly read the whole draft of the book at a very early stage. I am also extremely grateful to all those who took part in a workshop on the manuscript at Harvard University in February 2011, especially Michael Szonyi, Nicolas Standaert, Eugenio Menegon, Lily Tsai, James Robson, Robert Weller, Mark Elliott, and Bonaventure Bai. Their comments, suggestions, and friendly discussion have immensely improved the final book.

The book has required me to translate from a number of languages in which I am by no means confident. I am grateful to Catherine Keen for help with the Italian (and for listening with interest to such a lot of conversation on Shanxi Catholicism over many years) and to Muriel Hall for help with the Latin. Librarians, especially at the Institute for Advanced Study at Princeton and the Harvard-Yenching Library, have been wonderfully helpful. Scott Walker of Widener Library created the maps. I also received very helpful research assistance: Luca Cottini transcribed some troublesome Italian texts, and Lucy McCormac and Ruyi Lu created the graphs.

Funding for the project has come from the Radcliffe Institute for Advanced Study, Harvard University, the British Academy, the Chiang Ching-kuo Foundation, and the Universities' China Committee (whose funds originated in the Boxer Indemnity). I am grateful to all these organizations and especially to the donors and taxpayers who have contributed to support them.

I am also grateful to successive parish priests of Cave Gully for welcoming me into the community and to all those whom I interviewed, both in Cave Gully and elsewhere. This book tells a story that is of great importance to the Catholics of central Shanxi and it is dedicated to them. Never before have I written history that mattered so much to anyone. The experience has been exhilarating and inspiring, but actually publishing the results is correspondingly nerve-wracking. I doubt the many Shanxi Catholics who have helped me will always agree with my conclusions, but they have been astonishingly open-minded so I hope that they will be able to accept this as a possible version of their history. I am more afraid that there are mistakes in the details. I have tried very hard to get it right, but there is still much I do not know. Now I can do no more than apologize in advance, while expressing my heartfelt thanks for all I have learned.

A Note on Terminology
and Names

Both Chinese history and the history of the Catholic church are vast fields and what may be basic general knowledge to one set of experts is often completely unknown to others. In the hope of making this book accessible to all I have tried to avoid using too much technical vocabulary, using the terms bishop, diocese, monk, monastery, nun, and evangelist in their most general sense. I have done this even though until 1946 Shanxi was a vicariate apostolic rather than a diocese, Franciscan religious men are called friars and their building a friary, the women missionaries mentioned in the story were religious sisters of the Franciscan Missionaries of Mary, and people employed to spread the gospel are called catechists in the primary sources. With the same aim I have translated the Chinese names of the villages into English, since these names are often descriptive and it matters to my argument that some of these places were in the fertile, well-watered plains (Nine Springs, Cold Springs Road) and others were up in the hills (Cave Gully, Red Gully). Interested readers can find the original Chinese names of the villages in the glossary along with the Chinese names of the missionaries and priests. The glossary also includes the various Western transcriptions used for these Chinese names. Chinese versions of book titles translated in the text are in the relevant notes. Finally, I have omitted from the main text the names of many Chinese Christians, missionaries, and others who enter the pages of this narrative but are not important to the particular story I am telling here. For those who are interested all the names can be found in the notes.

Introduction

The village streets are dry and rutted, flanked by high walls stained yellow by the dust. The sky too is a grayish yellow with the pollution brought by coal mining, steel mills, and the rapid industrial development of the surrounding area. A painted notice running along one wall calls on people to observe the one-child policy. Here and there the gates of courtyards are ajar. The passerby can catch glimpses of shady trees, women preparing vegetables, old people chatting, and children playing. On a summer afternoon Cave Gully is much like any other north China village, but it is also different. An auspicious phrase written in tiles over a doorway reminds people to "Believe in the Lord and Honor the Commandments." Up the street is a church, where women are bustling about preparing for the next group of tour buses bringing pilgrims to the magnificent new shrine of Our Lady of the Seven Sorrows. For the people here are Catholics and as such they are part of a history that goes far beyond north China.

The villagers remember the history of their community in stories. Everyone in the village seems to know some of these, but few could tell them as well as an old man who until his death a few years ago was the orphanage gatekeeper. His stories spanned the village's history from the conversion of the first impoverished settlers three hundred years ago, to the Cultural Revolution when his brother came under attack and tried to commit suicide by jumping into the well in the church courtyard. The old man tells of how, as his brother jumped in, he was shouting, "Holy

Mother of God, I don't want to die, I just can't bear it, let me get out!"
The Virgin Mary saved him and he was able to climb out and run off.
But most of the village's stories are not set in any particular historical
time; instead they are just-so stories of how things came to be. The story
of the missionary who cursed the village with seven years of bad weather
explains the origins of the shrine to Our Lady of the Seven Sorrows,
built to remove the curse. Another story relates to why the Chinese
priests are buried at the feet of the missionaries in the village cemetery.
It tells of a Chinese priest who could not accept the missionaries' ill
treatment of the Chinese clergy and ran away to Rome to complain to
the pope. There he knelt in the pope's way with his petition pasted to
his hat, so that the pope saw and the priest was eventually able to come
back to the village justified. This tale takes a classic Chinese form in
which a petitioner appeals to a just official or even the emperor, but is
set in a world where Rome seems as close as Beijing.

And it is in Rome that the early history of the village is recorded. In the
archives of the Congregation for the Evangelization of the Peoples, bound
together into huge white leather volumes, are letters sent to Rome by
missionaries and priests over hundreds of years. Reading through from
the seventeenth century, the world that gave rise to these stories comes to
life: the diligent and kindly Chinese priest who never spoke ill of anyone
and who, in 1781, was the first to record a visit to the Catholics of Cave
Gully; the enthusiastic Franciscan who infuriated his congregation by
bringing two live sheep into church at Christmas; the Chinese priest who
got into trouble for betting a girl a considerable sum of money that she
would not dare take a look at her future husband; the missionary who
was driven mad by his experiences, chained up by the bishop, and wrote
desperate and largely illegible pleas for help with a Chinese writing brush
on tiny scraps of paper. And then in the files for 1873 there are four long
letters, pages and pages of neatly written Latin, from a priest who signed
his name Josephus Van and had come to Rome to complain about the
European missionaries' ill treatment of the Chinese priests.[1]

To write the history of one village over more than three hundred years
is unusual: historians mostly write about larger spaces or shorter time
periods.[2] Shifting away from this pattern opens up the possibility of
new ways of seeing what is happening. Imagine yourself looking at a
series of maps of the same place, each using a different scale. They all
show you the same thing, but changing the scale alters the context and

therefore the meaning. For historians too, choices about scale, both geographical and temporal, greatly affect what we see. Shifting the scale can change the stories we tell in illuminating ways. In this case, it helps us to see Cave Gully as part of global and local narratives as well as the more dominant national story of Chinese history. Each of these narratives then affects the way in which we interpret the others.[3]

In 1907, Léon Joly, a French priest who never left Europe, published a history of missions to Asia that asked the question that lies beneath almost all later studies of Christianity in China: why after hundreds of years of missions have so few Chinese converted to Christianity? Why has the Christian mission in China failed? Joly's answer was simple: the mission has failed because Christianity is seen as a foreign religion. The solution he proposed was a Catholic church run by the Chinese themselves and not by European missionaries. Joly's work provoked a storm of protest. Indeed, he wrote a second book subtitled *Sufferings of an Old Canon* in which he defends himself against attacks by the missionaries and their supporters. He died shortly afterwards, but his ideas proved to be hugely influential.[4] He articulated what was a widespread feeling of dissatisfaction with the missions, and in 1926 the Vatican began to appoint Chinese bishops for the first time since the seventeenth century. One of these early bishops, Chen Guodi, had been a Franciscan novice in Cave Gully and we will follow his story later in this book. Despite this symbolic gesture, real power remained with the missionaries until the 1950s when the Chinese Communist government took matters into its own hands, expelled the missionaries, and imposed an independent Chinese Catholic church.

Joly's great question and his answer have remained at the heart of much scholarship, which sees the story of Christianity in China as one of failure and argues over the extent to which this was due to the incompatibility of Christianity with Chinese culture or to its association with Western imperialism. These debates over the compatibility of Chinese and Western culture and the impact of Western power are also part of broader questions about how we understand modern China's relations with the West.[5] At the center of those relations is the question of how Chinese people have responded to and adapted ideas, practices, and institutions that originate in the West. From this point of view Christianity is an ideology that can be seen alongside science, democracy, communism, and contemporary ideologies of global capitalism, while the Catholic church can be compared to institutions as varied as the Comintern and the Red Cross.

So how does shifting the scale change how we understand this history? Firstly, focusing on a Chinese village that has a long history of Christianity reminds us that in some places Christianity has become part of Chinese culture. China did not convert to Christianity as the ancient Roman Empire did, which was Joly's standard for comparison, but there were places where people became Christian and the communities they built have lasted for many generations. Understanding this forces us to question the idea that Christianity was incompatible with Chinese religious culture. In recent years many scholars of religion have moved away from studying religions as philosophical and doctrinal systems, and have instead focused on how religions are experienced in everyday practice.[6] If we think about Chinese religion and Christianity in this way we begin to see firstly that each of these great traditions contains an immense variety of different practices, beliefs, and ideas, and secondly that the two traditions sometimes overlap. The Chinese religious scene included practices and religious experts drawn from Confucianism, Buddhism, Daoism, and the huge variety of temples, cults, and local religious figures usually known as Chinese folk religion. Each of these traditions changed over time, and they also varied between north and south China, between educated elites and impoverished peasants, and between different sectarian groups. The practice of Christianity too varies widely. Most of the missionaries who came to Cave Gully were Italian Franciscans, and if we look at everyday religious practice in the village we see similarities between the religious culture of rural north China and that of southern Italy: lists of commandments, regular fasting, group chanting of litanies and rosaries, village pilgrimages to pray for rain, expensive and elaborate rituals to help a departed parent's soul reach the final paradise, and visionary trances which give ordinary people special knowledge of the divine. These practices may not sound Christian to Protestants, or even to most Catholics today, but they would have been deeply familiar to southern Italian Catholics a few generations ago.

Most of the scholars who have looked at Christian practices and local religious culture in China have assumed that the two systems were originally different. They have been interested in the similarities mainly as a way of examining the process known as acculturation, through which as a foreign religion is absorbed into a culture it gradually adopts elements of that culture.[7] This idea is pervasive in studies of global Christianity. It is used to counter the argument that Christianity is a foreign religion alien to local culture, and to claim instead that

Christianity may become an authentic local religion. Since the 1970s acculturation has also been the official position of the Catholic church, which lays down that Christianity ought to be expressed through local culture and should not require those who convert to adopt foreign cultural customs.[8] Thus while Cave Gully's parish church was built in the Italian Romanesque style, the new shrine to Our Lady of the Seven Sorrows is in an ancient Chinese style with carved wooden dragons flanking the cross on the golden-tiled roof of the main hall. This book makes the opposite argument that there is significant overlap between Christianity and Chinese religious culture, and that in this area the differences between Catholic practice and local folk religion have actually increased over the centuries.

Scholars of China who are interested in acculturation have mainly studied the missions of the seventeenth and eighteenth centuries. The earliest records of Christian activity in China actually date back to the seventh century, but these communities died out, so our story begins with the arrival of the Jesuit Matteo Ricci in 1582. As in Europe, where they ran elite schools, the Jesuits in China used their learning to build connections with members of the elite. They went on to work at the Ming and later the Qing court as astronomers, teachers, and painters. Theologically they were influenced by the idea that all peoples have a natural understanding of God, so when they spoke of God they used the word *tian,* which means "heaven" in the sense of the sky above, but also refers to one of the most ancient high deities of the Chinese pantheon. They also developed a policy of presenting Christianity in ways that were acceptable to China's Confucian elite. So, for example, they emphasized the commandment to honor one's parents, which fitted closely with the high value Chinese society placed on filial piety. This then allowed Christians to take part in funerals, rituals honoring their ancestors, and other Confucian rituals. These methods encouraged the absorption of Christianity into Chinese culture, but were extremely controversial in Europe. In the disputes that followed, Rome renounced the policy, and in China the Yongzheng emperor banned Christianity altogether. The Jesuit order was under attack from all sides during this period, and was soon abolished altogether. It was later revived and the emperor's ban was largely ineffective, but in the meantime other missionaries who opposed the Jesuit policies had taken over the China mission. Scholars have traditionally seen this as the end of an early period of gradual acculturation before the new era that arrived with Western imperialism in the mid-nineteenth century.[9]

However, when we look at religious practice in Cave Gully over the centuries we begin to see that other explanations are possible. Cave Gully was established as a Catholic village during the period of the Jesuit missions and the villagers' religious practices at that time were indeed very close to those of the surrounding culture. There was no sudden change when the Jesuits left or indeed with the later arrival of a new generation of missionaries backed by Western imperial power. Instead each change making local practice more similar to Catholic practice elsewhere in the world was a matter of negotiation between ordinary Catholics, Chinese priests, the Franciscan missionaries, and the church hierarchy. Although some of the players have changed, this process continues today. Differences between Catholic Christianity and Chinese local religion have been created over the centuries as local Catholicism has gradually been bound into global networks and institutions.

This brings us to the second way in which changing the scale changes our understanding of the history of Christianity in China: it makes us rethink how Chinese Christians related to Western missionaries during the period of high imperialism in China, from the Opium War in 1838 until the Communist revolution in 1949. In recent years many scholars have attempted to write histories of global Christianity that play down the role of missionaries and emphasize the local growth of the religion instead.[10] Missionaries were often ineffective as evangelists, but as Westerners they had a huge impact on how the church was perceived. After 1840 Britain and France forced the Qing dynasty to legalize Christianity and remove constraints on missionary activity. Missionaries arrived in large numbers, and now included Protestants as well as Catholics. As citizens of the great powers, they were essentially outside the law and when disputes arose they could appeal to government representatives in Beijing. In these circumstances, while their motivations remained similar to those of the missionaries of earlier periods whose safety and survival had depended totally on good relations with local Christians, their behavior was often dramatically different. Meanwhile Western diplomatic and military power continued to grow, and in 1900 violence broke out: groups known as Boxers formed around temples across North China, attacked foreigners, and massacred large numbers of Chinese Christians. They were encouraged by support from the Qing court, which incorporated them into militias and declared war on the foreign powers.

The Boxer Uprising was the background for Joly's question about the failure of Christian missions in China, and its causes have remained a major topic of historical debate.[11] There is general agreement that the Qing court's support for the Boxers was important, but beyond this scholars disagree as to why ordinary people in the north China country- side felt such fear and hatred for the Christians who lived among them. There are two major lines of explanation, though they are often found intertwined. The first is that the hostility was the result of cultural dif- ferences between Christianity and the folk religion of north China, but in that case why did it not occur when Christianity was first introduced in the seventeenth and eighteenth centuries? Looking at Christian prac- tice rather than doctrine undermines the idea of cultural differences, while taking a long view makes it obvious that much of the most violent fighting occurred in places like Cave Gully where Catholicism had existed for centuries and there was very little growth. The second line of explanation is that ordinary people attacked the missionaries and Chinese Christians because both were associated with the expansion of foreign power in China. Accusations that missionaries were complicit in Western imperialism were then and have remained politically powerful in China. These debates are highly charged and since they involve the missionaries' motives as well as their behavior any agreement is unlikely.[12] However, looking at Cave Gully we see that Chinese Catholics actively resisted the growth of missionary power.

Imperialism matters in this story, but it is not inherent in the mission- ary enterprise, nor did Chinese Catholics necessarily benefit from the growth of missionary power. Before the Opium Wars missionaries were dependent on the local Catholics for support. Then from the 1840s onwards the disparities of political power between China and Europe gradually gave the missionaries power over Chinese priests and villag- ers. In Cave Gully the Italian missionaries controlled the money from Europe and later the money that the foreign powers extorted from the Qing government as an indemnity for the Boxer Uprising. The mission- aries used this money to build institutions through which they main- tained their own authority. The village had an orphanage, seminary, and monastery, and it was through these institutions that Chinese came into contact with the mission, when they handed their children over to the orphanage, studied in the seminary, or disputed the water rights of the monastery vineyard. Non-Catholics driven by poverty to abandon their children to the orphanage often disliked and feared the missionar- ies' power, but so did many Catholics who rented land or borrowed money from the mission. Chinese priests resented their exclusion from positions of authority. In the story of the priest who ran away to Rome to appeal to the pope, the villagers remind their children that they belong to a great global institution, but they also remember a history of resistance to foreign missionary control.

If we now return to Joly's question we may be puzzled, since it appears that neither cultural incompatibility nor complicity in Western imperialism has ever been an essential characteristic of Christianity in China. But then again, perhaps the question was wrong: perhaps Christianity did not fail. Certainly, looking beyond the Communist revolution of 1949, we see that a key question concerning scholars of religion in China today is why Christianity has grown so spectacularly since the 1980s. This growth far exceeds any achievements of the missionaries. Suggestions for its causes range from admiration for powerful Western countries to government policy that discriminates against Chinese folk religion.[13] The history of Cave Gully suggests that we should also consider Christianity's long history in the area and the role of the suppression of religious practice during the 1960s in transforming the church into a dynamic and expansive institution. The imprisonment of priests and a campaign to compel Catholics to leave the church created an atmosphere of impending catastrophe in which ordinary villagers took responsibility for resistance and found strength in visions, intimations of supernatural power, and a certainty of divine providence. It was these people who went out as evangelists and drove the conversions of the 1980s and 1990s. As in the Protestant churches, the lay evangelists who drew authority from their experiences of suffering under the state are now growing old and the institutional church is increasing its authority so that it seems likely that the period of most rapid conversion is over, though growth continues.[14] A recent government survey suggests that there are around twenty-nine million Christians in China today (twenty-three million Protestants and six million Catholics), which is about 2 percent of the population.[15] By Joly's standards of comparison with the conversion of the Roman Empire the Christian mission to China has still failed, but in absolute terms the number of Christians is both large and growing.

Looking at the history of Christianity in China from the point of view of Cave Gully, we might want to ask a different question, not "Has Christianity become a Chinese religion?" but "How have Chinese related to Christianity as a world religion?" By changing the perspective, the micro-historical approach allows us to look beyond imperialism and see both the many different ways in which the grand narratives of history have interacted with local experience and the connections that have linked this inland Chinese village to the wider world. The early converts were traders who brought the products of Siberia and Central Asia to Western merchants on China's southern coast. Later, Italian unification shaped the behavior of both missionaries and Chinese priests: the Chinese priest most active in resisting nineteenth-century missionary control had personally experienced the revolutions of 1848 in Naples, while the missionaries who supported the Japanese invasion during World War II were affected by the growth of Italian Fascism in Bologna. Today, global mass communications link ordinary Catholics into transnational Catholic communities, and the rhetoric of anti-imperialism has little relevance to their lives. At the local level we see the different histories of Catholics living on the plains and in the hills: in the villages of the Fen River valley the Catholics were descended from merchants and lived in mixed communities, whereas in the hill villages founded on abandoned land by impoverished migrants Catholicism was often essential to full membership in the village. It suited both missionaries and Chinese officials to describe Catholicism as a religion of the poor and dispossessed, but the provincial capital and the plains villages maintained an elite Catholic culture over the centuries. Even after the collapse of Shanxi's economy in the early twentieth century and the Communist takeover, the two types of community had different experiences: the Catholics of the plains villages feared attack by their neighbors whereas some of the Catholic hill villages formed closed communities highly resistant to the state. Recognizing these different experiences, we see more clearly the way in which the threads of local history are interwoven with global connections.

So instead seeing a process of acculturation, we find that Catholic practice in Cave Gully has moved ever closer to global norms. People tend to adopt local practices over time, but as members of a world religion Catholics also wish to share in the practices of the worldwide church, so that the processes of localization and globalization are in constant tension. However, it is the forces of globalization that have come to dominate, as inland Chinese villages like Cave Gully have become more closely linked to the outside world over the centuries. When the first inhabitants of Cave Gully called themselves followers of Heaven in the seventeenth century, they adopted fragments of Catholic practice that they may have garnered from the words of a visiting missionary, but more likely from other Chinese who had attended Catholic rituals, or met missionaries, or come across missionary publications. Only later was the village linked into the networks along which missionaries and Chinese priests traveled between

China and Europe. But these early travelers were isolated from their home-lands, exiles in a land where they had little influence or control. Then in the nineteenth century came the rise of Western power and the technolo-gies associated with it: banks, postal services, remittance agencies, and steam shipping lines. Chinese priests, and through them the villagers they served, saw themselves more and more as part of an institution headquar-tered in Rome. In arguments over correct religious practice, whether these involved limits on usurious interest rates or the proper conduct of the Christmas mass, both priests and laymen now wrote letters to Rome. As factions formed, merged, and formed again in various disputes, Catholics began to demand their rights as members of this global institution, even as they found themselves under attack at home as members of a foreign reli-gion. The policies of the Chinese Communist Party since it came to power in 1949 have had the effect of fossilizing the remnants of these disputes in the institutional structures of the church and state, but with the develop-ment of global communications technologies they are rapidly becoming irrelevant. Cheap air travel, labor migration, tourism, study abroad, and the Internet bind the villagers to the popular culture of global Catholicism even though their church remains formally separated from Rome. Thus what might look like the gradual development of a local Catholic church is far more commonly experienced today as progress towards authenticity defined in terms of global Catholicism. As the world has become increas-ingly globalized, Catholic practice in the village has become more like the practices of Catholics in other parts of the world. Through this same pro-cess, villagers have come to see themselves as members of a community that stretches far beyond the nation-state: as they often say, in words which the Chinese Communist Party fought hard for many years to sup-press, "All believers under heaven are one family."

A history that covers three hundred years must be selective. In this book I have chosen to focus on events that the Cave Gully villagers them-selves regard as important and have remembered in stories handed down from one generation to another. Each chapter of this book begins with a folktale told by the villagers, then follows its themes and under-lying events through the archives and other written sources. Often the events described took place outside the village and were driven by larger historical forces, but the focus of the story is the church as the villagers have seen it. This is a history that is present in the villagers' conscious-ness today, shaping how they think about themselves and the decisions they make in their lives. The past lies in layers beneath those lives and is experienced through the stories as it is through the everyday practices of their faith. Founding ancestors, Chinese priests, foreign missionaries as figures of fearsome power, accounts of miracles, and dramatic incidents of persecution take center stage, while the history of church institutions and a number of major political events such as the Taiping Rebellion, World War II, and the Great Leap famine retreat into the background. Allowing this oral history to interact with the book has the advantage of integrating the community's view of itself with our understanding of it, but the oral history as well as the professional historian's ideas are transformed in the process. The stories help us cut across existing arguments and assumptions to reveal aspects of the Christian experience in China that have often been neglected.

The living oral history of a Chinese village is something very different from a book published in English about Chinese history. The transmission of memories in the form of folktales is a way in which communities create a sense of identity by constructing a vision of the past. Professional historians are at odds with this process, because writing a story for an anonymous reader is very different from telling it to someone. Every time a story is told it is recreated in a process that involves the audience as well as the storyteller. All the stories used here have circulated widely. Some versions were collected in interviews, but others were sent to me by email, and many have also been published. As a foreign, Protestant listener with only a limited grasp of the local dialect and Catholic terminology, the versions I collected myself were clearly not the same as those that would be told if only the storyteller's grandchildren were present. Nor will those be the same as versions told to a priest from another village, let alone the version which that priest then publishes in a government-sponsored local history journal. There is no single authentic version. Indeed, telling competing versions of these folktales is one of the ways in which people debate and come to terms with their identity and the proper place of their community in the world.[16]

Combining the oral history with a temporal framework also poses practical difficulties. In the community these stories are not told, as they are in this book, as events that follow one after another and illustrate the characteristics of different historical periods. Instead they describe how things came to be, and how things were. Thus there are many stories for some periods and none for others. I have inserted the story of the bishop and the wolf, which no longer circulates today, to cover the period of the early nineteenth century. It comes from a collection of local oral histories made by a missionary in the 1890s, which includes many stories about the persecutions of the early Qing, stories which were then in circulation but have since been forgotten. At the other end of the spectrum there are a great many stories about the Cultural Revolution in circulation and I have selected the story of the four women who had the word *fragrance* in their names because it is well known and deals with themes that illuminate the events going on at that time.

Unfortunately, when studying China there is also a final level of negotiation about what it is or is not safe to say about recent history. Since this book uses numerous easily available written sources it is impractical to conceal the name of the village, which is in any case well-known in Shanxi and identifiable by its shrine. But the tensions between Beijing and the Vatican are an ongoing political issue, which make this what the Chinese call a "sensitive" subject. Everyone I spoke to was aware of this and talked about it, and there were a number of people whom I did not speak to because of it. To protect those who spoke to me, I have avoided using the names of anyone who is now alive, unless the material is taken from published sources or I have their explicit agreement for what I say.[17] Where possible I have referred to written documents, but have read and interpreted these in the light of the oral histories. For the same reason I have not mentioned many of the village's contemporary links with the worldwide Catholic church. The reader should be aware that these are considerably stronger than I have described.

There were also many people I interviewed who very much wanted their stories and those of their families and their community to be told, whether or not it was dangerous. Cave Gully and other Christian villages like it are omitted from the grand narratives of Chinese history that the village children study in school, or appear only as the villains, as in the case of the Boxer Uprising. When young people from these communities enter the Catholic clergy and study church history they find their story is missing again, since the events they study are concentrated in Europe, and China plays a role only in the story of the Jesuit missions. This version of the Chinese church, with its emphasis on emperors, high officials, and the transmission of scientific knowledge, seems a world away from the villages where these young people grew up. In classic narratives of both Chinese history and church history, a village like Cave Gully is utterly peripheral, but if we shift the scale of our enquiries and look at Cave Gully for itself it has the potential to cast light on both Chinese history and church history, and also to tell us something about how the interconnected world in which we now live was built.

CHAPTER I

The Ancestors Who Founded the Village

There are three different stories about how Cave Gully was founded. Many people will tell you that the village began when a foreign missionary settled there, but the Duan and Wu families both claim that their ancestors were the first to arrive, some eight generations ago, and that they settled land occupied only by abandoned tombs. The ancestor of the Wu family is said to have come from a nearby village called Wu Family Cliff. Like many poor people, he made his living pushing coal down from the hills in a barrow to sell to the people of the plains villages. His wife used to bring him lunch, which he ate at the foot of the hills where a stream flowed out onto the plain. After a while he saw that the land was abandoned, so he planted some crops, and when some of his crops were stolen he put up a hut so he could stay overnight to keep watch. Eventually he and his family moved to the site. The Duan family say that their ancestors came from Mu Family Village in nearby Qingyuan county and did business in Beijing where two brothers, Duan Tianhe and Duan Wanhe, converted to Christianity. When the brothers came back home they were persecuted by their neighbors, so they left the village to found a new settlement. They arrived as traveling doctors and built a four-room cave dwelling, which gave the new village its name of Cave Gully. The Duan provide evidence for their early arrival by saying that the original cave dwelling survived until recently and must have dated back to the Ming because the chimney was built into the wall, as the Ming emperor decreed for commoners, rather than outside as was done later.

They say that when this building was recently demolished to make way for a new highway, a picture of an angel (or maybe Jesus, the accounts vary) was found under the plaster on the wall.[1]

Stories like these about the first ancestor of a family to settle in a community are common across China and can give us important insights into a village's history. This does not mean that all the events in them took place exactly as described: the stories of the Duan and Wu families disagree about which family arrived first, there is no evidence for a Ming dynasty chimney regulation, and the wall painting has not been seen in living memory. On the other hand several elements have been part of the stories told by many Catholic families in this area since at least the nineteenth century and are important for understanding their history. Firstly, conversion to Christianity marked a new beginning for the family, who now remember their history starting with the ancestor who converted. Secondly, the people who converted had left their homes: they were merchants who joined the religion in Beijing or migrants founding a new community. Thirdly, and most surprisingly, there are no missionaries in the stories.[2]

Eight generations takes us back to the eighteenth century. At that time Cave Gully was far from any centers of missionary activity. So why did families there join this new religion? What did it mean to them? And why did it then matter so much that they remember this event as the beginning of their family history? Some time after the first conversions, when Cave Gully had grown to eight families and we meet its villagers in the archives for the first time, they were willing to suffer flogging rather than renounce their religion. To understand why, we need to know what it was that they believed and practiced and how it reached them.

It was at the intersection of two great trading systems that Shanxi people first encountered Christianity. The province is shaped by river systems that wind through uplands and mountains between the Mongolian steppe in the north and the ancient Chinese heartlands of the Yellow River in the south (see map 1). For centuries the Mongols were a major military power, a constant threat to the Chinese state, and Shanxi was the corridor to the Mongol frontier. Beginning in the fourteenth century, merchants selling provisions to the frontier armies were paid with certificates allowing them to trade salt under a government monopoly. This drew them into long-distance trade, not only in salt, but also buying the sheep, horses, furs, and medicines that were products of the steppe and selling the Mongols grain, cloth, tea, and other products from China.[3] Shanxi merchants spread over all the major cities of the empire. Naturally there were large numbers in the capital, Beijing, but in the sixteenth century they were also working in the distant southern city of Guangzhou where they sold their furs and medicines to Portuguese merchants who were buying tea, porcelain, and other valuable items for the European market. It was these Portuguese merchants who brought the first European missionaries to China.

The stories that families have passed down suggest that most often the Shanxi merchants first encountered Christianity in Beijing, which was the major commercial hub for north China and where, in 1601, the Jesuits established their largest and most influential mission, using their knowledge of mathematics and astronomy to win the support of the Ming court. In the open intellectual atmosphere of the time many educated men were curious about the foreigners and drawn to the new forms of practical learning. Like the schools of Confucian thought fashionable at the time, the new Western learning was associated with a cosmology, rituals, and rules for living; soon the missionaries gathered groups of converts who not only learned from them but also shared in their rituals and listened to their ethical teachings.[4] Some Shanxi merchants living and working in Beijing became part of these groups. Like the missionaries, the merchants spent most of their lives far from home: to ensure their loyalty to the firms they served, they left their families behind in Shanxi and lived in their place of business, returning home only once every few years.[5] Much Chinese religious practice was built round the family and local community, but merchants far from home were more likely to worship deities whose cult spread beyond a single locality. Joining such a religious group could also offer them useful business links and a close new community. Some Chinese deities like Guandi or Mazu filled this role, as did Buddhism, but the Teaching of the Lord of Heaven, as Christianity was known, was apparently also an attractive option.

Men who had been baptized in Beijing were eager to invite the Jesuits to visit them and their families back home. One of these was a wealthy man named Duan Gun from a village just outside the prosperous southern Shanxi town of Jiangzhou, who had returned home and persuaded his family members to join the new religion. Among Duan's friends were the sons of another Jiangzhou merchant who had made a fortune and bought an official title. These young men had been well educated and had

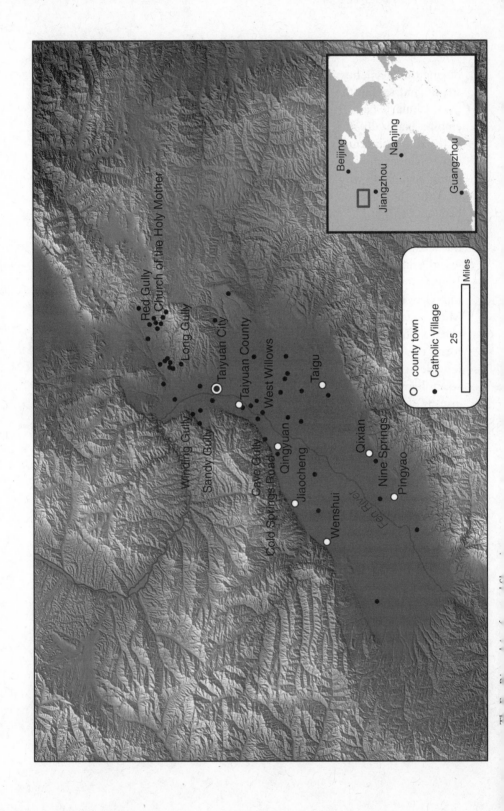

county town
Catholic Village

25
Miles

Red Gully
Church of the Holy Mother
Long Gully
Taiyuan City
Taiyuan County
West Willows
Taigu
Winding Gully
Sandy Gully
Cave Gully
Cold Springs Road
Qingyuan
Jiaocheng
Qixian
Nine Springs
Pingyao
Wenshui
Fen River

Beijing
Jiangzhou
Nanjing
Guangzhou

military interests. They were initially drawn to Christianity through the Jesuits' knowledge of mathematics, the science of ballistics, and newly imported Western armaments. The first missionary to visit Shanxi came to this community in 1620. He was a Jesuit who had left the major southern city of Nanjing after a series of attacks on the missionaries by a high official there, and was traveling with an official posted to northwest China. His aim was to find grapes that could be used to make wine for the mass, because the Chinese did not drink grape wine and shipping bottles of wine from Europe was extremely expensive. Grapes were in fact grown in Shanxi, but this first trip was a failure and the visit to Jiangzhou did not last long. It did, however, inspire the Jiangzhou converts to provide a house and to press for a resident Jesuit.[6]

The missionary who arrived was Alfonso Vagnone, a flamboyant character who had been at the center of the trouble in Nanjing. He had been arrested, flogged, shipped to Macao in a wooden cage, and expelled from the country, but had returned secretly using a new Chinese name. Now he needed to keep out of official view and Jiangzhou, which had good connections with Christian groups in the neighboring province of Shaanxi but was many days' journey from any major city, was a good place to hide. But that was not Vagnone's style; instead he used his learning and his excellent Chinese skills to build links with local officials and he made Jiangzhou a center of Christian writing, publishing, and charitable works. Duan Gun worked closely with Vagnone and was described in letters to Europe as an exemplar of romantic baroque piety, going out on the winter streets to rescue an abandoned infant that had already been buried, and when his disgusted servants refused to take the child, personally washing and caring for her. Vagnone and various Jesuits sent to help him traveled from time to time to other parts of the province including Taiyuan city, but the center of their operations was Jiangzhou.[7]

Vagnone was a strong supporter of Matteo Ricci's policy that missionaries adapt their evangelism to Chinese culture. This was justified by arguing that all peoples share an understanding of God that can be achieved through reason and that in China this rational understanding of God could be found in orthodox Confucian philosophy. The Jesuits intentionally presented Christianity in a way that was compatible with Confucianism. Thus they initially translated "God" as "Heaven" (*tian*) or the "Emperor on High" (*shangdi*), names given to the highest god by the two earliest Chinese dynasties. Using the names of ancient deities made it possible for them to present Christianity as the pursuit of an authentic Chinese past rather than an imported religion.[8]

The ethical content of Vagnone's teaching was also familiar and close to the orthodox tradition of Chinese thought. In Jiangzhou he edited several volumes of ancient Greek and Roman philosophy that were selected and organized according to Chinese categories.[9] For those who had converted, his focus was on the Ten Commandments, which played an important role in basic European religious teaching at the time. He explained that the commandments begin with honoring the Lord of Heaven: honor one Lord of Heaven who is above all things; do not call out the name of the Lord of Heaven or use it to swear oaths; keep the days for observing rituals. Next comes the first commandment for one's relations with people: honor your father and your mother. Explained in this way, with filial piety as the first commandment for how people should behave to one another, the commandments are very close to the ethics of Confucius, honoring filial piety as the primary human virtue. Both Confucian filial piety and the commandment to honor parents were also extended to cover obedience to rulers, masters, and teachers.[10] Soon this commandment was used to justify poor and illiterate followers of the new religion in keeping tablets in honor of Confucius, which were normally kept only by the educated elite.[11] The rest of the Ten Commandments express basic social morality: do not kill, do not steal, do not commit adultery, do not bear false witness, do not covet another man's wife or possessions. These are very similar to the lists of commandments (jie) common to various religious traditions in China (though Vagnone does not comment on this). The Buddhists and Daoists shared a list of five: do not kill, do not steal, do not commit adultery, do not speak falsehood, do not take intoxicating drinks.[12] The only difference is the command not to take intoxicating drinks, rather than not to covet another man's wife or possessions. The similarities with conventional morality were such that Vagnone, who went by the Chinese name Gao Yizhi, was honored by the county magistrate with an inscribed proclamation describing him as "a Western Confucian, Mr. Gao, who cultivates himself to serve Heaven, loves others as himself, and makes it his priority to teach loyalty and filial piety."[13] Vagnone spent twenty years in Jiangzhou and died there shortly before the great rebellions that brought about the fall of the Ming dynasty in the 1640s.

The early years of the Qing dynasty were the great age of conversion in Shanxi. This was the time when Cave Gully was founded and the period shaped the area's Christian communities for generations. Shanxi's vital position as a corridor to the north had long brought war as well as trade: during the sixteenth century there had been repeated Mongol attacks and many of those who fled to the hills survived by raiding the remaining settled population. This violence then contributed to the rebellions that led to the fall of the Ming, when rebel armies fought their way north through the province, gaining many adherents including the leading Christians in Jiangzhou. When the rebels were defeated in Beijing, they retreated south again followed by the invading forces of the new Manchu Qing dynasty bringing yet more devastation. One of the early Qing governors reported that more than half of the province's population had been killed, and nearly all property had been stolen or destroyed. Homes were empty and fields uncultivated, while the few people who were left had fled to fortified villages. Worse still, there had been several years of poor rainfall and the crops had failed. As a result the new government implemented a policy allowing people to cultivate abandoned land.[14]

Although we do not know the exact date of its foundation, Cave Gully was this kind of new settlement founded on land abandoned after the wars. Nearby Qingyuan township had been a base for groups fighting against the Qing in the 1640s and the devastation was terrible. The township's registered population (a figure used for tax purposes) dropped from 29,051 in the late Ming to 9,962 in the reign of the first Qing emperor.[15] An illustration from a nineteenth-century edition of the township gazetteer (figure 1) shows the hills just south of Cave Gully, with the lowest hill land used for graves, and cave dwellings built into the side of the hill. A stream flows down from the hill and grape vines grow over a trellis in a walled yard. In the foreground we can see the walls of Qingyuan town. The fortified farmhouses with their towers were characteristic of the area, with its long history of violence: in Taiyuan county immediately to the north nearly all the large villages close to Cave Gully were listed as being walled in an 1826 survey.[16]

Perhaps, as the story of the Wu suggests, the first settlers in Cave Gully were simply poor local people occupying abandoned land, who adopted the new religion after they arrived. Or perhaps, like the ancestors of the Duan, they had already converted in Beijing, but after the Yongzheng emperor's ban on Christianity in 1724 they had left the city, then been driven out of their original villages, and so settled in this new community bringing their religion with them.[17] The earliest reference to Cave Gully in the archives occurs in 1781 when the new

FIGURE 1. Hillside south of Cave Gully. From *Qingyuan xiangzhi* (1882).

village was visited by a conscientious Chinese priest who sent a table of statistics to Rome every year listing, in minute handwriting, every village he had visited, its size, and any baptisms he performed. In Cave Gully he baptized four adults and their two children, as well as seventeen children who had been born to already Christian families. The village must have been in existence for a considerable time at this point, for it had grown into a sizable community of 136 adults and 63 children, all of them Christian. This made it the largest Christian community in the local area: only two other villages had more than fifty adult Christians. It was also growing rapidly: a priest visited roughly once every two years throughout the 1780s and there were usually several adult baptisms.[18]

A map of the surrounding area shows the contrast between the fertile plain with its winding rivers and the steep mountains where coal was mined, with Cave Gully nestled in a small valley on the edge of the hills (see map 2). The twentieth-century Catholic parishes are marked with the dates of the first recorded visit by a priest. It is clear from these dates that all the major Catholic communities were in existence by the late

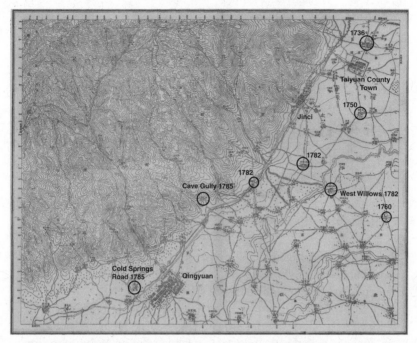

MAP 2. Qingyuan county showing Cave Gully, Taiyuan and Qingyuan county towns, and the Jinci temple complex. Adapted from Academia Sinica, Jindaishi yanjiusuo P/04-B-0920.

eighteenth century.[19] The communities fall into two types distinguished both by their geography and by their process of conversion. On the one hand there are relatively wealthy plains villages where a family or a branch of a family converted to Christianity. Most of the Catholics in these villages are the descendants of individual merchants who converted away from home and Catholics usually remained a steady minority of the village's population. On the other hand there are villages like Cave Gully, often little more than hamlets, built on marginal land available to migrants after the destruction of the seventeenth century. These villages were often entirely Catholic since they were founded by believers and new migrants converted as part of the process of joining the community. Cold Springs Road just outside Qingyuan county town, which is now the largest Catholic community in Shanxi and will play a major role in our story, is an exception to the rule in that it was a migrant community built not on hill land but on a marsh. Over the centuries Shanxi's climate has become increasingly arid and Cold

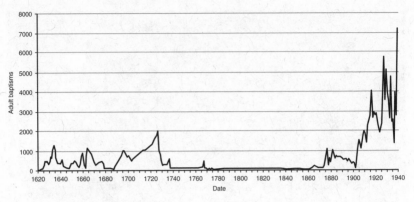

FIGURE 2. Adult baptisms in Shanxi province, 1620 to 1940.

Springs Road developed into a prosperous village on fertile land. Like the merchants, the migrants who came to these villages were separated from their homes, extended families, and local deities and thus were more likely to be willing to join a new religion.

Statistics for adult baptisms also suggest that the early years of the Qing dynasty were the great age of conversion. Figure 2 shows the number of adult baptisms that took place in Shanxi each year from the beginnings of Christianity in the 1620s until the start of World War II. These are not the figures for total numbers of Christians (they do not include children of already Christian parents baptized as infants), but rather for adults baptized by missionaries or Chinese priests. There are many problems with such statistics especially in this early period: some figures appear to be guesses, the missionaries were prone to exaggerate their achievements, and baptisms performed by lay people were not included. Nevertheless baptisms were easier to count than total numbers of Christians and the pattern fits with what we might expect from the political history of the period: for example, the drop in baptisms during the dynastic transition of the 1640s and the sudden collapse after the ban on Christianity in 1724. Overall these statistics show that there were more adult conversions in the seventeenth and early eighteenth centuries than at any time until the twentieth century.[20]

It is very unlikely that these Cave Gully villagers were directly converted by a missionary, since missionaries were eager to report their achievements to their superiors in Rome and there are no reports of baptisms in Cave Gully before the 1780s. An interested observer in the 1930s noted that many Catholic villages in this area had iron church bells with seventeenth-century dates cast into them even though there was no record of a Christian community in that place until considerably later.[21] When the Jesuit Christian Herdtrich visited Taiyuan city in the 1670s to reclaim property lost during the dynastic transition thirty years earlier, he reported that: "Because there are people who have already heard the trumpet sound of the gospel in the cities with their noisy markets and busy trade, people have gone out far from the city to the surrounding villages and towns by Christ's example, so that in fact the Holy Spirit breathes in the wilderness like a whisper or a gentle breeze."[22] This is phrased very differently from the folktales, but it describes the same process by which merchants in major cities came into contact with the religion and then it spread to remote villages.

Of course such conversions through local networks are seldom recorded in the missionary archives, but we do hear a story from the 1640s of a man of official rank from the mountains of northern Shanxi who met a Christian visiting on business. The Christian persuaded him to join the religion and baptized him. The man then went to Beijing, where he was baptized again by a missionary and bought some Christian books. On his return to Shanxi he persuaded the rest of his family to join: they worshipped Christian images, recited Christian prayers, and kept the Ten Commandments. These people's contacts were with the church in Beijing through their trading networks, but the missionaries thought in terms of provinces and thus made all Christians in Shanxi the responsibility of the missionaries in Jiangzhou. For twenty years these converts wrote to Jiangzhou from time to time asking for a missionary to come and baptize them, but none came. Eventually one of the older women in the family became ill and wanted to be baptized before she died, so her husband took her to Jiangzhou. The missionaries there were much impressed by the devotion that had brought the couple on such a long journey through the mountains in the middle of winter, so three years later one of them finally traveled north to the family's home town and baptized two hundred people. Another missionary visited sixteen years after that and baptized eighty people.[23] In this case Christianity spread through merchants, books, and visits to Beijing; the missionaries did come, but only twenty-three years after the conversion and then the people waited many more years before they saw a missionary again.

People who built a community on the basis of a few days intense conversation and some published books naturally adopted elements of the religion that could be easily remembered and understood: the list of ten commandments, the names of the divine figures, and the words of the prayers. In the absence of the missionaries they reassembled these fragments on the basis of their own previous experiences. The result was a religion shaped by local expectations, but within that context it also had a strong appeal. Firstly honoring the Ten Commandments was a way of intensifying existing morality: this was a religion, as Christians would always claim when they were arrested, that exhorted people to do good. Secondly, it was a religion honoring a great deity of the classical canon, Heaven, who was served by priests holding prestigious positions in the imperial court. And thirdly it was a religion that built new communities in a familiar form: Christians met regularly to pray in much the same style as other groups of devout religious believers. While the first two factors linked the religion to orthodox Confucianism and were due to the Jesuit policy of presenting Christianity in ways that were acceptable to China's Confucian elite, the daily religious practice of the new communities was much more similar to popular Buddhism and Daoism, which the missionaries roundly condemned.

There was much debate within the wider church over Ricci's policies, but the influence of Vagnone and the Beijing Jesuits meant that they continued to shape Christian practice in Shanxi. There were particularly strong objections to the terms Heaven and Emperor on High for God and the church formally adopted the new term Lord of Heaven (tianzhu) instead. However Shanxi Christians remained committed to the old terms. When the Kangxi emperor presented the Beijing Jesuits with the words "Honor Heaven" (jing tian), written in his own hand, the Austrian Jesuit Christian Herdtrich brought a copy with him to Taiyuan city, had it engraved on a wooden plaque, and installed it with great honor over the entrance of the church. Other Shanxi churches had the words "Emperor on High" hung over the entrance or above the altar.[24] A little handcopied book by a Chinese author that circulated among Shanxi Christians in the mid-eighteenth century gives a sense of how the use of these terms linked Christians to the Confucian canon. The author quotes from the Doctrine of the Mean (one of the Four Books used as the basis of Confucian education since the twelfth century), to explain why the proper man should serve Heaven: "Hence the gentleman may not neglect the cultivation of his own character. Wishing to cultivate his character, he may not neglect to serve his parents. In order to serve his parents, he may not neglect to acquire knowledge of men. In order to know men, he may not dispense with a knowledge of Heaven."[25] From this he argues that only someone who both knows and serves Heaven, or in other words is Christian, can be a true Confucian. For any who might object that the Christian teaching was foreign, he explains that *Lord of Heaven* is merely an alternative term for Heaven, the deity honored in the Chinese classics, not some new idea from the West. Indeed, he explains, every country gives its own name to the Lord of Heaven. In the Western lands he is called by the Latin term *Deus*. In China there are several different names: *Tianzhu* (Lord of Heaven), *Shangdi* (Emperor on High), and *Tian laoye* (Old Master Heaven); the Muslims call him *Allah* and the Manchus *Abka*.[26]

The link between Christianity and state orthodoxy was reinforced by the position of Christian priests at court. The Jesuits presented themselves as members of an elite whose status was intimately linked to recognition by the state and when men like Christian Herdtrich visited Shanxi from the court in Beijing their impact was immense. Herdtrich was a scholar and intellectual of the highest caliber. He was one of a group of Jesuits who made the first translation of the Four Books into Latin and published them in a magnificent volume dedicated to Louis XIV of France under the title *Confucius the Chinese Philosopher*. He was also a competent mathematician, and though he had originally been assigned by the Jesuits as the missionary for Shanxi, he spent most of his time working in Beijing as an astronomer. For several years he made only brief visits to Shanxi. One opportunity came when the Kangxi emperor received a pair of beavers from the Russians as a gift. The emperor asked the Jesuits to come and identify them, and laughed as he wrote down the names of the animals in Chinese, Manchu, and the Latin that they suggested. At this auspicious moment the senior Jesuit present brought Herdtrich forward to ask if he could go to Shanxi to convalesce from a recent illness. So Herdtrich arrived in Shanxi as a man who had personally been received by the emperor in an informal context: no wonder when he presented his official papers to the governor he was warmly received. During his visits he reclaimed property that the mission had lost and entertained the local officials with displays of optical illusions and performances on the harpsichord.[27]

Many years later when a group of Shanxi Christians was accused of complicity in a White Lotus uprising and all sects in the area, including Christianity, were banned, a missionary noticed that the rich, who had bribed their way out of trouble, were not too worried: "'What do these dogs of mandarins know?' they would say, 'I know that the Europeans are getting along fine in Beijing without any opposition.'"[28] Another later missionary complained that during the reign of the Kangxi emperor people converted not out of true zeal but because they saw how the European missionaries were revered by provincial and city officials.[29] By presenting Christianity in a form that fitted with Confucianism and was accepted by the state, Herdtrich and the other Jesuits employed at court played an important role in the spread of the religion even though their actual visits were few and brief.

But as the reference to the White Lotus suggests, many people thought that Christianity looked much more like some kind of Buddhist group. There was a huge range of such groups, which officials often labeled White Lotus. This term implied that the group believed that the end of the world was coming and that only those who adhered to the messengers of the Eternal Mother would be saved; but since Christians were quite often, as in this case, identified with the White Lotus, doctrine was clearly not the government's main concern. Uprisings related to these groups were a major problem for the Qing government in the eighteenth century, but far more people were members of a wider range of lay Buddhist groups characterized by prayer and fasting that were entirely peaceful and never came into contact with the government.[30] Ordinary people as well as officials noticed the similarities between these groups and the Christians. It was customary for local people to put on skits on topical subjects as part of temple festivals and one show included a scene of a Christian teacher debating with a Buddhist. Each was urging the other to join his group. The Christian claimed that his people did not fear demons and could exorcise them, to which the Buddhist replied, "Hah, hah, your Lord of Heaven can't rescue a mouse from the cat's mouth, so how can he free men from the talons of demons? Beware, for if you provoke these fierce spirits to anger they will torment you more than anyone else."[31] At this point demons rushed onto the stage to seize the Christian and lead him down to hell. The story was reported by a missionary because the actor playing the Buddhist suddenly collapsed and died (presumably as a divine punishment), but the skit was clearly intended to satirize both the Christians and the Buddhists.

People made these comparisons because the practices of Christians and members of lay Buddhist groups were indeed similar. The most characteristic practices of Christianity were community prayer and regular fasting, which were also typical of lay Buddhist groups. When the governor of Shanxi province investigated the followers of the Lord of Heaven in 1785, he concluded that people had joined the new religion "to do good deeds and bring down blessings," had passed the religion on to one another and had no contact with foreigners, but just "keep vegetarian fasts, recite prayers, and print a list of dates which they call the Calendar for Observing Rituals."[32] An Italian Franciscan, who had come to China after working in Jerusalem and had just spent a month in West Willows village agreed. He complained that in these villages "the essence of being Christian is the recitation and chanting of many prayers and the external observation of fasts."[33]

When Qing officials arrested a group of Christians in the 1780s they confiscated several prayer books, mostly handcopied booklets but also one printed volume with woodblock illustrations. Apart from this they found only wooden crosses and a calendar. The Christians reported that they said prayers together every morning and evening, and that those who did not have prayer books knew the prayers by heart. These were literate merchants; the impoverished Cave Gully villagers were probably more like the people of another Catholic hill village, Winding Gully, who told officials that they only knew prayers that had been passed down by word of mouth. Generations of hand-copying meant that no two Shanxi prayer books were the same, but they were descended from the *Daily Exercises in the Holy Religion* produced by the Jesuits in Beijing in the 1660s. The Our Father was the prayer which Qing officials most often reported after examining the prayer books and the prayer they most often heard from those who had no books. Perhaps it was presented to them because it reinforced the Confucian image of the religion, with its focus on Heaven and its request "Thy will be done" which Vagnone explains as meaning that we should obey the Ten Commandments.[34]

The Christians chanted these prayers together in a style drawn from Buddhist practice. Missionaries differed in their opinions of this. A French Jesuit who visited Shanxi wrote positively that those who assembled for morning and evening prayers sang in two choirs with great devotion. They did not know plainchant or European music, but used quite acceptable tunes and sang better than many communities in Europe. The bad-tempered Franciscan who condemned the ignorance of the West Willow villagers complained that people turned up to funerals carrying little handcopied prayer books which looked just like the Buddhist prayer books, and that they sang the prayers in imitation of

Buddhist monks. One of the most characteristic types of Buddhist monastic chanting does not have a fixed melody: there is a regular beat and one syllable falls on each beat, but after an introduction by a congregational leader the singers diverge and each person sings a different line. Chanting in this style infuriated one much later missionary who got into a dispute with his congregation when he demanded that they sing in unison with the leader. They complained to the bishop that he was trying to change the ancient way of praying and singing. This was not the only type of chanting: in both Buddhism and Shanxi Catholic practice some prayers had fixed tunes. Catholic chants collected in the early twentieth century used the Chinese pentatonic scale and mixed Chinese tunes, Gregorian chant, and Italian songs (the last probably dating from the nineteenth century). Whatever the style, chanting meant that prayers were not a matter for private communion with God, but a public group activity. Daily chanted prayers brought families and villages together and gave their members a physical and emotional experience of community.[35]

The types of prayers used were also strikingly similar to those used by Buddhist monks, Daoist priests, and local devotees. When Christian Herdtrich visited Jiangzhou he reported that the Christians there recited the rosary, chaplets in honor of the Virgin Mary and Jesus, litanies, and other prayers daily with their families. Many of these prayers were lengthy, highly repetitive, and characterized by strings of incomprehensible words. Chaplets, of which the rosary is the best known, are sets of prayers, usually with multiple repetitions of the short Hail Mary and Our Father, which are counted on beads. The strings of beads with a small attached crucifix were worn round the neck and have occasionally been found when early Catholic graves in Shanxi have been moved. In Buddhist practice too beads were used to count prayers, and Buddhist rosaries were widely worn as part of formal dress.[36] The Christian prayers were in Chinese, but since the translators had left key terms, such as *grace* and *church* in Latin they made little immediate sense. So, for example, the beginning of the Hail Mary, "Hail Mary, full of grace"—in Latin "*Ave Maria, gratia plena*"—became "*Yawu Maliya manbei elajiya zhe,*" where only the word "full" *(manbei)* is Chinese. Many of the best loved and most commonly used Buddhist prayers were transliterated from Sanskrit and similarly incomprehensible: the morning prayer service used by Buddhist monks from the seventeenth century began with a set of lengthy mantras that represent the sounds of the Sanskrit and make no sense at all in Chinese. Daoists too conducted morning prayer services with chanted invocations that were seen as reproducing the sounds written by Heaven rather than conveying meaning.[37]

Another popular form of prayer was repetition of the names of Jesus and Mary. People kept copies of these names and of the monogram IHS, which represented the name of Jesus, over their doors and in their houses. Such practices were common in southern Europe at the time, but they were also very close to the Buddhist prayer to Amitabha: the repeated recitation of his name was an essential part of all Buddhist traditions in China by this period, ensuring that the believer would be reborn in the Western Paradise.[38]

Buddhism, Daoism, and Christianity all also made use of litanies confessing sins, expressing repentance, and calling for protection. Christian litanies are long prayers in call and response form, and were popular with both Catholics and Protestants in Europe at this time. The lists of names meant that the leader usually needed to read from a prayer book; in old prayer books from Shanxi, the Litany of the Saints is so well thumbed that the edges of the pages are translucent from the grease on readers' fingers. After an invocation calling on God for mercy, the call and response continues: "Holy Mary, *pray for us*. Holy Mother of God, *pray for us*. Holy Virgin of Virgins, *pray for us*. St. Michael, *pray for us*. St. Gabriel, *pray for us* . . ." This goes on through fifty-seven more angels, prophets, and saints, and is followed by a list of sins and disasters: "From all evil, *Lord, deliver us*. From all deadly sin, *Lord, deliver us*. From thine anger, *Lord, deliver us*. From sudden death, *Lord, deliver us* . . ." and so on.[39] Buddhists and Daoists made much use of similar lengthy prayers in which those present repent of their sins and invoke a long list of divine names and titles.[40] Litanies were so popular with Shanxi Catholics that in the nineteenth century Bishop Grioglio, who objected that the Christians did not understand what they were saying, removed several from the prayer book.[41]

The centrality of these prayers to Christian practice in Shanxi is suggested by the story told about a man whose parents had converted to Christianity, but who had himself refused to be baptized. He died, but then, as everyone was wailing over his coffin, he suddenly spoke asking to be baptized. He explained that he had died and been compelled to take the path to hell but his way had been blocked by a young man with a spear in his hand who asked him why he had refused to embrace the Holy Law. He replied, "Because I do not know the prayers and I cannot say them from memory." The young man then asked him, "Is it so hard to call on the names of God and of the Virgin Mary and seek help from them so that you should not be constrained to sin?" He then explained that God had permitted the man to return to life and be baptized. After these dramatic events the man was indeed baptized and a few days later he died. Journeys to the underworld were an important genre of writing in both China and Europe, but this tale got the missionary who reported it into trouble with his superiors, since church officials thought the story implausible and indeed ridiculous. He excused himself by explaining that he had merely translated it from Chinese.[42] The clerics in Rome objected that there was no purpose to the miracle since there was no evidence that anyone had converted as a result, but for the Shanxi people who swore to its truth the moral of the story was quite clear: reciting prayers is essential to being Christian but you should not put off being baptized because of its difficulty, since simply invoking the names of Jesus and Mary will also be effective.

The other characteristic Christian practice was fasting. European Catholicism during this period had elaborate rules about fasting, especially the avoidance of meat on Fridays and during the season of Lent. Another story about someone who is saved from hell at the point of death comes from Vagnone's popular *Acts of the Holy Mother,* which continued to circulate in Shanxi into the twentieth century. Part of the book is made up of stories taken from the medieval European tradition illustrating the power of the Virgin Mary, including one which tells of a robber whose head is cut off. As the head fell to the ground it called out asking to be allowed to confess. A priest was summoned. The robber's head and body reunited, and he knelt and made his confession. The priest then asked how the robber had obtained this grace of a dying confession. He explained that as a child he had learned that all those who fasted in honor of Mary on Thursdays and Saturdays would obtain complete forgiveness of their sins and avoid eternal damnation. Despite his many wicked deeds he had never ceased to do this.[43]

Fasting was also an important part of Chinese Buddhist and Daoist religious practice. In Buddhism the command not to kill was understood as requiring a vegetarian diet, but it was common only to eat vegetarian food on certain days (a practice that paralleled the Catholic pattern of weekly fasting). More devout Buddhists and many sectarian groups abstained from eating meat at all times. Daoists fasted to purify the body, avoiding all stimulating foods including garlic as well as meat.[44] Chinese followers of the Lord of Heaven interpreted the Catholic church's practice of fasting in the light of this cultural background, and were often strictly vegetarian. Missionaries, officials, and some elite

Christians all objected to this. The Chinese author who argued that only those who worshipped the Lord of Heaven could be proper Confucians devoted a whole section of his book to telling Christians not to fast like Buddhists, saying that "to keep Buddhist fasts is to rebel against Heaven."[45] Some missionaries required people to eat meat before baptism and refused to baptize those who were not willing to do so, others demanded that people eat meat before they could receive the sacraments.[46]

The stories of the man who came back from the grave and the head that spoke remind us that the ultimate goal of both prayer and fasting was salvation after death. In practice people hoped to achieve this salvation through devotion to the Virgin Mary. Heaven is a high and impersonal deity in Chinese tradition, and the missionaries in their writings often equated Jesus with Heaven in order to prevent readers from thinking that Christianity had more than one god. Indeed Vagnone usually refers to Jesus either as the Lord of Heaven or as "the second person" (of the Trinity). Thus Jesus was understood as God the creator and judge, and Christians focused their prayers and litanies on the Virgin Mary and other saints who might intercede with God for them. Another story in the *Acts of the Holy Mother* tells of a Chinese scholar who had been devoted to Mary in his youth but had turned away from her to worldly things. He became very ill and as his illness came to a crisis he saw a vision of God seated on his throne with the Virgin Mary and St. Ignatius. The scholar heard God hand down the sentence of eternal damnation for his sins, so he threw himself at the feet of Ignatius, begging that he plead for him. The saint did so, and God agreed to Mary's petition, allowing the scholar to recover and make his confession before he died.[47] The same emphasis on Mary as a way to salvation—or as she was titled in a popular litany, "the Gate of Heaven"—was reinforced by the much repeated Hail Mary, which ends by calling on Mary to "pray for us sinners now and at the hour of our death."

In her cosmological power and compassion for humanity the Virgin Mary depicted by Vagnone is similar to the Buddhist deity Guanyin. Mary was chosen by the creator God before eternity to be his mother: miraculously born, never growing old, and untouched by Satan. God was a great and powerful judge, but because of his great love for her he would grant her compassionate requests, and thus she had the power to aid those who pray to her. Vagnone does not refer to her as the Virgin, instead he uses the title *shengmu*, with which he translates the term

Mother of God, but which could also mean *Holy Mother* or even *Mother of the Sage.* It is a title used for the highest ranking female deities in the Chinese pantheon, and is still today the name by which Mary is most commonly known in Shanxi. Guanyin is not given this title, but she shares the combination of power and compassion. In Shanxi temples, Guanyin was a distinctive and regal figure surrounded by the thousand arms with which she helps those who honor her, but in domestic contexts she was also depicted as a beautiful woman, her robes flowing in the wind.

A Chinese-style scroll painting of the Virgin Mary from Shaanxi has many similarities with a famous wonder-working picture from the church of Santa Maria Maggiore in Rome, which is said to have been painted from life by St. Luke. The Jesuits brought copies of this painting to China and for a time one of them was displayed over the altar of the church in Beijing. The folds of Mary's headdress, the red halo, the child's book, hand gesture, and glance up towards his mother are all found in the Roman icon and repeated in the Chinese painting even while the style and feel of the image is Chinese. But the image is also like pictures of Guanyin, who is sometimes shown with a child on her arm to symbolize that she will give sons to those who pray to her. Indeed in some parts of China at this time same craftsmen may have been commissioned to make images of both Guanyin and the Virgin Mary. In the case of this painting the iconography is so similar that there is a minority opinion among scholars that this particular image is not the Virgin and Child at all, but simply an image of Guanyin Who Brings Sons.[48]

Thus the early Shanxi Catholics built their communities out of fragments of religious practice culled from prayer books, devotional writings, meetings with other Catholics, and occasional brief visits by missionaries and Chinese priests. The missionaries had adapted elements of Christianity to fit with Confucian philosophy, but local Catholic practices also reflected a popular religious culture which had been profoundly shaped by Buddhism. However this Chinese religious culture was openly syncretic in a way that European Christianity of this period was not.

A few miles north of Cave Gully (see map 2) lies the Jinci Shrine, famous for its magnificent twelfth-century temple to a goddess known as the Holy Mother *(shengmu).* Dragons, revered as bringers of rain, wind up the columns of the temple and decorate her throne, for the Holy Mother was the spirit of the river whose streams flowed from a spring in front of the temple and irrigated the farmland of the surrounding villages.

FIGURE 3. Virgin and Child, Shaanxi,
variously dated between 1500 and
1850. Used by permission of The Field
Museum, #A114604_02d.

Every year farmers came in procession from each of these villages to worship her. Officials and some of the local elite also honored her in Confucian style as the mother of an ancient Shanxi prince. Her temple is surrounded by many other religious buildings including a large and ancient
Buddhist monastery, a Daoist cloister built into the hillside above, a temple to the Black Dragon King and another to the god of the Fen River,
and in a side hall a shrine to a folk deity, the Goddess Who Brings Sons
(song zi niangniang). It was possible to distinguish Buddhist and Daoist
clerics, but ordinary people might attend both Buddhist and Daoist
services, participate in sacrifices to the Holy Mother and pray to the
Goddess Who Brings Sons, in what was effectively a single religious site.[49]

Occasionally Christianity was absorbed into this kind of religious culture, as in a case where a Christian became the head of an existing Buddhist group and was very successful in expanding it. The members called themselves followers of the Lord of Heaven and a visiting missionary found it impossible to work out who was Christian and who was not.[50] Christian practices could also merge gradually into folk religion: in the 1830s a Christian peddler in the mountains of Shanxi came to a house with an old cross outside it, with sticks of incense burning in front of it. The people of the house, who were not Christian, explained simply that they had inherited the cross and that it was a defense against evil.[51] But while Christianity might look to outsiders very much like other local religious practices and might sometimes fade away into them, its devout believers rejected the idea that the Lord of Heaven was simply part of a larger local pantheon. In a mountain village a small number of Christian families dug a cave into the hillside as a chapel and installed a statue of Jesus. In response, the rest of the villagers came in procession carrying the statue of the deity from the local temple, which they placed before the statue of Jesus as was done in ceremonies of friendship between gods. They prostrated themselves before the images and said that all the villagers should worship both gods. When the Christians refused to cooperate there was a fight and an expensive legal case, which the magistrate refused to adjudicate on the grounds that it was a religious dispute unrelated to government.[52]

The clearest illustration of this Christian rejection of local deities is the figure of Michael the Archangel, quite possibly the angel that the folktale records as being painted on the wall of the first house in Cave Gully. Michael was a winged warrior and protector of Christians against the devil, as in the Book of Revelation where war breaks out in heaven and Michael and his angels drive out the red dragon that is Satan. Over the altar of the church in Beijing, where many of the earliest Shanxi converts would have seen them, was a picture of God flanked by images of the Virgin Mary and the Archangel Michael.[53] A seventeenth-century Portuguese statue from Macao shows Michael dressed in armor, raising a fiery sword, and holding a pair of scales, for he was also believed to fetch the souls of the dying to judgment (see figure 4). This is an object made in Europe, but it is very similar to the kind of small, portable wooden statues of folk religious deities that were popular in China. The Archangel Michael also served much the same function as the Bodhisattva Weituo (in Sanskrit, Skanda), who was depicted as a divine warrior protecting the Buddhist monastic

FIGURE 4. St. Michael the Archangel, seventeenth century. From the Museum of Sacred Art, Macao.

community. His statue guarded the entrance to temples and Buddhists sang praises to him in their daily prayers, just as Christians invoked the Archangel Michael in the Litany of the Saints.[54] But there was one crucial difference: Weituo was incorporated into the pantheon of popular Chinese religion, but the Archangel Michael was thought of as fighting against that pantheon. The classic depiction shows him holding a spear and crushing a dragon beneath his feet. Dragons decorate the temple of the Holy Mother at Jinci, and Dragon Kings who control rainfall are some of the most powerful deities in Shanxi. In the picture of the hillside near Cave Gully (figure 1), beside the graves is a small building labeled Temple of the White Dragon. Conversion to Christianity did not mean that converts ceased to believe in the power of these Dragon Kings, but rather that the converts put themselves in opposition to them. In a theology that dates back to the Roman empire the church taught that "the gods of the gentiles are devils" (Psalms 95:5).[55] Such a hostile relationship with powerful deities could be terrifying. One account tells of a Shanxi man who became very ill and awoke one night shouting that he had seen the dragon from the image on the altar in the room rise up from under the feet of the Archangel Michael, flashing its forked tongue and breathing fire, and descend on the door of the missionary's room to devour him.[56]

During the eighteenth century the Shanxi Christians' practices came under attack from both the Qing state and the church hierarchy. New missionaries arrived in the province, determined to make changes, but they could visit only occasionally and were in no position to enforce church rulings that were unacceptable to the wealthy Christian merchants. Local officials had great power if they chose to exert it, but generally had little interest in religious practices that were not an immediate threat, let alone those of communities as small and poor as Cave Gully. It was not until the 1780s that pressure from the central government began to make them take action. Meanwhile the Shanxi Christians continued in the practices that they had inherited from the first converts.

In 1724 the Yongzheng emperor issued a ban on the practice of Christianity, placing it alongside the White Lotus and other illegal but familiar Buddhist groups. Official tolerance of Christian communities had depended heavily on the patronage of the Jesuit officials at court and this fragile balance collapsed as the Jesuit order came under increasing criticism in Europe. As the papacy was forced into action against the Jesuits, the church hierarchy concluded that parts of Chinese funeral and lineage rituals should be classified as ancestor worship and therefore Christians should not be allowed to participate in them. This was entirely unacceptable to the emperor, as indeed similar papal decisions on local practice often were to European sovereigns. It also brought Christians into conflict with the basic values and structures of local society, since funerals and ancestral rituals were important representations of Confucian filial piety. Because of close personal relations with the Kangxi emperor and a series of rather confused rulings from Rome, the Jesuits managed to continue their mission for a while. But when the Yongzheng emperor came to power in a court coup, all the missionaries outside the court were ordered to leave the country. The emperor also issued a new edition of the Sacred Edict, on which all candidates for government office were tested, which included a clear statement that the Teaching of the Lord of Heaven was not in accordance with the classics and its priests were employed at court only because they happened to be skilled in astronomy and mathematics.[57]

The Shanxi Christians also found their practices under attack from new Franciscan missionaries, who arrived as a result of the defeat of the Jesuits. The funerals that they were faced with, like other elements of Christian practice, interwove elements drawn from European and Chinese ritual. An altar with a cross was placed in front of the coffin with incense, candles, and sometimes dishes of food on it. Guests would prostrate themselves in front of this altar, honoring both the cross and the deceased lying in the coffin behind it. Rules from Rome banned prostrations to the coffin, so the first Franciscan missionary issued a rule that the coffin should be moved away from the center of the room, so that the prostrations would be made only to the altar and the cross. This was not a success.[58] As one bishop wrote to Rome some forty years later, in the wealthy merchant towns of Shanxi, "it appears to be humanly impossible to enforce a command so opposed to the sensitivities of the people."[59]

A more immediate problem was the ritual in honor of ancestors. Some families honored wooden tablets on which the names of the ancestors were written, but most often Shanxi families kept a scroll painting depicting all the generations, which they brought out and honored at New Year. Since the Franciscans had to travel secretly and usually stayed in the homes of the wealthy Christians they were more likely to come across these objects than they were to attend a funeral. When the first Franciscan to tour the province found tablets in Christian homes, he took them and burned them.[60] This stern policy ended in fiasco. The leading Christians in Shanxi had opposed the new policy and supported the Jesuits from the start. Indeed they had written to the pope's representative in Beijing saying that when they were told to throw out and destroy their ancestral tablets, "We were terrified to do it. Our faces paled and we sweated all over, thinking that our ancestors and parents are our roots and although they have died we cannot forget their kindness to us."[61] They went on to say that anyone who destroyed his ancestral tablets would be despised by his relatives and neighbors, and would inevitably be reported to the local official. According to the Qing legal code the punishment for destroying one's own ancestral tablets was beheading, and the punishment for destroying another family's tablets was beating. If the church's ban on ancestral tablets was enforced then Christianity would be "a teaching that denies both father and monarch, and those outside the religion will take it as proof that members of the teaching are not filial to their parents."[62]

With this confident moral stand, the leading Shanxi Christians refused to allow Franciscans who were bent on enforcing the new policies to operate in the province. After a Franciscan destroyed the ancestral tablets in the house of one of the leaders of the Taiyuan city Christians, most of the other Christians there and in the nearby villages refused to attend the rituals he performed. When he wanted to visit the Christians of the merchant town of Qixian two leaders came to find him and told him that Christians could not receive the sacraments from the Franciscans. They insisted on writing to the Beijing Jesuits before they would allow him to practice in their area, and even then they refused to allow him to take down the board engraved with the words "Emperor on High" from the church, would not allow him to visit any of the Christian communities in villages outside the city, and soon forced him to return to Beijing.[63] When another Franciscan tried to do the same a few years later, the heads of twenty Christian communities near Taiyuan city held a meeting at which they decided to expel him. He went to take the last rites to a man dying in an outlying village, but the head of the Christians there refused to allow him to proceed and he was so badly treated that he knelt down (to prepare for death, he says). In the end other people intervened and he was released.[64] As a practically-minded Chinese priest wrote to Rome, some Christians did have concubines and ancestral tablets, but there was nothing that could be done about it.[65] Christianity was marked by its strong accepted morality. It was impossible for the missionaries to enforce a policy that was seen as immoral and to exclude from the community those who refused to conform.

These disputes probably meant little to the villagers of Cave Gully since ancestral tablets and the rituals that went with them, which had long been widespread in southeast China, were only just coming into fashion in Shanxi. They were a sign of social status: poor people in the hill villages told the missionaries that it was not their custom to keep such tablets.[66] In any event until the 1780s there is no record that a missionary visited Cave Gully at all. The government's ban on Christianity did affect the villagers, but not until 1784 when they were unfortunate enough to be formally accused of being members of an illegal religious group. The county magistrate went in person to investigate. According to the bishop as soon as the magistrate entered the village,

> He saw the miserable circumstances of these poor people, and realized quite clearly the treachery of the pagans. Nevertheless he imprisoned eight of the Christians, that is, one from each family, but without putting them in chains or fetters. And after two days they were all called for an interrogation that lasted several hours, during which the preacher of this congregation disputed so well on the subject of the existence of God and other points of religion that the mandarin and all those standing around appeared convinced. But nevertheless, since power always prevails over clear and evident reason, the official then began to beat and persecute the poor Christians, pressing them to leave the religion, but they remained constant in the confession of the faith. So the mandarin, so as not to make the affair more criminal, decided that they should be sent home the next day as foolish people.[67]

Clearly the magistrate did not really think these poor migrants worth his attention, but two other things are also obvious from this account. Firstly, someone in the village was an effective speaker who could present the teaching of the Lord of Heaven in sufficiently Confucian terms to make it acceptable to the magistrate and his staff. Might this perhaps have been one of the Duan brothers who had come from Beijing as traveling doctors and built the first house? Certainly the image of an angel on the wall of the Duan family's home suggests that it was being used as a chapel. The village's growth and its regular adult baptisms also suggest the presence of an effective religious leader. Secondly, the villagers were extremely loyal to their religion, refusing to deny it even when they were imprisoned, interrogated, and beaten. Clearly their allegiance to the Lord of Heaven mattered to them and their loyalty suggests the power of the belief in salvation that lay behind everyday Christian practice. At the same time these eight men were representatives of each of the families in the village and in refusing to deny their religion they were also being loyal to their community, a community which had been constructed around the worship of the Lord of Heaven.

The beliefs and practices of this first generation of followers of Heaven were to shape much of the later history of Catholicism in Shanxi. After this period Catholicism was a religion passed down through the families of those original founders. Of course women married into these communities, migrants joined the hill villages, and not all converts produced many generations of Christian descendants: one missionary lamented that many families ceased to practice after three or four generations and another report explains that the number of Christians has dropped because of ignorance, persecution, and migration beyond the Great Wall.[68] Nevertheless later generations were born into the faith and inherited the practices of the early converts which were so strongly influenced by Confucian philosophy and Buddhist religious practice: the emphasis on the Ten Commandments and filial piety, the chanted prayers, the vegetarian fasting, the Chinese-style images, and the devotion to Mary Mother of God, all of them tools for the salvation of the soul. They also inherited communities that had much in common with the more widespread Buddhist devotional groups, but carried in them a strain of hostility to the Dragon Kings and other local deities that could be found in the anticlericalism of some elite Confucian thought but was utterly alien to the culture of folk religion. Many of these practices have continued until today; what has changed over the centuries is the creation of ever stronger links between the followers of the Lord of Heaven and the institutions of the global church. This process began to affect the people of Cave Gully at the turn of the nineteenth century with the intensification of government persecution and the arrival for the first time of resident priests.

CHAPTER 2

The Bishop and the Wolf

A Franciscan missionary who lived in Cave Gully in the early twentieth century published a story he had heard about a Chinese priest sent by Bishop Giovacchino Salvetti in the early nineteenth century to give confession and communion to Christians who had been exiled to Yili, beyond the Gobi desert. The priest set off, riding a mule, and came to the Great Wall.

> But then seeing before him an immense desert, it was unclear which way he should go, and he hardly expected to find the guide that the bishop had promised him. And then, lo and behold, a great wolf came from the other side and set out. The mule which the priest was riding followed the wolf of its own accord all that day, and at dusk the priest came to a place where some herders had pitched their tents. The wolf disappeared and that night the priest was a guest there. The next morning he set out and there was the wolf who had led him to the tents.[1]

The wolf led the priest for sixty days until he came to the place where the exiled Christians were living, and then brought him safely home again. When the priest returned, he went to report to the bishop, but before he could speak Salvetti asked him, "Was the wolf a good guide?"[2] The Christians debated whether the wolf was really an angel, a demon, or a soul from purgatory, but the bishop said that it was simply a wolf acting according to the will of God.

The wolf is the stuff of legend: a magical creature that guides the hero across the desert. Barnaba Nanetti, who collected many oral histories in the area in the 1890s, heard another version of the story in which the wolf follows the priest's mule, making itself "a companion like a faithful dog, so he was also pleased since he was sure that no rogue would dare accost him in the sight of such a terrifying animal."[3] Wolves were much feared in Shanxi for snatching children and causing serious injuries to adults. People called them spirits *(shen)* and they fit easily in a folktale.[4] But the story of a wolf sent to guide the priest also has another source in the legends of medieval Europe, which tell of how Francis of Assisi spoke to a wolf that had been attacking the townsfolk of Gubbio. The saint persuaded the wolf to promise, by raising its paw, that if the people fed it every day it would no longer attack them.[5] Chinese villagers who told the story of the priest led by a wolf were also comparing the Franciscan missionary bishop, Giovacchino Salvetti, to Francis. The story shows his holiness and spiritual powers, but it was also handed down because after his death praising Salvetti was a way of criticizing the behavior of later missionaries.[6]

This is a story about the clergy. Jacobus Wang, whose name had been forgotten but whose letters in the archives in Rome tell us that he was the priest who made this dangerous journey, did so to provide rituals that only a priest can perform: confession and mass. These are rituals that are often seen as central to Catholicism, but they were largely absent in the early Catholic communities in central Shanxi. The first priests to live permanently in the area arrived in the second half of the eighteenth century. Like Jacobus Wang most of them were locally trained Chinese men, though there were also Chinese priests who had been trained in Naples and a few European Franciscan missionaries. Their presence made confession and mass possible: they spread these new rituals and they earned their living from them. So a story about the holiness and courage of priests is also inevitably about the importance of confession and mass.

Long and dangerous journeys shaped the lives of these priests and of the merchants for whom they worked. We too easily assume that Chinese Christians stayed in one place and European missionaries came to them. In fact Christian conversion had been built along existing networks of long-distance trade that linked Europe to China and exile spread some Christians into parts of Central Asia and beyond. The followers of the Lord of Heaven in a poor inland village like Cave Gully were linked to the wider world by the European missionaries, but also by Chinese priests and by Chinese Christian merchants. The priests were aware of European politics and corresponded with the papal bureaucracy in Rome in Latin. Some of them had even studied in Europe. The merchants carried letters and made travel possible even when it was illegal. Both Italians and Shanxi men studied foreign languages, learned about distant cultures, and crossed the globe. The difference from later periods was the difficulty and expense of travel, the associated expense of correspondence, and the dangers of Qing persecution. The travelers, whether European or Chinese, were few, and they experienced danger, isolation, sometimes severe mental illness, and almost always the powerlessness of exile.

The arrest of the Cave Gully villagers in 1784 was only the beginning of the Shanxi Catholics' troubles. In the decades that followed their everyday lives were repeatedly interrupted by an erratic and unpredictable succession of official crackdowns on Christianity. We next meet them in the archives in 1810 when Giovacchino Salvetti, who had just arrived from Europe, came to the village to be with Luigi Landi as he lay dying. The two men were both from Tuscany and Salvetti had already been appointed to succeed Landi as bishop. In fact Salvetti had only come to China because Landi had written home to his Franciscan brothers asking them to send someone competent to take over. It was not a desirable post: the last seven bishops had all been captured or died shortly after their appointment.[7] Now Salvetti and Landi were in Cave Gully because they were in hiding.

This was the time when missionaries first became a regular part of the lives of Catholics in central Shanxi, but because of the lack of funding from Europe and the Qing ban on their activities they were seldom powerful figures in the community. Instead they were dependent on the local Catholic merchants for financial support and often for their very survival. In these circumstances they had no opportunity to evangelize and spent most of their time hidden away in the wealthy Catholic villages on the plains, supporting themselves by providing rituals to the people there and fitting easily into the familiar social order.

Landi had been living in the village of Nine Springs, just outside the city of Qixian, which was one of the rising centers of Shanxi's trade with Mongolia. Members of a branch of the Fan family had converted as merchants in Beijing during the Ming dynasty. Nine Springs people today claim that their village, not Jiangzhou, was the first Catholic community in Shanxi, but explain that this is not widely known because at that time their ancestors were not rich enough to bring in a missionary.

Since the Qing conquest, however, the Fan, like many Qixian families, had grown wealthy from trade with the newly opened territories beyond the Great Wall. An old rhyme describes the village packed with fine houses with tiled roofs, quite unlike the flat roofs and cave dwellings of villages like Cave Gully.[8] The Christians of Nine Springs could afford to support a missionary, but Landi had to flee when one of the Chinese priests he had trained was captured in Shaanxi province and tortured. The priest managed to convince his interrogators that the foreign missionary was actually in Pingyao, which gave Landi a chance to flee, but the homes of the Pingyao Christians were ransacked and their leaders pulled in for questioning. Landi was already dying and was smuggled out of Nine Springs in a cart by night. Cave Gully was the safest place the cart could reach before dawn and Salvetti followed him there.[9] It was a good place to hide: poor, insignificant, on the borders of two counties, backing onto mountains riddled with coal mines, and entirely Christian.

As government crackdowns on Christianity become increasingly intense, simply reaching Shanxi was extraordinarily difficult and dangerous for European missionaries. Landi's arrival in 1784 (just after the arrest and release of the Cave Gully villagers) had caused a major persecution. He came with a group of Franciscans who had been transferred from Egypt and Palestine. They were frightened, could not speak Chinese, and did not trust the Shanxi Christian merchants who made the travel arrangements. In the end they quarreled so badly that the party split up and they came to the attention of the authorities. When the Qianlong emperor found out about them, he suspected that they were involved in some way with a Muslim rebellion in northwest China, which had been fanned by new currents in Islam that were spreading along the trade routes of central Asia, so he ordered officials across the country to find and arrest all foreign missionaries and their Chinese followers. Chinese Christians who refused to leave the religion were exiled, while the missionaries were sent to Beijing, where most of them died in prison. Landi, who was still young and strong, was one of the few who survived long enough to be expelled from the country. He spent three years in the Philippines, and then returned most unwillingly to China (he wanted to go home to Tuscany) and this time made it to Shanxi.[10]

Salvetti too was arrested on his first attempt to enter the country. The Shanxi man who had come down to Macao on business and was to escort him north was sent into exile, while Salvetti himself was imprisoned in Guangzhou for three years. He was kept in chains and his suffering was successfully used by his jailers to extort money from the European traders in bribes: a total of 1,900 pieces of silver was paid, about half of it collected from the staff of one of the British merchants. The chains were removed for a while, but for the rest of Salvetti's life his legs remained swollen from the injuries and he knew that if he were captured he would be executed rather than expelled. However, Salvetti's philosophy of life was summed up by one of his favorite quotations from the Bible, "The Lord gave, and the Lord has taken; blessed be the name of Lord" (Job 1:21). These are the words in which Job accepts his sufferings and they were to characterize Salvetti's whole experience of life as a missionary. When he was released he set off almost immediately on a difficult journey to Shanxi through Vietnam and the remote mountainous areas of southwest China.[11]

In Cave Gully, Landi and Salvetti were joined by the other missionary living in the area. He had made the same dangerous journey as Salvetti, and from their first meeting Landi thought that the heat and the journey must have "struck a blow to his heart, so that I say nothing against the poor man, and nor does anyone else speak against his behavior, which I am absolutely sure could not be produced by a healthy mind."[12] Landi took him in to live in Nine Springs, but he fasted for days, spoke of the Bible and the saints with his own strange interpretations, and was terrified that the ground was going to give way beneath him. One night he tried to run away: he changed his clothes, slipped out of the church compound, and made his way to the main road to Beijing, which ran past the village. He was found by the villagers, who brought him back, telling him that if he tried to travel like that he would certainly be captured and start a great persecution. After that the Nine Springs people refused to allow him to stay there. He came to attend Landi's deathbed from Winding Gully, a Christian hamlet in the hills near Taiyuan, where he lived for many years as a hermit in a cave above the village (where he is still remembered today).[13]

Landi was buried in Cave Gully, which suggested to later generations that missionaries had lived in the village in this period, but this is misleading: it was a good place to hide, but too poor to support a missionary. The missionaries needed to live in wealthier places because subsidies they had once received from Europe had all but ceased. Soon Salvetti was back in Nine Springs where he began the letter he wrote to Rome to report Landi's death by urging his readers, surrounded by the tumultuous events taking place in Europe, to remember that "in China too the devil is not sleeping."[14] Rome needed to be reminded because the princes of the church were overwhelmed with their own troubles: after the French Revolution of 1789 the new government confiscated church property, abolished tithes, and expelled monks and nuns from their institutions. The governments that followed were not quite so hostile, but the wars they unleashed devastated the economy of Catholic Europe and spread republican ideals. In Italy Pope Pius VI was taken from Rome when a republic was briefly declared, then an invasion by Napoleon removed his successor. For several years starting in 1808 the papal bureaucracy that ran the missions simply did not exist: its property was confiscated and its papers were carried off to France.[15] In time these disasters would invigorate the church with a new generation of leaders passionately opposed to revolution, Enlightenment values, and the rationalism of their eighteenth-century predecessors. These were the men and women who would launch the great missionary endeavors of the nineteenth century, but for the present the European church was absorbed in its own woes. Very few men volunteered for missions and any remaining funds were used to pay for their journeys to China. Once the missionaries arrived they were on their own.

The obvious solution to the shortage of manpower and money was to train Chinese priests. The first Shanxi man to train for the priesthood had traveled to Europe with an Italian Jesuit in 1708. On his return to China he wrote a long account of his journey for the Kangxi emperor, describing the islands of Indonesia and their spice trade, Portuguese colonies on the African coast, an audience with the king of Portugal, Rome with its palaces, aqueducts, fountains, and magnificent churches, and finally the Holy House of the Virgin Mary at Loreto (said to have been brought by angels from Palestine).[16] Later a college was set up in Naples for students from the Chinese and Ottoman empires to study for the priesthood. The number of Chinese studying there was never large, but most of them returned to serve in the Franciscan dioceses of north China.[17] After their time in Europe, speaking fluent Italian and Latin, they considered themselves the elite of the Chinese clergy and many years later one of their number, Wang Tingrong, would campaign passionately against European missionary power, but that is the subject of the next chapter.

The journey to Europe was both expensive and dangerous, so Landi's predecessor as bishop had decided to send students to study for the priesthood in Beijing. There was no shortage of either applicants or local funding, and a seminary was set up with donations from Shanxi and Shaanxi merchants. When the few remaining Jesuits in Beijing got into financial trouble the students were brought back to Shanxi, where they settled down in Nine Springs. Both Landi and Salvetti spent their lives as missionaries hidden away in relative safety, teaching these students.[18] Jacobus Wang, who made the journey across the desert to the exiles, was the last priest to be ordained by Landi before his death. Like most Chinese priests of this generation (and indeed like Buddhist monks) he used a religious name, James (Latin: Jacobus, Chinese: Yage). Perhaps he was inspired by the tale of this disciple of Jesus who traveled beyond the Mediterranean to take the gospel to Spain. Though he himself had never been overseas, he was aware of what was going on in Europe. Indeed he wrote to Pope Pius VII congratulating him on being returned to his throne after the revolutions of the Napoleonic wars.[19]

Landi and Salvetti chose to live in Nine Springs even though the wealthy Christians around Qixian were far from obedient to the missionaries: it was they who expelled the first Franciscan missionary in the 1730s. The struggles continued in later years: the Fan family in Nine Springs had a scroll painting of their ancestors that circulated between the four branches of the family and was honored at New Year. The Christian branch of the family was still taking part in these rituals in 1798 despite fierce missionary objections.[20] The missionaries had to accept this because the Fans' wealth, connections, and power were essential to their survival. Nine Springs was a busy commercial community on the main road from Beijing to Xi'an, so there was an endless stream of all sorts of people passing through and visitors were not likely to be noticed.[21] If the presence of foreigners did come to the attention of officials the village leaders had the wealth and position necessary to bribe their way out of trouble. One of Landi's predecessors was arrested in Qixian, but only after he walked into the government offices and handed himself over. He had hidden for months in the home of a merchant family. Afterwards it was said that soldiers had searched the house and had not seen him, even though he was right in front of them saying mass. This was attributed to his miraculous powers, but the power and wealth of his hosts was surely important too.[22] On another occasion a Christian from Pingyao was invited to a party in the offices of the county government, presumably got drunk, and declared that there was a foreign Christian leader in Qixian and that another foreigner had just arrived. This should have led to an investigation but it was hushed up by the man's brother and the other Christians and nothing further happened.[23]

The merchants not only kept the missionaries safe, they also supported them financially. They built and paid for the seminary, which had rooms for six students and their teachers, a chapel, a garden (where the homesick Landi hoped to grow Italian vegetables) and a surrounding wall. Landi and Li Zibiao, a Naples-trained priest usually known as Jacobus Ly who ran the church in southern Shanxi, also raised three thousand taels, an immense sum, which was invested to provide a regular income to support the students and teachers. They got some additional funding by writing to church authorities in Macao, who provided money from a donor in Manila, but this was only a small portion of the total. The Shanxi donations were invested locally with a merchant (who did very well but was then exiled), a grain dealer, two water-mills, an oil shop, and in a moneylending business giving mortgages for land. Gradually these investments became the primary financial support for the bishop and his establishment.[24]

The missionaries' dependence on the Shanxi merchants for both funding and their own safety naturally affected the way in which they worked. There were already local Christian men who were accustomed to lead prayers, preach, baptize, and manage any church property. The missionaries usually called them "prefects of the Christians," but they are often referred to as "catechists," which misleadingly implies that their duty was to provide basic Christian education. In Chinese they were known as *huizhang* (literally, leaders of the association) and their role in the disputes with the early Franciscans was much more similar to that of the men (also known as *huizhang*) who manage Chinese temples and invite Buddhist and Daoist clergy to provide various rituals.[25] When a Qixian merchant was found to have escorted a group of missionaries from Macao to Shaanxi, his business partner's son told officials that the two men went regularly to Guangdong and "last year I heard them discuss how the Western Ocean men in Guangdong were good at praying and they would like to invite two or three to come and teach."[26] He speaks very much as if the merchants were members of a temple committee employing ritual experts, rather than messengers fetching clergy allocated by Rome, which is the impression given in most church documents. Moreover, it was the custom among Chinese Catholics at this time for some of the daughters of well-off families not to marry but to become sworn virgins who lived in their parents' home and dedicated their lives to prayer and good works, something that was also quite common in Catholic southern Europe at this time. The period of persecution with its intense religious commitment, saw an increase in the number of these Christian virgins as well as the number of priests.[27] Together the leading Christian merchants and the sworn virgins provided the leadership and rituals to which the community was accustomed.

Priests needed another role and this centered around the spread of the mass and confession, rituals that could only be performed by a priest and provided a source of income. One of the first accounts of these rituals in the archives comes from the official who in 1810 made the arrest of a Shanxi priest that led to Landi taking refuge in Cave Gully. The official did not realize the man he had arrested was a priest, but when he asked about the religion he was told about confession and communion, rather than the prayers and fasting described by most Catholics who were arrested. He reported to his superiors that "to take the Holy Body" meant to offer bread and wine to Jesus then divide them between those taking part. After the priest chants the Lord's Prayer, Hail Mary, and other prayers, "the bread and wine change into Jesus' flesh and blood which can help men gain understanding and increase their strength." In confession the Christians who have not obeyed the Ten Commandments beg for pardon from the priest. They kneel and secretly say what they have done, then the priest begs the Holy Mother to entreat the Lord of Heaven to forgive their sins. He added that the power to perform the ritual belonged only to priests.[28]

Since there were still few priests, most Christian communities experienced confession and communion only once every few years. The process began with the individual confessions of the whole community. The priest would sit before the altar while the people came in turns to kneel on either side of him. They listed their sins according to the Ten Commandments, saying which commandment they had sinned against and how many times, as was the practice in Europe. For those who made a formal preparation by enumerating their sins according to the commandments, the process was similar to the practice popular at this time of keeping moral accounts, known as ledgers of merit and demerit, in which good and bad deeds were tallied up regularly with a points score. A bilingual manual for missionaries listed a set of questions for each commandment. For the first commandment, to honor God, the priest could ask whether the person had used divination, had denied that they were Christian, had burned paper money, had kept an image of the stove god in the house, or believed that souls live in ancestral tablets and can help people (a list that suggests interesting continuities with folk religion in Christian households). In practice, since the priest was usually confessing the whole community and any other Christians in the local area in a short time, it is doubtful that he could have spent a great deal of time questioning people. After hearing the list of sins, the priest would set an appropriate penance, then pronounce a Latin formula of absolution. Confession immediately before death was believed to be crucially important for salvation, so attending the dying was one of the most important duties of the missionaries in Nine Springs.[29]

Mass was said immediately after the confession, because to pollute the sacred with the profane by eating the Holy Body while in a state of sin could bring down dreadful punishments after death. While the Christian theology of atonement that underlay the mass was very different from Chinese religious traditions, the ritual itself had much in common with services provided by Buddhist and Daoist clergy: the participants were not supposed to have eaten since the previous evening; the priest put on special garments and a high embroidered hat (worn by Zhao Yuqian, whom we will encounter in the next chapter, see figure 6); the words were spoken in Latin and the priest faced the altar, with his back to the people, to perform the central ritual while the men knelt on one side of the room and the women on the other chanting prayers. Fasting, elaborate embroidered vestments, incomprehensible ritual language, and the separation of the priest from those for whom he performs the ritual are characteristic of much Buddhist and Daoist ritual practice. They were also common in Europe at the time, where the mass was proceeded by a strict fast, the liturgy was in Latin, and parts were said under the priest's breath so that they would not be heard. Men and women also sat on different sides of the church in some parts of Europe, though this practice was dying out. Congregational chanting of prayers throughout the mass was a Chinese innovation. The prayer book provided various prayers for use during the mass, including a set derived from Spanish baroque meditations, but less literate congregations might simply chant the rosary. Europeans too prayed aloud during the mass, saying the rosary or the Stations of the Cross, but they did so as individuals. In both China and Europe the actions of the priest and congregation came together when the priest raised the bread and wine transformed into the body and blood of Christ, and the congregation on seeing them struck their breasts three times and lamented their sins. The priest consumed the bread and a sip of wine during the ritual, and afterwards the remainder of the bread was distributed to those who had confessed and been absolved.[30]

Saying mass was a source of income for priests because the benefit of the ritual could be transferred to others, and especially to one's ancestors who might otherwise be suffering in the afterlife. This was a familiar idea in China since in Buddhism too merit earned through prayer and good deeds is frequently transferred to others. Catholic theology taught that for the mass to benefit someone, the priest should say it with that intention in his mind, so since the medieval period people have often paid the priest for the ritual. For the missionaries and priests dependent on the wealthy Chinese merchants of central Shanxi, these masses were an important source of funding. The standard fee in Shanxi was somewhat higher than the three hundred cash which had been set for China as a whole and masses performed by the bishop would probably have been worth more than this. Landi wrote in 1806 that for the previous thirteen years he had lived entirely on money for masses. Earning money for saying masses was another way in which the missionaries acted as ritual experts like the many Buddhist monks or Daoist priests who made their living as paid service providers for families and temples.[31]

In theory priests could exclude people from the community by refusing absolution and not allowing them to receive communion, a practice which was quite common in Europe.[32] The Fan in Nine Springs were excluded from communion because of their ancestral scroll painting for some years, but with the rise in persecutions this power was seldom exercised. Priests knew that their congregations might betray them to the state at any time if they were angered. A Chinese priest, trained in Naples and known derisively among the Italian missionaries as "that well known Neapolitan gentleman," described what had happened when he refused to give someone absolution. After the mass, the man came up to him, grabbed his Latin prayer book, which would have proved his contact with foreigners, and tried to drag him off to the government offices. He said that the priest had dishonored him by not allowing him to receive communion with the rest. The other Christians wanted to beat the man up, but the priest was terrified, convinced he would be martyred, and fled all the way from Shanxi back to his family in Beijing.[33]

Christians who became alienated sometimes also simply blackmailed the priests and missionaries for financial advantage. The seminary was particularly at risk because of its wealth: after a case in which the blackmailer extracted two hundred taels it had to be moved to another village. The worst case involved a Christian who was blackmailing the missionaries in Beijing, trying to extract five hundred thousand taels, and told the authorities there about the Europeans in Shanxi. Salvetti, who had to go into hiding while the man went on to extort money from the Shanxi Christians, explained to Rome that this was why it was essential to treat

Chinese Christians with patience and caution, "since it is all too easy to create a situation where one hears threats of accusations."[34]

The fragility of the missionaries' situation meant that they could not implement the papal rulings against Christian participation in ancestral worship and Confucian rites and Christians continued to justify their faith in terms of the Chinese classics. Tablets with the Kangxi emperor's inscription "True Origin of All Things" *(wan you zhenyuan)* hung in most churches and Christians told people that Heaven and the Lord on High were the same as the Christian God. Salvetti wrote repeatedly to Rome to defend the Christian use of the ancient Chinese divinatory classic the Book of Changes, arguing along with Jesuits of the early eighteenth century that, like the Sibylline oracles of ancient Rome, it was prophetic and foretold the truths of Christianity. Christians kowtowed in front of the coffin at the funerals of their parents and Salvetti wrote again to Rome to defend their need to give money when they attended pagan funerals, because otherwise their neighbors would raise a tumult against them. All these practices had been forbidden in earlier papal rulings but continued nevertheless.[35]

The remaining differences between the missionaries and the merchants who funded them, especially those concerning personal morality, were smoothed over by a system of monetary penances. This was common in Europe at the time and was another important source of income for priests. Believers who confessed their sins were allocated a penance by the priest. Such a penance could involve the return of stolen property, but for most sins the penance was either prayer or almsgiving, which meant giving money to the church or paying for masses to be said. In practice people often gave the money to the priest who had heard the confession. In Shanxi the sums involved could be sizable. One missionary was accused of having told a merchant to pay five hundred taels for the sin of usury, without having investigated exactly how much profit the man had made. The money raised by Landi and Li Zibiao for the Nine Springs seminary was said to have come partly from fines paid by those who had married their children to non-Christians, worked on Sundays (or made their family and employees do so), or failed to give their children a Christian education. The church official in Macao who reported this explained that it was the traditional way of funding the mission and that the one bishop who had tried not to use it had failed.[36] This was hardly surprising since the practice benefited both the priests and the rich merchants, who could remain part of the Christian community while continuing to take part in activities which created and maintained their social status, such as arranging marriage alliances for their children, trading at the times that others did, educating their sons for the examination system, and lending money at interest. The fines also functioned as the kind of donations to which elite Chinese men were in any case accustomed as an expression of their status. In this case the money paid for an educational institution, at other times for rituals performed for the souls of the ancestors.

Like much illegal but widespread religious practice at the time, the delicate balance between Christians and local officials was subject to occasional violent interruptions. Mostly this happened when there were wars or rebellions and local officials came under pressure from above. The crackdowns led to the arrest and exile of many Christians to newly conquered lands beyond the borders of Chinese culture. Their stories show how not only missionaries and priests but also ordinary Christians traveled vast distances, lived among different peoples, and understood what was happening to them in ways that were shaped by their membership in the church as a global institution.

One of the most severe crackdowns came in 1816, when there was a major White Lotus rebellion and Shanxi Christians were accused of involvement. Even those not convicted were required to leave the religion; those who refused were exiled, though women were usually exempted on payment of a fine. Nearly forty men from Qixian county were arrested, all of them the employees of trading houses. The members of one family agreed to leave the religion and trod on a cross that was put on the ground in front of them, but twenty others, mostly from the Fan family of Nine Springs, refused. All but two of them were sentenced to be tattooed on the face with the words "sent beyond the border" *(wai qian)* and exiled to Kashgaria as slaves to the local Muslim aristocrats who had allied themselves with the Qing dynasty during the recent conquest. Sending people to Kashgaria was a change of policy, since previously Christians had been exiled to Yili which, though distant, was the base for Qing operations in the area and for many Shanxi merchants. Salvetti reported that the news of the sentences caused utter panic. The men of Winding Gully and another hamlet near Taiyuan decided to report themselves to the county magistrate and renounce their religion as communities, handing over their prayer books, images, and crucifixes. The magistrate accepted these symbolic actions, though he quite rightly did not believe that they were genuine.[37]

A few years later Salvetti sent Jacobus Wang to visit the exiles. It was a journey that required great courage and Wang was known afterwards as "the Tartar" for his exploit. He was a passionate man later described by one of the European missionaries as "that famous fanatic."[38] His passion comes across in a letter he wrote to urge the pope to forbid Catholic women to bind their feet. He described this custom as "a great and most enormous evil invented by the devil."[39] He had known, he said, that footbinding was wrong when he was a child still too young to know the difference between putting stones in his mouth and bread. The binding of a little girl's feet brought curses and blows and made mothers and daughters hate each other. It was done only to cause lust in men and to incite them to break the commandments. It damaged the body, since it was begun for girls as young as two years old, blocking the circulation of the blood so that many became sick, died young, or became lame or disabled, and later in life had miscarriages. Even when the binding was successful it made it difficult for women to walk on a flat surface, let alone on rocky or wet ground. So they often fell and their feet then became so inflamed that they fell off and the woman died; indeed he had given the last rites to many women who had died like this. He had made repeated efforts to get his superiors (the missionaries) to ban the custom, but had failed, so now he asked that the church bureaucracy forward his statement to the pope. This letter probably did not reach the pope and certainly had no effect (the church saw footbinding as a local custom and did not condemn it until the twentieth century), but it is a most effective piece of writing, which conveys Wang's passionate, emotional commitment to the idea that footbinding was morally wrong.

This Chinese man who argued with bureaucrats in Rome against Chinese custom now set off to travel to the furthest reaches of the expanding Qing empire. The whole journey took more than two years. He had a map, possibly something like the early nineteenth-century map of Asia on which the places he visited are shown (map 3). In his report to Rome he described how his map showed that the Christians were in places along the borders of Russia, Armenia, and even India. His colleague Li Zibiao commented that the exiles were being sent to a place that might be closer to Palestine than to China.[40] Wang traveled along the old Silk Road through Shaanxi into the province of Gansu. Because much conversion had occurred through merchant networks, there were Christian communities along the main trade routes and he could make his way from one to the next, but it was still risky. A few years earlier when the Nine Springs Christians had been arrested, Wang himself had been denounced to the authorities as a priest by a Christian in Shaanxi and had had to go into hiding.[41] He can only have assumed that the authorities in Shaanxi still had his name. In Gansu he had to pass through the Great Wall, which divided China proper from the territories that lay beyond. This was something Shanxi priests sometimes did when they traveled to Mongolia, and it terrified them. An Italian who went as far as the Wall in the mid-eighteenth century, when the Qing were still at war with the Zunghars, described how the gates were staffed by officials, soldiers, and customs officers who questioned all who came about where they were going and why. The Italian himself did not dare step forward, though he thought he might have done it with a large group of Christian merchants passing through at the time.[42] The Chinese "Neapolitan gentleman" had to go through quite often, since he was priest to communities on either side of the wall. He needed to carry his prayer book and missal, both written in Latin, his vestments, chalice, and crucifix for the mass, and he was terrified that some Christian would betray him. He said that every time he had to pass through he prayed to the Virgin Mary, Paradise, the Souls in Purgatory, the Holy Trinity, and Maria Maddalena Sterlich (a nun in Naples famous for her holiness).[43]

Beyond Gansu and the Great Wall was the vast area known as the New Territories (Xinjiang), which had been conquered by the Qing only seventy years earlier and where the state authorities were more vigilant and active than they were in the interior of China. The native population of the northern pastoral area known as Yili were Mongols, though their population had been decimated in the wars against the Qing. To the south round Kashgar there were Muslims who spoke a language related to Turkish and had close ties with central Asia. Between these two areas lay the Taklamakan desert. Chinese were supposed to enter these territories only as officials, soldiers, exiles, state-sponsored colonists, and merchants. The merchants traveled across the vast distances with camel caravans and were required to have passes listing the number of men in their party and any distinguishing features, which were to be countersigned by officials along the way.[44] Jacobus Wang, who presumably traveled with one of these merchant caravans, adapted the familiar Latin of Paul's Letter to the Corinthians to describe his experiences: "Also going to those parts there is no shortage of perils from robbers, perils from waters, perils from mountain precipices, perils from wild beasts, perils from tax collectors, perils from false

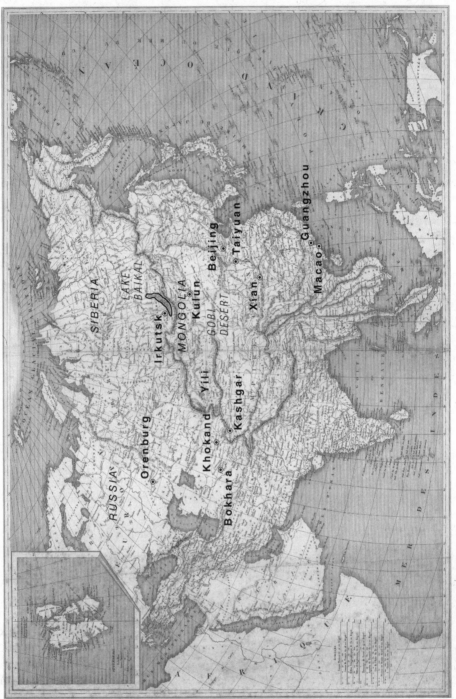

MAP 3. Asia in the early nineteenth century, showing places visited by Shanxi Catholics. Adapted from map of Asia by Charles Monin

brethren, and perils from enemies both visible and invisible. I cannot fully express all these perils with my pen, but nevertheless by God's protecting grace I escaped unhurt."[45]

The wolf that accompanies and protects Wang in the folktale resembles the dogs that ran with these caravans. They were savage and dangerous, but they acted as guard dogs, even sometimes as messengers, and were part of the business. An explorer who traveled with one of the last generation of camel caravans in the 1920s described how it was the caravan cook's job to feed them and to call them when the caravan set off. One dog moved into his tent after he fed it and would savage anyone else who came there. The best caravan dogs were said to come from the great Dashengkui firm, which dominated the trade with Mongolia and was partly owned by investors in Qixian.[46]

Wang's journey was made possible by the Shanxi trading network that spread across the newly conquered territories. Shanxi merchants began by provisioning the Qing armies during the conquest, but then expanded into much the same kind of business that they had in Mongolia. They imported tea from south China, bought grain from the Yili valley to sell in China, and smuggled rhubarb roots through Kashgar into the Fergana valley on the first stage of their journey to Beirut and then across the Mediterranean to Europe. As business expanded they built temples to the Chinese military deity Guandi that functioned as native place and business associations. Qixian was one of the wealthiest Shanxi cities and its merchants were especially active in Xinjiang, to the extent that part of one of the major market towns in the north was actually known as Little Qixian.[47]

Christians were part of these expanding networks. When the Qing launched a nationwide manhunt for a Qixian Christian merchant who was one of the escorts for Luigi Landi and his companions in the 1780s, they failed to catch him, but they found out all about his business dealings. Like many Shanxi merchants he worked far from home, in this case in Xi'an, the capital of Shaanxi province, where a small group of traders closely bound by their shared Christian faith used the same building as both church and warehouse. From there he traveled every year to Guangzhou to sell the products of northwest China and the Mongolian steppe: rhubarb and leather. On the trip when he met Landi, he was said to have purchased eight hundred taels worth of rhubarb. The root of the rhubarb plant, which was used as a purge, was a popular drug in eighteenth-century Europe; the Russian state, which controlled the caravan trade across Siberia, had a monopoly on its sale. Shipping low quality rhubarb to Europe through

Guangzhou was a profitable way of undercutting this monopoly.[48] Another Christian merchant family, the Tian of Pingyao county who made a major donation to the seminary in Beijing, traded in European novelties (clocks, pictures, and ornaments), and in the late eighteenth century opened a famous fur store. The furs suggest that as well as traveling to Guangzhou the Tian were doing business in Mongolia, where furs from the newly opened Siberian wilderness were sold south to the Chinese market.[49] Members of such families often lived and worked for long periods in Mongolia and Xinjiang. In the 1790s Shanxi Christians in the salt trade in "Tartary" (a European label that included everything beyond the Great Wall) asked a missionary whether they could follow the example of the Muslim merchants and use money from a special price increase to pay their contribution for a temple to a Chinese deity being set up by all the merchants.[50] Today there are branches of the Catholic Fan family in both Inner Mongolia and Xinjiang. Those in Inner Mongolia came as merchants, but the family in Yili remember that their ancestors arrived as exiles.[51]

So the exiled Shanxi Christians were not sent beyond the borders of their known world, as exiled officials often felt they were.[52] Instead they entered a space structured by the same long-distance trade networks that had formed the channels for the earlier generation's conversion to Christianity. The first group to be exiled in the 1780s were sent as slaves to the recently conquered Oirat Mongols. Their slavery was supposed to be permanent but the Oirats were apparently willing to take cash rather than to try to extract agricultural labor from unwilling prisoners. Within six months five exiled Chinese priests had been redeemed for a total of one hundred taels and brought into the city by a rich Christian exiled from Shanxi. On his instructions one of the Naples-trained priests, who knew how to repair clocks, managed to earn enough to redeem eight more of the exiles. Another Shanxi priest, whose accounts of the Chinese system of pulses had intrigued the intellectual elite of Naples, practiced as a doctor.[53]

Jacobus Wang traveled south from Yili to the area round Kashgar to visit the most distant exiles. Although the first news that people were to be exiled to Kashgar was greeted with horror, later reports of life in these oasis towns were positive: Li Zibiao reported to Rome that the area had a temperate climate, abundant fruit, grapes, and wine, and the people were not barbarous but of a vigorous constitution and followed the Muslim religion. He thought that it was "certainly much better for the convenience of human life than the kingdom of China, which has more hunger than anywhere else."[54] It was also known that the exiles in

Kashgaria were not in fact enslaved and were free to practice their religion. But this comfortable life was not to last. Shortly after his return Jacobus Wang heard that the Russians had joined with the Muslims to occupy the cities there. What had in fact happened was an invasion from Kokand (in what is now Uzbekistan) led by a descendant of one of the area's former leading clans. The invaders were supported by the local population and both Qing dynasty forces and Chinese residents were massacred. When the Qing needed to bring in reinforcements, Chinese exiles in the north became potential soldiers: about forty Christian exiles were allowed to return home to Shanxi as a reward for fighting for the Qing in this war. Their leader was a priest who had been trained in Naples, though the Qing never discovered this. He had had a mixed career: when he first returned to China, he got into trouble for seducing women and was suspended for several years before being sent off to work as a priest in Gansu. He was captured, refused to recant, and was sentenced to exile plus the *cangue,* a heavy wooden frame which he wore round the neck for the next eight years. Then the *cangue* was removed and his sentence was commuted to exile. In Yili he became friendly with a military officer who got him released by enrolling him among the troops sent to fight the invasion. As another Chinese priest commented, "Behold a soldier of Christ and of the Chinese Emperor!"[55]

Hardly any of the Christians who had been exiled to Kashgaria survived the war, but one man, who came from Qixian and had been exiled with the group from Nine Springs, was thrown into a yet more distant journey. He was captured and carried off by the invaders across the mountains to the khanate of Kokand. There he was sold into slavery, but escaped along with one of the Chinese Muslim merchants who had been captured at the same time. Dressed in local clothes and wearing turbans, they begged their way from village to village until they reached Bokhara, where they met up with some other Chinese Muslims who had also been captured and escaped. The group planned to get back to China by taking the trade route to Russia, so they followed a caravan, scraping a living by leading the camels, working as porters, and begging for food. When they reached the Russian border near Orenburg they handed themselves over to the border guards. The Russians were bound by treaties to return subjects of the Qing found on their territory, so they provided a cart and the men set out across Siberia to Irkutsk. By the time they arrived their clothes were in rags and a kindly Russian official got a local nobleman to give them clothes and some cash, and provided them with food until winter set in, Lake Baikal froze over, and they could set off across it. When the Russians handed them over to Qing officials in Kulun (today Ulaan Bataar) the Muslims were questioned and allowed to return home, but the Qixian man still refused to renounce the Christianity for which he had originally been exiled, so he was sent back into slavery in Kashgar.[56]

Jacobus Wang was only one of the priests, missionaries, and exiled Shanxi Christians who traveled immense distances in this period. Their journeys were linked to their religion, with its close ties to global trade, but they took place at a time when such long-distance travel was extraordinarily hard. Few returned to their homes: missionaries from Tuscany died in Shanxi, Christian merchants from Shanxi died in exile in Xinjiang. The survivors often felt isolated and powerless in a foreign culture.[57] Jacobus Wang's letter to Rome about his journey ends with a request that the missionaries selected for future missions be wise, since those who have recently arrived have distressed Salvetti. This was a polite way of saying that there were now three Europeans in the province, and two were entirely unable to cope. The newest arrival tried to run away, and when he was caught he became violent. He later explained that he had wanted martyrdom, which suggests that his flight was an essentially suicidal gesture, but it was terrifying for the people of Nine Springs, who knew that they could easily be arrested and exiled. Salvetti, acting in a way that was not uncommon among bishops in Europe who had to handle problem clergy, had him locked up and even put in chains. From his prison he wrote desperate and increasingly wild letters to the pope, in uneven brush strokes on tiny scraps of paper, complaining that he had been persecuted because he objected to the failure to implement papal rulings. He described the Shanxi Christians as "impertinent," suggesting that he found their claims to authority within the church unacceptable.[58] After a while, Salvetti gave up hoping this unfortunate man could work as a missionary and took him into his household, using the seminary money to provide for him. Only ten years later was the political climate safe enough for some of the Christians to agree to take him back to Macao. He was one of the very few missionaries who returned to Europe. Salvetti, who was endlessly charitable, wrote to Rome to say what a pleasure it had been to be able to send him off, since it made him so happy.[59]

From Salvetti's point of view there was a striking contrast between Chinese priests like Jacobus Wang, with his courage, passion, and the discretion needed to make such a difficult journey, and the two Europeans, neither of whom were able to work at all. As bishop he was in the habit of writing once a year to Rome listing all his clergy and their achievements.

In 1825 he began with the two Europeans and their many problems, then listed the Chinese priests, beginning with Li Zibiao ("the most able of all for intelligence and wisdom") and ending with the other six Chinese priests, all of whom he declared to be good.[60] Salvetti greatly admired the Chinese priests who had endured exile and who returned after many years of hardship. He wanted to put one of them in charge of the seminary, though this came to nothing as the priest died only a year after his return. He also treated the priest who had suffered exile and the *cangue* for so many years with immense respect as a "Confessor of the Faith."[61]

Government crackdowns went on into the 1830s and the threat of them continued to shape the Shanxi church. Salvetti survived into old age, living in Nine Springs and working closely with a small group of Chinese priests. Under their leadership the sacraments of confession and communion had become a major part of local religious practice, but between occasional visits from priests Catholic practice remained much as it had been in the seventeenth century, with its similarities to lay Buddhist groups and its emphasis on Confucian moral values. Since the clergy remained dependent on donations from wealthy Christian merchants, rules about ancestral rituals and funerals imposed more than a century earlier were largely ignored.

In 1835 a Shanxi Buddhist sectarian group called the Teaching of Former Heaven *(xiantianjiao),* which had been growing rapidly, was suspected of rebellion, threatened with arrest, and fought back. They captured Zhaocheng county town, burned the government buildings, and murdered the magistrate and his family before enough government troops arrived to put down the rebellion. The arrests that followed inevitably included a nearby Catholic village. Jacobus Wang happened to be there and was among a group of Christian men paraded through the crowded streets of the county town with their hands tied behind their backs. When they got to the government buildings, the investigating official wanted to know if the Teaching of the Lord of Heaven was related to the Teaching of Former Heaven. He took Wang aside and asked who his group's leaders were and what prayers they used. Wang replied that they worshipped only one God, so there was only one teaching in the whole world, and its leader was in Rome. He also called up the whole panoply of Confucianism with which Christianity could still be defended. He asserted that Christians prayed once every seven days because that was what was laid down in the Book of Changes,

wrote out a set of prayers for peace and for the emperor and his officials, and told the magistrate about the Ten Commandments. He admitted that Christians fasted but claimed that they were doing so now
because of the troubles (which any Confucian official could expect
would be aided by a ritual of sincerity). The magistrate was evidently
not concerned with the idea of Christianity as a foreign religion headed
from Rome but only about its connections with the Teaching of Former
Heaven, so his anxieties were calmed. He told Wang that the Christians' only error was not to worship Buddha, and that was not of great
importance compared to Confucius, so he released Wang and the other
Christians. Wang's fear comes across in the exaltation of his report:

> Then I thought I would be martyred, even though I am unworthy of such a
> gift. Since I was captured on Passion Sunday, I hoped to be placed in a
> wooden frame and strangled on the Thursday of Holy Week, because that is
> the penalty for missionaries in this kingdom. Oh how unfortunate I am and
> unworthy of such a favor, for which reason I passed unharmed through this
> great opportunity. So I beg Your Eminence on my knees to intercede for me
> to our merciful Father, by the merits of his beloved son our Lord Jesus Christ
> who died on the wooden frame of the cross for me and for my sins, that I too
> should die in that way for my sins.[62]

These events set off another wave of arrests which involved Christians as well as Buddhist sectarians. When not long afterwards a church
messenger had some Latin books stolen and reported the theft to the
local magistrate, there was a major investigation. Once more those who
refused to tread on a crucifix were exiled to the area round Kashgar,
including this time three women who were sworn virgins.[63] Meanwhile
Salvetti transferred Jacobus Wang to the relative safety of the villages
round Cave Gully, where he was described as both "indefatigable" and
broken by his labors. He died in 1841 in Cold Springs Road.[64]

Salvetti too survived into old age. He often had to go into hiding, but
he was never betrayed. Whether as a result of his personality and religious formation or as a matter of conviction, he was willing to conform
to the situation in which he found himself, spending his life largely in
providing rituals for the wealthy Christians who supported him. After
his death he was praised for his careful and precise observance of all the
rituals and ceremonies of the church and his obedience to the Franciscan monastic rule. This, not conversions, was what he considered to be
his task as a missionary: when a charismatic young Italian who had
been sent off to Hubei province converted 185 people in one year,
Salvetti wrote to remind him of a regulation that adults should not be

baptized in China unless they were prepared to submit to torture and death rather than deny the faith. In cases where the desires of the Chinese Christians disagreed with church rules, he wrote to Rome on their behalf and allowed the practices to continue in the meantime. He was also generous. When the seminary was unable to continue in operation because of persecution, he distributed its income, which amounted to the considerable sum of three hundred taels each year, in charity. It was said of him that people never left him with empty hands and that many were entirely supported by him.[65]

From this behavior Salvetti won a reputation for holiness that made it easy to credit him with supernatural powers. Another folktale told of how one day he was preaching when he suddenly stopped and wept. He was asked what had happened, but would only groan and reply, "They are adding another fault to their sin." Later it was discovered that at that moment a Christian virgin who had been seduced and abandoned had procured an abortion rather than lose her honor.[66] Virgins were a point of tension in a society where a family with an unmarried daughter was always concerned for its honor, but where religious fervor made people accept exile for their faith and where virginity was seen as a route to salvation. The tensions were particularly severe because some women chose the religious life as an alternative to an unwanted marriage and in these cases the woman's fate might be decided by throwing lots to determine God's will for her. Some women who swore virginity did later marry, but to do so was a loss of honor.[67] The story of Salvetti's foreknowledge depicts him as sharing in the community's concern for family honor in his reticence while at the same time it provides a disciplinary tale for virgins, whose wrongdoings can be sensed by the virtuous bishop even at a distance.

Salvetti's reputation for holiness was made possible by his humility, but this was a double-edged sword for a missionary bishop. Humility was perhaps Francis of Assisi's most characteristic virtue and certainly one strongly inculcated in eighteenth-century Italian Franciscans during their training. Salvetti was praised for treating children seriously as if they were adults and being humble even with his staff, whom he called assistants rather than servants. He never learned to read Chinese and by the 1830s he was heavily dependent on a man named Wang who managed the diocese's property, dealt with the correspondence, and advised him on difficult cases. A saying went round that "Wang is the bishop, Salvetti the servant."[68] Another folktale about Salvetti told of how he was hidden under the awning of a cart, like a dog it was said, and driven into the city with a young bride sitting up in front. Even at the city gate no one could touch a bride and thus he was safe.[69] Holiness and humility might be linked, but humility was not always admired.

In the late 1830s one of the Chinese priests who had returned from exile died and his body was laid out in the Nine Springs residence. The death coincided with the arrival of a young Italian who had been sent to take over from Salvetti and who was horrified by the failure to enforce papal rulings banning kowtows to the deceased at funerals. He persuaded Salvetti to send someone to watch over the coffin to ensure that no one kowtowed as the prayers for the dead were being recited. This plan failed: at least one of the Christians kowtowed not only in front of the body but also at the grave. Under pressure over this and another funeral, Salvetti simply announced that in general he ignored these rules.[70] The criticisms shook the diocese and disputes of every kind broke out, with many detailed letters of complaint to Rome, on which much of the material in this chapter has been based. What is most striking is that the young European did not win the arguments, but was forced to leave Nine Springs and retreat to Shaanxi. His perception of what was going on was that the Chinese priests were running things and unless there was some change "it is finished for the Europeans."[71] Salvetti died in 1843 and left the diocese in the hands of another newly arrived European Franciscan, Gabriele Grioglio.[72]

The villagers of Cave Gully were peripheral to the world described in the stories of this period, which were centered in the merchant towns of the Taiyuan plain and the Catholic villages near them. Even so they would have known the characters: Landi died in Cave Gully and Salvetti was present at his death, while Jacobus Wang would have visited to say mass when he was living in Cold Springs Road. The Cave Gully people told tales about them that reflected the world they shared with the wealthier Christians of the plains villages. They remembered it as a world of miracles, a time of intense religious commitment and a time when Chinese priests and European missionaries worked in harmony. Giovacchino Salvetti was admired for his holiness while Jacobus Wang was honored for his courage. This world had already ended when Salvetti died, though the Cave Gully villagers surely did not know that at the time. In 1840, with British victory in the Opium War, everything about Catholicism in Shanxi was about to change, and Cave Gully would become not an impoverished peripheral community but the heart of the story.

CHAPTER 3

The Priest Who Ran Away
to Rome

The orphanage gatekeeper in Cave Gully used to tell the story of a Chinese priest who entered the seminary late, after he had been married and widowed. He had very good grades so he did well, but he could not accept the low status of the Chinese priests. The Chinese priests were not treated with respect: at meals they sat at seats below the foreigners so when there was chicken the best bits were all gone before it reached the Chinese, and when they died they were buried at the feet of the foreign priests. So after hiding for three years, this priest ran away to Rome, but it was very difficult to get to see the pope, so he wrote his petition out and wore it on his head to attract the pope's attention. The pope saw it and was convinced. He ordered that in the future, relations between the Chinese and foreign priests should be equal: they should eat facing each other and be buried head to head. When the priest got back to Cave Gully he entered on his knees with his back towards the bishop. The bishop asked why he did this, so he explained that it was because the Chinese priests' position was low. Then he handed over the letter from the pope.

This tale has a variety of endings, all of them demonstrating the priest's success in his campaign for equality between the Chinese and foreign clergy. Wang Tingrong, who is often called Wang Ruose (Joseph), had already become a folk hero only a few years after his death: in the version collected by Barnaba Nanetti in the 1890s, he emigrates to America. In versions circulating today he becomes parish priest of a wealthy village, repeatedly refuses positions offered to him by the missionary bishop, and even introduces to Shanxi the foreign practices of growing tomatoes and smallpox vaccination.[1] The story follows the form of many Chinese folktales, in which the hero undergoes many trials but finally reaches the virtuous ruler and is justified. It also fits into a pattern of popular stories of modern Chinese nationalism: to Shanxi Catholics today Wang Tingrong is a familiar nationalist hero who resisted the demeaning treatment of Chinese by foreigners. After many years of propaganda by the Communist government accusing Catholics of subservience to the foreign powers, the story of a priest who persevered in such difficulties to resist foreign oppression proves the strength of Catholic patriotism. But this is not simply a tale of Chinese nationalism, but also one about being part of a great transnational institution: Wang makes his petition not to a Chinese official but to Pope Pius IX in Rome.

The global aspect of the story becomes even more important when we know more about Wang Tingrong's life. He was born in Newtown, a Catholic village where the leading inhabitants were large-scale merchants in cloth and medicines. Far from being someone who resisted foreign control because he became a priest later in life, he entered the seminary in his early teens, presumably because his uncle was a priest. The priesthood was a lucrative and well-respected occupation, so there was considerable competition for seminary places and they often went to the relatives of priests and Christian leaders. Family connections made it very hard to ask these boys to leave the seminary if they turned out not to be suited for the priesthood. There is no evidence that Wang Tingrong was ever particularly devout, but nevertheless in 1838, during the last of the major government crackdowns against Christianity, he was among a group of seminarians sent first to Macao for safety and then on to the College for Chinese in Naples to continue their studies.[2] In Naples he experienced the rising tide of Italian nationalism and the dramatic European revolutions of 1848. His later Chinese nationalism was shaped by the Italian south, a complex world where clergy were inspired by the ideals of the Enlightenment but struggled against the modern state; resisted the growing dominance of the church hierarchy over their lives, but shared the longing of many European Catholics for the elevation of the pope. When Wang came back from Naples he brought these ideas with him, but in China they were played out in the quite different context of growing Western imperialism.

Shortly after Wang Tingrong left for Naples, Gabriele Grioglio arrived to replace Salvetti as bishop and took up residence not among the wealthy merchants of Nine Springs but in the poor hamlet of Cave Gully. The move was the result of political changes driven by the rise of European power that transformed the context of Catholicism in China. A new generation of missionaries received money and protection from Europe, and were thus no longer dependent on the support of wealthy local Christians. Grioglio did not need to live in Nine Springs. Instead he moved into Cave Gully, a poor community that he could more easily dominate. He imposed not only the long postponed papal rulings about ancestral worship and funerals but also his own rules that would make Catholic practice in Shanxi more similar to Catholicism in Europe.

The changes began with British merchants in Guangzhou who were increasingly dissatisfied with the terms of their trade with China, while in Beijing officials worried about the impact of British opium imports on the exchange rates between silver and copper, which was making it hard for the poor to pay their taxes. In 1839 these tensions exploded in the first Opium War. Although the war itself was fought far away in the southeast and had little direct impact on people in Shanxi, the treaties that followed China's defeat transformed the lives of the missionaries. They did not explicitly permit missionary activity, but they included clauses stating that foreigners found outside any of the five new treaty ports were to be taken back to those cities, and any illegal activity by foreigners should be dealt with by their consuls rather than by the regular legal system. In effect these two rules meant that the penalty for a European missionary discovered in Shanxi was no longer painful imprisonment and probable death, but merely temporary removal to Shanghai. Moreover, as a result of French pressure in the aftermath of the war, the emperor issued an edict permitting Chinese to practice Christianity. A Catholic working in the provincial government saw this edict when it arrived and immediately made a copy. It was greeted with "indescribable joy" and was put into use a few days later when a man who had been arrested successfully quoted it to an official who had told him to leave the religion. No longer would Catholics live in fear of blackmail, persecution, and exile.[3]

The Opium War also transformed the financing of the Catholic missions in China. With the end of the Napoleonic wars, the French economy was reviving and there was a new group of Catholic clergy whose ideas, formed in reaction to the revolution, would come to dominate the church of the nineteenth century. Their vision was conservative in that it recalled past glories, but it was also a response to ongoing social and political changes. Two new charities were established in France whose priorities were to shape the operations of Catholic missionaries in China for the next century. The first was known as the Propagation of the Faith (l'Oeuvre de la Propagation de la Foi) and its primary goal was evangelization. It provided funding for church buildings, religious schools, and the employment of local evangelists. The money was sent to missionary bishops and they were required in return to send reports and statistics of conversions for publication in the charity's journal. The second great missionary charity was the Holy Childhood Association (l'Oeuvre de la Sainte Enfance), which began as a project to rescue Chinese babies from infanticide, baptize them, and if they survived, raise them. It later expanded to include work with children in other countries, but it always devoted a large amount of its resources to China. The treaties that followed the Opium War made it possible for these charities to send money to the missionaries in Shanxi: the first annual payment from the Propagation of the Faith arrived in Shanxi in 1845 and was for the considerable sum of 834 taels. Money from the Holy Childhood Association arrived the next year. By the 1860s the Holy Childhood Association was sending nearly as much money as the Propagation. Combined with income from the investments belonging to the seminary, this money meant that the Shanxi missionaries were no longer dependent on local Christians for funding.[4]

The money was a huge windfall for Cave Gully, where Grioglio built a church and then a residence for himself and the seminarians he was teaching. The church replaced the chapel in the home of the Duan family, but belonged to the mission, not the family, making it a striking symbol of the changes that were taking place. Grioglio told the Propagation of the Faith, who had provided 474 taels to fund the new building, that it could be considered "the cathedral of Shanxi."[5] The Cave Gully villagers also benefited for a time from a subsidized school attached to the seminary. All this building drew new settlers: one family remembers that their ancestor moved to the village at this time as a craftsman who came to work on the new seminary, married a local girl, and stayed.[6]

With the money from the Holy Childhood Association, Grioglio established institutions to care for unwanted children and these too were based in Cave Gully. He began by employing four women as wet-nurses to care for eleven children and paying families to look after other children. Being given money to raise little girls who could later become brides for their sons was popular with the villagers and Grio-

FIGURE 5. Cave Gully orphanage circa 1900. Courtesy of Archivio Fotografico, Centro Studi Confortiani e Saveriani, Istituto Missioni Estere, Parma.

glio could say proudly that he only gave the children to devout parents. The competition for boys, who had a higher market value as adopted sons, was presumably even more intense. The sums involved were considerable: at one point ten taels was being paid each year to support two boys being raised in the village. Then in the 1860s an orphanage was built to care for forty-five girls. The building cost around 650 taels, spent on repairing the courtyard, wages for workmen, furniture, carters, medicines, clothes, bedding, fittings for a chapel, books for the girls to learn to read, a donkey, a grindstone, and a wheel.[7] While some of these things must have come in from outside, much of the money was clearly spent locally. Figure 5 shows the orphanage around 1900. There are about a hundred toddlers and older girls arrayed in rows in the courtyard, displaying spinning wheels that are a symbol of the women's work they are learning. Off stage and inaudible to one who sees only a photograph are the babies, many of whom arrived in the orphanage sick and soon died.

The orphanage drew the Christian virgins, who up until this time had lived with their families, into the institutional structure of the church.

The first director was a sworn virgin in her forties; she was the daughter of a well-known doctor and was both literate and learned in medicine. She was praised for leaving a comfortable home to come to devote herself to the children. As the orphanage expanded, more virgins joined. In the photograph they are standing on a step behind the children, wearing distinctive black clothes and headgear. When additional orphanages were established, they too were administered by sworn virgins who left their families, taking their dowries with them, and worked for the clergy. All this was strongly influenced by the expectations of the French charities providing the funding, so it is not surprising that it was similar to what was going on in France at this time: a wave of new church buildings, the founding of church welfare institutions, and the absorption of independent religious women living at home into new religious orders.[8]

With money, buildings, and staff at his base in Cave Gully, Grioglio was in a very different position from his predecessors who had been dependent on the merchants of Nine Springs and he behaved accordingly. Where Salvetti saw himself as the patiently suffering Job, the Bible quotation most characteristic of Grioglio is one of the harsher sayings of Jesus, "It is not good to take the bread of the children and cast it to the dogs" (Matthew 15:26), which was widely understood at the time to mean that the holy bread of the eucharist should not be given to those who went against the church's teaching.[9] By controlling access to the eucharist Grioglio banned a wide range of practices ranging from participation in non-Christian funerals to painting images of saints wearing Chinese-style shoes. Like many of the rising generation of priests in Europe he believed in rigid obedience to the church hierarchy with the pope at its head and aimed to unify Catholic practice far more than had ever been contemplated by earlier generations.[10] His rules were so different from previous practice in Shanxi that he wrote to Rome for permission to collect and burn the sermons of one of his predecessors.[11]

Grioglio began, as a number of his predecessors had tried but failed to do, by implementing earlier papal rulings about Chinese funerals and ancestral rituals. He banned Catholics from attending non-Christian rituals for their ancestors, or any non-Christian funerals. Since most Catholics were now the descendants of Catholics, ancestral rituals were not so much of an issue, but the ban on attending the funerals of non-Christians was deeply unpopular. He also declared it a sin for Christians to pay the levies raised by villages to put on festivals in honor of local deities or watch the operas that accompanied these festivals. Whether or not Christians should contribute to festivals had been an ongoing problem since the time of the Jesuits, but after the religion was made illegal contribution had become inevitable because Christians could so easily be blackmailed: they explained to Grioglio that what was done with the money was none of their business. Some Christians even became professional actors who could expect to spend much of their lives performing at temple festivals.[12] Now in order to satisfy the bishop, Christian communities would have to negotiate some kind of new arrangement with their neighbors.

Grioglio also introduced a strict ban on usury, something the seventeenth-century Jesuits in China had fought hard within the church bureaucracy to avoid. He ruled that Catholics in his diocese were not to receive the sacraments if they were borrowing or lending money at interest rates of more than 5 percent. The medieval Catholic church had taken Jesus' statement "Lend hoping for nothing thereby" (Luke 6:35) as a total ban on interest payments, but in Europe the growth of an increasingly monetized economy had led to the development of elaborate contractual arrangements that allowed interest payments in fact though not in form. After centuries of dispute, Rome had decided in favor of the Jesuits, who claimed that the risk of default in China was particularly serious and should be considered a reason for charging for a loan. This decision turned out to be the thin end of the wedge that eventually destroyed the church's ban on usury in Europe: by the early nineteenth century the church accepted that loans made at moderate legal interest rates were not sinful. However, Grioglio was a conservative who remained hostile to interest payments in principle, and he was shocked by the level of Chinese interest rates, which often included an element of insurance, as the Jesuit case suggested, and could go up to a legal limit of 30 percent. This was a major issue for the Catholic merchants of the plains villages like Nine Springs because many Shanxi businesses were developing at this time from long-distance trading houses into banks that provided moneylending, pawnbroking, and remittance networks. The Tian family of Pingyao developed their fur-trading business into a bank, but this now put them, and others like them, in conflict with the church. Some Catholics avoided confession for years, while others withdrew from the business. One man who had opened a pawnshop in Beijing closed it and lost his capital, so that he was unable to pay his creditors and he had to go off to work as a merchant beyond the Great Wall.[13]

Churches were still built in the courtyard style used for houses, but Grioglio campaigned to change the interior decoration to make them look as much as possible like Catholic churches elsewhere in the world. He banned inscriptions over the altar, not just the inscriptions saying "Honor Heaven" but any inscriptions, explaining that they were not used in the worldwide Catholic church. He also banned the use of paper flowers to decorate the altar. Any devotional images where the clothes, beards, or shoes were different from those seen in Catholic images all over the world were to be removed not only from churches but even from people's homes. The Christian painters who made them were warned that in the future they must not produce images in this style. The ban on inscriptions failed, but from this time on Catholic devotional images would be visibly foreign.[14]

Grioglio was able to enforce these bans because with the new legal situation and the flow of European money he could safely refuse absolution and the eucharist to leading Christians. Earlier bishops who had tried to do this had not survived for long, but now Catholics discovered that their relation to the missionaries had changed. One old man came to Cave Gully to ask for confession and communion before death (something that elderly Christians often did quite early in case a priest was not available later). He was refused because he was not complying with the new rules and, annoyed, went straight to one of the nearby villages where he announced that horrendous deeds were being committed in the foreigner's residence. This was reported to the county magistrate and in earlier years would surely have resulted in arrests, but now the government clerk was not interested and just locked the man up as a trouble-maker. Clearly blackmail by Christians was no longer an effective way of controlling the missionaries. This did not mean that the Christians always felt safe: during the great Taiping Rebellion, with its Christian teachings and emphasis on the Ten Commandments, Grioglio went into hiding in the mountains, but the state never took action against him.[15]

Grioglio could also enforce these new rules because, with the money from France, he did not need cash penances. Where he was determined to make changes he declared the sin involved to be a "reserved case," which only he as bishop could absolve, and he demanded not cash but a publicly performed penance before he would do so. These public penances, such as kneeling outside the church throughout the mass, were designed to humiliate, so they were much more problematic for elite Christians who were leaders of their congregations than for the poor. It was the elite who were more likely to want to take part in ancestral rituals, attend the funerals of business associates, and lend money at interest.[16]

Grioglio's later story suggests that he was quite popular both with the most devout believers and in poor hill villages like Cave Gully where people benefited from his institution building. In the plains villages where many Christians were the descendants of merchants, the campaign for low interest rates was destructive of family businesses, but in Cave Gully it may have appeared an obviously righteous act. Early Confucianism, born out of an agrarian state, shared with medieval Christianity a distrust of trade as a way of earning money, which was most famously expressed in the occupational hierarchy of gentlemen, farmers, craftsmen, and finally merchants. By the nineteenth century in both China and Europe economic development had changed the attitudes of the elite, but the rhetoric remained. It could be used by the rural poor, who suffered from high interest rates and often saw them as unfair and wrong, as became clear in the twentieth century with the success of communist campaigns for interest-rate reductions and the popularity of attacks on moneylenders.

On the other hand many wealthy Christians were clearly strongly opposed to the new rules. Instead of trying to dispute Catholic teaching on the Chinese rites or usury, they focused their objections on changes Grioglio made in the prayer book, and used these to criticize his whole attitude towards local practice. Disputes over ritual as a way of debating larger issues are of course characteristic of both Christianity and Confucianism, and the prayer book was the Shanxi Catholics' central ritual text. Grioglio's problems with it arose because, unlike Salvetti, he could read Chinese. He had, in fact, studied the language with a former missionary in Rome for two years before setting out for China. When he arrived in Shanxi, attempted to read the elegant but archaic language of the prayer book and heard the largely illiterate villagers of Cave Gully and other communities chanting the words, he came to the conclusion that they were "praying like so many parrots."[17] So he decided to rewrite the prayers himself and make them simpler, explaining in the preface of his new prayer book that prayers would not work unless one held the meaning in one's heart and thus it was essential to understand them. The task he had undertaken was particularly hard, since in order to avoid changes to the chanted rhythm he tried to avoid changing the number of characters. Moreover what was simpler and easier for Grioglio to understand was certainly less elegant and not necessarily any easier to the ear of a native speaker of Chinese.[18] Not surprisingly the enforcement of new, mangled texts of familiar prayers was extremely unpopular.

Grioglio's rigid character was important in the disputes that followed, and explains why ultimately they were more spectacular in Shanxi than elsewhere in China, but the underlying problem was not the attitudes, character, or theology of the missionaries, but the drastic change in their status brought about by the Opium War. In 1848, less than ten years after the war, a group of men from six provinces including Shanxi decided to write to Rome to complain about the changing behavior of missionaries across China. The Shanxi signatories to this letter were men closely associated with Salvetti. They described how in the past "the Western gentlemen treated people most harmoniously, and with loving kindness and transformed the people through their virtue." The new missionaries, by contrast, have failed to understand that "what is suitable for foreign countries is not suitable for our land." They have issued illiterate and embarrassing prayer books, made conversion too easy, caring only for the statistics that they are submitting to Europe, and above all they are no longer respectful of the Chinese priests and Christians. They ban things that should not be banned with no attention to local custom or proper human relations and exclude from the church anyone who criticizes them. In sum, "they treat our Chinese priests as slaves and look on the Christians as insects."[19] The writers conclude by asking that in the future the Western missionaries should set a good example to the Chinese rather than using power to humiliate them.

Into this already inflamed atmosphere came Wang Tingrong, returning from his studies in Naples in 1852. His experiences in the Italian south, where many of the clergy were resisting the imposition of papal control, had given him very different ideas from Grioglio's about church hierarchy, and the two men immediately came into conflict. The disputes escalated over several years, ending only when Grioglio was recalled to Europe. Although the ultimate cause was the rise of European power and the actual debates were often about Grioglio's attacks on Chinese customs, the issues at the core of the disputes were initially about church hierarchy rather than national identity. Wang Tingrong was driven by ideas drawn from his experiences living in Italy and was allied with the other Italian missionaries, while Grioglio had considerable support from local people and from the priests he had trained in Shanxi.

Naples, when Wang Tingrong first arrived there, was the capital of the Kingdom of the Two Sicilies and the third largest city in Europe. He entered the College for Chinese, which had been founded in the early eighteenth century for Chinese students studying for the priesthood. Alongside the Chinese and Ottoman students, the college consisted of the fellows, who were local priests responsible for teaching, and seminarians preparing for missionary work in China. The rules when the college was first founded were extremely strict and intended to isolate the students from outside influences, but since then Naples had undergone a Republican revolution and nearly ten years of Napoleonic rule when church property was confiscated and religious orders suppressed. The College for Chinese had survived by exempting its local students from the requirement to work as missionaries and transforming itself into one of the city's top private boarding schools. It was known for the fine food enjoyed by the fellows and for musical performances put on at Carnival by the schoolboys with adult professionals in the academic theatrical style. The Chinese priests offered classes in Chinese language, published a Chinese grammar, and were employed on a major French project to produce a Chinese-Latin-French dictionary. They spoke to each other in Latin, the first foreign language which they had learnt in the seminary in China, but they also picked up Italian.[20] A senior cleric in Macao who met many of those returning from Naples complained that they what they spoke was the worst Neapolitan street slang. He said that the students went out walking in the city so that they saw the prostitutes for whom the city was famed and the free manners of even the respectable women. People visited the seminary to look around, chat, or sing, and the students themselves were frequently invited out and were treated with honor at public events. The students became familiar with the local clergy and saw how they ate, traveled, joked, and lived with women.[21] Chinese priests newly returned from Naples were the group of clergy in Shanxi by far the most likely to be accused of misconduct with women.[22]

Many of the southern Italian clergy were engaged in long-running battles to resist the increasing control of the church hierarchy. During centuries of Spanish rule the clergy had been a privileged class with high status, great institutional wealth, and important exemptions from taxation, but from the eighteenth century on governments confiscated much church property and suppressed religious orders. Monks, especially the numerous and powerful Franciscans, were accused of idleness, extravagance, cruelty, and sexual exploitation, and for a time all monasteries and convents were abolished. Priests lost the right to receive tithes and were gradually impoverished, but there were still very large numbers of them. Many belonged to property-owning collegiate churches, where the priests had to be from the local area, were often entirely untrained, wore ordinary clothes, lived with the families into which they had been born, and worked the land belonging to their church or traded on its behalf. It was common for priests to have mistresses and even bishops campaigned against the rule of clerical celibacy. After the end of the period of French rule the government and the church hierarchy worked together to reduce the numbers of these priests and impose a new discipline on those who remained. They agreed that priests must pass a test set by their bishop before they could be ordained and that the bishop would then give them an appointment. This was a huge change from a system where local families had placed sons in steady positions in the collegiate churches, where they had few duties and could control their own lives. Bishops also used religious orders to help them get control over the local clergy: they would allow the order to reopen monasteries and then use the monasteries to sideline the local priests, leading to great hostility between diocesan priests and the religious orders. By the mid-nineteenth century priests, who had seen their standard of living collapse with the abolition of tithes, were facing unprecedented discipline and outside interference and many were resisting the changes.[23]

The College for Chinese was actively involved in these disputes. The fellows of the college were educated men known for their liberal ideals, but the institution's structure was the same as that of the many collegiate churches that were under attack. The fellows owned the revenues from several valuable benefices (hence their fine dining) and they were fighting to defend their autonomy and their common property against control from Rome. Some years after Wang's departure they accepted state control and the college became a school of oriental studies (today called the University of Naples L'Orientale) with two of the remaining Chinese priests taking responsibility for teaching Chinese.[24]

In 1848 a year of revolutions began in Sicily and spread across Europe. Priests throughout Italy sympathized with the revolution and for a brief period the newly appointed Pope Pius IX was an important symbol of the movement. Since the late eighteenth century, priests in southern Italy inspired by Enlightenment ideals and feelings of Italian nationalism or resentful over their poverty and increasing control by bishops had been participating in the radical associations that characterized the political life of the period. Some joined Jacobin clubs, which supported the ideals of the French Revolution, and later some even joined the Italian nationalist Carbonari. In 1848 Italian priests joined political associations and blessed revolutionary militias. Elsewhere in Europe priests formed groups to demand higher social status for clergy and elected church councils to reduce the power of bishops. This was combined with huge popular excitement over the potential of Pius IX, who had a reputation as a liberal reformer, to act as a figurehead for national unification, leading a federation of Italian states as in the Middle Ages. The revolutions soon collapsed: Pius IX refused to back the war against Austrian rule in the north and fled from Rome in disguise, while in Naples street fighting was followed by violent reprisals against all those involved.[25] At this point Wang left Naples to complete his studies in Rome, where Chinese students were now being accepted into the Collegium Urbanum, which specialized in training missionaries. There Wang studied with Grioglio's former teacher and was ordained.[26] The revolutions had failed, but the nationalism of this period, the participation of priests in demands for political change, and the idea of Pius IX as a symbol of reform were all to influence Wang Tingrong in years to come.

Wang traveled back to China taking ships from one bastion to another of the growing British empire (Malta, Alexandria, Cairo, Suez, Penang, Singapore, Hong Kong, and Shanghai), but without realizing the impact that British power had had on the church of his childhood. As priests and missionaries had done in the past, he waited in Shanghai to be met by a merchant employed by the mission to escort him back to the province. No one came. Eventually he set off on his own, taking with him three boxes of books that had been sent to the Franciscan bishops of north China. Given the persecution the year he had left China, which had been started by the discovery of a foreign book, he was understandably anxious. However, the action that he took to avoid capture is evocative of his character and suggests the high value he put on his European education: he dressed himself as an official, with an official hat, two red lanterns carried before him, and a red banner with the words "Hanlin Academy."[27] The Hanlin Academy employed only scholars who passed the top level of the imperial examinations with the highest grades. Clearly a Hanlin academician was unlikely to have boxes of books investigated, but it seems unlikely that Wang Tingrong with his entirely European education could have passed for an academician. He traveled like this to the residence of the bishop of Shandong, who presumably disapproved since afterwards Wang dressed as a merchant. When he got to Shanxi he went first to visit his parents, then stayed for a while with his uncle, before reporting to Cave Gully to meet Bishop Grioglio.

Wang Tingrong's problems with Grioglio began at that moment, since the bishop was angry that he had not come straight to Cave Gully. Despite the seriousness of the dispute, which was to destroy both their careers, there was never really any objective cause. Instead each resented the other's lack of respect. Grioglio complained that Wang used the familiar form of language when speaking Italian to him and did not address him when he came into the seminary garden. Wang complained that Grioglio did not greet him personally when he arrived and did not visit him when he was ill. The bad feeling was exacerbated when Grioglio sent Wang to Cold Springs Road and was told that he was being too familiar with the women there. One of the European missionaries, who later tried to find out what had happened, concluded that all Wang had done was to talk to the women, but however common this might have been for a priest in Naples it was shocking in a Shanxi village and instantly suggested more serious misdemeanors. Grioglio's response was a public investigation: he sent one of the other Chinese priests to question the women involved and write a report. This uncovered nothing, but Wang felt humiliated and was convinced that the community would now never respect him as a priest, so he went home to his family in Newtown.[28]

Over the next few years Grioglio repeatedly required Wang to come to study in Cave Gully, attributing all his problems to the inadequate education he had received in Naples and Rome. An Italian priest whom Grioglio treated in much the same way because of his rural background and low level of education, described being given very little food and shut up in one room with everyone watching him, straw and flies blowing about in the wind.[29] Wang was also required to do public penance: he had to go to three parishes and proclaim in the churches "I beg all you Christians not to look at my bad example, in that for more than a year I have not been in accord with my bishop."[30] Even after this Grioglio did not allocate him a parish, and from time to time forbade him to say mass so that he had no source of income. Instead he sent him up into the hills to work as an evangelist trying to convert people to Christianity. For a priest to be required to spend his time attempting to convert people was regarded by both Wang and Grioglio as a degrading punishment. When one of the other missionaries pointed out to Grioglio that his strict regulations were preventing conversions, Grioglio simply replied that conversions were not important.[31]

While on the surface the disputes were about matters of pride and respect, the underlying issue was clearly Wang's European experience.

Grioglio wished that no priest in his diocese had been to Europe and "seen with his own eyes the innumerable scandals of the Europeans."[32] As this suggests, both Grioglio and Wang expected the church to operate as it did in Italy, but they had very different ideas about what that meant. Grioglio, who came from northern Italy, believed strongly in the idea of the church as a single hierarchical institution demanding absolute obedience. Wang, on the other hand, had experienced a quite different side of the European church: in Naples clerical elites were still influenced by the ideas of the eighteenth century, the lower clergy were struggling to defend their prerogatives from control by bishops, and Pope Pius IX had briefly been the symbol of hopes for a national constitutional government. For Wang the European church provided examples of resistance to the new institutional controls.

Meanwhile, Grioglio's policies and his personal control over the money coming in from Europe had also angered the four other European missionaries in the province. Their leader was a man named Domenico Cannetti, who had arrived in Shanxi not long after Grioglio. Initially the two had got on well: Cannetti was a competent missionary whose severity, zeal, and excellent Chinese were long remembered by the villagers. Many years later they would say to Barnaba Nanetti, who preached especially well, "Eh, Father Liang was like you."[33] But by that time Cannetti had been so thoroughly written out of the diocese's history that Nanetti had never heard of him. Cannetti was also an enthusiast. One year, when he happened to be parish priest of Nine Springs, he organized a group of men wearing sheepskins, holding shepherds' staffs and carrying boxes with small gifts of bread, sweets, and coins, to lead two live sheep into the church up to the altar during Christmas mass. No doubt he was inspired by Francis of Assisi, famously the inventor of the Christmas crib scene, and wanted to bring the Biblical story alive, but what happened in fact was chaos and laughter. Afterwards people were furious that the ritual had not been performed properly: two different groups complained about it in letters to Rome.[34]

The European missionaries' dispute with Grioglio began over very much the same issues that were a problem for Wang Tingrong: status, money, and the authority of the bishop. They complained that Grioglio kept them waiting in an outer room when they came to Cave Gully to see him, rebuked them in public, and moved them from one parish to another without consultation.[35] He did not give them any of the money he received from Europe, but expected them to live from payments for saying mass.[36] They also objected to the rules he had issued allowing only the bishop to absolve certain sins. While this was a common arrangement, Grioglio had expanded the list of these serious sins to include any form of participation in ancestral ceremonies, temple festivals, and funerals, all of which had previously been dealt with through fines paid to the parish priest.[37]

At this stage in the dispute there was no pattern of hostility between Chinese and Europeans. Some of the policies the missionaries complained about were those that were particularly unpopular with the Shanxi Catholics, such as the ban on contributions to temple festivals and on married women spending more than three weeks at a time with their parents. Grioglio thought that this latter practice put them at risk of "diabolical abuse" (presumably incest), but Shanxi women whose husbands were away on business for years often spent a large proportion of their time in their parents' homes and the ban had caused uproar.[38] On the other hand, another of the missionaries' complaints was that Grioglio had not allowed them to relax the strict rules on fasting. The Chinese Catholics were strongly attached to these rules, but several of the Europeans suffered from swollen legs and intense fatigue which left them bedridden for months at a time. They attributed this to malnutrition created by combining the local diet with rules of fasting which banned meat during the forty days of Lent. In Europe this rule was not particularly severe since fish was permitted, but this was not a practical exception in much of Shanxi, and the local Catholic practice was to be strictly vegetarian. The missionaries wanted to be allowed to eat meat in Lent, and this shocked their parishioners. A joke passed round that Cannetti had once bought a pig's liver and heart and cooked it secretly in his rooms. Of course the smell filled the courtyard, where the women laughed and said that he might be able to deceive the wise, but he certainly could not fool them.[39] However, the problem which headed the missionaries' list of complaints, when eventually three of them ran away to Shanghai to launch a formal accusation against Grioglio, crossed national lines: it was Grioglio's treatment of Wang Tingrong and one of the other Naples-educated priests.[40]

In these early stages of the dispute there is no suggestion of nationalism or of hostility between the Chinese and European clergy, but all that was to change because of what Grioglio did next. When the church authorities ordered the missionaries back to Shanxi and sent in an elderly Franciscan from another province to mediate, Grioglio went off on a tour of his diocese, leaving one of the older Chinese priests as his deputy

FIGURE 6. Zhao Yuqian.
Courtesy of Provincia di
Cristo Re dei Frati Minori
dell'Emilia Romagna.

and putting Zhao Yuqian, a young man he had trained himself, in charge
of the seminary. Zhao was Grioglio's best student: he could write Latin,
and had excellent Chinese literary style. He also accepted without complaint the public humiliation which Grioglio had dealt out to ward off
any sense of pride in his achievements. A photograph (figure 6) shows
him in later life dressed in his ritual garments: a surplice and embroidered stole and hat. The hat is of the kind adopted in the Jesuit period so
that priests could cover their heads as they made the sacrifice of the
eucharist, in accordance with Chinese custom. It was designed according
to images of ancient Chinese headgear and gives Zhao an official air. The
full beard, on the other hand, was a matter of nineteenth-century European fashion, and considered very striking in Shanxi: many years later in
the Boxer Uprising he had shave it to avoid being noticed for his foreign
appearance. As a young man Zhao was serious and devout. Grioglio
trusted him. When he banned Cannetti from working as a priest, he sent
Zhao to investigate his behavior. This whole situation appalled Grioglio's superiors, who saw it entirely in terms of European prestige: four

missionaries and a senior Franciscan were shut up in a Chinese house (the residence in Nine Springs) while "the Chinese priests are acting as masters."[41] Grioglio was removed from his position as bishop and recalled to Europe in disgrace. He left attributing his misfortunes to Rome's decision to allow ruinous rates of interest, and saying to the Chinese only that he was going to Tianjin. Ironically, given the image of European Catholicism that he had tried to present, he ended up being expelled from his monastery when the Italian government closed down many religious orders.[42]

In the years immediately after Grioglio's departure Western pressure on China grew. A second Opium War broke out and this time the French, who saw Catholic missionaries as an important part of their imperial project, fought alongside the British. The treaties that followed in 1860 allowed foreigners to travel anywhere in the country, to own property, and to evangelize, and they required that Chinese Christians be allowed to practice their religion without interference.[43] It was in the aftermath of these treaties that European imperialism became a major issue for Shanxi Catholics and Wang Tingrong's disputes with his superiors were transformed from battles over the authority of the bishop into a struggle by the Chinese clergy for independence from Italian missionary control.

The changes in the behavior of the missionaries that followed the 1860 treaties horrified the Christian elite of Shanxi, whose model for relations between European missionaries and state was still that provided by Jesuits like Christian Herdtrich. Domenico Cannetti pasted up an announcement of the treaty with France claiming that henceforth priests were the equals of county magistrates. According to a group of Shanxi Christian leaders, who wrote to Rome to complain, he then burst into the provincial governor's offices with banners and gunfire. The governor was so angry that he wrote to Beijing and got a ruling that missionaries should be treated like Buddhist monks or Daoist priests and should not be allowed to see officials whenever they wished, a result that the Shanxi Christians thought could easily have been anticipated. They also complained that the elderly Franciscan mediator, who was now running the diocese, wrote to the governor signing himself "your younger brother," a familiarity resented by both the Christians and officials in Beijing.[44] Similar problems were repeated at the county level. The magistrate of Qixian reported that he was visited by three missionaries whose cards bore the title "Great France Missionary Department Shanxi priest" and that they had established a church in Nine Springs (thus ending two hundred years of official ignorance of the missionary residence less than two miles along a main road from the county government offices). Zhao Yuqian and another Chinese priest wrote to Rome requesting Cannetti's removal and saying that the officials so disliked his angry speech and excessive pomp that they had taken to harassing the Christians as a result. They suggested that Cannetti had gone mad.[45] Forty years earlier under the threat of state persecution, accusations of insanity had been an effective way of controlling the radical actions of foreign missionaries, but now they were simply ignored.

The missionaries also circulated a new set of church rules saying that Christians should no longer contribute to temple festivals. When the provincial governor saw these rules he wrote to Beijing to say that as far as he was aware the treaties did not mention this subject at all, only that the French could buy property and preach in the interior. From the Catholic point of view the freedom to be Christian necessarily included the freedom not to contribute to sacrifices to other gods, but that this should involve refusing to pay local levies was not immediately obvious to Chinese officials.[46] The year after the treaties were published, the Shanxi missionaries took four legal cases to the new office in charge of foreign affairs in Beijing. Three of these cases were about Christians being required to make contributions to temples. One came from Upper Mines, one of the largest Catholic communities in the hills north of Taiyuan, where there was a longstanding arrangement for splitting taxes, corvée duties, and temple levies between Catholics and non-Catholics. The village had a total land tax responsibility of seventy units of grain, of which the Catholics paid thirty and the rest of the villagers forty. They then split other levies according to the same proportions. At some point there had been a dispute because a newly converted Catholic family had refused to contribute to temple fairs and sacrifices for rain, so mediators had been called in and it had been agreed that the Catholics would get a discount of 50 percent on the amounts the village had to contribute, an arrangement which was in itself longstanding by 1860. Temple festivals were hugely important for village life, but the case of Upper Mines suggests that the disputes that arose over Catholic refusal to pay for them in the late nineteenth century were the result of the treaties rather than simply the strength of local feeling.[47]

Certainly, as far as the Chinese leadership of the church was concerned, these legal cases were an entirely unacceptable flaunting of European power. The sixteen Chinese priests in the diocese got together to sign a joint letter to Rome asking for the removal of all the European missionaries and the return of Grioglio. The letter was composed by Wang Tingrong and one of the other senior priests who had studied in Naples. Zhao Yuqian and a companion were sent off as their representatives to deliver it to the church authorities in Tianjin. In the letter the Chinese priests imagine the missionaries' superiors in Rome feeling sorry for them and saying, "My poor brothers, how they suffer for the honor of God, in that vast empire of China, abandoning their homeland of coffee, wine, cheese, and parma ham, and not finding any food there suited to them, but God will reward them in Paradise."[48]

This sympathy, they say, is entirely misplaced, since the missionaries' behavior is appalling, though they naturally do not report this to Rome. So now the Chinese priests have decided to write and ask that all the Franciscans, or in other words all the Europeans, should be removed. The situation is urgent because of the recent war between China and Europe, which has caused Chinese officials and commoners alike to see the missionaries as spies for a foreign invasion, an attitude that is likely to cause a persecution. After lengthy criticisms of individual missionaries, the letter ends with a declaration of what they call "ecclesiastical war" against the Franciscans,

> Namely by expelling them and resisting them by every means possible, whether formally or, if the need arises, materially or morally or physically. In a word we will do whatever God permits against those seducers and hypocrites, without any mercy. Why? In accordance with justice, in accordance with the strictest obligations, we national priests are bound through the conviction that for the glory of God we must protect our religion with all our strength, to defend our fatherland from every assault, even at the risk of our own lives, to prevent them destroying it by their arbitrary actions which oppress and harass our Christians. This is our sole aim, for the blessing of peace, the salvation of souls, and indeed for the conversion of the pagans.[49]

This letter mixes the new with the old. The references to persecution hark back to the world of Salvetti, where threats of persecution enabled the Chinese Catholic elites to control mission policy. At the same time the writing is clearly inspired by the rising Chinese nationalism of its time, with its references to foreign invasion, popular fears of foreigners acting as spies, and the Chinese priests' determination to defend their country. But the means of resistance to their clerical superiors come from the culture of early nineteenth-century Naples: the open declaration of hostility between diocesan priests and members of a religious order, the stereotypical accusations that the Franciscans are seducers and hypocrites, and the formation of an association of priests for a political goal. Even the nationalist language of giving one's life for one's country seems likely to have been influenced by the rhetoric of 1848 and Italian unification.

Church officials in Rome merely filed this letter, but unfortunately for the Chinese priests one of their number, an endlessly talkative man, betrayed its contents so that they came to the attention of Luigi Moccagatta, the new bishop who had been sent in from neighboring Shandong province. As in Europe the church hierarchy was committed above all to retaining control and Moccagatta was sent to put an end to the trouble in the diocese. His first act was to get rid of Cannetti, who was blamed for everything and packed off to Shandong. He wanted to go to America or back to Italy, but the threat of being sent to New Zealand with its foreign language and strange food was so appalling that he pleaded to be allowed at least to remain in China. Moccagatta then moved to reassert control over the Chinese priests by demanding that each of them send him a written explanation of what had happened. Wang Tingrong replied demanding a regular stipend and a meeting at which the Chinese priests could negotiate as a group. Meanwhile about a hundred leading Catholics, presumably acting in concert with the Chinese priests, came to Cave Gully to ask Moccagatta to bring back Grioglio. When he agreed to see them, they knelt down and refused to rise, so that after shouting and threatening he had to defuse the situation by explaining that he was a former classmate of Grioglio's and he too wanted his return. This dramatic scene did nothing to shift Moccagatta's tough line and he now announced that he would suspend from office all those Chinese priests who refused to cooperate with his demands. Wang Tingrong immediately left for Newtown where he bought some land. Several others were also suspended, leaving them unable to make an income from saying masses, so that most eventually gave in.[50]

Up to this point Wang Tingrong's difficulties with Grioglio and Moccagatta had much in common with disputes between priests and bishops in southern Italy, but in China the political context was profoundly different. The treaties gave foreigners powers that bishops simply did not have in Europe, while new colonial ideologies suggested responses based on ideas of essential cultural differences. It was at this point that Moccagatta imposed the rigid hierarchical order between European and Chinese clergy that is described in the folktale: the Chinese priests were seated at table below the Europeans, during prayers the Europeans sat on chairs and the Chinese priests on benches, and in the diocese of Taiyuan no Chinese priest would again fill a senior administrative position until the arrival of the Communists in the 1950s. Such practices became common to many Catholic missions in China in the late nineteenth century, but it seems likely that the Italian missionaries in Shanxi implemented them unusually harshly in part because in the ideology of the dominant European powers Italians too were a backward and uncivilized people. For the Chinese priests Zhao Yuqian, who took a strictly orthodox line, summed up the crisis in words from the Breviary, "because of all our sins the scourge of God's wrath has come upon us."[51]

At the same time, the link between the longstanding Catholic villages and the foreigners came to public attention with the construction of a huge new church in Taiyuan city, the first to be built in a Western architectural style. The missionaries moved their headquarters from Cave Gully to Taiyuan as a statement of their new rights under the treaties and so that they could more conveniently deal with provincial officials. Soon it was said that children had been buried alive under the cathedral's foundations and by the end of the 1860s there were constant rumors against the foreigners: China and Europe would go to war, the churches in Beijing had been destroyed and the foreigners expelled, the Christians and missionaries in the province would all be executed by the provincial governor.[52] In Tianjin in 1870, claims that Catholic orphanages were buying kidnapped children to steal their organs exploded into rioting in which the French consul and several other foreigners were killed. After that, Shanxi people became even more afraid: there were rumors of war with France and parents in Taiyuan would fix yellow paper talismans to their children's clothes to prevent the missionaries stealing them.[53]

Wang Tingrong's problems with Moccagatta came to a head in this context. For years Wang had spent most of his time at home farming and engaging in business, but Moccagatta now felt strong enough to demand that Wang work full time as a priest under his direction. So he told Wang to wrap up his business affairs and come to stay in Cave Gully where he would be supported by the mission. When Wang arrived, Moccagatta brought in a tough young missionary, Francesco Fogolla, who was later famous for his daring in taking court cases to Beijing. He was nicknamed "the terrible" after he took out his gun and shot dead a dog that barked at him in the mountains at night. As Fogolla and another young missionary stood over Wang, who felt thoroughly intimidated, Moccagatta tried to get him to sign a document handing over control of any remaining property to the mission while he worked as a priest. This was the breaking point for Wang.

Church rules did not allow a bishop to take over a priest's private property, and Wang with his experience in Naples knew all about those rules. That night he left the seminary and set off for Rome to take his case to the pope.[54]

Wang Tingrong wrote a ballad about his journey to Rome which many north China Catholics can still sing. It is written in the style of a southern Chinese folksong:

> In the first month it is New Year for the tea pickers.
> I say farewell to Guangdong and board a foreign ship,
> For days I vomit as if I were drunk,
> Who knew that the waves of the sea really are like mountains!
>
> In the second month the tea bushes sprout for the tea pickers.
> My sufferings in the ship are like being stabbed with a knife,
> Spinning head and sick stomach are really hard to bear,
> My tears fall uncontrollably as I long to go home.[55]

After six months of sea voyage with rotten meat and stinking water, seas reaching to the horizon, and no hope of ever seeing his parents again, he arrives in France and travels south. Eventually he reaches Rome,

> In the ninth month it is Double Ninth festival for the tea pickers.
> Rejoicing in the blessed city, I see the pope,
> I behold the churches and all the relics,
> I thank the Lord for his great gift of boundless grace.

Wang did not in fact see Pius IX, who had been transformed by his experiences from a symbol of liberal reform and Italian nationalism in the 1840s into one of the leading forces of conservative reaction by the 1870s. Instead he submitted a series of formal letters of complaint to the Propaganda Fide, the church bureaucracy in charge of missions. In these letters he distinguishes his personal dispute with Moccagatta from the more general issues that he raises on behalf of all the Chinese priests in Shanxi, but it is clear that the two cannot really be separated. The Chinese priests were demanding autonomy from the new rules that made them perpetually subordinate to the foreigners and that autonomy depended on their having separate financial resources.

Wang demanded equal status between Chinese and European priests. In the standard format of canon law his letter was phrased as a set of questions beginning, "Do native *Chinese* priests, ordained either in the Collegium Urbanum or in their provinces and sent out under the jurisdiction of the Propaganda Fide, have the same status as the missionaries

of the Propaganda belonging to other nations?" Later questions press
the same point:

> Is there any difference in the dignity and honor given to European missionar-
> ies and indigenous priests? If so, what difference?
>
> Is it true, as some say, that the European missionaries are *all* without excep-
> tion the superiors of the indigenous priests?
>
> Should the European missionaries, whether in public or in private places, in
> their functions and in all their actions, hold a superior position by law? And
> on the other hand should the indigenous priests, even the older ones, take the
> lower place for their whole lives?[56]

The claims are made on the basis of reason and justice rather than piety
or emotion. This is characteristic of Wang's writings, which totally lack
the pious formulations used by the other priests and missionaries. When
he did not receive an answer to this petition, Wang wrote, "I must in
conscience say that I came to seek justice. In my country, China, when
an appeal is made to a superior court, the cause is always adjudicated
and the reasons are laid out to both parties."[57]

Wang knew well that the status he was demanding depended on the
priests having a secure income. He asked for an annual stipend and
demanded that Chinese priests should be able to bequeath property to
their heirs, in other words that their personal finances should be separate from the diocese. The idea of an annual stipend had its origins in
the eighteenth century when both missionaries and the Chinese priests
received such stipends from Rome. These ended during the financial
crisis of the early nineteenth century and were never reintroduced. However, Wang also had startlingly high expectations, claiming that he
needed the equivalent of four hundred taels per year to live respectably
and if not he would need to farm or go into trade. By contrast one of the
older Chinese priests had calculated that he needed less than forty taels,
an income roughly equivalent to that of a country schoolteacher.[58]
Inheritance was an important issue since the Shanxi mission had long
received significant income from taking over the estates of Chinese
priests, which was not in accordance with church rules. On this issue
and his own financial disputes with Moccagatta, Wang was knowledge-
able of European precedents, framed his appeal carefully, and won the
case.[59] Wang's other financial demand related directly to the connection
between missionary power and European funding: Shanxi had eight
European and nineteen Chinese priests, could the Europeans keep all the
money sent by the Propagation? Could the Chinese priests have a share

in it? And if not could they form an association to apply to the Propagation for their own subsidy?

Wang Tingrong never obtained an audience with the pope, though
he asked most persistently, nor did he win the equality that he wanted
for Chinese priests. On the other hand he was successful in that he was
sent back to Shanxi over the strong objections of the missionaries there,
who knew that his return would be seen as a victory, and the diocese
was required to pay for his journey.[60]

> In the tenth month it is like spring for the tea pickers.
> I receive great kindness and am enlightened by the elders of the church,
> But getting this personal favor I have nothing to offer,
> So from day to day I rely on all the saints to entreat for me.[61]

On his return to Shanxi Wang Tingrong continued much the same life
he had had before his departure. Moccagatta grew old and handed the
diocese over to his nephew, a gentle and unassuming man who complained occasionally that Wang was too fond of the country air and the
company of his nephews, but employed him to oversee some of his new
building projects.[62]

This ambiguous result reflected tensions within the church hierarchy.
Wang traveled to Rome shortly after the First Vatican Council, an
immense gathering of bishops in Rome that famously confirmed the
nineteenth-century trend towards uniformity of Catholic practice, clerical hierarchy, and the power of the pope, by endorsing the doctrine of
papal infallibility. These developments had contradictory implications
for the European missionary establishment in China. On the one hand
they tended to strengthen the power of bishops against their clergy. But
on the other hand this was a struggle in which the papacy was competing for power against other Catholic institutions including great religious orders like the Franciscans. The Propaganda had long hoped to
introduce the practice of appointing local bishops in mission lands, who
would then be directly controlled from Rome, rather than having a primary loyalty to a religious order. As a result Wang's letters were officially debated at a meeting of missionary bishops that followed the
Council. Unsurprisingly his proposals suffered a resounding defeat. Not
only were the missionary bishops, who included Moccagatta, strongly
opposed to any reduction in their own power, they were already
appalled by the spread of Wang's campaign against European control
from Shanxi to the provinces of Hubei and Hunan. In their response to
Wang's documents they declared that Chinese priests like the rest of the

Chinese people were "inconstant, lazy, ambitious, idle, thieves, hypocrites, liars, ungrateful, very greedy for money, likely to rebel, and very weak in matters of chastity."[63]

The Catholic church was an institution deeply embedded in Chinese society that was transformed by the new international political structures of the nineteenth century. The missionary bishops' response to Wang Tingrong would have been unthinkable before 1840. The growth of Western imperialism changed the context in which Europeans in China acted and made it possible for missionaries to claim extensive new powers while also providing an ideology of racial and cultural differences that justified those powers. At the same time growing Western power, new and cheaper transport and communications technology, and the security provided by the treaties strengthened the ties binding the church together as a global institution. People in Cave Gully and other Shanxi Catholic villages were no longer linked to the church elsewhere by isolated travelers and exiles, but instead gradually came to see themselves as part of a global organization: when they disapproved of how the missionaries were behaving, their response was to write a letter of complaint to Rome. The priests who resented the new missionary bishops came to think of themselves as Chinese resisting foreign control, but their sense of nationalism was developing in relation to a transnational institution. For Wang Tingrong the church was a bureaucracy within which he as a Chinese claimed justice and equality, but he was also deeply affected by his years in Naples and his struggle reflected ongoing differences within the European church.

A further layer of complexity is added by the fact that for all the nationalism and very real sympathy with Wang Tingrong felt by Chinese Catholics, imperialism also had its advantages for them. When Grioglio was sent back to Italy there was genuine popular feeling for his return. One group of Shanxi Catholics wrote in a letter to Rome that they were stunned when they realized he was not going to come back. Grioglio, they said, had thought of Shanxi church affairs day and night, built churches, organized an academy to train seminarians, written and published religious books, and brought people to repent of their sins and change their evil customs, while the orphanage he built was still caring for the sick and poor. "All his actions were for the glory of the Lord of Heaven and to save men's souls, so how can he go back to Rome without a word like a thief taking to his heels?"[64] Such advantages were particularly obvious in Cave Gully where Grioglio with his European funding brought job opportunities, investment, and impressive new buildings. From being a huddle of impoverished cave dwellings, the community had now become a real village.

In the long term the struggle between the Chinese and European clergy in the mid-nineteenth century set the stage both for the years of high imperialism and for the development of a Chinese church hierarchy that would replace the missionaries after the communist revolution of 1949. More immediately, less than ten years after Wang Tingrong's death came a crisis that proved the missionary reliance on foreign power unrealistic. Zhao Yuqian, who had predicted that the missionaries' behavior would lead to a new persecution, would be proved right, but would lose his life in the process.

CHAPTER 4

The Boxer Uprising and the Souls in Purgatory

All the Catholic villages of central Shanxi have tales of the Boxer Uprising. Often it is the first story the villagers tell about themselves, and the focus is on how few people survived the terrible massacres. The Cave Gully people do not have a story like this because there was no massacre. When asked about the Boxers, the orphanage caretaker told instead a story that explains how the village was preserved by figures dressed in white who appeared so that the Boxers did not dare fight. The priest had given communion to all the men of the village, so that Jesus would protect them; the figures in white were souls in purgatory come to their aid. When I then asked what he meant by "souls in purgatory" (*lianyu-hun*), since this is not a common Chinese term, he explained that people offer masses for them and they often appear; they are very powerful in their ability to rescue you from danger and protect you. You invoke them by putting your hands together and praying: "I beg the souls in purgatory to protect me." You might need their support in a fight. You cannot see them but it is as if many people appear. They can help because God has a special love for them, since they are not like people on earth who commit sins. People also ask the angels, Jesus, God, and Mary but that is more formal; asking the souls in purgatory is more like asking a person who is close to you.[1]

The Boxers began as martial arts groups that gathered in temples in Shandong province. In 1900 they developed into militias that won central government support and aimed to drive the foreign powers out of

China, beginning with the missionaries and Chinese Christians, who were seen as their representatives. Shanxi was one of the parts of the country where the violence was most intense, with approximately two thousand Christians killed in the center and south of the province and many more in the northern areas bordering Inner Mongolia, as well as an unknown number of Boxers, and most of the Catholic and Protestant missionaries living in the province.[2] Interpretations of these events have focused on the social tensions caused by the spread of Christianity in the years preceding the uprising. In other words they assert that the underlying cause was the conversion of Chinese to an imported Western religion that was alien to Chinese culture.[3]

The story of the souls in purgatory who saved the people of Cave Gully suggests quite a different interpretation, for the souls are the Catholic ancestors of the villagers. In this story the Christianity of those who come under attack is at once rooted in European Catholicism and strikingly similar to local religious practice. Ideas about the role of the living in shaping the experience of the dead have long been part of Chinese religious culture. The dead were believed to have power over the living, but also to be dependent on their offerings: the dead worshipped by their descendants became ancestors, while those who were abandoned became ghosts. This is very similar to the medieval Catholic doctrine of purgatory, a period after death during which souls are punished for the sins they committed in life but can be helped by the prayers of the living. In the nineteenth century, European Catholics earned indulgences through prayer and rituals which they could then transfer to the dead. In China, Buddhist and Daoist religious specialists conducted rituals to transfer merit to souls and save them from punishment after death. In both China and Europe the souls who received these benefits were felt to be under an obligation to respond to their devotees. The streets of Naples were scattered with little shrines depicting the souls in purgatory, their bodies rising from the flames. Because the souls depended on the prayers of the living to shorten their sufferings, they were willing to grant the requests of those who prayed or offered masses for them.[4]

A popular Italian collection of stories about the souls in purgatory includes the tale of a certain Duke of Sardinia who had given the revenues from one of his richest cities for the benefit of the souls in purgatory. The duke's lands were invaded by the king of Sicily, but as the battle was about to begin another army approached whose banners and uniforms were entirely white. Four knights came forward to announce that they were from the heavenly host and led an army of those the duke had freed from purgatory, who had come to recover the city given to them. Tian Fenglan, a priest from the wealthy Tian family of Pingyao, compiled a similar volume in Chinese which was read aloud every year during daily prayers in November, the month dedicated to the souls. The book includes the story of the Duke of Sardinia and the army of souls, though with some minor changes. In the Italian version the Sicilian forces retreat at the mere sight of the ghostly soldiers, but Tian has the army of souls fighting alongside the Sicilians to defeat the Sardinians. He also explains that the revenues of the duke's city were used to pay a priest to say a mass for the souls each month. The offering of masses for the souls in November was (and remains) a significant source of income for Shanxi priests, so that they had an interest in these stories. The tale of the souls in purgatory dressed in shining white who drive away the Boxers from Cave Gully clearly comes from this tradition.[5]

However similar Catholic practices actually were to local religion, when people at the time talked or wrote about Christianity in China they usually did so in terms that made the two seem entirely different. Both missionaries and members of the Chinese elite nearly always depicted Catholic religious practice as foreign to Chinese culture and symbolic of Western power. For the missionaries this was a way of dealing with the pressure to make conversions. When few people converted they could argue that the key problem was the hostility of the Chinese state to foreigners, an argument that had several significant advantages for them. For one thing it was readily accepted in Europe, where governments and traders already saw the Qing government as intransigently resisting European expansion. Secondly it allowed the missionaries to continue to avoid evangelism, which was hard and often unrewarding work. Fiery young men arrived in China determined to convert the pagan, but they were told first that they must learn Chinese and then later that local preachers had a better understanding of people's customs. Instead the missionaries were employed teaching in the seminary, acting as priests for the old Catholic parishes, or administering the diocese and its institutions. Most eventually came to believe in the importance of the institutional work they were doing and evangelism was left to the locals. Thirdly, when the Chinese preachers came into conflict with the authorities, the missionaries had the challenging and high-status task of taking the resulting legal cases to the provincial authorities and sometimes to the European diplomats in Beijing. Francesco Fogolla, nicknamed "the terrible," was appointed to assist Luigi Moccagatta's nephew as bishop. He liked to quote Jesus' injunction sending his disciples out to preach the gospel, "Be ye therefore wise as serpents and simple as doves" (Matthew 10:16), with an emphasis on the serpents. He often took disputes as far as Beijing where they could be dealt with by the foreign consuls, giving the foreign powers the ability to intervene directly in local administration and set precedents for the rest of the country. As Italians, whose country had only recently emerged as a nation-state, the missionaries in Shanxi also used these cases in their search for equality with other Europeans, hoping that eventually they would be allowed to operate under Italian rather than French consular protection.[6]

Chinese officials too saw Christianity in the light of China's struggle against the Western powers. In the aftermath of the Boxer Uprising, the provincial governor summed up the official view of the problem by saying "after the country was opened to trade, large numbers of missionaries came to the province, forests of churches were built, and more and more of the foolish people joined the religion."[7] For officials who had previously ignored the existence of Catholic villages their sudden appearance looked like massive growth and they hoped that this might be an arena in which to resist foreign intervention. In 1881 the young and dynamic Zhang Zhidong was appointed governor of Shanxi, then just recovering from severe famine. He launched a crackdown on government bureaucracy and corruption alongside policies aimed at strengthening China against foreign interference, which included a new provincial office for dealing with missionaries. This had dramatic effects for members of the Catholic elite who participated in the examination system. Since the examinations were a major marker of local status, wealthy Catholics had always put their sons in for them, though a number of eighteenth-century missionaries had vociferously disapproved (failure to provide a Catholic education for one's children was one of the sins dealt with by cash penances). Now lower-level officials suddenly prevented these men from taking part in the exams. In Wenshui county a Christian from the Ren family was removed from the list of lower degree holders. Then another member of the family went to the trading city of Pingyao to attempt the lowest level of the exams and was asked if he was Christian. When he admitted that he was, his script was removed, and he was not allowed to continue. The Ren were descended from merchants who converted in Beijing in the eighteenth century and since that time the family had consistently produced civil and military degree holders. There was nothing new about either their religion or their participation in the examination system, but such pressure on Catholics was one of the few ways in which officials could express their support for the governor's policies and their hostility towards the unequal treaties the Qing had signed with the foreign powers.[8]

The problem with depicting Shanxi as a place where conversions to Christianity were linked to the expansion of Western power is that there were not in fact very many conversions. Going back to figure 2, we can see that the arrival of more missionaries and their European funding initially had almost no effect on the number of adult baptisms, which remained minimal until the 1870s when persistent drought led to the great north China famine. This was one of the major global disasters of the nineteenth century and brought an outpouring of donations both from China and from overseas. Protestant missionaries came to Shanxi for the first time, bringing aid to the famine victims, but the famine relief committee in Shanghai also handed over very large sums to the Catholics to distribute. To these were added the considerable sums the Catholics themselves raised in Europe. Between 1877 and 1879 the diocese of Taiyuan gave approximately thirty-five thousand taels in cash to the hungry. Not only did the bishop restrict distributions to Catholics, which naturally encouraged conversion, but money that arrived after the famine ended was used to pay for evangelism.[9] However figure 7 shows that the total number of Catholics actually declined during the famine, presumably because conversions were outnumbered by deaths and emigration.[10] As prosperity returned and the money ran out conversions dropped: in 1900 the number of Catholics had only recently recovered to 1877 levels. These figures are for the whole province of Shanxi, but the absence of conversions was even more striking for the central Shanxi plain, where the Boxer fighting was to be most intense. Almost all the conversions in the aftermath of the great famine took place in the impoverished mountain areas of the north and west of the province.[11] Nor were there many Protestant conversions, since the new Protestant missionaries were starting from scratch: in 1898 there were 1,513 Protestants in the province, compared to 25,147 Catholics.[12]

Conversions were difficult because of the increasing separation of Catholics from the wider community and growing hostility towards the foreign powers. The conversion manuals published by the diocese responded to the changing popular image of Catholicism. In an old-fashioned woodblock printed booklet called *Straight Talk from a Farmer,* the

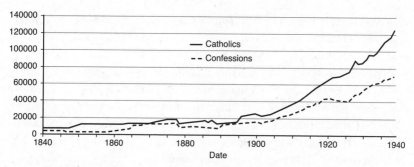

FIGURE 7. Total numbers of Catholics and annual confessions reported in Shanxi province, 1840 to 1940.

narrator describes three occasions during the course of his life when he discussed Christianity and succeeded in convincing elite men that it was not a bad practice. On one of the occasions his listener says to him "Since you are so talented, why are you still selling vegetables?" and the narrator is able to remind him that the ancient emperors Yao and Shun were farmers too and that farming is not something of which one should be ashamed.[13] The farmer does not attempt to persuade his listeners to convert, instead he defends Catholics by explaining that their religion is in conformity with Confucian orthodoxy. The first conversation begins "I hear you believers do not honor Confucius, is it really true?"[14] The farmer answers that Catholics are in fact the true Confucians since they honor what Confucius taught rather than just worshipping him as a god. The second conversation is set in the marketplace, with a lower degree holder who begins, "I hear that your family lives in Newtown . . . . Since you live in Newtown you must be a Catholic." When the farmer admits this, the scholar continues politely, "Your religion has a very deep and mysterious spirit and I have not looked into it, but I hear that you Catholics are not filial to your parents and do not worship the gods and buddhas, and hearing this makes me very sad."[15] The farmer succeeds in convincing him that followers of the Lord of Heaven are in fact more filial than others since they honor not only their parents but also the creator of the universe. The final encounter is with an official who says that Christianity is heterodox, to which the farmer replies that the Catholic God is the same Heaven worshipped in the Chinese classics. These arguments date back to the seventeenth century, and are presented as much to defend believers from criticism as to make new converts.

A new manual by Tian Fenglan (who also wrote the book about the souls in purgatory), assisted by the older Zhao Yuqian, takes a quite different line. It begins by explaining who the Lord of Heaven is, then immediately deals with the question "I am afraid that when the Westerners come to China they have ulterior motives and are deceiving our Chinese people, so how can I trust them?"[16] The answer is that the Westerners do not like to come to China at all: many of them die on the journey, once they arrive they find it difficult to learn the language and adjust to the living conditions, and they often become ill. Clearly Tian and Zhao were all too familiar with the lives of missionaries. They then describe the contributions of the early Jesuits who served the Qing by making explosives and calculating the calendar, before going on to other topics: Why can't we see God? What is the difference between the Lord of Heaven and the Daoist Supreme Ultimate? Since Catholics worship the Lord of Heaven (presumably a weather deity) why does it not rain more on their land? Much of the argument remains highly Confucian, such as the explanation that Christians are not allowed to contribute to operas because operas are lascivious, performed by low people, and men and women mix together watching them (rather than because operas are put on to worship other gods). The answer to "Since I was born in China why should I believe in a foreign religion?" is that Chinese should believe in Christianity just as foreigners should listen to the words of Confucius.[17] Towards the end the questioner announces, "Now that I hear the truths of the religion I really want to join, but I am afraid people will say I have joined a foreign religion. How should I reply to them?"[18] This prompts a detailed discussion of the impact of the treaties, with an explanation of why the foreign powers think they should protect Christians, which ends with a lengthy quotation from the imperial edict authorizing Christian belief. The authors of this booklet were both from families that had been Catholic since the early Qing: Tian Fenglan was descended from the wealthy Christian merchant who had funded the original Beijing seminary, while Zhao had been engaged in the struggle against missionary control of the diocese in the 1860s. They knew the deep local roots of their religion, but they also understood that people thought of it as foreign.

So why were Christianity's links with the foreign powers now such a major issue? If the answer is not that there were more converts, then it must be that the missionaries and their works were becoming more visible in other ways. From the 1860s the foreigners themselves were much more commonly seen. The Italians who had previously been hidden away, first in Nine Springs and then in Cave Gully, established a large complex in the provincial capital. Then the Protestant missionaries began to arrive and they came in much larger numbers than the Catholics. By 1899 there were twenty-six Catholic missionaries but eighty-nine Protestants, many of whom had also brought their families.[19] More visible even than the foreigners themselves were their new buildings. The late nineteenth century was a great age of religious building in Europe and America and the missionaries brought these ideas with them to China. They built churches, orphanages, seminaries, and in the case of the Protestants, schools, clinics, and hospitals, and they themselves were in charge of most of these new institutions.

Between 1870 and 1900 more than sixty Catholic churches were built in central Shanxi using European money and often in something approximating Western styles. There was also a growing complex round the new cathedral in Taiyuan city, with a seminary, orphanage, school, and finally a convent for a group of newly arrived missionary nuns. The pace of construction increased through the 1890s: one provincial governor estimated that the province had 119 churches in 1892 and 226 in 1898. A few of these buildings were strikingly Western in appearance, like the pilgrimage church of the Holy Mother in the mountains north of Taiyuan, which had a baroque façade modeled on the church of St. Louis at Versailles. Far more of the churches were built in local styles, but were nevertheless striking and highly visible.[20]

A monastery was built on a rocky outcrop just above Cave Gully in the 1880s. Like many of the new churches it was on a highly conspicuous site: its fine brick buildings could be seen for miles across the plain, and people said that the rock had once been the lair of a terrible bandit who had resisted all assaults of his enemies. The building was in a mixed Chinese-Italian style, but looked very foreign at the time. It cost seven thousand taels, much of it spent locally on the purchase and transport of building materials, bringing wealth as well as prestige to Cave Gully.[21] Two young Franciscans arrived from Bologna to take charge: Barnaba Nanetti and Francesco Saccani. Nanetti was one of seven children of a lower middle-class family and had a history of epilepsy and mental instability. Often at odds with both his Italian and Chinese colleagues, he was clever, could be charming, and soon spoke good Chinese. When he was sent as parish priest to Nine Springs, it was he who collected the area's folktales and family histories and was complimented for preaching as well as Cannetti. Saccani was a peaceable man who also later became known for his good Chinese, but he had wanted to go to America and, like his eighteenth-century predecessors, wrote home asking for the seeds of Italian vegetables. For the Italians the monastery was a place of refuge with Italian food, vegetables, flowers, and games of lawn bowls, where the Chinese novices would be "staying in Italy" (though without the danger of actually seeing Europe).[22] The younger generation of Chinese priests, on the other hand, hoped the monastery would finally open up paths to positions of authority hitherto monopolized by the Italian Franciscans. One of the first two novices was Chen Guodi, an immensely able and devout young man who had already been thrown out of the south Shanxi seminary run by Dutch Franciscans for having a bad attitude, almost certainly code for nationalism. The Italians responded to such attitudes with such a strict regime for the Chinese novices that even one of the younger missionaries regarded it as barbaric.[23]

The diocese also spent large sums of money on orphanages, which often had fine new buildings. Through these orphanages the church also came to touch the lives of many families in a way that was often traumatic. By 1892, the Cave Gully orphanage was taking in six hundred children each year, not including those who died shortly after their arrival.[24] The story of how one little girl entered the Cave Gully orphanage suggests how frightening the experience must have been. The author was a French Franciscan, excluded by his nationality from the Italian and Chinese diocesan politics, who wrote frequently for the European mission press describing life in the villages where he worked and gently satirizing his own failure to live up to popular images of the heroic missionary. The little girl he describes had lost her sight from smallpox. Her father, who went by the nickname Black Ox, came from West Willows, but was not a Catholic. He worked as a laborer and when his wife died he could not keep his blind daughter with him. So he handed her over to her maternal uncle, who cared for her for several years, until his wife died too. The twelve year old was sent back to her father, who simply could not care for her. One day he put her in a wheelbarrow and set off down to the river, apparently with the intention of drowning her, but on the way he met one of the Catholic villagers. The two settled down to smoke a pipe together, and the Catholic suggested giving the little girl to the orphanage in Cave Gully. Black Ox set off at once with some money to offer the orphanage if they would take her in. When he arrived, he signed the usual contract which absolved the church of any responsibility if the child got sick or died, then left. The little girl's uncle was horrified when he found out what had happened, convinced that the Catholics would already have killed her and mutilated her body by taking her eyes and heart. The missionary, who knew all about these fears, was not at all surprised when the two men reappeared at the orphanage. He got one of the sworn virgins to fetch the little girl and then, when the two men could see that she had not been harmed, he threatened not to keep her. Since neither Black Ox nor her uncle could care for her, negotiations followed and the next day her grandfather came to sign a statement praising the orphanage's work. The little girl was baptized, taught to chant prayers, and set to work in the kitchen.[25] As in other orphanages at the time the vast majority of children died: the babies were mainly fed on gruel and sugar, which was likely to cause malnutrition and infections, while the older children succumbed to croup, smallpox, cholera, and typhus, diseases which Cave Gully's inadequate water supply made particularly common. But this little girl may have survived: older children who were not sick when they arrived had much the best outcomes. The church would give them a small dowry and the blind girls too were married.[26] The missionary published this story in the French press to show how people were beginning to learn that the orphanage was safe, but it also suggests the desperation of the poor who placed their children in such an institution and the terror they felt about the results.

The missionaries also became more visible as ordinary Catholics displayed the foreigners' power and prestige for their own ends. It was not only the poor, the marginal, or converts who did this. Barnaba Nanetti recorded how he was asked to take the last rites to a dying man from a prosperous family in a village just outside Qixian (very likely Nine Springs). When he arrived he found that the old man was not quite on the point of death, so he guessed that something else was going on. Then, over a meal, he overheard one of the family say how good it was that a foreign missionary had come. They explained that a local Catholic employer had got into a brawl with one of his laborers and the case was about to go to court. Nanetti did not want to get involved and refused the family's offer to lend him a fine gown and cap to enter the government offices, but he did agree to go into town with them the next day. Once there, he was pressed to enter the outer courtyard of the government buildings, "Oh, just so they can see you (as if I were some strange animal) and they will know that there is a foreigner among us. Then they will be more afraid and we will have a bit more courage."[27] Francesco Fogolla served the Cave Gully people in a similar way by visiting the Taiyuan county magistrate to complain about the villagers being required to provide carts for military transport. Before they got to the real business, the magistrate and the missionary drank tea together and chatted. Fogolla, who had said he came from "Great Italy," was annoyed when the magistrate asked first if it were near Japan and then if it were the same place as France. Fogolla blamed Chinese official ignorance, rather than the insignificance of Italy on the world stage, and gave the magistrate a lecture on the subject.[28] Unlike Nanetti, who disliked being manipulated, Fogolla was very willing to display Italian prestige and was correspondingly popular. In 1899, when he came back from a trip to Italy, he visited Cave Gully and the Catholics of Cold Springs Road decided to welcome him with the full ceremony permitted by a recent Qing government ruling that made bishops symbolically equal to provincial governors. They got hold of a sedan chair of the sort used by high officials, the bearers put on ceremonial dress, and musicians accompanied the procession. Shots and firecrackers were fired as they set off and again along the way. Curious onlookers were told, "This is the lord of our Holy Religion."[29]

At the same time that the missionaries and their institutions were becoming more visible, the Catholic communities were also becoming more exclusive. Grioglio had banned Catholics from taking part in ancestral rituals or attending non-Catholic funerals. He was also much stricter than his predecessors about marriages between Catholics and non-Catholics, demanding that these have permission from the priest. Women who married without this were condemned as concubines and both they and their parents were held responsible. In the 1850s one of the Naples-trained priests got into trouble for giving communion to a Cave Gully woman who had married a non-Catholic, a couple who had married their daughter into a non-Catholic family, and a woman who had allowed her son to sell his wife. By the 1890s missionaries refused to give people confession and communion before death if they were in breach of the rules.[30] The Catholic communities were already tightly bound together. Under this additional pressure from the church nearly all the marriages arranged by Catholic parents for their children were with other Catholics. After 1900 when Barnaba Nanetti compiled lists of all those killed, the information he collected included not only the natal villages of the women killed but also in many cases their mothers' natal villages. The data shows that by this time in central Shanxi, 77 percent of women who had married into Catholic villages came from places where there was a longstanding Catholic community.[31]

The missionaries also encouraged forms of public religious practice that emphasized the separation of Catholics from the surrounding communities. By the late nineteenth century many people in Europe who disliked both the rationalism of the eighteenth century and the social changes brought about by industrialization were looking back with romantic nostalgia to the Middle Ages. For Catholics this was a time when Christianity had been politically powerful and had permeated all aspects of daily life. This ideal they summed up in the Latin term *christianitas*, which meant both "Christendom" as an area of Christian rule in the medieval sense and modern attempts to rebuild the all-encompassing Christian world of the that time. The missionaries sought to create such a Christian world through their institutions, but they also found it existing already in the religious practices and social order of the Chinese Catholic villages: *christianitas* was the word used for a Chinese Catholic parish.[32] These late nineteenth-century missionaries, inspired by romantic ideals of the Middle Ages, were far more sympathetic to the religious practices that bound the Catholic villages together than their immediate predecessors had been. The long, chanted prayers and rigorous fasting were no longer evidence of ignorance but models for Europeans.

A Chinese priest who worked in Cave Gully told a story about an old woman living up in the hills and how he discovered she was Catholic. One day a man came down from the mountains and told the priest that there was an old woman who wanted to speak to someone from the Western religion. So the next day the priest set off on a mule into the mountains. He arrived in a hamlet where two of the woman's sons came to meet him and took him to speak to their mother. She told him that as a child she had lived in one of the plains villages, but her father was a bad man and her mother often wept. Then one evening her mother told the little girl that she had been sold to a family up high up in the mountains as a bride. Before she left, her mother told her never to raise her hands or kneel in front of statues and to recite two formulas daily. The old lady had followed these instructions all her life but she did not know what the words she was reciting meant. Now, she said, she would soon die, so she wanted to speak to someone from the foreign religion. The priest asked the woman what the formulas were, and she began to recite *"Zai tian wo deng fu zhe . . . "* He recognized the Our Father then the Hail Mary and, deeply moved to have found a lost Christian, explained some basic doctrine, to which she smiled and agreed. He returned a year later to give her the last rites before she died.[33] This story was published in the European mission press as an example of the power of prayer: daily recitation of simple prayers, even without understanding the meaning, had brought great fruits and ultimately, salvation.

The missionaries also admired and encouraged the close bonds that linked Catholic communities together. When Barnaba Nanetti visited

Tian Fenglan's family, he noted with admiration that any Catholic who came to the city on business could stay at their shop. He also described in an article for a European mission journal how, when Catholic villages held festivals, visitors did not bring any money with them because they stayed in the homes of the Catholics and were fed by them. In one village he asked one of the leaders why his household was preparing so much food, since his family was not large, and was told that it was for those who would come at the feast of Epiphany. Nanetti asked, "But they are not all your relatives, are they?" The leader clearly he thought it was a foolish question, for he replied, "Father, the Holy Church is Catholic." The Chinese word *gong*, which he used for Catholic, means literally "public" or "for the whole community."[34]

Missionaries expected strong Catholic communities to be hostile to the state because that was how it was in Europe. There, the world that Catholics were trying to build was one that looked back to medieval Christian rule but was in opposition to governments of the day. In both Europe and China processions at festivals were a particular source of friction. One missionary described a new procession that he had introduced in Cave Gully, for the feast of Corpus Christi. It included the big drums characteristic of Shanxi folk music, village men and children chanting prayers, a band of musicians, the seminarians, the clergy in their robes, and clouds of incense. The women, he said, did not take part because their feet were so tightly bound that they had to move their arms for balance when they walked and to lean on something when they stopped. He pointed out that the procession would have been illegal in Europe. It was also common for Catholics to compel all onlookers to kneel as the Corpus Christi procession passed, which they certainly could not have done in France.[35]

Group pilgrimages to pray for rain demonstrate the public drama of Catholic processions, but also their similarity to local temple cults. The best description of these pilgrimages comes from Winding Gully in the 1880s. That year, drought threatened the millet that was the staple food and the main crop on most unirrigated land. In response the magistrate had banned the sale of meat, thus enforcing vegetarian fasting, and temples were holding rituals. The bishop had also issued a statement, probably written by his secretary, Tian Fenglan. It begins,

> Director of Shanxi northern district religious affairs, Bishop Grassi, proclaims prayers for rain:
> This office is aware that the weather has been dry for a long time and there is fear of famine, which is a cause for serious concern. Christians are

well aware that the lives of the myriad souls, the cycles of the myriad kinds of matter, the changing seasons, cold and heat, wind and rain are all controlled by the Lord of Heaven. The Lord of Heaven loves mankind and wants humanity to do good for which they will later receive their reward, but only a few do as the Lord wishes; many are distracted by the pleasures of this world and do evil provoking most justly the Lord's wrath so that he sends disasters to awaken them and bring them quickly to repentance, to make them follow the commandments and do good, and so avoid eternal punishment after death.[36]

The proclamation goes on to command people to go to church and to pray to Mary Mother of God, St. Joseph, St. Francis, the Five Wounds of Jesus, their patron saints, and the souls in purgatory for three days. It is written and presented just like a government document and the bishop lays claim to what sounds like an official position, which would have been normal in a Daoist religious text but had imperialist overtones for a foreigner in China at this time.

Meanwhile the people of Winding Gully planned a village pilgrimage to the shrine of the Holy Mother high up in the mountains north of Taiyuan. The church there was a magnificent new Western-style building, but the shrine was older: Catholic prayers for rain had been held there since at least the 1850s. Just as groups of villages turned to a particular Dragon King temple to pray for rain, over the years a cluster of villages in the valley below the temple had become Catholic, affiliated with the shrine of the Holy Mother (see map 1). The shrine also drew pilgrims from much further away: Winding Gully was two days' journey on foot. For the pilgrimage, as for temple processions, each household sent one man to represent it. A group of men went to fetch banners and a portable shrine containing a statue of Jesus that was kept at the cathedral in Taiyuan. A music group began rehearsals in the vinegar-maker's courtyard. The village schoolmaster, who held an official degree, wrote an announcement of the prayers for rain on red paper, attached a pigeon feather as a sign that it was to be passed on, and sent it to the villages that the procession would pass through. On the morning that the pilgrimage was due to set off, the parish church was full for mass. Then the men gathered and organized themselves for the procession, which was led by a team playing a huge drum, cymbals, and other percussion instruments. Following them were the men of the parish chanting litanies and carrying the processional cross and three ceremonial umbrellas, another group of musicians with pipes and stringed instruments, more men carrying wooden boards with Catholic teachings, and at the end the banners and the portable shrine. As they passed through each village the musicians struck up and the men chanted. In response to the pigeon-feather letter, the villagers had put out jars of water, and the pilgrims drank a little before they went on. They passed the night at Red Gully, a Catholic village up in the mountains, before making the final ascent to the shrine, where they said the Stations of the Cross and spent the night.[37]

These prayers to the Holy Mother of God were similar in form to those of villagers who worshipped the Holy Mother at Jinci or the Dragon Kings who brought rain for their crops. At Jinci the Holy Mother was the goddess of the stream that irrigated their farmland and dragons twined up the columns of her temple. In the mountains, Dragon Kings were worshipped at shrines where there was a spring, or where a cave where dripped water to form a pool even in the driest weather. Each year in the spring, the village went in procession to fetch the statue of the Dragon King down from the mountains; after the harvest the deity was ceremonially returned. The statue of the Holy Mother was escorted in the spring from her temple to visit a nearby temple of the Dragon Kings. The processions included drums, cymbals, performers, ceremonial umbrellas, and a large group of village men; the women watched from the side. The deity was carried in a portable shrine near the end of the procession. In times of drought there were other processions as people went up to the mountain shrines to pray. One man from each village family took part and other villages were informed by the same pigeon-feather letter. Those taking part recited the name of Amitabha Buddha and villagers dipped willow branches into the jars of water to scatter on the procession. When these processions arrived at the shrines of the Dragon King, the rituals were structured around drawing water from the pool and were very different from the eucharist at the church of the Holy Mother, but the level of emotion was much the same: the worshippers would walk with bare feet, carry heavy iron implements, and stay awake all night reciting the name of Amitabha Buddha. At the annual festival at the Catholic shrine, pilgrims would stay awake all night praying to the souls in purgatory and sometimes whipping themselves.[38]

On the day of this particular Catholic pilgrimage heavy rain fell and by the time the Winding Gully villagers traveled back, the rivers were swollen. In one large village that had only two Christian households, a crowd gathered in front of the temple and an old man made a speech thanking the Catholics for their successful prayers. The village's own musicians even came out to join the procession. When the procession got back to Winding Gully the women were so moved by the rainfall and the arrival of this band of musicians that they were trembling and murmuring "Jesus and Mary." Firecrackers and guns were fired, as was also the custom in southern Italy. Indeed Winding Gully had a parish shotgun for this purpose, an 1882 British model. (Another parish had three small cannon which they fired off during Christmas midnight mass, breaking the paper in the windows of the priest's residence.) Temples might not usually keep firearms, but processions of the gods were demonstrations of local power relations and were often the occasion of disputes. The mountain shrine of the Holy Mother with its network of Catholic villages was one of many pilgrimage sites with networks that bound some villages together and separated them from others. This network of cults was never uncontentious, but it was part of the fabric that made up the Chinese countryside.[39]

So perhaps it was after all similarities, not differences, that made temples a flashpoint for the troubles that followed—but it was also because officials had built an alliance between the state and temples against the Christians as a way to resist foreign interference. Temple cults were powerful and longstanding markers of local identity, with the gods' processions and annual festivals being major local holidays, but the state's relationship with them was problematic. The deities and rituals were often closely linked to state orthodoxy and had the effect of legitimating the social order, but there was also a long history of Confucian criticism of communal celebrations focused around temples whose organizational structure was largely outside the state's control.[40]

The organizers of temple festivals expected each household in the community to contribute to the cost. Given the general unpopularity of taxes and the fact that the Ten Commandments clearly banned Christians from worshipping other deities, it is not surprising that disputes over Chinese Christians refusing to contribute to temple cults date back to the early Qing. The records of several early cases suggest that when such disputes were taken to court at that time the results were unpredictable. One missionary wrote that although the legal code banned festivals that involved opera or processions, Christians who refused to pay and were persecuted by their neighbors could not get redress in the courts. However, some officials did rule in favor of the Christians: one judge commented that the Christians did not expect other people to pay for incense for them, so they should not be expected to pay for the temple. Often the officials simply negotiated deals dividing the community into two groups and fixing the contributions to be made by each side. Legal cases ended with the first large-scale crackdown on Christians in the 1780s, after which people could simply blackmail their Christian neighbors to make them pay. But in 1843, with the ban on Christian practice newly lifted, a Taiyuan city official again ruled against a temple in a dispute over contributions, saying that the law did not require anyone to contribute to temples.[41]

After 1860, cases of Christians who refused to contribute to local temple cults were dealt with quite differently: officials nearly always ruled in favor of the temples and their judgments were phrased in terms of China's international position. One magistrate asked a Catholic who refused to contribute where he was from, then said, "Since you are a Qing subject, why are you following the foreign devils' rebellious teaching? You are a rebel . . . . You people should definitely pay the money for the operas. If not we won't let you live in the Qing country and you can go abroad."[42]

In a case where an official ruled in favor of the Catholics and accused the village head of extortion, as had been common in earlier years, people interpreted the decision not as Confucian hostility to superstition, but as evidence of foreign missionary power.[43] This shift in official attitudes was a response to increasing Western power in China, though it also reflects local governments' growing reliance on elite organizations, including temple cults, to provide services after the wars of the Taiping Rebellion. In any case, the new alliance between officials and temples against the Christians was potentially extremely powerful, for it combined deeply felt markers of local identity with issues of national sovereignty. That power also made it dangerous, for the temple cults and their networks were never really under state control.

The tensions provoked by the increased visibility of their missionaries and their works, the growing exclusivity of Catholic communities, and official recognition of local temple cults set the stage for the violent attacks on Catholic villages that broke out in 1900, but the immediate impetus came from outside the province. News arrived from over the mountains in Shandong province that groups had formed to practice martial arts and destroy the foreign religion. Soon similar groups began to meet at Jinci and other temples, where they conducted rituals, were possessed by the gods, and practiced martial arts. They saw themselves as a militia resisting foreign control and expected a return to the old order in which Christianity was illegal: what purported to be official announcements circulated, telling Christians to leave the religion and threatening those who refused. But times had changed and what followed was very different from the old order, when Christianity had been condemned as a heterodox teaching alongside the White Lotus and local people had paid little attention except when they used blackmail to take advantage of the situation. Now Christianity was condemned as a foreign religion, a foreign army was moving inland towards Beijing, and local people took up arms against neighboring Catholic villages. Soon flyers reported that Boxers were fighting alongside the regular army around Beijing and had been praised by the court. In Taiyuan city the new provincial governor began to enroll some members of local Boxer groups into the army and regular militia; they camped outside the city and he was said to have inspected and drilled them.[44]

On the central Shanxi plain, the killing began with the murder of a Catholic butcher from Cold Springs Road, whose job made him liable to accusations of magic involving smearing blood. The murder was not investigated, and the same group of Boxers took advantage of the situation to strengthen their own position. About a hundred men entered Taiyuan county town to demand that they be provided with grain by the local government. The magistrate went out to welcome them, but they came into the government offices, occupied the magistrate's seat, drew their swords, and cursed him. He was horrified and wrote to the provincial government asking for military support.[45] Most officials of the central government would have been hostile to such groups, but the central government was divided over how to respond to the crisis, so local officials waited for a clear policy, and allowed the violence to grow.

In Cave Gully people were terrified. A messenger arrived with news that a church in the north of the province had been destroyed and that handbills denouncing Christians were circulating. There were rumors that the cathedral in Taiyuan city had been burned, that the Westerners had been massacred, and that Boxers were planning to come in the night to attack the village. The village men began to collect together possible weapons: farm tools, long poles, swords, knives and spikes, but also rifles, pistols, and revolvers of various kinds, sacks of gunpowder, bullets, nails and anything else that might serve as ammunition, paraffin, and tin cans and iron vessels that could be used to make bombs. The cast-iron vessels were filled with earth and crushed stones, which were rammed down and covered with grapeshot, a fuse and another layer of earth and stones. The young missionary whose room in the monastery was used to manufacture them noted that they worked quite well, scattering a hail of projectiles at a great distance, but were very dangerous to use. He regretted that it was not possible to use nitroglycerin, but it was in Taiyuan (presumably in the cathedral compound). Families buried their valuables. Women left to hide in the mountains. The men set up guard posts and a group went in to Qingyuan to buy gunpowder.[46]

The neighboring villages and towns were thrown into a panic that the Catholics would attack them. In the late nineteenth century members of the local elite began for the first time to refer to Catholics in their writings. Now Liu Dapeng, a degree holder living near Jinci, recorded rumors that the Cave Gully Christians were coming to kill everyone. In some nearby villages people hid all of one night in the fields. In Taiyuan county town, a strange hissing sound like the Chinese word "kill" *(sha)* was heard at night; the magistrate sounded the drum and set a guard on the town walls and at the gates. As well as fearing an outright attack, people were terrified of magic: the strange hissing, poisoned water in the wells, blood scattered on doorways to make the household within go mad, cut-out paper figures which would turn into soldiers. A green hand as big as a wheel appeared in the night sky over the wall of a city across the plain. People looking towards Cave Gully were said to have seen balls of fire and men dressed in white on white horses threatening them with fiery swords. These were the shining figures the Catholics identified as the souls in purgatory, to whom they had been praying for aid.[47]

While the surrounding villages were terrified of Cave Gully with its defensible position and warlike preparations, for many Catholics from the plains villages getting there seemed to be their only hope of safety. A member of the Fan family of Nine Springs, known as a collector of children for the orphanage, was murdered on his way across the plain. Zhao Yuqian arrived dressed as a porter, almost unrecognizable without his beard, and soaking wet because the ferry had refused to take him across the river. He had traveled from Taiyuan city across the plain amidst all the chaos to attend the deathbed of another priest, who had once been his pupil, and then come on to Cave Gully. He was carrying rings, earrings, and silver head ornaments given to him by the women of one of the Catholic villages he had passed through as payment for masses, and he told stories of miracles performed by holy water and an amulet that protected against demons. A few days later he went off to hide in the hills, taking the young Chen Guodi with him, but they were discovered and had to return. Ordinary Catholics also flocked to Cave Gully, though the women were turned away unless they had brought food with them. Soon the village's army had grown to two hundred men (though Liu Dapeng heard that there were two or three thousand) and Nanetti led them out to fire on an approaching group of Boxers, who rapidly retreated.[48]

The next day the head of the neighboring village arrived with an announcement from the county magistrate that Catholics must leave the religion on pain of death. Two armed men went out to meet him, brought him in, and offered him tea, listening courteously as he said that he knew it was pointless to ask the Cave Gully people to leave the religion but urged them to live at peace with their neighbors. A couple of days later he came again, to say that government troops would soon be arriving. Nanetti and the other missionaries in the monastery fled to the hills, taking all the church funds with them. The only missionary to remain was too sick from typhus to be moved and was hidden in a cave in the hillside. A few days later in Taiyuan, Bishop Fogolla was killed along with all the other Catholic and Protestant missionaries in the city.[49]

Nanetti succeeded in making his way to Inner Mongolia, but fleeing into the hills was just as dangerous as remaining in the village. Zhao Yuqian and his nephew left a second time with the parish priest of Cold Springs Road and a group of strong young men. They got through to the Yellow River and into Shaanxi province, but there they separated from the rest of the group and were robbed. Alone and penniless, they turned to beg their way back through the high mountains, where the people were poor and violent at the best of times and now were so desperate because of the drought that even Liu Dapeng was afraid to send his family to hide there. Like many an unfortunate traveler that year, Zhao found himself accused of poisoning wells. He fled but was caught and beaten till blood ran down his face. Then he and his nephew were bound by the hands and feet, slung over carrying poles, and taken to another village. The nephew agreed to renounce Catholicism and was released, but Zhao refused and was left hanging by his hands and feet from a beam in the village temple. The next day he was taken down, apparently dead, and told to leave the religion, which he again refused to do, saying that his family had been Christian for seven generations. The following day after further torture he was killed with a sword to the stomach and his body dismembered and burnt.[50]

Soon the killing shifted from murders to fighting as the Boxers increasingly took on the role of an official militia supporting the Qing against the foreign powers. The fighting was particularly intense because this was an area with both large Catholic communities made visible by their fine new churches and a weak county magistrate. Liu Dapeng saw the Boxers gathered at Jinci: a huge crowd of men and boys with red cloths on their heads, red sashes round their waists, and red puttees. They worshipped at the temple of the god of drought, then formed up to leave bearing banners with the slogans "Support the Qing and destroy the foreign! Implement the Way of Heaven!" Later he stood at his door and watched Third Prince, the Qingyuan Boxer leader who led the attack on Cave Gully, pass leading an army of about a thousand, all arranged in orderly troops and units.[51] All the old Catholic communities around Cave Gully came under attack. In some villages the Catholics took refuge in their new churches and fought to defend them, but if the church was taken almost the whole community would be slaughtered. In West Willows, people got news that the Boxers were coming and fled, leaving their church and homes to be burned. Sometimes the Cave Gully villagers came out to help break the sieges. In one wealthy village across the plain, the Catholics were besieged in their fine, solidly built, stone church by more than four hundred Boxers. The Catholics had hired mercenaries from Shandong and Zhili, and the fighting went on for six or seven days. When the Cave Gully fighters managed to break in, those who were strong enough to escape fled with them, leaving only the old and weak, who died three days later when the church was burned and thirty-three Catholics and two Boxers died.[52]

As the other villages fell one by one, groups of Boxers from across the plain converged on Cold Springs Road, where some of the most severe fighting in the province took place. At one point a force of one thousand Boxers launched an attack, but the Catholics managed to kill the Boxer leader and capture five cannons. Many Catholics were killed too, but at the high point of the fighting they saw a vision of a great light and in the center of it, the arms of God. They fell to their knees and prayed. When the vision ended they rang the church bell, rose up, and drove the Boxers back. As the battles at Cold Springs Road intensified the Boxers also gathered at Cave Gully, but the defensible site and the villagers' preparations made it a discouraging target. The villagers attempted to exorcise the Boxers by making the sign of the cross, calling on the holy names of Jesus and Mary, and sprinkling them with holy water. Guns were fired, but no one was killed. This may also have had something to do with the fact that the Boxers managed to get hold of the communion wine which the missionaries were manufacturing in the village and drank seven thousand pounds of it. The Qingyuan gentry called in the regular army, but they marched as far as Taiyuan county town, then turned back. It became obvious that the political situation was shifting and the Boxers gradually dispersed.[53]

By the time the fighting ended two months after it started, nearly a thousand people had been killed in the area.[54] More men were killed than women, especially men of fighting age. This was partly because some women were treated as property and sold rather than killed, but it was also because explicit choices to die for the faith were quite as likely to be made by tough young men as by an elderly priest like Zhao Yuqian. One man from a longstanding Catholic village is described in the list of martyrs as "a bad Christian and opium smoker who did not attend the annual confession and communion." The Boxers caught him, took him to the village temple, and said "You have not been Christian for a long time, so if you just say one word against your religion, we will set you free straight away." At which he shouted "You can tear my heart out of my body but I won't say that word. I am and will always be Christian." The Boxers hacked him to death then and there.[55] But the age group killed in the largest number was children, who were simply least able to get away. In the province as a whole, 562 children under ten were listed among a total of 1,820 martyrs.[56] The Cave Gully villagers survived, but did so when their friends and relatives died: one member of the Wu family lost his daughter, who had married into a nearby village, along with her fifteen-year-old daughter and her four sons ages thirteen, ten, seven, and four. Later, the coffins from villages all across the plain were collected in Cave Gully for burial.[57] As the villagers watched them pile up whatever sense of separation from their neighbors they may have felt before that terrible summer was inevitably multiplied.

Far away in Beijing, the foreign forces had sacked the city and compelled the government to condemn the Boxers. As the allied army moved on across the north China plain towards Shanxi, government policy suddenly and drastically changed. The provincial governor was removed and forced to commit suicide, county magistrates were dismissed, and Boxers began to be arrested and even executed. The foreign troops massed in the mountains that bordered the province and waited. Liu Dapeng reported the general local opinion, which was that the Cave Gully Catholics were in league with the foreign armies and were now buying grain and weapons for an uprising. The missionaries also began to return. Saccani, who had escaped from Taiyuan by climbing the city wall on ropes at the dead of night and hiding in the mountains near the shrine of the Holy Mother, arrived back in the monastery. Nanetti, who had reached Beijing and was seeking help from the Italian consular officials, asked for photographs of the warrior Saccani on horseback: a heroic image of the Italian missionary. In a surviving photograph, a group of men and boys are posed for the camera in front of the monastery (figure 8). The missionary is on horseback directing them, pointing

FIGURE 8. A missionary, probably Francesco Saccani, with Cave Gully seminarians and villagers drilling outside the monastery, 1900. Courtesy of Archivio Fotografico, Centro Studi Confortiani e Saveriani, Istituto Missioni Estere, Parma.

forwards with a trumpeter beside him. A flag flutters in the wind. A Chinese priest wears an embroidered stole as a mark of his office. In front of them kneel the seminarians, in their matching long robes with guns pointing out, then a group of younger boys in ordinary clothes, and a crowd of men with guns, many of them wearing the white headbands of local mourning dress. Liu Dapeng reported that they drilled daily and that the sound of guns and cannon could be heard across the plain.[58]

The fighting of the Boxer Uprising separated Catholics from their neighbors in an entirely new way, even though Catholics continued to share the core values of the surrounding society. Many of the memorials that they set up describe the dead in strongly Confucian terms. One says that the martyrs "willingly gave their lives for the Lord, perfecting loyalty and filial piety for all generations."[59] Other memorials praise the martyrs for their loyalty to the nation. Zhao Yuqian's epitaph praises him for having "shed his blood for the enlightenment of China" (though there is no mention of his resistance to foreign missionary control in his youth).[60]

However for many, Catholics had become a group almost entirely identified with foreign power. Cold Springs Road and Cave Gully were the only Catholic communities in the area to survive the Boxers unharmed. Cave Gully, once a huddle of cave dwellings on the side of the hill, was now a powerful and impressive village. A couple of years later Liu Dapeng happened to pass by on his way to Qingyuan. He wrote,

> From afar I could see Cave Gully village about half a mile to the west. All the villagers follow the foreign religion. The village is at the foot of the hills and the church is built on the side of the hill and surrounded by a wall. Within the wall there are many fine large buildings all in the foreign style. The foreign barbarians use it as their hideout and seduce people into joining their sect. Those who join are all disloyal subjects who do it for the foreign money to support themselves and their families, not because they really like this religion and want to follow it. So the foreigners are stupid and the believers are even more stupid. . . . Everyone who goes by points and stares at the place saying "This is Cave Gully. We have all been harmed by them and do not know when we can wipe them out." If passersby speak like this, I don't know what it is if not hatred.[61]

This alienation was matched in the Catholic villages. Cave Gully had existed for two hundred years with no recorded trouble with its neighbors, its people too poor and too unimportant to be of interest to anyone. Since the 1860s it had gradually become more separate from the surrounding communities as the missionaries imposed bans on Catholics attending funerals or temple festivals and marrying outsiders. But it was the fighting and killings of 1900 that really isolated the Catholics. The memories of the survivors bound the villagers together into the strong and exclusive community of the twentieth century. Through the 1960s there would be people alive who could remember the massacres, and knew what had happened when the state had turned against them in what they called not the Boxer Uprising but the Great Persecution.

CHAPTER 5

The Missionary Who Cursed the Village

There was once a French priest called Fa who brought a beautiful statue of Our Lady of Lourdes to the village. Some years later he was transferred to another parish and wanted to take the statue with him. He got a wooden box ready to pack it in, but the Christians prevented him: they blocked the church door with stones and refused to let him in. The priest became very angry. He called the villagers Judeans, and as he left he took off his shoe, shook off the dust, and prayed to Heaven to punish them with seven years of bad harvests. The next year, as the fields were ripening, black clouds came from behind the mountain and hail fell, destroying the standing crops. But the Christians did not believe, so the following year it happened again, and then the next year again, until the villagers were so poor that they had to go to nearby Christians and beg for food. Then they remembered the priest's words so they built a chapel to Our Lady of the Seven Sorrows on the mountain. After that there was no more hail.[1]

This is the best known of all the Cave Gully folktales and the one that is most strongly associated with the village. Like other tales the villagers tell, it has a familiar plot: the story of the outsider with dangerous powers who must not be offended. People used to tell similar stories about the skilled foremen employed to direct the work in the coal mines, who could destroy the whole mine if they were offended.[2] But the story of the missionary's curse is also shaped by Cave Gully's Catholic history. The statue whose theft is prevented is Our Lady of Lourdes and help is granted by Our Lady of Seven Sorrows, both of them important figures of the Virgin Mary in the late nineteenth and early twentieth century. Moreover the priest's dramatic gesture comes directly from Jesus' words as he sends out the first missionaries, "And whosoever shall not receive you, nor hear your words: going forth out of that house or city shake off the dust from your feet" (Matthew 10:14).

For the Cave Gully people today, the story explains the magnificent shrine to Our Lady of Seven Sorrows on the mountain and its purpose is to demonstrate her great power. The shrine caretaker tells it alongside other miracles: causing snow to fall, bringing about the conversion of two women, and curing an AIDS patient in a distant city. Elsewhere in central Shanxi the story is used to illustrate the character of Cave Gully and its people. For these Catholics the point is not the power of Our Lady of the Seven Sorrows, but the comparison of the Cave Gully people to the Judeans, who they explain are "the people who killed Jesus." Similar stories exist about other villages: the people of Nine Springs are also labeled Judeans and the Newtown people are compared to Peter, who denied Jesus three times, because they were never attacked by the Boxers. Thus local Catholics condemn the people of these dominant villages, with their longstanding close relations with the church, for disloyalty and disobedience. When non-Catholics tell the story of the missionary's curse they skip both the Judeans and the power of the Virgin Mary, but emphasize the curse, which to them explains why the Cave Gully villagers are such strong Catholics and so obedient to the church. This can be used to compliment them on their morals, but it also expresses the widespread hostility and fear that has existed since the Boxer fighting.

Underlying all versions of the story is tension between the power of the missionaries and the poverty and dependence of the villagers. This tension reached its height in the early twentieth century when the Boxer Indemnity gave the missionaries of central Shanxi great wealth at a time of growing Chinese nationalism. The overthrow of the Qing dynasty in the 1911 revolution motivated by republicanism and nationalism caused these tensions to blow up into a series of disputes between the villagers and a bad-tempered Italian missionary, Francesco Fazzini. These disputes (in which Fazzini is remembered as a Frenchman because his Chinese surname, Fa, is the word for France) gave rise to the story of the missionary's curse. The ending of the folktale with the building of the shrine to Our Lady of the Seven Sorrows suggests how investment that followed the village's new position as the headquarters of a new diocese in the 1920s resolved some of these tensions, but the fact that the story was handed down suggests that the struggles it described continued to be relevant. Although people in Shanxi do not connect the Judeans *(Rudiya guo ren)* in the story with Jews *(Youtai ren)*, it is possible that Fazzini's words were related to the growth of anti-Semitism in Europe and support within the Italian Catholic church for Fascism. Both Italian and Chinese nationalism grew in the 1920s and 1930s and the two countries fought and suffered on opposite sides during World War II. When central Shanxi was occupied by the Japanese in 1942, the missionaries, as Italians allied to Germany and Japan, had the power to protect Catholics. They did so at the cost of ever more severe tensions with local Chinese nationalism.

The statue of Our Lady of Lourdes first came to the village in 1901 during the negotiations over the Boxer Indemnity, which were to make the diocese wealthy and give the missionaries great power over ordinary Catholics. After the defeat of the Boxers, Barnaba Nanetti, who had managed to reach Beijing, took responsibility for dealing with the Qing government on behalf of the diocese. In compensation for the deaths and the property that had been destroyed, he demanded not only a huge sum of money but also that the shrine at Jinci and its water should be handed over to the church: the Jinci shrine was where the Boxers had gathered before marching out to attack the Catholics, so he argued that the Buddhist monks should be held responsible and the shrine removed from their control. Controlling Jinci, the church would have been able to provide irrigation water for Cave Gully and other Catholic villages, allowing a shift of the balance of local wealth and power in their favor. The missionaries could also take over the shrine of the Holy Mother of the Jin River and presumably convert it into a shrine to Mary the Holy Mother of God.[3] As the negotiations were going on, Francesco Saccani arranged for a statue of Our Lady of Lourdes to be brought in a triumphal procession through the countryside to Cave Gully.[4] We think of Lourdes as a healing shrine (and indeed Cave Gully people today explain that the villagers probably wanted to keep the statue because of its healing power), but Lourdes was also associated with springs of water. When the Virgin Mary appeared to a young girl in the French Pyrenees in 1858, she told the child to drink from a spring that appeared nearby. Statues showed Our Lady of Lourdes as a young woman wearing a blue sash, holding a rosary, with a stream flowing from beneath her feet.

A couplet written to adorn shrines to her in Shanxi begins, "With plentiful water and beautiful mountains, what is as efficacious as Lourdes?"[5] In 1901 bringing Our Lady of Lourdes in procession to Cave Gully was not only a symbol of the Catholic victory, it could also be understood as a symbol of the missionaries' determination to get water from Jinci for the Cave Gully farmers.

But Nanetti's negotiations failed. This was partly because he was simply too angry and upset to behave rationally. Among those who died, when he had fled, were not only his friends and colleagues but also his younger sister, who had come to Taiyuan as a nun at his suggestion. He insisted on negotiating through the Italians rather than the official French protectorate, a choice which was bound to alienate both the church bureaucracy and the French. As a result he was criticized for making the Catholics look bad in comparison with the Protestants, who had asked that most of their indemnity be used for the construction of a university, and he was sent back to Italy in disgrace.[6] The French then negotiated a much lower deal: there would be no transfer of property and the total cash payment for Taiyuan diocese was greatly reduced.

Nevertheless the indemnity that was finally agreed was a huge sum: one million taels to be paid to the diocese over four years. The provincial government raised the money by forced contributions from the local elite and an increase in the salt tax. Salt was both a daily necessity and a state monopoly, so in effect the entire population of the province was forced to contribute. A further 1.25 million was paid to the Catholic dioceses in southern Shanxi and north of the Great Wall, which were run by Dutch and Belgian missionaries. All this was in addition to the much larger indemnity paid by China to the foreign governments, which was still being paid off in the 1940s.[7]

The diocese's indemnity was calculated in relation to the number of people who had been killed and the property that had been destroyed, but it was paid to the bishop and very little reached individual Catholics: for each room destroyed, they got five taels or in some cases ten taels. Those who had agreed to leave the religion to save their lives, or who smoked opium, or who did not participate regularly in religious activities, received nothing. All this was very different from the arrangements made by the Protestant missionaries, who made payments of up to five thousand taels to the families of those Chinese Protestants who had died.[8] The Shanxi merchants were already in decline as a result of the growth of coastal shipping and modern-style banks. For those Catholics of the plains villages whose homes and businesses had been destroyed by the Boxers it was all but impossible to recover their former wealth. The Catholics of the hill villages like Cave Gully, which were less attractive for the Boxers to attack, simply remained poor. Since Grioglio's time the missionaries had claimed that the Catholics were poor and dependent on the mission: the decline of Shanxi's merchant economy, the destruction caused by the Boxers, and the way in which the indemnity was used finally made these statements true.

Instead of being distributed to Catholics, the indemnity was invested and it made Taiyuan one of the richest dioceses in China. In time the diocese came to own seventeen properties in Taiyuan city, including the main post office, a major hotel, and a commercial center, as well as a valuable portfolio of properties in the industrial cities of Tianjin and Wuhan. Other funds were invested with local businesses or lent out at interest. The growth in the income from these investments coincided with a decline in charitable funding from France as a result of the 1914–18 European War and the collapse of the French franc. Money extracted from the local economy by the foreign powers, not foreign donations, funded the diocese in the early twentieth century.[9]

The demonstration of foreign military force in 1900, combined with the diocese's new wealth, made the missionaries extremely powerful. A photograph taken in 1914 shows a group of Franciscans from Bologna apparently gathered in the home of a wealthy local Catholic (figure 9). Like all Franciscan missionaries in Shanxi from the eighteenth century through to the 1940s they wear Chinese clothes: matching white summer gowns, dark jackets, and caps, although Giovanni Ricci, seated in the front holding a pipe, is still wearing a dark padded winter gown. In Italy they would have worn the familiar brown Franciscan habits (see figure 13), but these had to be imported and the woolen cloth was uncomfortably cold in winter and hot in summer, so they were kept for special occasions and use within the monastery. Although the missionaries wear Chinese clothes, only Francesco Saccani—squarely seated with his hands on his knees, looking away from the camera—has a posture that goes with his Chinese clothes. He had been in China for nearly twenty years by this time and had become strongly committed to the newly fashionable idea that missionaries should become like the Chinese. As he grew older, he was known not only for his kindness to his colleagues (he was nicknamed "everybody's mother") but for his knowledge of Chinese customs, which made him a popular mediator of local family disputes.[10] Ricci, leaning against the ornamental table, and the four younger men, with their full beards and their chests forward in

FIGURE 9. Group of missionaries from Bologna. Left to right: Eligio Ferretti, Giovanni Ricci (seated), Ugolino Arcari, Ermengildo Focaccia, Francesco Saccani (seated), Patrizio Ventura. Courtesy of Provincia di Cristo Re dei Frati Minori dell'Emilia Romagna.

the fashionable European posture of the day, look like Italians and are somehow ill fitted by their fine Chinese clothes. The sense of traditional wealth and power is palpable, but so is the feeling that these people identify themselves with a different culture.

The missionaries controlled the lives of vast numbers of people, since the wealth from the Boxer Indemnity meant that the church came to have a great many employees and dependents. In 1918 the bishop in Taiyuan made a rough estimate that he was feeding five thousand people, including one thousand orphanage children. He did not include the approximately three thousand younger children whom the diocese placed with foster families, so the total of those being supported was nearer to eight thousand. Some of these were religious professionals: 376 priests, nuns, sworn virgins, seminarians, and evangelists. The rest were presumably converts receiving a subsidy while they prepared for baptism, old people cared for in the orphanages, and employees such as teachers, carpenters, cooks, caretakers, carters, mule-drivers, messengers, water carriers, and coal haulers. Since Taiyuan diocese at this point had a total of approximately fifty thousand Catholics and converts preparing for baptism, we can conclude that something like one in six was at least partially supported by the diocese; there were many more who relied on the church because they rented its land, sold it goods or services, or borrowed its money.[11]

The orphanage in Cave Gully was one of the places to which the church's new dependents came. In addition to accepting babies and children, the orphanage now took in significant numbers of adult women. Being able to send women to the orphanage made it easy for the clergy to intervene in families. In one case a family had adopted a girl from the orphanage to work for them and ultimately to marry their son. They were poor people and when a missionary visited them he was shocked to find that the girl was sharing a bedroom with the boy she was going to marry. When he questioned her she wept and said that she was poorly clothed, ill treated by everyone, and did not want to marry the boy. The missionary decided (in a strikingly European fashion) that not only were the living arrangements unacceptable, but the young man did not love the girl, so he sent her to the orphanage. Such interventions could be a way of controlling women. One girl who was not Catholic was taken to the orphanage after trying to break off her engagement to a young man who was in the process of converting. Her prospective mother-in-law dragged her into the church, where she absolutely refused to kneel. So she was packed off to the orphanage to learn about the religion. On the other hand the orphanage could also be a refuge for women who had nowhere else to turn. A Chinese priest wrote to the bishop to apologize for sending a young woman there without permission. She had lived in the orphanage for a few months as a child and had now run away from her husband. She made her way to the priest as a beggar, and when she arrived she knelt at his feet and told him that if he did not send her to the orphanage she would kill herself.[12]

The girls who grew up in the orphanage could choose to remain there as sworn virgins, since the church's new wealth meant that girls who did this no longer needed their families to support them. However, if they chose to marry their husbands had to be Catholic. The vast majority of children in church orphanages were girls, since families were more likely to abandon a daughter than a son. Because many of them came from families that were not Catholic the community had a surplus of brides and bride-prices for Catholic women dropped. In one county a missionary noted that the standard price for a bride was forty strings of cash but that Catholic men were only prepared to pay thirty. This differential provided an incentive for Catholics to marry their own daughters outside the religion and then get cheaper orphanage girls as brides for their sons, a practice to which the clergy strongly objected. The missionaries demanded that local officials ban people from marrying their sons to Catholic girls, which was possible because if the officials refused the legal cases would go to Beijing, where the consuls would argue them as questions of freedom of religion.[13]

The missionaries also used their position as foreigners to intervene with the government over how much tax Catholics paid. During the last years of the Qing dynasty, Catholics continued to claim exemption from local levies on the grounds that they were used to pay for temple rituals. Since this tax exemption was backed up by the foreign powers, in practice it was received at the discretion of the missionary. One missionary reported that he had sent someone to compile a list of all those preparing for baptism. The plan was that if any of the converts behaved badly they would be removed from the list and the magistrate would be informed that they should not get the tax exemption, "and thus, I think, they will be in holy fear so that they are good and observant converts."[14] When the magistrate failed to cooperate with this scheme, sending only a brief acknowledgement of the list, the missionary wrote a fierce letter accusing him of being anti-European.

The church also collected taxes of its own. The practice of levying a contribution from members of the community to pay for the priest's visit for mass and confession dated back to the eighteenth century. In those days people paid a Catholic priest when they wanted rituals, just as they might a Buddhist monk or Daoist priest. Later bishops had tried to impose a regular schedule of visits, so that by the end of the nineteenth century most Catholic communities would have mass once a year, but the resulting compulsory levies were the subject of many disputes.[15] The Cave Gully villagers tell stories of how the rich people of the plains villages were punished for their wickedness. One of these concerns Eligio Ferretti (one of the younger Bologna missionaries in figure 9), who was trying to collect contributions according to the size of each family's landholdings. A rich man refused to pay and asked, "Are you making a mission to the people or the land?" The missionary responded by threatening that God would take away the man's wealth. That summer his barn caught fire, then his two sons became addicted to drugs, leaving only a daughter who had to take refuge in the orphanage.[16] Refusing to make the contributions was also a way of articulating other problems. The Nine Springs villagers were horrified to discover that those who had smoked opium or gambled would not be allocated any money from the Boxer Indemnity. A number of them refused to pay the church levies and the case went to the local magistrate. The missionary, who had refused to confess them unless they paid, summed up their attitude as, "Who is this Westerner? We've already told the bishop about him. He is obstructing confessions, that's what the bishop says. He's just stuffing a sausage full of sins. Who cares if he's shocked and torn apart and so on? When he hears someone confess he should absolve them—that's his duty. . . . You'll see if the Christians of Nine Springs are afraid of a missionary!!"[17] He ended his letter, as he had a previous one, by urging the bishop to give him permission to have one of the leaders beaten.

The power of the missionaries and their relative immunity from the state meant that priests did indeed sometimes beat their parishioners. In the eighteenth century there had been a case where a missionary had beaten Catholics, including women, as a penance after confession, but the bishop at the time was appalled and threatened to leave unless the missionary was removed. Priests had also been banned from beating or striking anyone in 1853, though there is no other indication that this occurred.[18] Indeed if the missionaries had been beating the Chinese Catholics in the 1860s it seems inconceivable that Wang Tingrong would not have mentioned it. By the 1900s, however, beating appears simply to have required permission from the bishop and this was sometimes requested after the event.[19] Penitences that were symbolic forms of criminal punishment were common, as when a group of senior Cave Gully men who were held responsible for the theft of the church candlesticks were required to come before the priests with ropes around their necks. Such penitences could be extended to physical beatings. One missionary demanded that some people who had renounced the faith should kneel outside the doors of the church saying prayers while a priest beat them with a rod. Priests also sometimes beat their parishioners out of anger. A Chinese priest reported that zeal for justice had led him to beat a man who sold his adopted daughter in marriage to a non-Catholic. Sometimes the missionaries simply became so exasperated that violence seemed the only solution. One described how a man had come to him bringing his little daughter for baptism. The child's mother strongly objected and tried to snatch the child away. The missionary grabbed the mother by the arm and dragged her out of the room. When she came back, still cursing, he took a riding whip which was handed to him and struck her. Then he performed the baptism. He was not comfortable with this, but excused himself by saying that he had been seizing an innocent soul from the devil.[20]

More serious accusations came from Barnaba Nanetti, who returned from Europe having received funding from an Italian national association for missions in order to make an official record of the Boxer martyrs. He traveled from village to village, even though the experience was so terrible for him that he had to lie down for hours, hardly able to breathe and shaken by vomiting and paroxysms, before conducting each hearing. Shanxi was the only place where so many of the Chinese Catholics who had been killed were officially recorded by the church and the process resulted in the church registering many of those who died as martyrs, but collecting the information that made this possible killed Nanetti. He died in 1911 and on his deathbed he wrote a long letter to the pope detailing abuses in the China mission. In it he denounces his former colleagues and claims that in some places missionaries beat their parishioners more than the officials did, and that some beatings were so severe that they risked killing the offender. He says that the French and German missionaries were the worst, and certainly the recorded cases in Shanxi did not involve that degree of violence. Nanetti's accusations suggest that it was not only Chinese villagers who felt that the missionaries now had too much power.[21]

The diocese's new wealth made it possible for it to support many more missionaries. Starting in 1903, for the first time since the 1770s, there were more European than Chinese clergy. By the early 1930s there were more than a hundred missionaries in the province and twenty-nine in Taiyuan diocese.[22] In the central Shanxi parishes, these men formed a tightly bound community with regular meetings and social occasions. As their numbers increased so did their tendency towards internal politics. They were divided into two main groups: those from northern Italy and Bologna, a prosperous city with a famous university at the heart of Italy's modern agricultural sector, and those from the countryside of Lazio, near Rome, which was much poorer and less developed. While the Bologna priests, who included both Nanetti and Saccani, were always in the minority, they were well educated and more likely to come from the urban middle classes. Northern Italians had controlled all the senior positions in the diocese until 1900 when several died and won glory as martyrs but the rest lost their reputations because they had hidden or run away. The priests from the Roman countryside, on the other hand, were much less well educated than most earlier missionaries, sometimes indeed scarcely literate, but they were an effective faction tightly bound together by hometown links: in the early twentieth century, sixteen missionaries came to Taiyuan from Artena and another six from the nearby village of Pofi.[23] These factions came to be aligned with differing attitudes towards modern Chinese nationalism, with the better-educated Bologna priests tending to side with the Chinese priests in support of reforms, while the Roman priests fought to maintain the power and status of the missionaries. Competition between the factions combined with money from the Boxer Indemnity to drive a new wave of conversions that were closely connected to the struggle over missionary power within the church.

The factional disputes among the Taiyuan clergy were part of wider struggles elsewhere in China and the world, inspired by the rise of anti-imperialism and connected to the development of a newly dynamic liberal wing in the church. Europeans read about the Boxer Uprising and admired its martyrs, but they also began to ask why it had happened and why Christians were so hated. Léon Joly's response, that missionaries in Asia needed to cede control to the indigenous clergy, was widely circulated. Wang Tingrong was not mentioned, but his cause was taken up across China not only by the Chinese clergy but also by a new generation of missionaries. The most famous of these was Vincent Lebbe, a Belgian priest who arrived in China and was appalled to find that the missionaries sat above the Chinese at meals, that some of the missionaries could hardly speak Chinese, that Chinese priests were always the subordinates of the missionaries even when the Chinese had far more experience, and so on. Working in Tianjin, he allied himself with the younger generation of Chinese priests and set out to modernize and nationalize the mission, with public lectures on a new national morality and a diocesan newspaper that became one of China's major national dailies.[24]

Similar ideas were spreading in Shanxi, where both priests and missionaries followed events through national and provincial newspapers and kept in touch with trends in the church through the European mission journals.[25] The genial Eugenio Massi, who came from the Italian Marche and was appointed bishop in 1910 as a compromise candidate between the Bologna and Rome factions, took a distinctly modernizing line. When he first arrived, he wrote from a remote mountain area, where he was only eating Chinese food, "I have become to the Chinese a Chinese, that I may win the Chinese" (echoing Paul in I Corinthians 9:20) and followed this by declaring that it was in fact possible to marry orphans without binding their feet.[26] Francesco Saccani was a close supporter and his very Chinese pose in the photograph of the Bologna missionaries is part of this missionary presentation of a Chinese identity. Missionary support for a modern, national, Chinese church was also taken up with enthusiasm by the Chinese clergy, who thus allied themselves with the new liberal tendencies in the global church.

Because the key accusation against the missionaries was that they had failed to make conversions, the reformers and the conservatives competed over how many people they could convert. For the first time since the seventeenth century, evangelism became a priority for the mission: the missionaries themselves now worked as evangelists and they devoted a large amount of the diocese's funds to the task. But with Christianity increasingly associated with the foreign powers and the dramatically greater exclusivity of the Catholic communities in the aftermath of the Boxer massacres, conversion was a much greater leap than it had been for earlier generations. In the eighteenth century people had joined a group that looked much like any other local sect; in the early twentieth century they were joining a tightly structured institution controlled by foreigners at a time of high nationalism. In the areas round the old Catholic villages it was almost impossible to persuade people to make this leap, so the missionaries went up into the mountains in the north and west of the province where the people were poorest and there were few existing Catholic communities. The results of their labors can be seen in the table of adult baptisms (figure 2 in chapter 1) which shows a spectacular increase in the number of adult baptisms from 1900. (The fluctuations after 1920 are due to warlord wars, the Japanese invasion, and administrative issues connected to the establishment of several new dioceses.)

Both the modernizers and their opponents concentrated their evangelism in the poor mountain districts, but the methods they used were significantly different. The modernizers emphasized conversion through preaching by the clergy and the cultivation of good relations with members of the local elite and officials. When Massi first arrived in Shanxi he was determined that he himself would preach to potential converts and sent for a newly published book of Chinese sermons so he would know what to say. Chen Guodi, who was bravely wearing his Franciscan habit when the missionaries first got back to Cave Gully, was sent out to the mountains to work alongside him. The two men were the same age and they got on well, presenting the church to officials and members of the elite as both modern and morally strict: they pressed officials, for example, to issue orders banning infanticide. They also built a major irrigation channel, schools, and a home for the elderly. Chen wrote dismissively of pagans who put on operas during a drought and bowed superstitiously in front of a branch that had caught fire spontaneously, saying "what we perhaps attribute to natural causes, the pagans really wonder at, thinking that it is due to a spirit."[27] Here, tentatively expressed, we see a Shanxi Catholic for the first time expressing the idea that local gods and spirits simply do not exist. Such modernizing ideas appealed greatly to many of the Chinese priests, who were enabled to join in the world of their educated, nationalistic peers outside the church. The greatest successes of this modernizing evangelism were in the 1920s and 1930s, when some Chinese priests formed close relations with local officials and elites. One priest boasted of having held an Easter mass that was attended by the district head, his staff, and all the teachers and pupils of the government higher primary school.[28]

But the modern style of evangelism was difficult if not impossible for most of the Italians. Almost as soon as Massi arrived he was critical of other missionaries who had not learned enough Chinese to be able to preach and lacked the cultural knowledge to understand the debating points needed for evangelism. He complained that there were too many Europeans and not enough Chinese priests and said that the Europeans should not be allowed to evangelize unless they could learn to preach in Chinese. This was an extremely unusual position to take, since after the Wang Tingrong affair most senior missionaries were determined that European missionaries must outnumber the Chinese priests in order to ensure continued European control.[29] Massi's proposal would also have removed many of the Italians from evangelism, since the majority of them in this period never really learned to speak Chinese. The old priests today recall that some of the missionaries who had spent many years in Shanxi spoke good Chinese, but the young men did not. Others came too late in life to be able to learn: one notable evangelist arrived in Shanxi after many years as a missionary in Bolivia. Until the 1930s new missionaries did not receive classes in Chinese but were supposed to study the language with the older missionaries or the Chinese priests wherever they were posted. They spoke to the Chinese priests in Latin, and stumbled through a few words of Chinese to communicate with the evangelists. They often did not speak to their Chinese parishioners at all, but had a Chinese priest to act as chaplain. Of course the Chinese chaplain was worked off his feet with all the parish problems, and here the resentment of the Chinese clergy, who did the work but would never be promoted, comes through even sixty years later.[30]

Francesco Fazzini, whom the Cave Gully people remember as having cursed their village, arrived in China in the last days of the Qing dynasty and had great difficulty with the language. When he was sent to the mountains of northern Shanxi he was desperately lonely and unhappy. He had begun his missionary career in Winding Gully and from there he could go into the city once a month to meet up with the other missionaries at the cathedral. But then he was sent to the mountains. "Where can I go," he wrote in a letter to the bishop, "and to whom? To Brother Cipparone who smokes, or to poor Brother Vanzolini who is in an even worse place than me?"[31] His underlining suggests that Cipparone had sought solace for his own troubles not in tobacco but in opium, which was very commonly used in the area. Fazzini does not appear to have taken drugs, but he was no better able to cope. He found himself in the midst of a complicated family dispute in which a Catholic father wanted to remove his daughter from her unhappy marriage. Her Catholic husband had signed a contract selling her to another man. The various parties to the dispute came to find the missionary to negotiate an agreement and the courtyard was packed with people who had gathered to watch. Fazzini tried to persuade the woman to go back to her husband, but he could not understand what anyone was saying and they could not understand him. The woman began to scream and curse, so Fazzini tried to send her out so he could settle things with the men, at which she threw herself on the ground, yelling over and over again, "I won't! I won't! I want to stay here." When he gave up and retired to his room she simply yelled louder. He summoned the village head, who refused to come. Finally he got a local Catholic leader to drag her out of the courtyard. Out in the street she continued to yell and beat on the gate with a stone. She stopped during the night, but the following morning Fazzini was writing to the bishop asking for advice, with the woman still screaming outside.[32]

These isolated Italian missionaries were the diocese's front line. They were under great pressure to report conversions, but were quite unable to use the methods suggested by the modernizers. Given the new wealth from the Boxer Indemnity, the easiest alternative was to pay people to convert. This worked in various ways and the attitude of the senior clergy combined acceptance, since they wanted to report conversions, with disapproval of certain methods. The simplest method was to employ evangelists who, since they were poorly paid, unsupervised, and had to report results, often gave people a small payment for registering their names. A more sophisticated method was to provide food for people studying the catechism and prayers in preparation for baptism. Eligio Ferretti (see figure 9), who made large numbers of conversions in northern Shanxi, reported that he had thirty men and boys staying in his residence to study prayers and requested money to feed them so that they could stay all day and the instruction would be quicker. Some Chinese priests also used these methods; one wrote to the bishop requesting 1,440 Chinese silver dollars to feed two hundred people for four months and later reported that he was expecting sixty to eighty baptisms.[33] Paying people to study was seen as better than paying them to register. In West Willows new conversions became possible after severe floods. A Chinese priest reported that the missionaries had employed forty-seven evangelists and entirely failed to supervise them, with the result that they had registered opium smokers, gamblers, and criminals, who were simply splitting the money and had no serious intention of converting. The evangelists had even registered fictitious names and names of people who were no longer in the village. The priest's proposed reform was to give five hundred cash to those who memorized the Lord's Prayer, Hail Mary, and main morning prayers, another five hundred to those who could recite all the morning and evening prayers, and one thousand cash to those who could recite the catechism. Chen Guodi was among those horrified: he argued that "money should not be given either to Christians or to pagans proposing to convert as a substitute for charity."[34]

Despite this kind of disapproval, paid conversions were sometimes done openly and even reported to Europe. During a severe food shortage that took place in 1932, one of the missionaries in Cave Gully wrote that more than two thousand people had come to the village seeking aid and that they had promised to convert if they received it. It was, he said, a poor motive but nevertheless the people were fed and instructed in the hope that their children at least would be tied to the church. In Winding Gully that year, people who were willing to convert and had regular attendance at classes were given one peck of millet for each family member every two months.[35] In addition to straightforward payments there were other material incentives for conversion, though these applied to fewer people: the destitute might be admitted into the orphanage, and men might receive land to farm or orphans as brides. Parents who had handed their children over to the orphanage often signed contracts that allowed them to claim the children back if they converted: "If the father hereafter converts, is baptized, obeys the rules, and respects God then this boy can return to his family."[36]

The diocese's new wealth was crucial to all these conversions. The mountain people in the north even had a proverb, "The Lord of Heaven is all knowing and all mighty, but even he doesn't know how much money the Franciscan order has."[37] They still remember the mule-loads of silver that the missionaries brought with them. Some missionaries went into banking, with the church functioning as a remittance network for local businesses, to avoid these dangerous journeys through the mountains.[38] Of course, this does not mean that all conversions were financially motivated. Some people still converted, as they had in earlier centuries, because they found work in a Catholic village, married a Catholic, were attracted by the prayers, had a significant dream, or hoped to be delivered from demonic possessions. Others presumably admired the church's charitable works and were convinced that Catholicism was a modern religion suitable for a new China. But it was the indemnity money that produced the statistics that made Shanxi famous among Chinese provinces for the number of conversions.[39] However, as figure 7 (see chapter 4) shows, the number of those taking part in annual confession fell well below the total number of registered Catholics, which suggests that many of these new converts had a very low degree of commitment. Fazzini, whose language problems made him especially prone to emphasize physical gestures, was said to have thought that it was enough for converts to be able to make the sign of the cross. In the end even those families who persevered with their new faith and handed it on to their children would later remember that their ancestors' conversions had been bought; indeed they sometimes remember the exact price.[40]

Most of the new conversions took place in the mountains, but they also affected the old Catholic communities. Cave Gully men worked as evangelists. The pay was very low, but these were difficult economic times and it was a reliable job: on at least one occasion, men turned up in mission parishes uninvited, hoping to be employed. Priests also began to recruit women and especially sworn virgins already working in the orphanages: Chen Guodi came to Cave Gully and persuaded a former orphan to go to the mountains to work with him, while Massi wrote requesting four chaste, elderly, dutiful, obedient sworn virgins capable of teaching women's work. Missionaries also encouraged converts to move to Cave Gully and other old Catholic villages, which effectively cemented the conversion by bringing them into a strong Catholic community. Families living in Cave Gully today can trace their origins to a man who came in this period to work as a miner, cart driver, cook, or a teacher, or because the church rented them land to farm. Many of the men then took advantage of the availability of Catholic women to marry into the village and remain there. For the earlier migrants, the arrival of newcomers to farm where there was a very limited supply of land and water inevitably led to tensions.[41]

The Cave Gully villagers' disputes with Fazzini were sparked by the 1911 revolution, when talk of a new republic brought the ongoing issues of missionary power, rising Chinese nationalism, and a growing village population to a head. The revolution combined a modern Westernizing style with strong anti-imperialist feeling. While the fighting was going on, the church provided a refuge for prominent figures on both sides: a Qing official and his family stayed in a house next to the church in Cave Gully, while Chen Guodi was said to have helped the revolutionaries, and one of their leaders stayed in the Taiyuan orphanage. This support for both the Qing and the revolutionaries reflected the different attitudes of the conservative and reforming factions in the diocese. In 1909 the conservative bishop reported that ideas of progress were not good for the faith, but there was no need for anxiety since the authorities were vigilant.[42] The next year he was replaced by Eugenio Massi, who worked closely with Chen Guodi after the revolution to use the Boxer Indemnity money to launch a series of modernizing institutions. Their flagship was an elite school in Taiyuan, which received a donation of science equipment from the new republican government and was headed by Chen. There was also a small hospital which was briefly staffed by an Italian doctor. Chen planned a newspaper which would provide news alongside Catholic doctrine and reprint material from the European press.[43] Massi sent the Chinese priests gifts of Western-style hats and trousers, the height of fashion at the time. The priest in Cold Springs Road wrote that he had put the new clothes on immediately and was sure they would be good for his health, while another priest wrote "I will never forget these kindnesses from Your Excellency but remember them for ever."[44] Massi also defended the Chinese priests against the fury of one missionary who found out that a nearby priest had told his parishioners that they no longer needed to kowtow to priests and missionaries, since under the Republic people were equal.[45]

The revolution was clearly an opportunity for all kinds of change, and longstanding tensions in the diocese over the power of the foreign missionaries blew up into a series of disputes. Since Cave Gully, with its orphanage, seminary, and monastery, was a center for church institutions, many of these disputes affected the clergy there. One conflict led to another and soon the whole village was involved. The first spark came in Taiyuan city, where a leading Protestant with close ties to the new republican leaders had established a Chinese Christian Independent Church in the offices of the new provincial newspaper and hundreds were leaving the missionary churches for its nightly meetings. This new Protestant church had explicit policies of not inviting missionaries to preach or accepting their money or leadership. Someone sent out an anonymous circular suggesting that the Catholics should try to follow the Protestant example. The plan horrified the missionaries and a new "Apostolic Union" created by the Chinese priests was closed down.[46] These events reverberated through the Catholic parishes, especially where there was already hostility towards individual missionaries. Francesco Fazzini's problems in the mountain areas started when he was sent to replace a young Chinese priest who had allied himself with Catholics trying to evict two missionaries, one of whom had drawn a revolver on his parishioners. Anna Gao, the Cave Gully woman sent in response to Massi's request some years earlier for chaste, elderly, dutiful, obedient sworn virgins to work in the area, found herself in the center of the dispute. Massi had been very appreciative of her work, saying that she did prodigies and behaved like a saint, and now she was torn between her loyalty to the mission and the general objections to Massi's disastrous successors. She came to Fazzini in tears with the posters that the two opposing parties had pasted up in the church, but as usual Fazzini was quite out of his depth.[47]

Fazzini was transferred to Cave Gully, which was considered an easier posting, but there too there was turmoil. In the spring all the students had walked out of the junior seminary as a protest against harsh discipline from their missionary teacher.[48] The following winter, there was what one missionary described as a revolution in the orphanage, over control by newly arrived foreign nuns and the pressure on the sworn virgins to work as evangelists. The new emphasis on evangelism brought huge changes in the lives of these women. Evangelism required a drastic reordering of their understanding of the Christian life, from an emphasis on prayer and personal salvation to a more outward-looking focus; many of them found the transition very hard. Even Anna Gao did not initially want to work as an evangelist, saying that evangelizing was not as good for her soul as being in the orphanage.[49] Another sworn virgin, who worked with a missionary in the mountains in the 1900s then returned to Cave Gully, wrote to him when she was asked to work as an evangelist again, describing the pressure she was under: "So I said, 'I am ill and the long journey will not be convenient, so I can't go.'

Father Zhang and Father Du said, 'You should obey.' I did not want to go, and did not know what I ought to do, but I had no alternative. So they told me to go to Shuozhou in the seventh or eighth month. A lot of people were to go: Father Duan's aunt, Fu Yinze, and Yuhua and some others I don't know. I was truly depressed and my illness got worse than before."[50] The missionary sympathized and wrote to the bishop on her behalf saying, "she writes to me in sorrow and very simply, knowing that I too had a lot of trouble in those places for nearly six years."[51]

Fazzini was very poor at dealing with these cases: one of the virgins he tried to send to the mountains wailed and then refused to eat for days, or if pressed to eat, vomited. Some of the other virgins were willing to go but turned out to be quite unsuitable. Girls became sworn virgins for a variety of reasons. Some were promised as young as eleven by their families. Others joined because they could not marry. Qin Zhanyu came from a very poor family in Winding Gully and her father had refused to attend confession for many years. As a result he was unable to find her a husband, so at the age of nineteen she decided to become a sworn virgin. She turned out to be extremely competent and successful, but others might not have been. Another problem group were those who swore virginity as a way of avoiding an unwanted marriage, both orphanage girls escaping from partners chosen by the clergy and girls resisting their families. Chen Guodi sent one of these virgins, a woman nicknamed for her unbound feet, back to Cave Gully with the simple complaint that she was frivolous.[52]

This unhappiness in the orphanage was exacerbated by the efforts of newly arrived European nuns to position themselves as the religious superiors of the Chinese virgins. The nuns were members of the Franciscan Missionaries of Mary, an order set up in the nineteenth century to work in the mission field and to direct the work of indigenous religious women. The French mother superior placed a strong emphasis on obedience and humility and was in constant conflict with the Chinese virgins, who had previously run the institution. Fazzini, who was a stickler for European prestige, supported the mother superior, but other missionaries were more sympathetic to the sworn virgins. Ultimately, the virgins succeeded where the Chinese priests had always failed, presumably because as women they were not a threat to the male church hierarchy: over the next few years the foreign mother superior left Shanxi altogether and a new Chinese religious order was set up for the sworn virgins. It was headed by Qin Zhanyu and given responsibility for teaching, evangelism, and the Cave Gully orphanage. A photograph (figure 10) shows two of

FIGURE 10. West Willows Catholic primary school girls with sworn virgins from the Chinese order. Courtesy of Provincia di Cristo Re dei Frati Minori dell'Emilia Romagna.

these virgins, dressed in the black garments that caused people to call them the "black nuns," with their class of primary school girls some years later. Apart from a few older girls in the back row who wear modern schoolgirl jackets and silver crosses, most of the little girls are dressed up for the occasion with skirts (to comply with European standards of modesty) worn over their jackets and trousers. The older virgin hides her bound feet discretely, as the sworn virgins had always done, amazing the missionaries because they appeared to have no feet at all. A similar photograph of the boys shows them with the missionary as well as their teacher, but the Chinese virgins are depicted as having complete responsibility for the girls.[53]

In addition to disputes within the institutions of the church, there was considerable anxiety over the potential economic impact of the revolution on the villagers. For fifty years Catholics had avoided paying the full rate of local taxation, but the new Republic had transferred the sums previously raised by temples to the education budget, so it was no longer possible to claim that the taxes were idolatrous. On the other hand the new schools were expensive, and the church already provided and subsidized much cheaper schools which taught traditional primers alongside the catechism and often ran only in the winter months when the children were not needed in the fields. In Cave Gully the girls were taught by the virgins and later by the black nuns to memorize the catechism and various prayers, but did not learn to read. With the exception of Chen Guodi's elite school in Taiyuan, diocesan schools were nearly all of this type. The missionaries defended them by arguing that Catholics should be allowed to have their own religious education. So in the early years of the Republic there were disputes as Catholics tried to preserve their lower rates of taxation by refusing to pay for the new government schools. In Cave Gully much of the tax resistance was simpler: people simply refused to pay the land tax, saying that the land belonged not to them but to the church, whether or not it actually did.[54]

All these disputes came to a head in Cave Gully over the issue of Franciscan winemaking. The first missionary had come to Shanxi to look for grapes and missionaries had been making wine for the mass in the area since at least the 1830s and possibly as far back as the 1760s. The vineyard in Cave Gully was both an escape from their difficult lives and a way of expressing their Franciscan commitment to manual labor. The uneducated Italian missionary who was confined in the Cave Gully residence by Grioglio ended up spending the next forty years in the village. He terraced part of the hillside and built a vineyard, a small lodge, and a cistern which was used for fish as well as to provide irrigation water. Later another Franciscan used skills he had learned in Assisi to engineer a pipe that would bring water across from another hillside. The very fact that the cistern was photographed and the image sent back to Italy shows how important it was for the missionaries (see figure 11). At first local people came to the cistern for healing, as they did to mountain pools, and one even left the plaque so often seen at Chinese shrines announcing that the donor's prayers had been heard. Later the water was enclosed behind the monastery wall.[55] By Fazzini's time the winemaking operation was much larger than could be supported by the monastery's own vineyard. Like other missionaries he enjoyed the winemaking, and operated on a considerable scale. In 1914 he bought nearly fifteen thousand pounds of grapes through leading Qingyuan Catholics. By 1924 the diocese was aiming to buy eighty thousand pounds. Some of the grapes were made into communion wine to be sold to other dioceses and the rest used for table wine. Although parts of the vineyard were rented out, the actual wine production was done entirely by the missionaries.[56]

Increased wine production and the arrival of new converts into the village put pressure on Cave Gully's limited natural resources. When

FIGURE 11. Monastery water cistern. Courtesy of Provincia di Cristo Re dei Frati Minori dell'Emilia Romagna.

combined with the church's control over the hillside spring and cistern, this inevitably led to tensions. In the winter of 1912 these tensions broke out into a dispute between the villagers and Fazzini. The trouble began with the failure of one of the church's tenants to maintain a water-course, followed by the repeated theft of sections of pipe. Fazzini ordered the church staff to detain the men of the family who were thought to be responsible. That night a crowd of women came up to the monastery and gathered outside the gates to demand that Fazzini hand over the staff involved. The staff fled and Fazzini thought the trouble was over, but a few days later another mob besieged the monastery. Things calmed down, but the next winter the pipes were stolen again. This time Fazzini no longer dared to act informally but instead reported the theft to the local official. The dispute continued over the summer with a lawsuit between the church and the villagers. This was particularly difficult for Fazzini because he could not read the court documents and did not trust the nearby Chinese priest who could have helped him. While the lawsuit was still going on there was heavy rain and the villagers lifted some of the stones in the dyke that protected the church buildings, so that their own properties would not be flooded. Water poured through the monastery garden, destroying the terraces and the vines, then through the orphanage, where the roof of the mother superior's bedroom collapsed. Fazzini and one of the Italian lay brothers went out themselves to repair the terraces, but it seems to have been at this point that Fazzini's superiors decided to transfer him again.[57]

When he left Fazzini decided, or maybe he was told, to take with him the statue of Our Lady of Lourdes that Saccani had brought to the village in 1901. Like the statues of deities in Chinese folk religion, which were occasionally stolen in inter-village disputes, the statue was seen as powerful in itself, so this provoked a lot of opposition. The villagers refused to pay their levies to the church or to repair the road using stones that had been washed down in the flood and had fallen near the church door. In the end two Chinese priests were called in to sort out the trouble. They persuaded the bishop not to remove the statue but also required the leading villagers to do penance by wailing publicly in two nearby churches and to repair the road with the stones.[58] It is impossible to know if Fazzini actually took off his shoe and cursed the villagers as he left, but he was emotional, extremely bad tempered, and had such poor Chinese that he was quite likely to use physical gestures instead of words.

In the folktale the resolution to the disputes comes with the building of the shrine to Our Lady of the Seven Sorrows, which was the result of a new wave of missionary investment in Cave Gully in the 1920s and 1930s, when the village became the headquarters for a new diocese. Tensions between the Chinese, Bologna, and Rome factions of the clergy were greatly reduced as Rome introduced a policy of creating new, smaller dioceses. Cave Gully became the headquarters for a new Yuci diocese under the Bologna Franciscans and the villagers benefited not only from the construction of the shrine and a new parish church, but also from new opportunities for their sons to enter the seminary. Nevertheless tensions over missionary power continued, and indeed were exacerbated in the 1930s when several of the missionaries were active supporters of the Italian Fascist government that was allied to the invading Japanese.

The policy of creating new dioceses, which was to have such an impact on Cave Gully, had its origins in the split between modernizing and conservative missionaries in China, which had reached breaking point when Vincent Lebbe, at the height of European patriotism during the 1914–18 European War, allowed the Catholic newspaper he had founded in Tianjin to take a patriotic Chinese line and oppose an expansion of the French concession in the city. He was dismissed and sent back to Europe where he continued to campaign for Chinese control over the Chinese church. At the same time Eugenio Massi was removed from his post as bishop in Taiyuan and sent off to a much smaller, poorer diocese in the neighboring province of Shaanxi. Massi's troubles were in large part due to competition between the Bologna and Rome factions, but the Chinese clergy appealed his dismissal and his supporters saw him as being on the same side as Lebbe.[59]

The war not only heightened European nationalism, it also caused a drastic decline in the number of young men entering the priesthood. Together these two factors influenced the Vatican towards a greater acceptance of nationalism and put pressure on it to start moving towards a fully Chinese clergy. New dioceses were created and each was allotted to a single group of clergy: there were now Chinese bishops but European missionaries still did not have to serve under them. One of the first of these new Chinese-run dioceses was Fenyang, which included Wang Tingrong's home village of Newtown. Chen Guodi traveled to Rome to be consecrated as Fenyang's bishop, fulfilling the ambitions of generations of Chinese priests. On his return he was greeted with great celebrations and the Cave Gully villagers went out to join the procession that carried him in a sedan chair from village to village across the plain, accompanied by musicians. Then he found himself living in rented rooms, because the new diocese had no money and most of it was in a poor mountain area. The Chinese priests did however manage to rebuild Wang Tingrong's grave.[60]

The Bologna missionaries were also allotted their own diocese, centered on the new industrial city of Yuci. Since there were no church buildings there, they initially set up their headquarters in Cave Gully, bringing with them investment and new buildings. A Way of the Cross had been laid out on the hill behind the monastery, where people could take part in a typically Franciscan group pilgrimage that imaginatively follows the steps of Jesus from the garden of Gethsemane to his death on the cross. When there was a drought in 1922 one of the missionaries suggested to the villagers that they perform the Way of the Cross to pray for rain. This was taken up with enthusiasm and for three days the men of the village did so at midday and the women in the evening. The next year the villagers were still suffering from the drought and, while some people traveled to the pilgrimage shrine of the Holy Mother,

FIGURE 12. Shrine to Our Lady of the Seven Sorrows, Cave Gully, circa 1924. Courtesy of Provincia di Cristo Re dei Frati Minori dell'Emilia Romagna.

many others performed the Way of the Cross on the hill behind the village. Soon the Franciscan superior decided to build a small chapel dedicated to Our Lady of the Seven Sorrows on the top of the hill to complete the pilgrimage site.[61] The newly completed buildings can be seen in a photograph (figure 12): in the foreground is the seminary, behind it two groups of villagers spread out along the paths that link the Stations of the Cross, and perched on the top of the hill is a little chapel.

The devotion to Our Lady of the Seven Sorrows suggests the richness and depth of the village's Catholic piety in this period and its close links with Italy. The Seven Sorrows of the Virgin Mary had been included in Chinese prayer books since the eighteenth century and the prolific nineteenth-century local priest Tian Fenglan had even compiled a short book about them. The first of the sorrows is the old man's prophecy to the Virgin Mary that her child is destined for greatness but also for suffering and that "a sword will pierce your own soul too" (Luke 2:35). So Tian's book encourages readers to think of their sins as knives in Mary's heart and in the shrine she was depicted with a ring of swords piercing her breast.[62] The rest of the sorrows follow Mary as she flees with her newborn child, loses him on a pilgrimage, and watches as he is put to death. They are emotional but also familiar scenes which suggest that no sorrow is greater than that of a mother and resonate with Chinese ideas of filial piety. But Our Lady of the Seven Sorrows was also associated with nineteenth-century northern and central Italy, where she became a symbol of grief for a vanishing Catholic society. In the 1890s an image of the Madonna of the Seven Sorrows in the village of Campocavallo near Ancona became a mass sensation when the Madonna's eyes were seen to move. Her images circulated in Shanxi; indeed one was reported to have performed a miracle when an old Catholic leader who had been beaten by a missionary was, according to the missionary, pretending to be in agony and the missionary was unable to calm him down until he saw an image of the Madonna of Campocavallo on the wall.[63]

The shrine was followed by a fine new parish church dedicated to Our Lady of Lourdes, paid for, it is said, entirely by one of the missionaries from his inheritance, since the village's expansion meant that the church built by Grioglio in the 1840s was now too small.[64] The seminary too had existed since Grioglio's time, but now for the first time several boys from Cave Gully entered it and were ordained; earlier students had nearly all come from wealthier places with better primary education. The first priest from Cave Gully was ordained in the 1900s, but four more, including Zhang Yonggu who was to be parish priest in Cold Springs Road in the 1960s, were ordained in the 1940s and 1950s.[65]

The Cave Gully villagers were undoubtedly pleased at these changes, but the 1930s was also the time of first a growing Japanese threat to China, then outright invasion, and this heightened nationalistic tensions between the Chinese Catholics and the Italian missionaries. In Europe nationalism was interacting with increasingly extreme left- and right-wing ideas and the Catholic church was strongly allied with the right. Longstanding opposition to republicanism had developed into resistance to communism after a series of violent campaigns in Russia against religious institutions. Then came the terrible violence of the Spanish Civil War, in which Republican forces backed by Russia fought against Nationalists closely aligned with the Catholic clergy. The hostility between communists and the church was brought home to Cave Gully when a group of Spanish priests arrived with seven trucks of orphanage children fleeing the Chinese Communists in Shaanxi. The Bologna missionaries also had their own grounds for allying with the right. Bologna, with its highly commercialized large-scale agriculture and impoverished rural proletariat, had been the scene of land seizures and violent labor conflict since the 1890s and its middle class was active in the rise of Italian Fascism. Support for the Fascists was encouraged by the Vatican, which negotiated an agreement with Mussolini that ended the active hostility between church and state that had existed since Italian unification. They did this—despite the Fascists' significant anti-clericalism—for various reasons including fear of communism, hope for greater influence in the Italian state, and financial problems, but it is hard to imagine that the decision was not influenced by the considerable popular support in Italy for Mussolini's regime at the time. The missionaries shared these widespread Italian attitudes: they told the Chinese Catholics about the revival of the Roman Empire, the greatness of Italian civilization, and the war in Abyssinia. One of the Roman missionaries planned to meet Mussolini on a visit back to Italy. As part of Mussolini's imperial ambitions, the mission for the first time received money directly from the Italian government: a large grant to rebuild the Cave Gully orphanage and old people's home.[66]

Italian Fascism became a major issue in 1937 when Japan invaded much of north China including the central Shanxi plain. The missionaries flew the Italian flag and used the protection of Italy's alliance with Germany and Japan to make churches and orphanages into places of refuge for those fleeing the fighting. The war ended the structured evangelistic campaigns, but the refugees under church protection proved a fertile ground for conversions. This was a violent and brutal invasion and the Italian flag was not always enough to protect the missionaries, their property, or parishioners from Japanese troops who smashed up churches, dragged off women, and shot people. One shocked missionary wrote that such a barbarous invasion could only foretell the imminent end of the world. But at other times the missionaries defended the Japanese on the grounds that they were fighting against communism. When the Franciscans sent back to Bologna a picture of themselves (wearing their Western habits) posed with the local puppet magistrate and Japanese soldiers in Cave Gully (figure 13), it marked an achievement as well as a simple expression of the Italian-Japanese alliance. The village was important to the Japanese because it was on the frontline between the plains, which they controlled, and the hills where Communist guerillas operated. Cave Gully was packed with as many as five thousand refugees and from time to time Communist troops raided it, at first in search of weapons and medicine, but on one occasion carrying off three of the missionaries for ransom.[67]

The missionaries' power in this situation exacerbated the Catholics' nationalist feelings. A seminarian in Winding Gully was expelled after he went out at night and cut down the Italian flag. Chinese nationalism

FIGURE 13. Franciscans in Cave Gully, with the Taiyuan county magistrate and soldiers from the Japanese occupation forces, 1938 to 1945. Courtesy of Provincia di Cristo Re dei Frati Minori dell'Emilia Romagna.

within the church was supported by the actions of Vincent Lebbe, who had returned to China to work for one of the new Chinese dioceses, and was passionately opposed to the Italian line. His preaching was welcomed in what were now three new Chinese-run dioceses in Shanxi. Later he joined the Nationalist Party forces as they retreated through Shanxi bringing with him a corps of stretcher-bearers that he had recruited. He also organized a company of Catholic guerilla troops to support the Chinese war effort, for which he received both financial help and high honor from the Nationalist government. He was hugely popular with the Catholic villagers of central Shanxi. So many came to make confessions to him that the local priest objected that Lebbe was exhausted, to which the villagers responded that he was a real saint and those who confessed to him received special graces.[68]

Wealth, power, and violence were not the cause of the Boxer Uprising but its result. The Boxer Indemnity made the church rich and therefore made the missionaries powerful, but while the people of Cave Gully welcomed the economic benefits this brought, there was always tension over foreign power. The hostility of the villagers to missionary power was also part of a struggle that increasingly integrated Chinese Catholics into the global church. Priests who supported Vincent Lebbe, and even the village Catholics who thought him a saint, were consciously or not aligning themselves with what was developing into the liberal wing of the twentieth-century church. Ironically the Chinese Communists who were about to take power were themselves members of transnational movement in which many of the same struggles took place, but they could never acknowledge that the Catholic church had a history that ran parallel to their own. Soon the Catholics of central Shanxi would have to turn from struggling for independence against the missionaries to defending themselves against the state for precisely those things that they had long resisted.

CHAPTER 6

The Four Fragrances and the Flying Bicycle

People say that during the Cultural Revolution, Catholics were forced to leave the church, so they thought that the end of the world was coming. A group of women known as the Four Fragrances went around the Catholic villages urging those who had left the church to return before the Day of Judgment. They were very brave. They even persuaded officials to hand over the letters of apostasy that Catholics had been forced to sign. One of these women was speaking when soldiers broke in and arrested everyone they found in the room, but one of the men put her on the back of his bicycle and pedaled away. The bicycle went so fast that it did not touch the ground. They were flying. It was a miracle! Even people who are not Christian saw it![1]

This is a familiar story to many central Shanxi Catholics, but people lower their voices when they tell it. In the face of state condemnation of religion as superstitious folly and Catholicism as a tool of foreign imperialism, it tells of the power of God to intervene in everyday lives and of ordinary people's courage and leadership. For that reason it matters greatly to those who tell the story that they should be believed. On one occasion an old man responded to my obvious doubt by saying that he had a photograph of the flying bicycle. A short while later he came back with a pile of old glass slides. As we hunted through the slides looking without success for a flying bicycle, I realized that they had in fact been made as part of the Socialist Education Movement not to prove that miracles took place but, quite the opposite, to show the villagers how the miracles of that time had been faked and thus to persuade them not to believe in Christianity. For the old man, the original intention of the slides did not matter, instead he was preserving them as a record of what really happened.

The story of the Four Fragrances reminds listeners of Catholic resistance, heroism, and supernatural powers, but it does so only by allowing its audience to forget much of what took place. Setting the whole story in the Cultural Revolution (1966–76), a chaotic period many of whose policies have subsequently been repudiated, conceals the fact that the events described actually took place in 1965 during the Socialist Education Movement, when the drive to get Catholics to leave the church began. Moreover the term *Four Fragrances* conceals the crucial role of one woman in opposing that campaign: Li Zhenxiang, the preacher about whom this story was originally told. And by ending with her miraculous escape the story blots out the events that followed her later arrest, when she played a part scripted by the government in a huge educational campaign that led into the attacks that caused nearly all the village's Catholics to renounce their faith. Telling the story of the Four Fragrances allows Catholics to remember Li Zhenxiang's courage but avoid speaking of what subsequently happened to her and to them.

Another effect of speaking of a group of women rather than of Li Zhenxiang alone is to foreground the role of ordinary people in what happened. By 1965 the Catholic hierarchy and institutions had virtually vanished, priests were effectively imprisoned, and the leaders of village congregations *(huizhang)* came under attack. So when government workteams began to pressure people to leave the religion, it was ordinary villagers who took the lead. Since they had no previous claims to power, their authority came from signs of divine intervention: visions, exorcisms, and miracles. The high emotional mood that made people willing to accept such signs was a product of the Communist state's threat to the most important and longstanding aspects of local Catholic faith: public prayer, traditional morality, and loyalty to the community. It was also a product of very different understandings of the community's history. When the workteams demanded that Catholics renounce their faith, they were acting on the narrative of Catholicism as a foreign religion introduced by imperialist missionaries. Ordinary Catholics, on the other hand, looked back through their own understanding of their history and heard the calls for them to renounce the church as the start of a persecution that would repeat the massacres of the Boxer Uprising and might even herald the end of the world.

Strong hostility between the Catholic church and the Communist Party, the expulsion of the Italian missionaries, and the confiscation of church property transformed the institutional context of religion in Cave Gully in the early years of the People's Republic. Everyday religious practice in Cave Gully, as in other old Catholic villages, continued relatively unchanged, but Catholic anti-communism and the government's hostility to the Catholic church set the stage for the events that followed.

As the Communist armies advanced through the province after the end of World War II, it was clear that much was going to change. Priests and missionaries retreated before the great violence of Land Reform in the mountains of northern Shanxi, bringing news of the confiscation of church property and violent attacks on the clergy.[2] Gathered in Taiyuan in 1947, the Chinese priests made a renewed effort to get rid of the Italians. They wrote letters to potential supporters, articles in the local press, and a letter to the Vatican asking to be allowed to take control of the diocese, all without effect. The bishop allowed them to sit in his presence and even offered them cigarettes, but he resisted appointing them to senior positions.[3] Meanwhile the diocese prepared to face the Communists. A Belgian priest, a member of the order founded by Vincent Lebbe, came to Taiyuan looking for funding to arm a Catholic group to fight against the Communists. The provincial government had no money to spare and the Italians had always opposed Lebbe so the plan collapsed.[4] However, the diocese did establish the Legion of Mary, a deeply anti-communist prayer group originally founded in Ireland whose members were given military-style titles. In Chinese the Legion was called the Holy Mother's Army *(shengmujun)*, with the result that the Communist Party later conflated it with the nonexistent Catholic fighting force that Lebbe's supporters had tried to set up.[5]

As the Communist armies approached Taiyuan, nearly all the clergy fled. Most of the missionaries left for good, but the Chinese priests and a few missionaries took refuge in Beijing or Hong Kong and returned after order had been reestablished. It was soon clear that the days of missionary wealth and power were over. One by one schools, hospitals, and orphanages were removed from church control by taxes, forced contributions, fines, and populist accusations of illegal activity. Leading members of the Legion of Mary were prosecuted, and all those who had enrolled were required to leave the organization. In Cave Gully people lined up to swear that they were leaving, but finished by saying that they were still members of the church.[6] In prison the Italian bishop had to ask for a spoon because, despite living twenty years in China, he had never eaten with chopsticks. In 1952 he finally appointed a Chinese priest to replace him as bishop. This new Chinese bishop inherited a diocese whose institutions were rapidly collapsing. It had no access to its investments outside the province and local property was heavily taxed or confiscated by local government. Meanwhile, the missionaries came closer to the Chinese than they had been since the early Qing. In Cave Gully, missionaries, Chinese priests, the remaining orphans, and staff all ate together. The last missionary is remembered as a kindly man who ran an eye clinic, cycled round the villages to see his patients, tossed children in the air, and slipped extra food to girls in the orphanage when they were sick. He was deported in 1953 and by the following summer all the missionaries were gone.[7]

After so many years of tension between the Chinese and Italian clergy, it is not surprising that when the new government insisted that the priests of central Shanxi reject the era of missionary control they were willing to do so. In 1951 all the priests in Taiyuan diocese subscribed to the creation of what is now generally known as the official Catholic church in China. In later years they would accept a bishop whom they themselves had elected and who was consecrated by the head of the official church. That did not mean that they were rejecting membership in the global Catholic community: the new bishop continued to send annual statistics to Rome at great personal risk until his arrest in 1955.[8]

The clergy entered the official church under pressure from the government and out of their own tradition of nationalism, but (unlike some leaders of the Protestant church) not because they shared the ideals of socialism.[9] Even after the departure of the missionaries the clergy encouraged forms of devotion in which anti-communist ideas were deeply embedded. In 1955, Taiyuan cathedral held regular services to consecrate the diocese's children, youth, and elderly to the Immaculate Heart of Mary. This was a ritual linked to visions of the Virgin Mary that had taken place at Fatima in Portugal in 1917, which were widely promoted by the church in the early years of the Cold War, when the surviving visionary revealed two of the three secrets that the Virgin had told her. Both turned out to be apocalyptic prophecies shaped by World War I and the Russian Revolution in which the Virgin asked that people should pray the rosary and prayers in honor of her Immaculate Heart; if they did not, then Russia would bring war and persecution. The visions at Fatima, devotion to the Immaculate Heart of Mary, and praying the rosary as a weapon against communism were an important part of the prayers encouraged by the Legion of Mary.[10]

The combination of the Catholic church's hostility to communism and the Communist Party's hostility to religion made it extremely difficult for the Party to penetrate Catholic villages. The Party saw religion as a human invention that legitimated unjust social systems, so those who wished to join had to abandon any previous religious beliefs. In villages where community and family identity were defined by Catholicism this made it almost impossible for people to become Communist Party members. The local police were sent in to set up a party branch in Cave Gully and with great difficulty persuaded one young man to join, but when they returned a few days later he had changed his mind. After that there were no party members in Cave Gully and the work that the village branch should have done was undertaken by the committee of the nearest small town. In theory more people should have joined mass organizations: the Peasant Association, Women's League, or the Young Pioneers group for children. But before he left, the last missionary bishop had banned Catholics from having anything to do with these groups: he even ordered priests to exclude from communion any parent whose children joined the Young Pioneers. As time went on, all this was to make it hard for Catholics to marry outside their community, so that the exclusive marriage patterns previously promoted by the missionaries were reinforced and the community became ever more closely knit.[11]

Faced with Communist attempts to transform rural society through Land Reform and the new Marriage Law, Catholic priests defended the traditional rural values embodied in the Ten Commandments. The Party's model for Land Reform was not simply to redistribute land, but to bring the poor to realize the exploitation they had suffered, struggle against the rich, and take the land for themselves. In the process they would align themselves with the new government. Similarly the new Marriage Law was promoted with calls on women who were suffering at the hands of abusive husbands or mothers-in-law to resist the power of the traditional family by demanding a divorce. Priests and the remaining missionaries condemned robbery, covetousness, accusations against other Catholics, and divorce. One priest told Catholics that dividing the land was wrong and anyone who coveted someone else's land should do penance, while another said that anyone who took someone else's property was committing a sin because the owner had earned it by his labor. Accusations for which one did not have strong evidence were condemned as breaking the commandment not to bear false witness. This too had the effect of blocking Land Reform because the Communist organizers used such accusations to find out about tensions within the community that they could then manipulate to induce villagers to attack landlords and others. Priests also condemned divorce and successfully prevented Catholic women from using the new Marriage Law, which was in any case very unpopular with rural families who had paid high bride-prices for their daughters-in-law. Some Catholic villages registered no divorces at all.[12]

With no party members, minimal mass organizations, and a strong commitment to the Ten Commandments, Cave Gully people never experienced Land Reform as a mass movement. This was unusual but by no means unknown, especially in poor and unimportant communities. In several non-Catholic villages in this area there was considerable opposition to labeling anyone a landlord or rich peasant: people were afraid that their community would lose land to other villages and knew that "there are families who have been neighbors for a thousand years, but officials don't last for ten."[13] Such attitudes were even stronger in Catholic villages, with their intense feelings of community and heavy investment in traditional morality. In Cave Gully people simply said that everyone in the village was poor, which, given their inadequate water supply and long history of accepting migrants, was not so far from the truth. The Land Reform workteam classified the villagers, but there were no struggle meetings and no one was labeled a landlord or rich peasant. A few families were labeled "rich middle peasants." Parts of their land and the Franciscan vineyard and vegetable garden were confiscated and redistributed to the poorest families. Moral opposition to communism did not prevent effective government: land was redistributed, meetings were held, and a few years later villagers' land was taken over by large-scale collectives. The difference was that the village did not go through the searing process of popular redistribution that bound so many Chinese peasants to the new regime. Today many Cave Gully people say that Land Reform never happened there.[14]

Cave Gully's experiences were not shared by all Catholic villages (in Winding Gully and Cold Springs Road, rich families were attacked as landlords), but in general the Catholics of the hill villages were more likely to resist than those of the plains villages and recent converts. The Catholic merchant families of the plains villages had ceased to be wealthy long before the arrival of the Communist Party, but they easily came under attack because they were a minority in their communities.

Relations with other villagers had been poor since the Boxers and they themselves could not join the Party or take up any key positions in the new political order. Because of these differences, Communist rule completed the transition of community leadership, which had begun when Bishop Grioglio moved from Nine Springs to Cave Gully in the 1840s. In 1965 it was to be the exclusively Catholic hill villages (and Cold Springs Road, with its similar history) that took the lead, rather than the formerly wealthy plains villages.[15]

In the areas evangelized during the early twentieth century, Catholicism almost entirely disappeared. The warfare, isolation, poverty, and inadequate government that had made the mountains of northern and western Shanxi good sites for Catholic evangelism also made them likely recruiting grounds for the Communist Party. Even if relations had been amicable, it was easy to set off attacks against the Catholic minority in these areas. One priest whose nephew had established a textile workshop in his parish was tortured to death by people trying to extort money from him. In such circumstances converts who had been attracted to the church by the wealth and power of the missionaries quickly left. In one intensely evangelized village where the first conversion had been in 1918, there were twelve paid evangelists and three hundred Catholics before the Japanese invasion in 1936. The last priest left at the end of the war and after 1949 there were no religious activities. By the 1980s only a few scattered families remained. The situation in Wutai county, famous for its great Buddhist pilgrimage site, was even more striking. The first conversions there had been in the 1870s, and during the Japanese occupation many people converted for protection, so that at the end of the war the county had 8,060 Catholics. By the early 1960s there was hardly a trace of these Catholics. In 1988, when Catholic religious activities began again, the church had 341 members. Across central and northern Shanxi, Catholics who had converted as a result of the missionary work of the late nineteenth and early twentieth centuries had mostly abandoned the religion by the 1960s.[16]

On the other hand, public religious practice in the old Catholic communities continued. When the last of the missionaries left Cave Gully, the monastery was taken over by the army as a convalescent home for soldiers returning from the Korean War, but a new Chinese parish priest arrived and the parish church still owned enough land to rent out and thus support him. A Cave Gully man was ordained to the priesthood as late as 1956. Industrialization and population growth meant that the total number of registered Catholics in some old Catholic villages actually increased. In one rapidly industrializing community so many new Catholics arrived from the hills that people had to kneel outside the church because they could not fit into it and in 1956 a priest was sent to live there for the first time. Catholics, like other people, were affected by the great political campaigns that swept the country: villagers left to seek work in Taiyuan during the Great Leap Forward in 1958 and suffered with others during the terrible famine that followed. Nevertheless, the Cave Gully parish priest continued to say Sunday mass, there were daily prayers in the church and a music group for festivals, and people continued to pay the priest for masses for the souls of the dead. Village pilgrimages to the shrine of the Holy Mother in the mountains north of Taiyuan ended in 1958, but small groups of young men continued to make the lengthy journey to pray for rain or offer thanks for healing. In other villages where there was no priest, daily prayers often continued even if masses were infrequent. There were even a few conversions.[17]

The pressure on Catholics to leave the church that is described in the folktale began with the Socialist Education Movement. In 1965 as Catholic villages became a target for the movement, rumors began to spread of a shining cross that had appeared on a cliff face in the hills north of Taiyuan. People flocked there and as they knelt in the dark many saw visions. Li Zhenxiang, who is at the center of the story of the Four Fragrances, was a young woman who emerged as a preacher at this time, urging Catholics to repent and return to God.

The crisis had its origin in Beijing. When China's leaders finally recognized the scale of the famine that had followed the Great Leap Forward, part of the blame was placed on low-level officials, village leaders, and opponents of the revolution. In response the central government expanded the longstanding Socialist Education Movement. In 1963 they began to send teams of educated people to villages all across the country to launch a new wave of revolution by persuading poor villagers to rebel against the village leaders. These workteams began by checking up on the village accounts and preventing petty corruption. Then in the last months of 1964 the campaign was widened to target "capitalist" and "feudal" practices, which meant such things as selling produce at markets, gambling, taking part in religious rituals, or paying a bride-price for a new daughter-in-law. Village leaders and others were forced to write confessions of their misdeeds, were criticized and beaten at mass meetings, and were required to repay any money gained in these ways. Poor villagers were expected to support the new revolution: the workteams organized Poor and Lower Middle Peasants' Associations and picked their most active members to take over from the former village leaders. The workteams' efforts fed on ordinary people's anger with low-level leaders, whom they blamed for the famine, and the campaign quickly became violent. Many officials were beaten and some were put under such pressure that they committed suicide.[18]

Catholic villages became a specific target of the Socialist Education Movement in 1964 when the central government circulated a report on Catholics in northeast China with instructions to use the campaign to extend government authority over Catholic villages.[19] This was followed by another report on the successful conduct of the Socialist Education Movement in a Catholic village near Jiangzhou (the site of the Jesuit mission in the seventeenth century) where, after months of education by the Socialist Education workteam, villagers had held a meeting to criticize and attack their priest and many had left the church. Religious affairs officials were told to use the Socialist Education Movement in Catholic villages to uncover class struggle and implement the policy of religious freedom, which in effect meant encouraging people to leave the church ("explain to the masses that one is free to believe in religion, but one is also free not to believe in religion").[20] A provincial meeting laid out a detailed framework for the campaign, focusing on teaching Catholics history and science. New workteams were to be sent to these villages, where they would begin by getting villagers to recall the past and then use the stories the villagers told to show how they had been exploited by the church. To provide a financial incentive, priests and church leaders would be required to repay any money that the villagers accused them of obtaining by exploitation. Those who resisted would be "counterrevolutionaries and bad elements hiding in the religion" and should be "struggled against until they are uncovered and stink."[21] Then the campaign would focus on scientific education to get the villagers to stop believing in God by teaching them about evolution and the natural causation of weather. Finally the workteam would explain the policy of religious freedom and then people should write letters announcing that they had left the religion.

History was at the center of this campaign and the trouble that followed was built around two entirely different conceptions of the history of the Catholic villages. The workteams, like many educated Chinese, saw the Catholic villages as the result of nineteenth- and early twentieth-century imperialist missionary activity. In this they inherited the ideas of Qing officials and late nineteenth-century local elites who after two hundred years of ignoring Catholic villages assumed that they had suddenly emerged in the late nineteenth century. For the Catholics, on the other hand, relations with the missionaries had certainly been fraught but the missionaries were gone. Far more relevant to them as they faced the Socialist Education Movement were stories of persecution by the government and especially the stories of the Boxer Uprising. Old people could still remember the Boxers and everyone had heard stories of the massacres. These memories had been reinvigorated in 1943 when the bishops, several missionaries, and the Chinese who died alongside them had been beatified in Rome as martyrs of the Catholic church.[22] Officials were horrified when two priests working on a history of the Boxer Uprising edited a text that seemed to imply a comparison between the Boxers and the Communists, but that comparison was immediately obvious to many Catholics.[23] If the workteams were motivated by a history of imperialism, the Catholics were spurred into action by stories of state persecution and Catholic suffering and resistance.

In November 1964 priests and nuns were ordered to leave their parishes and attend a "study class" in the cathedral compound in Taiyuan.[24] Soon workteams arrived in the Catholic villages to enforce rules made in 1958 closing churches and banning collective prayers in the absence of a priest. They also announced that heads of families must write statements renouncing the religion.[25] They did not at this stage enforce this demand, but they said enough to make people anxious. Then in the early spring of 1965, people in Cave Gully began to hear reports that a cross had appeared on a cliff face near the village of Long Gully in the hills north of Taiyuan city (see map 1).

Among the many who went to see the cross was a middle-aged woman called Zheng Fentao whose family had been struck by tragedy (figure 14). She was hard working, outspoken, and popular, and had been a leader of the village's women workers, but that winter she did not work at all. First she had cared for her elderly father-in-law, who was dying of cancer. Then her mother-in-law also became ill. The family was very poor with a small, dilapidated house and many debts. Their son was training to be an electrician, but was not yet bringing in any income. They were relying on his young wife to do the farming while Zheng Fentao stayed at home to care for her husband's sick parents. After the expense of her father-in-law's illness, she could not even afford to take her mother-in-law to the hospital. In April, after the death of

FIGURE 14. Zheng Fentao. Private collection.

both her parents-in-law and shortly after the shining cross first appeared, her husband too died. Perhaps, like others, she first went to the cliff in search of healing, or perhaps so much tragedy made her feel the need for supernatural help.[26]

Because the early spring days were short, and people were under pressure not to waste work time on religion, most people came to Long Gully after dark. As the news spread more and more people came and there were large crowds. The cross was a loess formation high up on the side of the cliff. Candles were lit at the foot of the cliff and some people brought burning torches, but all around was pitch dark. The people knelt in the fields, looking up at the dark cliff where something miraculous had happened, and chanting prayers. A few individuals were rhythmically beating themselves across the shoulders in penitence for sins. Many prayed all night and saw nothing, but from time to time others would shout out the visions that they saw on the face of the dark cliff. Most saw a cross radiating light, but some people saw visions of heaven and hell, a priest saying mass, or the Virgin Mary. Sometimes the crowd would start to call on the Virgin Mary to come down and allow herself to be seen.[27]

After praying overnight at Long Gully many of the pilgrims then went on to another village in the hills where a young woman had begun to preach. Li Zhenxiang was a sworn virgin, so to some extent a religious professional, and had worked closely with the bishop, but that was not how she struck those who met her at this time. Instead what they saw was an ordinary village woman, wearing a black jacket, her hair in long plaits, someone who could be, and was, easily mistaken for any young village wife. She put her message in the most commonplace terms, telling people that in the past she too had done bad things like stealing a piglet from another house. The message too was simple. She called on Catholics to pray with sincerity, to live together in harmony, and to return anything they had stolen or acquired dishonestly *(bugong-dao)*. She warned that God would punish those who failed to do these things, and especially those who left the religion by ceasing to pray. People were moved by her courage in speaking out so directly against the policies of the Socialist Education Movement, which called on Catholics to deny their faith, break all ties with other Catholics considered class enemies, and repay profits made by taking goods to market. Soon she was being invited to come to other villages to preach.[28]

Li Zhenxiang arrived in Cold Springs Road on April 1, 1965 and went to the church. The doors were locked, but she wailed and made a commotion demanding that they be opened. A crowd gathered and as they stood, tightly packed in the church courtyard, the great doors suddenly opened and the people flooded in. Word spread that a miracle had taken place in which the church door opened on its own, a bell rang on its own, and a candle lit on its own. Meanwhile inside the church, Li Zhenxiang began to preach and the dramatic events of the day continued as she called on people to act out their repentance: those who had accepted money or goods from the workteam should repay it and those who had left the church should return. But some people had already handed over letters renouncing the church, what should they do? The answer seemed simple, though it demanded courage: late that evening Li Zhenxiang led a large crowd out of the church to the offices of the workteam to demand the letters back. It is said that the leader was wearing a leather coat because of the cold, but even so he was sweating and trembling with fear as he handed over a pile of letters.[29]

The people prayed all night, and early the next morning Li Zhenxiang led a noisy crowd of more than a thousand carrying the village's processional cross to the shrine of Our Lady of the Seven Sorrows. As they passed through Cave Gully one of the women let her hair loose and ground her teeth, so that people understood that she was possessed by a demon. Someone called to her husband and he took her out of sight around the side of the hill, but there, with no one to pray for her, she ran around crazily. In an intensely dramatic context this woman was acting out not only the power of the supernatural, but the sense that people were out of control and that the evil they faced could make them behave in ways that were irrational and unpredictable. Only the united prayers of the community could counter such evil. But how could the community be united in the face of a powerful and hostile state? When the Cold Springs Road people reached the shrine, they saw that the courtyard was full of police and some went home. Some of those who entered the church to pray were arrested as they left. Li Zhenxiang stayed that night in Cave Gully and early next morning one of the men from Cold Springs Road fled with her on his bicycle towards West Willows. Soldiers followed them and she was arrested later that day.[30]

From the start there were stories about Li Zhenxiang's arrest, though they did not initially involve a flying bicycle. Instead people said that the car taking her away broke down before it reached the town and Li fled. In another version, when the car got stuck Li asked the driver if he believed in God. He said he did, and when he looked up Li had vanished. As time went on and people wondered what had become of her, the stories became more elaborate. It was said that she had gone to Beijing to hold talks with Chairman Mao, even to persuade the Chairman to believe in Catholicism. When he refused, God punished him by leaving him paralyzed on his bed unable to speak. Meanwhile Li had disappeared again to help the Americans in Vietnam or to hold meetings in Rome. A girl who came from one of the few families in Cold Springs Road that were not Catholic, told her Catholic friend as they chatted together in the fields, "Li Zhenxiang was caught by the government ages ago, and tomorrow she is coming back to confess her crimes." The Catholic girl responded firmly, "If they can bring Li Zhenxiang to our village to confess you can chop off my head!"[31]

During the summer after Li Zhenxiang's arrest other people began to preach. Many of them were young men and women who went into trance states. A man from West Willows who preached in Cave Gully in his youth remembers today that while he was preaching for a few minutes it was as if he was sitting before Jesus and was unaware of the everyday world. Through such experiences the divine began to intervene directly in people's lives and gave quite ordinary people an extraordinary new authority.[32] These visionaries began to take over the ritual roles of the absent priests: they blessed water to make it holy, could tell people's sins by looking at them and assign penances, blessed bread for people to eat, and performed exorcisms. They made holy water by speaking prayers and making the sign of the cross over it. The young man who preached in Cave Gully was believed to be able to tell people their sins by looking at them. He assigned penance, as a priest would do at confession, to someone who had said that Li Zhenxiang was a counterrevolutionary and to a child who had renounced the religion. In Cold Springs Road another young man blessed packets of dry flatbreads for people. Yet another of the Cold Springs Roads preachers saw demons everywhere in his house and was famous for dramatic exorcisms. These were practices that defined priests and the visionaries could only perform them because people believed that the supernatural was present all around them.[33]

One of the other women subsequently remembered as the Four Fragrances, Han Qingxiang (Clear Fragrance), was a middle-aged Cold Springs Road woman who was remarkable for her supernatural powers at this time. She lived in a mud-brick house with an electric light from a wire that came in through the window. People remember seeing her peel the covering off the live wire with her teeth. They say that she could tell her visitors about their lives even though they came from the city. Her visitors gave her bread, which she blessed for them to eat. An image of Jesus was miraculously discovered in her family's cesspit and people went to see the angels which had been seen floating over the water in her storage jars.[34]

Many of those who preached spoke of how the Day of Judgment was coming. God would punish people for their sins by sending fire, or possibly an atomic bomb, to destroy the world. They called on women to cut off their plaits, which were a sign of female vanity, and to destroy plastic goods, which they thought were made of bones. People burned plastic sheeting, nylon socks, and rubber-soled shoes, and threw away plastic cigarette lighters.[35] These apocalyptic themes drew on the traditions of European Catholicism and may have been linked to new revelations about the third secret of Fatima. Since the mid-nineteenth century, there had been visionary moments in which the Virgin Mary had foretold the imminent destruction of the world, and the Cold War and fears of nuclear apocalypse had produced a rash of visions in the 1940s and 1950s. In 1963 the European press published what was said to be the third secret of Fatima, a brief text in which Mary threatened punishment for all mankind and foretold terrible persecutions for the church in the second half of the twentieth century: the leaders of the church would turn on one another, Satan would rule, a great war would break out and finally God would destroy the earth, sending fire and smoke from the sky that would vaporize the oceans. One of the written texts that circulated during the visions in Shanxi was called "A Startling Piece of News" and was said to have come from Rome. It may have contained part of this text or simply echoes that had reached the Shanxi Catholics as rumors originating in Hong Kong or Macao.[36]

In preparation for the Day of Judgment the preachers called on Catholics to make reparation for their sins by returning anything they had stolen or acquired dishonestly. Sometimes people handed these things over to the preachers as they might have done to a priest after confessing a theft: Han Qingxiang received two gold rings which she later passed on to a Cave Gully woman. Other people returned items of clothing and quilts directly to their neighbors. Families who had been given aid for cooperating with the Socialist Education Movement handed money and goods back to the workteam. Just as workteams required church leaders to repay money gained by exploitation and those in charge of village finances to repay money they had obtained through corruption, so the preachers demanded that Catholics repay money and possessions they had gained by cooperating with the government. Cold Springs Road villagers returned 2,425 yuan (at a time when 300 yuan was a high family income for the year), 651 pounds of grain, 473 farm tools, oil, vegetable seeds, a leather jacket, and a large quantity of vegetables.[37]

People also beat themselves to make reparation for their own sins and to redeem the sins of others. Tian Meixiang (Beautiful Fragrance), another of the Four Fragrances who came from Red Gully village in the mountains near the pilgrimage church of the Holy Mother, placed slivers of glass in a ball of cotton so that blood ran as people beat themselves and swore to be loyal to the church.[38] This intensified Catholic traditions of self-flagellation, which the Franciscans in Cave Gully had practiced on Fridays using a knotted rope. It also had clear links with the confessions and beatings of village officials that were central to the Socialist Education Movement. A government booklet, published as part of the crackdown on Catholicism the following year, shows the emotional scenes in the pilgrimage church of the Holy Mother (figure 15). This booklet told the story of a young man who was said to have beaten his sick mother to death while trying to exorcise her. The young man, who later spoke out against the church, is standing at the church door uncertain how to respond. According to the story, his mother's sickness had been caused by drinking unboiled holy water,

FIGURE 15. The Church of the Holy Mother at the height of the movement. From *Kongsu—shi shei haisile wo ma?* [Accusation: Who killed my mother?] (Taiyuan, circa 1965).

and behind him in the church two men can be seen pouring holy water over a kneeling figure. In the text the young man describes how he went to the church and found it full of people, some praying, some wailing, some beating themselves. There were also some men standing in the middle saying that because their sin was great it was being punished by Heaven. When holy water was poured over them they instantly fell to the floor.

The focus of all this collective emotion was on what the preachers called living together in amity, in other words bringing back into the community those who had broken with their Catholic neighbors. In Cave Gully the visiting preacher from West Willows sent for a young man who had ceased to attend prayers. When the young man arrived, the preacher went into a trance and demanded to know why he no longer prayed. He then rebuked him for his ill-gotten gains and sprinkled him with holy water. He told a young woman who had divorced that God would punish her. In this atmosphere of high emotion and powerful community feeling many of those who had been cooperating with the workteams began to call them devils and returned to the church.[39]

Towards the end of May the police came to arrest one of the leading preachers in Cold Springs Road. He was a young unmarried man who preached powerfully on the Passion and death of Jesus as well as about the Ten Commandments. He battled with devils and spoke of the value of suffering, whipping himself daily, wearing a belt to mortify the flesh, and even placing hot coals on his bed and lying on them. When the police arrived to arrest him the villagers came out onto the streets in protest. The bravest lay down in the road in front of the trucks or climbed up onto the vehicles. The police had to fire their guns in the air before they could get through.[40] By this time talk of the end of the world had passed and people already knew there would be a massive government crackdown. On July 9, crowds gathered at the shrine of Our Lady of the Seven Sorrows in Cave Gully to pray for rain. The next day it rained. On July 11, five thousand people gathered to carry the cross and a statue of the Virgin Mary up the mountain. They went in procession accompanied by one of the local church music groups, and the mountain was so packed with people it was difficult to get through. People went to give thanks for rain, but as they remember today they also turned to Our Lady of Seven Sorrows because they knew that suffering was to come and they were afraid.[41]

What followed is what the story of the Four Fragrances omits: a massive government crackdown and educational campaign that lasted for more than a year, involved Li Zhenxiang and other leaders of the previous year making public accusations against the church, and ended with most Catholics formally renouncing the church. There are many stories about these events, but they focus on the heroism of those few who firmly resisted the state, rather than the many who conformed and the minority who became activists for the government. During this period the workteams succeeded in splitting the Catholic villages, fracturing the community loyalty that had characterized them since the eighteenth century.

The crackdown began four days after the great pilgrimage to Our Lady of Seven Sorrows, when the provincial government sent two thousand members of the militia to surround Cold Springs Road, while another thousand people went from house to house to register every person as present or absent. For the Cold Springs Road villagers this was a time when they sought and received divine aid as they had done in the time of the Boxers. A policeman remembers that the villagers scattered holy water on them (to exorcise them as they had the Boxers). There are also many accounts of the involvement of the souls in purgatory. It is said that even the militia heard strange voices praying and that the police pointed to photographs on the wall, accusing this person or that of having been involved in the earlier resistance. These were photographs of the dead whom the police had seen standing alongside the villagers. That night several Cave Gully people and many others from outside the village were rounded up and taken to the local courthouse. Most were released the following day, but some, including Zheng

Fentao, were taken to a chaotic mass trial in one of the villages near Cave Gully and then imprisoned.[42]

New workteams were sent into the Catholic villages and all religious activity was banned. Cave Gully was treated as a center of the trouble and its workteam came from the Public Security Bureau. Several of the villagers were sentenced to lengthy prison terms, though who was imprisoned and how long they were held depended as much on the logic of the Socialist Education Movement as on what one had done. The workteam made endless efforts to persuade Duan Runcheng, a poor peasant. Because he had been only partially sighted since childhood, he was illiterate, but he was also tough, determined, and very intelligent. He protested the closure of the village church, asking his sister to write a statement for him, and argued with the workteam on the basis of the official policy of freedom of religion. This is how he remembers the debates:

> The next day the workteam called me to the office and said, "We hear you are illiterate. You are too stubborn but your background is good, so we will pardon your dreadful ideas, but can't you be a little flexible?" I asked, "What do you mean 'flexible'?" The workteam told me, "If you believe in the Lord of Heaven in your heart we can't see that, so just as long as you say the words 'I don't believe' and you admit you are mistaken then we won't pursue the matter and we'll make an exchange." I immediately spoke out saying, "Chairman Mao teaches us, 'All over the world people most fear those who take things seriously and the Communist Party takes things most seriously.' I believe in the Lord of Heaven, so how can I not say what is in my heart." The workteam said, "Aren't you afraid of going to a labor camp?" I said, "I haven't broken the national law, so there is no reason for me to be in a labor camp."[43]

Meanwhile a middle peasant who had done little more than visit Long Gully and receive one of the preachers in his family home received a ten-year sentence. For similar reasons the clergy were held responsible in order of seniority, even though the bishop of Taiyuan had been in prison since 1955 and other priests who were accused had been confined in the study class throughout the trouble. As head of the Franciscan order, the Cave Gully parish priest was counted among the senior clergy and was formally arrested and taken to prison. The rest of the clergy remained confined in the Taiyuan cathedral compound.[44]

The experiences of those who were imprisoned varied. At first many of the Cave Gully people were locked up together in the same local prison. One man remembers that his task was to sweep the courtyard and that when the guard wasn't looking he used to sweep cabbage stalks into the room where the parish priest and the village's former Nationalist Party branch head were being held with nothing to eat. A Cave Gully woman recalls being interrogated for seven nights, being punished for throwing her food at the red demons with tails that she could see accompanying the prison guards, being tied up on a wall outside in the heat of the day, having handfuls of her hair pulled out and given electric shocks, so that when she was released three months later her children could scarcely recognize her. She steadfastly refused to cooperate and claims today that miraculously none of this caused her pain. (Others made similar statements at the time.) Most of those arrested were released after a few days or weeks, but a few remained in prison. Zheng Fentao, who had not been a leader in the movement, was one of them and stories began to circulate about her total refusal to cooperate.[45]

However, there were also people who agreed to make public confessions. Huge mass meetings, each involving twenty thousand people, were staged in the Catholic hill villages that had been at the center of events: Cave Gully, Cold Springs Road, Winding Gully, Sandy Gully, and Red Gully. Li Zhenxiang and other key figures were taken around to the meetings to confess their crimes and accuse others. The young man who had confessed to beating his mother to death spoke out passionately against the church and was treated as a model. These mass meetings were recorded and the tapes then used throughout the rest of the campaign. There were also smaller village meetings. A young visionary who had been taken to the police station where he was tortured by being beaten with rods, given electric shocks, and deprived of sleep, confessed, most implausibly, to sleeping with two unmarried girls and a young wife during the two days he spent in Cave Gully. The Cave Gully parish priest, who was thought to be very timid and had a reputation for never even speaking to a woman, was not only accused of rape, but of concealing a radio transmitter in a well. People recall that when he was ordered to climb down into the well to fetch it, he was so frightened that he just stood there trembling, until eventually someone else went down.

After a period of this education each villager was required to make a written statement detailing exactly what Catholic activities they had participated in, where these had taken place, and that they now understood this was an illegal counterrevolutionary movement hiding under the cloak of religion and they would not be deceived again. In Cave Gully the meetings culminated in the demolition of the shrine to Our Lady of the Seven Sorrows on the feast of the Immaculate Conception in December 1965. All the villagers went up the hill and dismantled the building, taking the bricks, wood, and tiles to use as building materials.

Apart from those who were still in prison it is said that the only people who did not participate were Duan Runcheng and an old woman who was in poor health.[46]

The workteams then moved on to educating the villagers on the evils of religion. A special set of textbooks rushed out for the occasion criticized Catholicism as a tool of imperialist invasion, attacked the papacy with references to the corruption of medieval popes, and discussed Marx's ideas of religion as a tool of class exploitation. The textbooks also discussed issues of more obvious local importance, criticizing the idea that "all Catholics under Heaven are one family" since "not only in the recent troubles were they 'as close as a single family' but in daily life and work too they cannot draw clear lines between classes."[47] One volume went through the Ten Commandments contradicting each in turn: the commandment not to kill belongs to a slave society and undermines patriotism, the commandment to honor one's parents is feudal, the commandment not to steal was used against Land Reform, the commandment not to bear false witness impedes the activities of the workteams and so on. Small-group sessions were held in which the leaders detailed the charges against the church and then all those present were asked individually and repeatedly whether in the light of these things Catholicism was a good or a bad religion. For those who said they did not know, could not understand, or that Catholicism was good but there were some bad people in it, the education sessions were simply repeated. The campaign was rounded up in the spring of 1966 with the registration of those who were considered "targets of investigation" and a report listing a handful of people who had been persuaded to apply for membership in the Party's mass organizations.[48]

Then that summer a massive new national campaign was declared: the Great Proletarian Cultural Revolution, which moved on from the Socialist Education Movement's attacks on lower-level officials, to attack senior party officials. At first the Shanxi provincial government resisted implementing this campaign and events moved slowly, but then in August the policy of encouraging students to travel in order to exchange revolutionary experiences was declared and thousands of Red Guards arrived in Taiyuan from Beijing. Because of the recent events the Catholic church was an obvious target for them and they organized a "living exhibition" of the clergy in Taiyuan cathedral. For three weeks the priests and nuns who had been gathered in the cathedral for the Socialist Education Movement were exhibited to the public. While the Red Guards yelled slogans at them, they were forced to kneel outside in the rain for days, poked with sticks and made to eat dirt by the audience, and beaten. One of the elderly priests and a nun died. Six hundred thousand people were said to have attended the exhibition: many non-Catholics in the city today remember going as children and groups were also brought in from the villages.[49]

Red Guards also went out to the Catholic villages in the surrounding area to educate the villagers. They attacked the village officials and anyone who had been in trouble during the Socialist Education Movement and also conducted classes for the Catholics. This time the vast majority of Catholics finally renounced the church. Many handed over written statements, though for most people the Red Guards were willing to settle for a spoken agreement that "Catholicism is a bad religion *(huai jiao)*." These written statements are headed "Statement of determination" or "Statement of apostasy" and are brief and highly formulaic. Here is a very poorly written example signed by a Catholic from one of the plains villages:

> I am a Catholic whose religion was handed down from our ancestors. Since I was a child my breast has been full of superstitious poison, which completely confused my thought. I only knew to hope to go to heaven and fear going to hell. I was a slave of foreign imperialism.
>
> With the patient help and teaching of the workteam, and after listening to the recordings, I finally understood that Catholicism is a bad religion, a foreign religion, a landlord religion, an exploitative religion, and a religion that harms people. In the future I will not pass it on and will not believe in this bad religion. Catholicism is a tool for the invasion of China. I want to cut myself off from it and wash my hands of it. I will not be deceived again. I will listen to the words of Chairman Mao, read the books of Chairman Mao, and do what Chairman Mao directs. I will stand together with the masses of workers, peasants, and soldiers. I will work diligently at production and strive to be a Five Good commune member.[50]

Another statement written in the name of an illiterate older woman says that she now understands that "Catholicism is an imperialist cultural invasion of China, its rules and doctrine are counterrevolutionary and opposed to the people, it is a reactionary fraud."[51] These are complex ideas, and it is easy to sympathize with the man who responded to the workteams and Red Guards by saying simply that he was not educated and did not understand all that about imperialism but he believed in the Lord of Heaven.[52]

As at the time of the Boxers, those who resisted and suffered for it were not always those who had been the most devout. In Cave Gully some of the devout resisted and those who came from rich middle peasant families were especially likely to suffer for it: one old woman was paraded through the streets with a big placard hung with wires round her neck because she would not stop praying. But the workteams tended to put more pressure on men than women, since as the heads of families they were held more responsible. Some of the men who resisted seem to have been motivated primarily by classic manly virtues of courage, filial piety, and loyalty. One couple were described as "very cold" Catholics both before 1965 and after 1980 when the church revived, but during the campaign even though the workteam beat them they refused to deny their religion. The father told his children that if they denied the religion he would kill them, so they did not dare do so even though they were too young to understand what was going on. Years later the parish priest asked this couple why they had been so firm. They did not find it easy to reply but eventually said that they could not turn their backs on their ancestors. Duan Runcheng too continued to refuse to cooperate and to insist that the policy of freedom of religion meant that he could believe in God. Because of his undoubted status as a very poor peasant he was not sent to prison, but for four years he worked in the village fields wearing a paper hat and a placard saying "Running dog of imperialism, counterrevolutionary element Duan Runcheng" and in the evenings he was subject to repeated struggle sessions in which he was beaten, kicked, and paraded through the streets.[53]

The campaign also allowed the workteams and later the Red Guards to recruit activists in Cave Gully for the first time. As with the resisters these were a diverse group. Some had been very devout, some had genuinely lost their belief in God, and a few young people hoped to improve their chances in life. For the workteam the most important targets were isolated women whose weakness could easily be exploited. The model was provided by an official report from Cold Springs Road, which told of how the workteam selected an extremely poor woman whose husband had died a few years earlier, leaving her with five children under twelve, so that the family was dependent on government aid. At the start of the Socialist Education Movement she had cooperated with the workteam and had written a letter stating that she was leaving the church, but then when Li Zhenxiang came she had taken part in going to the workteam's offices and demanding her letter back. Afterwards one of the workteam members went to carry water, sweep the floor, and grind grain for her almost daily for two months to win her over. Eventually she gave in and began to speak out publicly, attacking people in meetings. The police and, later, soldiers who formed the Cave Gully workteams followed this model by seeking out another poor widow with young children. They convinced her that the Party's teachings on religion were correct, paid her a large monthly salary for making secret reports, and gave her children the opportunity to leave the village to join the army and the Communist Party, but they also exploited her sexually.[54] Recruiting government activists in Cave Gully still required effort and persistence, but the intensity of the campaign against Catholicism made it possible.

The crackdown ended public Catholic practice in Cave Gully for the next thirteen years. However, unlike the Socialist Education Movement, the Cultural Revolution in Shanxi was not focused on the Catholic villages. Those who had been imprisoned for their activities or resisted the workteams continued to suffer, but provincial elites and Red Guards alike were primarily concerned with their own increasingly violent struggles for power. After three weeks the exhibition of clergy was brought to an end. They were removed to a Buddhist temple where they were locked up for the next twelve years, operating a small workshop making protective gloves.[55] In the villages the pressure continued for a few more weeks, but then the Red Guards began to turn their attention to the provincial government. In January of 1967 the provincial authorities were overthrown, and soon the former provincial governor was dead. Over the next three years the central government lost control of Shanxi and there was large-scale fighting between factions. Finally in 1969 the military was sent in and a new provincial government was established.

In the spring of 1970 the main leaders of the defeated Red Guard factions were shot and a crackdown was launched against any possible opponents of the new regime. The campaign was called Struggle, Criticize, Reform, and officials were told to conduct it as if the nation were preparing for war. Across the province, 154,000 people came under attack and city governments were allowed to execute people on the basis of a popular vote. Among the many people caught up in this campaign were some of the Catholics who had been imprisoned in 1965. Cave Gully's timid parish priest had at first given in to the government's pressure and written a long report, but his sister who was a nun living at the family home in Cold Springs Road had been one of those who resisted fervently. Her head was shaved, then at a struggle meeting her clothes were torn off and she was punched and shoved from one person to another, desperately trying to cover herself. Afterwards her whole body was so badly swollen that she could not get up from her bed. She died a few days later from her injuries and her body was thrown into the river. Perhaps moved by his sister's terrible death, the priest recanted his confession and from then on astonished everyone who knew him by his courage. He was publicly executed alongside the first two Chinese bishops of Taiyuan. One of those who saw the parade passing slowly through the main streets of the city on the way to the execution ground reported that he shouted out once "Long live Catholicism! Down with Communism!" and an activist jumped up onto the truck and drove the metal wires that were supposed to gag him through his cheek so that he could no longer speak. His body was dug up at night by a Catholic who reburied it but later, fearing it would be found, kept the bones in a sack at home where he prayed to the martyr.[56]

Zheng Fentao too was executed, though as a poor village woman she was shot in prison rather than receiving the full panoply of public execution. She had been given a twelve-year prison sentence for her participation in the "Catholic counterrevolutionary disorder," but under the new campaign she was sentenced to death on the charge "ongoing counter-revolution." Specifically she was accused of refusing to accept her sentence, of saying once that former president Liu Shaoqi was a just official, and of continuing to say that "Catholicism was a good teaching."[57] Her terrified daughter-in-law could not even find out which grave was hers and never managed to retrieve the body.

It was at this time too that Duan Runcheng was finally sent to prison. He had taken advantage of a power cut to run away from a struggle session conducted by a group of laborers who had been brought in to work on a new military highway being built through the village as part of the country's defenses against war with the Soviet Union. When the lights went off just as the road workers were about to start beating him, he ran away. As a result the different factions present at the meeting got into a brawl. Three days later he was arrested for counterrevolution and he was later sentenced to twelve years in a labor camp.[58]

By the early 1970s the original goals of the Socialist Education Movement appeared to have been achieved. Several Catholic communities had demolished their churches. The pilgrimage church of the Holy Mother was too remote for its stone walls to be removed but the Catholics of Red Gully took away its furnishings, stripped the timber from its roof, and left it as an empty shell. All across the province church towers were destroyed and other church buildings taken over to use for clubs, granaries, housing, offices, schools, and small-scale industry. Cave Gully's parish church was used as a granary.[59] Public religious practice ceased. People remember being afraid even to eat good wheat noodles or dumplings at Christmas. Images, devotional books, and rosaries were confiscated, destroyed, or hidden. Some families continued their morning and evening prayer, but they did so at home and often prayed silently rather than with the familiar chants.[60]

Catholics were also divided. The clergy confined together in Taiyuan had lost the unity they had maintained since the Communists arrived. There had always been tensions between different groups of clergy, especially between the Franciscans, who had been considered as an elite by the Italian Franciscan missionaries, and the diocesan priests. New divisions were created over how far each member of the group was prepared to cooperate with the workteam's and ultimately the government's demands. The tensions were exacerbated by the workteam, which put the priests under huge pressure to criticize, bully, and physically assault one another. Some broke altogether, lost their faith, married, and denounced the church. Two of those who resisted were persecuted so badly that they committed suicide. Cave Gully too was divided into hostile camps. Some of those associated with the workteam became Red Guards and even joined the Communist Party, while the families of the resisters were isolated. Duan Runcheng's younger sister, who had helped him write the poster in which he initially protested against the closure of the church, lost the residence permit that gave her a grain ration and had to leave the village. His wife and five children had nowhere to live, as the Red Guards tried to drive them too from the village. When they worked in the fields the activists shouted at them, and when his daughter took food to Duan in prison she still had to do a day's work in the fields after she got back.[61]

Duan Runcheng was one of a number of those who understood their experiences through the idea that God chooses some individuals who are strong to suffer for the sins of others and thus make atonement for them. This concept was popular in early twentieth-century Italy, where it was associated with women who were recognized as saints because though incapacitated by illness they accepted their sufferings and saw them as God's will for the world. In the villages of Shanxi these ideas enabled those who continued to resist to make sense of their sufferings and to be seen by others as people who had been chosen by God. After his arrest, Duan Runcheng remembered two dreams he had had years earlier. As a child he had dreamed that a figure in shining white took his hand and led him before a statue of the Virgin Mary. Years later he dreamed that a voice spoke to him saying, "The Lord will let you make atonement."[62] A similar thought occurred to the sister of one of the young Cave Gully men who had become a priest and who had been arrested in 1965. Ten years later he was transferred to a prison in the mountains on the east side of the province where he worked in a coal mine and was allowed visitors. His sister, who had refused to deny the church, made the long journey to see him and found the man who had been her handsome brother dressed all in grey, his hair grey, almost too weak to walk. She wept, but the words she spoke to console him were "the Lord is letting you make atonement."[63]

Towards the end of the 1970s the Communist state also finally succeeded in achieving some of its goals for economic development. The villagers tell stories of a good policeman: a white-haired, kindly old man from across the plain. He tried to mediate when Duan Runcheng was in trouble with the Red Guards and took responsibility for telling some young men to rescue a woman who had tried to kill herself by jumping into a well. They also give him the credit for finally getting the Jinci water for the village. Qingyuan county government opened a series of new, deep, self-pumping wells and the largest of them was in Cave Gully. Industrial extraction had already depleted the aquifer so that far less water was flowing from the springs at Jinci. The new wells in Qingyuan meant that hardly any water flowed from the temple springs at all and people said that the Cave Gully Catholics had broken the Jinci water. What the missionaries had tried and failed to give the villagers after the Boxer Uprising, finally came to them at the gift of the Communist state. Even this water would not last, but nevertheless it transformed the village as farmers began to change from growing millet and date trees, which could resist drought, to more profitable vegetables and fruit trees.[64]

By 1979 the Communist state had succeeded in penetrating the Catholic villages and was bringing significant economic development to Cave Gully, while pressure from workteams in the Socialist Education Movement and Red Guards in the Cultural Revolution had fractured the church community. The state had succeeded in the aims of the Socialist Education Movement, but it was also laying the foundations for the religious enthusiasm, the church building, and the wave of conversions that followed in the 1980s and 1990s. The community had been broken, but the Catholics' sense of their own identity as a group had been reinforced by the very exclusion and persecution that broke it. As soon as they were allowed to, the villagers began to rebuild. They had destroyed their churches with their own hands, but today what was once a little gothic chapel to Our Lady of the Seven Sorrows is a spectacular pilgrimage site built in the style of a Chinese palace. The many who had not dared to speak out admired the fortitude, loyalty, and filial piety of the few who resisted. Duan Runcheng's sufferings were to give him the prestige to become a well-known and effective evangelist far beyond the village.

CHAPTER 7

The Village Since the 1980s

The return of a Cave Gully priest to his family in the mid 1980s is not a folktale that belongs to the whole village, but a story told by his family. He had been in prison for many years far from home in the mountains east of Shanxi and his release took place quite unexpectedly on a winter evening; the old man had nothing but a quilt and a few personal possessions, and he was very weak. The only person he could think of to ask for help was one of the prison guards who came from a village near Cold Springs Road. After toiling through the darkness and some difficulty explaining the situation to the guard's wife, who had never met him, they welcomed him into their home. The next day the guard made a telephone call to the village office in Cave Gully, but the man who took the call went out to work in the fields without informing the family. When the family eventually got the news several of them went to fetch the old priest. They stayed with the guard, then took the train back to Taiyuan. At the station they saw a bus to Qingyuan, which happened to have a Catholic driver from Cold Springs Road. He did not recognize the frail old man, but when he was told who it was he set off immediately, not waiting for any other passengers or following the bus route, but driving straight to Cave Gully. The old man lived with his family for three years while he recovered his health, then moved back to Cold Springs Road to resume work as a priest. He had emerged from prison a stern, unsmiling man, not someone people found easy to get along with, but with an enviable reputation for never having bent.

The bus driver in this story represents the warm welcome the priest's family thought he should have had, but the reaction of the man in the village office reminds the listener that there was also denial, fear, resentment, and hostility from those who had been closer to the government.

More difficult for the community were the priests who had broken under pressure: those who had denounced the religion, denied the existence of God, or betrayed others. Another Cave Gully priest was released several years earlier and his story, though perhaps even more tragic, is far harder for people to tell. The story begins with his childhood, when his family was confident the bishop had been right to choose him for the priesthood because he did not cry in the seminary even though he was only ten years old when he entered. Then he was imprisoned and tortured and under great pressure agreed to marry a nun. At the end of the Cultural Revolution she returned to her family and he went back to Cave Gully. As soon as he could, he wrote to Rome to get a dispensation to leave the priesthood. He was so happy on the day that it finally arrived that he had a stroke. For the last ten years of his life he was paralyzed, living in a little room his parents left for him, while the rest of the household said that the stroke was God protecting him. This is a strange story, for why should a paralyzing stroke be considered God's protection? Other scraps of information hint at another story lying behind the one that is told. The old man was indeed confined with the other priests, but he had the good job of being their cook. After they were all released the nun returned to her family. The document that came from Rome was not a dispensation to leave the priesthood, but rather an annulment of the marriage, obtained by the nun's brothers, who were also priests. He stayed in the cathedral for two years, before coming home because of ill health. There are also accusations that after his return his family did not treat him well. One can guess that he collaborated with the authorities during the Cultural Revolution and then wanted to continue to practice as a priest despite his marriage but was rejected by the people. Unlike the missionaries after the Boxer Uprising, the Catholics after the Cultural Revolution were not so much concerned with whether people had denied their faith *(beijiao)*, though they greatly admired those who had not. Instead they fiercely condemned those who had actively given reports *(jiaodai)* that destroyed the reputation of the community and betrayed others. For priests the great symbol of this betrayal was marriage. To the Communist authorities in the 1960s and 1970s, marriage was the key symbolic act through which a man renounced the Catholic priesthood and aligned himself with the state; now the Catholics treated it in the same way.[1]

These stories are too close in time, too tightly bound to men and women still alive, too closely linked to everyday parish politics to represent the whole community; instead they lay out the issues and tensions that have shaped the church since 1980. At the core of all these tensions is how to come to terms with the events of the 1960s and 1970s. At the time these events involved many ordinary people, but the old priests have become symbols through which people discuss and debate what happened. By the end of the 1970s pressure from the state had broken the community, but the very same process had increased the separation between Catholics and other people. When religious practice was allowed again, the Catholics rapidly began to rebuild their communities. This meant literally rebuilding churches, but also the far more difficult task of reconstructing damaged human relationships and making sense of the past. The same intensity of feeling that made people donate eagerly for new churches often made it very hard for them to come to terms with the clergy and their neighbors. The result was a community characterized by great religious devotion that produced a new wave of evangelism for the first time since the eighteenth century, and one in which numerous young men and women entered the church as priests and nuns, but a community that was also soon divided between official and underground churches.

In 1979 the government permitted public religious activities again at the same time that it abolished collective farming, freeing villagers from control over how they spent their time and money. The 1980s was a period of rapid reconstruction: priests returned to the parishes, churches were rebuilt, the vast majority of those who had renounced the church in the 1960s returned, and the pilgrimage networks that bound Catholic villages together were reconstructed. But the divisions and betrayals of the 1960s were not forgotten and the end of the decade also saw the development of an institutionally separate underground church.

In Cave Gully those who had been sent to prison for their beliefs were gradually released starting in the late 1970s: a few of the clergy who had conformed most obediently to the authorities were sent back to the newly reopened cathedral and given small stipends. Public prayers began in Cave Gully in 1980 in people's homes and courtyards. People put up sacred images in their houses, though these were hard to obtain until 1984 when a priest in Taiyuan city succeeded in ordering supplies of images, crucifixes, rosaries, and medals from factories which had already started up in southeast China.[2] The first churches were reclaimed and rebuilt in 1982, the year when a new policy on religion was issued. The parish church in Cave Gully was relatively easy to reclaim, because it had not been badly damaged and the end of collective farming meant that such large storage spaces were no longer needed. The process was more contentious where churches had been adapted for use as government offices, factories, schools, or housing. Most often the local government provided an alternative site and the Catholics collected the money for construction. In Cold Springs Road, where the church had been completely demolished, it was rebuilt using local donations. The new church was large enough to seat the whole community of four thousand people and cost three hundred thousand yùan (at a time when annual incomes in the area were little more than five hundred yuan).[3]

The speed with which all this took place was striking, especially compared to the much slower revival of Buddhism and folk religion in this area. It was not just a result of people returning to their old ways: rather the devotion in the 1980s was something quite new, at least in recent history. Thirty years of state discrimination had increased Catholics' sense of community and their separation from their neighbors. Then the events of 1965 had led to intense experiences of divine presence and the persecution that followed had made those who resisted hugely respected. When religion was allowed again the vast majority of those who had written statements rejecting the church were eager to rejoin it and to reclaim their reputations by contributing generously.

Catholics who had been activists came under huge pressure to confess that they had been wrong and rejoin the church, but often found it very hard to return to the church because they could not face meeting those they had attacked. If they did not return to the church they had to deal with considerable hostility: in Cold Springs Road in the late 1980s a man who had left the church and joined the Communist Party had to put up shutters on his house to prevent his windows being broken. The same hostility was expressed in the many stories that circulate in Cave Gully of divine punishment for families that had taken an active role in attacks on the church. One such activist went to work in the mines and was killed by an out of control coal wagon. A man who had accused the parish priest of raping his wife had a son who quite unexpectedly tripped, broke his leg, and died. A family who used materials from the tombs of the smashed-up cemetery to build their house suffered from strange mental conditions and birth defects. Often when people are asked about the activists from that time, they simply say that the activists are all dead: they died young as a punishment. This closes down discussion and protects the community's reputation, but it also has the effect of incorporating those activists who are still alive into the community: since they are still living they cannot actually have been so wicked.[4]

While villagers condemn the activists, they are often also very critical of the surviving visionaries. Several who were widely accepted at the time are now said to have had longstanding mental health problems. People criticize them for causing trouble for the church and harming others. When the workteams forced the visionaries to recant at mass meetings, many people were left horrified and confused, but criticizing the visionaries today is also a way of separating the community from that moment when the divine was directly and unpredictably present in people's lives. Those who continue to see visions know that these are unlikely to be widely accepted and are hesitant even to speak of their experiences. One Cave Gully woman was introduced to the visionary Han Qingxiang as a young child. Since then she has on occasion seen visions and the souls from purgatory come to her at night. The messages that the souls bring her are about rebuilding the community: they want her to tell their families to leave off bad habits, repay debts, get on with each other, and attend prayers. More specifically the souls want their family members to repent, confess, and take communion. These are messages with which almost everyone in the village would agree and some of the families to whom she has spoken have been startled but convinced, but even so neither she nor her family wants her to have a reputation for being a visionary.[5]

The Catholic villages reconstructed the networks between them by cooperating to rebuild the shrine to the Holy Mother in the mountains north of Taiyuan. In 1982 thousands of Catholics from thirteen villages took a statue of Mary up the mountain to the roofless shell that was all that remained of the shrine. The next year the city government persuaded the priests to tell them not to go, but then in 1984 there was a drought and village pilgrimages went one after another to the shrine to pray for rain for nearly a month. After that the government agreed to allow the church to be rebuilt and provided twenty thousand yuan. Given that it cost three hundred thousand yuan to rebuild the church in Cold Springs Road, the Church of the Holy Mother must have cost a great deal more money than the government provided. The priest who was in charge of the rebuilding had a brother who was a priest in Hong Kong and probably provided some of the money, but what is now remembered is the symbolic participation of the whole community. Each village organized people to take part in carrying the building materials up the mountain. Today the shrine's brochure tells the story of a four-year-old girl who was carrying sand for cement in her schoolbag when the strap broke, so she carried some of the sand in her hands for the Holy Mother.[6] This story suggests the new social position of women and indeed children, compared to the past when the community was represented by its adult men. It also marks the great importance that was placed on every single member of the community taking part in the rebuilding.

Tensions between Catholics and their neighbors became visible as the rebuilding took place. In one village near Cave Gully the Catholics rebuilt their church and its tower in the late 1980s, but the other villagers were angry that the tower made the new church higher than their temple. They put ropes round the tower to pull it down, so the Catholics gathered in the church to express their willingness to die if the whole building collapsed. In the end the police came and arrested the Catholics, and the tower was demolished. After that people expressed their feelings by lobbing stones over the wall of the church courtyard. When a newly arrived priest went to complain to the village leaders, they asked him to tell the Catholics not to call on the people of Cave Gully and Cold Springs Road to come and attack them.[7] It was not just Catholics who remembered the Boxers.

There were also tensions within the Catholic community, especially over how to relate to priests who were seen as having betrayed the faith. These disputes over priests had much wider implications for how Catholics should relate to the government. Officials, often the same people who had been in power in the 1960s and 1970s, continued to distrust the Catholics and were determined to maintain control over them. In other parts of the country where the history of local relations with missionaries had been different, an underground church had existed since the 1950s. In Shanxi, where all the priests had entered the reformed church in 1951, the underground church had its origins in these tensions and in the struggles between the clergy while they were imprisoned together during the Cultural Revolution. One of the priests released from prison in the mid-1980s refused to cooperate with the church hierarchy, and thus to acknowledge the state's claim to control his right to practice. He was much admired and many people shared his distrust of the government-sponsored church hierarchy, but it was not until 1989 that the underground church as a separate institutional structure reached Shanxi. That year the social and economic tensions that had been growing across the country came to a climax and all kinds of people began to hope for a different political order. In the aftermath of the crackdown on the Tiananmen Square protesters, when the international legitimacy of the Chinese Communist government was at a low point, a group of underground clergy organized an alternative national bishop's conference in the neighboring province of Shaanxi. All those who attended were soon arrested, but the meeting had been inspirational and the movement rapidly spread. An evangelist who was also an effective healer arrived in the villages of central Shanxi and was successful in per-suading some Catholics to set up separate, underground church congre-gations. The suppression of the democracy movement is still remem-bered within the underground church, where people tell a story about a young soldier from Cold Springs Road who was dragged from his tank and demoted when he refused to drive it against the protesters.[8]

The new underground church soon became tightly embedded in the local community, though it was—and remains—led from outside the province and there has never been an underground bishop in central Shanxi. Underground congregations have lay leaders and chant the old Catholic prayers with an emotional fervor that Westerners might more easily associate with Protestant evangelicals. The priests tend to be young, thin, and often on the move. They change quickly out of their vestments after saying mass and join quietly in the prayers that follow. The atmosphere is quite different from the more formal official church and many Catholics who attend the official church rather admire it, but there are also important costs to membership: underground Catholics not only risk trouble with the government but also split the local Cath-olic community and indeed sometimes their families with their refusal to take part in community rituals. In Cave Gully, which never had to deal with parish priests who had especially problematic histories, very few people joined. The histories and character of individual priests matter because although there are two separate hierarchies, nearly all the priests of the official church continue to assert their loyalty to Rome. The Vatican, which has been dealing with similar disputes over national churches ever since the French Revolution, has issued repeated injunctions to the two sides to cooperate.[9]

The 1990s brought two other major changes in the lives of Shanxi's Catholics: a spectacular wave of new conversions and the rebuilding of the structures of the institutional church. The conversions were driven by ordinary Catholics, especially those who had suffered for their faith in the 1960s and whose experiences then had given them experience of speaking in defense of their faith and great respect in their communities. Like the first evangelists in the eighteenth century, they taught a faith that was deeply embedded in the local culture, with healings, exorcisms, and an emphasis on filial piety, but also provided a structure for new communities and addressed people's everyday problems.

At the beginning of the decade almost all Catholics in central Shanxi belonged to families or villages that descended from the first great wave of conversions in the eighteenth century; by the turn of the millennium there were large and growing communities of new believers. The total number of Catholics in Taiyuan diocese when the Communists took over in 1949 was 40,429, but less than half of these attended annual confession. With the disappearance of nominal Catholics and recent converts in the 1950s it seems likely that no more than 20,000 remained. Neither the diocese nor the government keeps reliable statistics, but priests estimate that by the end of the century this number had quadrupled to 80,000.[10] Some of this was due to population growth in the old Catholic villages, but much of it was due to new conversions. When religious practice was first revived in the 1980s the government made it clear that it would not tolerate evangelism. Most converts at that time were young people who joined the church in order to marry a Catholic. This grew more common as young Catholics increasingly worked or studied away from home, but even so the numbers were small.[11] However when people realized that some local governments were ignoring evangelism, the passionate devotion of the 1960s and the strong communities that were being rebuilt came together and laid the foundations for numerous conversions.

One of the best known local evangelists is Duan Runcheng of Cave Gully. Because of his poor eyesight, Duan Runcheng had never been much use in the fields. After he came out of prison he farmed for a while, but then left the family's fruit trees to his wife and found a job as church gatekeeper in Sandy Gully. There he met an educated convert who read to him a history of Christian missions. Duan was inspired. He left his job and started on life as an unpaid evangelist. Since then he has spent most of his time in the mountains to the west of Cave Gully. This was an area of evangelism in the early twentieth century, but the only church was destroyed during World War II and there had been no community religious practice since that time, though a few people did still identify as Catholics. Duan went from village to village staying in people's homes, telling his own story, healing, and preaching to small groups. He claims to have converted three thousand people and in 2005 a training meeting took place in Cave Gully for the leaders of forty new Catholic communities he had founded.[12]

Duan has published a conversion manual which brings together his life story and his teaching and illustrates how his successful evangelism works. The booklet begins with his own story. He tells of his debates with the workteam in the 1960s and his experiences in prison without rancor. Indeed in person he likes to add cheerful little details such as how he used the placard he had to wear reading "Running Dog of the Imperialists" to rest on when he was working in the fields. His evangelism is certainly not hostile to the authorities—indeed he is very proud that his son is a policeman—rather the point is that his willingness to suffer establishes the sincerity of his faith. Then he combines ethical teaching based on the Ten Commandments with demonstrations of the existence of God from first principles, linking the two together with the requirement to be filial to God the creator of all. As in the nineteenth-century conversion manuals the rest of Christian theology is understood to follow naturally from this filial love for the creator God. Obedience to the Ten Commandments and especially filial piety remains a key feature of Catholic practice in the area: the triple kowtow to the coffin, against which missionaries so long campaigned, is now a practice that Catholics describe as a distinctive feature of their funerals.[13]

In the preface to his booklet Duan writes that without God's grace "I would still be the despised and illiterate old blind Duan in the little mountain village of Cave Gully."[14] In his T-shirt and plastic sandals, speaking with a strong local accent, traveling by bus and on foot, he is indeed like any other elderly villager. Like his ancestors in Cave Gully in the early eighteenth century, he preaches a Catholicism that fits easily into the world of the mountain villagers, but now that is a world where the global reach of Christianity is also part of its appeal. Unlike the writers of conversion manuals in the late nineteenth century, Duan never considers the possible objection that Christianity is inappropriate for Chinese because it is a foreign religion. The only glancing reference to this issue is in his description of his debates with the workteam in the 1960s, where he explains that Jesus had fair hair and blue eyes because he was born in a climate that produced those looks, and that if he had been born in China he would have looked Chinese.

Instead of defending Christianity against accusations that it is foreign, Duan links it to science and technology. He suggests the question

"Why do 80 percent of scientists believe in the Lord of Heaven?" and explains that this is because science and faith correspond.[15] He talks about nuclear power, genetics, and climate change, arguing that scientific knowledge of each leads us to understand the important role of God in the universe. The modern world of science and technology is part of the daily lives of the people to whom he preaches, providing them with links beyond their remote towns and villages, links which symbolize status and desirable lifestyles. He tells the story of a young man who went to Taiyuan to buy two satellite dishes. On his way home, the truck he was traveling in overturned on a mountain road. It was wrecked, but none of the six men in it were hurt and the satellite dishes were not damaged either: afterwards they were attached to televisions and worked perfectly well. The mother of the young man wanted to thank God, so she donated several rooms of her house to use as a small church and a place for the priest or evangelist to stay. Evangelism, technology, and links to the outside world are all different aspects of this one event.[16]

Duan's booklet also includes lists of the many miracles and acts of divine providence that he has seen. This is quite different from the nineteenth-century conversion manuals, which were largely restricted to argument, but very similar to the actual practice of evangelism in earlier centuries. One story of Duan's concerns a shepherd who was coming home with his flocks when a demon followed him, so that afterwards he could not eat, drink, or speak. The local doctor said that there was nothing wrong, so the man's family took him to hospitals in the nearest town and then in Taiyuan city. This was extremely expensive for them, but useless since the doctors there too denied that the man was sick. Eventually Duan was called in. He prayed and sprinkled the man with holy water. The next day the man could put on his clothes and in two weeks he was cured. As in the past conversions take place within a world in which spirits and ghosts are widely accepted and evangelism often goes along with driving out demons.[17]

Prayer and divine intervention are combined with community building and practical help in the crises that afflict families in these poor mountain areas. One of Duan's miracle stories tells of how Catholics not only gathered to pray for a neighbor facing financial disaster when someone who owed him money absconded, but also managed to find the debtor and get back the money. Duan prays with couples who cannot conceive a child and for problem children. He gives advice for how to raise a child who will do well in school: don't smoke or drink from before conception, the family should be at peace, pray together and avoid arguments during the pregnancy, let the fetus listen to music in the third trimester, and breastfeed the child for the correct length of time. He mediates disputes with neighbors, as when the police invited him to settle a dispute in which a Catholic was accused of poisoning his neighbor's pig. All these events demonstrate God's providence and his direct intervention in the world, and Duan quotes Jesus as saying, "If you knock at the door I will open it for you" (Matthew 7:7).[18]

Duan Runcheng is famous as an effective evangelist, but his relations with the clergy and diocese are checkered. Priests who are highly educated, live in urban areas, and deal with a secular urban elite do not always feel comfortable with Duan's miracles and his preaching. Recently he published a new edition of his conversion manual that omits some of the elements they most object to including the instructions on how to perform an exorcism. Such exorcisms act as dramatic proofs of the power of the Lord over other spirits, and the first edition of Duan's manual gives specific instructions on how to do them. The evangelist should sprinkle holy water on the possessed person and the family, and call on Jesus who defeated the devil through his suffering on the cross to drive out the demon, then he should hold a crucifix over each of the five organs of the body (as described in Chinese medicine) and call on Satan to leave.[19] In the 1960s and 1970s, with the clergy absent, ordinary Catholics were recognized as receiving divine inspiration and took on themselves roles that the church normally limits to priests. That inspiration and authority empowered them to take responsibility for their faith, to suffer for it, and later to become powerful evangelists drawing large numbers of new converts into the church, but once the priests had returned it also created a situation where they were likely to come into conflict with the institutional church.

The 1990s also saw another trend that was pulling the church in a very different direction. This was the reconstruction of the institutional church through the ordination of a new generation of priests. These young priests launched a new wave of church building and introduced new rituals drawn from a changing global Catholic church. As the institutions they controlled expanded, some of them became very powerful in their villages. While they welcomed the church's ongoing growth, with their modern education and global links they were moving the church in a very different direction from that of the older evangelists.

Almost as soon as the clergy were released from prison they moved to regularize their situation with Rome: the new bishop asked the Vatican for recognition in 1980. The clergy also worked through the government to reclaim some of the property the diocese had lost since 1949. This included buildings on the site of the cathedral compound in Taiyuan but also eight buildings on three sites in Tianjin from which the diocese received rent until 2003 (when they disappeared in a major property redevelopment). Another urgent need was for more priests: the seminary was quickly reestablished with a grant from the government and running costs that ultimately came from the Vatican.[20] With legitimacy as part of the global church, a steady income from property rentals, and a group of active young priests, the leaders of the diocese in the 1990s found themselves in a very similar position to the missionaries of the 1840s as they struggled to take control after many years of lay leadership. As had happened then, they did so partly by rejecting some of the community's traditional practices and imposing new practices that they defined as belonging to the global church. Confusingly these global norms came in under the label of "localization" (bendihua) and were explained as restarting the process of acculturation that had been mistakenly ended by papal rulings against the Jesuits in the eighteenth century. Their effect however was to move Catholics away from historic practices, such as their long chanted prayers, and towards practices used by Catholics elsewhere in the world, such as the new vernacular mass.

The first class of young priests graduated in 1989 and one of them was assigned to Cave Gully. He came from the world of the old Catholic communities, indeed his family traced its history to an official in Taiyuan who had converted in the Ming. He had grown up listening to his grandmother telling him stories about the Jesuits, singing Wang Tingrong's song about his journey to Rome, and describing the circumstances of her own dramatic birth in the mountains when the women of the family were hiding from the Boxers. He had even been warned that Cave Gully would be a difficult parish because the villagers there were Judeans. But he had also been educated in the revived seminary, which was rapidly moving from the intensive Latin that the old priests taught (an early exercise required students to write an annual report on their activities in Latin for God), toward a quite new curriculum that brought in the major changes that had taken place in the worldwide Catholic church since the 1940s.[21]

The most dramatic of these changes were connected to Vatican II, a huge congress of bishops in the 1960s that moved the Catholic church away from its longstanding conservatism and adopted policies intended to open it to the modern world. From the point of view of the Shanxi priests the key changes were related to localization: the translation of the mass into the vernacular and a stress on the need for the church to adapt to local cultures. There was also a new emphasis on the figure of Jesus and a move away from reciting prayers and devotion to the saints. When these changes were implemented elsewhere in the world in the 1970s, some of them provoked resistance from both priests and congregations. Similar resistance might have been expected in Shanxi, where Catholics were not only deeply committed to devotional practices criticized by the reformers, but had also been heavily influenced by the conservative Catholicism of the Cold War. Moreover, by the time Vatican II reached Shanxi in the 1990s, the global church under Pope John Paul II was moving back to a more conservative position, and the independence from Rome forced on the diocese by the Chinese government meant that Rome had no means of enforcing its wishes. But Shanxi's Chinese priests had been aligned with the liberal wing of the church ever since the time of Wang Tingrong and his journey to Rome, and the emphasis on adaptation to local cultures was precisely what they had long demanded. So the young seminarians were taught the new policies, and teachers came in from Shanghai and Hong Kong to instruct them on the new Chinese mass. Then the old priests laid the groundwork for their congregations to accept the new practices by publishing key Vatican II documents, playing tapes of the Chinese mass alongside the Latin mass, and circulating a video recording of Pope John Paul II saying the new mass.[22]

The new rituals demanded significant changes from ordinary Catholics. Many churches, which had just been rebuilt, were now also redecorated to bring the altar forward into the church so that the priest could face the congregation as he said mass. The congregation, who had been accustomed to chant prayers in local dialect throughout the service, were now expected to listen to what the priest was saying in standard Chinese and respond. The chanted prayers had mostly been addressed to the Virgin Mary, but the focus of the new mass was Jesus and for several years the clergy insisted that this should be reflected in the decoration of the churches: in Cave Gully the image of Our Lady of Lourdes was moved from over the altar to the side of the church and replaced by a white plaster statue of Jesus on the cross. Naturally there were many people who were unhappy with these changes. For a while some devout Catholics even separated from the church to form a group called the Holy Mother Teaching, which worshipped the Virgin Mary and expected the world to end in the year 2000. Other people simply continued to pray the rosary and other prayers through the mass. Today there are still old women who stand up to bow towards the images on the church wall as they say the prayers for each of the Stations of the Cross, a practice that was entirely in harmony with early twentieth-century Catholic teaching but to which the younger priests often object. But the vast majority of Catholics today hardly remember church services before 1965 and for them the new rituals are simply their experience of the mass, though most congregations now chant the traditional prayers for an hour or more before the mass begins and resume their chanting after it ends.[23]

The arrival of the new young priests also sparked a second wave of church rebuilding and the idea of localization meant that some of these churches were constructed in explicitly Chinese styles. It was characteristic of the clergy's response to Vatican II that they chose to interpret localization to mean that Catholic practice should represent Chinese national culture. In Cave Gully the new priest decided to rebuild the shrine to Our Lady of the Seven Sorrows, but instead of restoring the little gothic chapel he replaced it with a spectacular Chinese-style building (figure 16).[24] Where the chapel once stood there is now a wide stone staircase leading to a monumental archway topped with the flying eaves of a blue glazed tile roof. The design was originally based on the Arc de Triomphe in Paris, but then the architect added a Chinese-style roof, so that the general effect is more similar to the mausoleum of Sun Yat-sen, modern China's "national father," built in Nanjing in the 1930s. Over the arch are inscribed the words "Gateway of Heaven," a title of the Virgin Mary from the litany in her honor. When the pilgrims pass through the archway they see before them the Altar of Heaven: the top of the hill has been flattened and across a wide open space, capable of holding thousands at festival times, stands a striking circular building with three ascending tiled roofs, modeled on the Altar of Heaven in Beijing, where the emperor made the annual sacrifices to Heaven. Beneath the roofs the sides have been left open to reveal a large stone altar that is used for open-air masses. Behind this, acting as a spectacular backdrop for the mass, is a great building with red columns, flying eaves, and golden tiles in the style of the palaces of the Forbidden City. On its roof are two curling golden dragons on either side of a cross, which are explained by the diocese as a symbol of China: as the dragons face the cross, so China will come to God.

FIGURE 16. Church of Our Lady of the Seven Sorrows. Photograph by the author.

The Cave Gully villagers had mixed feelings about this spectacular new complex. Like the institutions built by the missionaries, it was impressive and added to the village's reputation. Moreover they got it largely for free, being asked to contribute only their labor. On the other hand many did not feel comfortable with a style they associated mainly with temples. This was a period when the Communist government had begun to promote a nationalism based on images of China's ancient glory that rapidly became extremely popular especially with the young. However, what enabled Cave Gully's priest to build a Chinese-style church was the arrival of a priest from Taiwan, who had been born in West Willows but had been evacuated with his seminary class before the arrival of the Communists in 1949. He had come to control a very large amount of money brought to Taiwan by a missionary bishop from northwest China, which he was now using to pay for new church buildings on the condition they were built in a Chinese style, which was popular in Taiwan where it fitted not only with the Vatican II emphasis on localization, but also with the Nationalist government's promotion of ancient Chinese culture. Little of this was known to ordinary Catholics. A few even saw the Chinese style as a capitulation by the clergy to a nationalism that ultimately reinforces Communist rule. If asked why the shrine was built in this way, they say that was what the government wanted, though in fact religious affairs officials disapproved since the style seemed to dispute the idea that Catholicism was a foreign religion.

The dragons became the point at which many local Catholics felt that the Chinese symbolism had gone too far and it is said that some people refuse to enter the shrine because of them. Today dragons are an important symbol of an ancient and enduring China, but that symbolism has grown out of the same dragons who decorate the columns of the temple of the Holy Mother at Jinci and are worshipped at shrines in the mountains, deities which Catholics reject. People from Cold Springs Road remember a preacher justifying the dragons to them by saying that they represented the devil beaten down by the cross, referring them back to images of the Archangel Michael impaling a serpent on his spear. This was a highly traditional interpretation, but was certainly not the original intention of the design, nor was it very convincing as a description of the proud dragons curling along the church roof.

Despite the complaints, the shrine is extremely popular. It draws a constant stream of daily visitors and crowds in the tens of thousands for its two major feast days. Devotion to the Virgin Mary as a caring and sorrowing mother continues to appeal to many, and local Catholics come to make the Way of the Cross here as part of their regular devotions. A few of the most devout Cave Gully people do this every day and many of the villagers do so after mass on Sundays. Families, youth groups, and busloads of older women come regularly from nearby Catholic communities, especially on the 13th of each month. It is impossible to visit the shrine without meeting pilgrims. Some come to this powerful and sympathetic Mother of God in times of crisis when they have nowhere else to turn, like the distraught elderly peasant who came because his son had just lost the unimaginably large sum of 250,000 yuan. A caretaker is employed to listen to their stories and to deal with the many people who come from long distances as part of the growth of both pilgrimage and tourism in recent years. Bus tours park regularly in the village and the visitors range from Catholics from Hebei who impress the locals with their devotion when they kneel and weep on the steps up to the shrine, to tourists who know nothing of Catholicism and have to be prevented from sitting on the great stone altar.

The shrine is only the most visible of the new institutions in Cave Gully. The same young priest also established an orphanage and a nursery school, paid for the rebuilding of the village primary school and for a deep well, campaigned to get the monastery buildings back from the army, and built a new cemetery. Much of the work was financed by a German Catholic charity, though some of the new institutions succeeded well enough to become self-supporting. The orphanage, which took in infants but also provided special care for disabled children, fitted with local expectations of the church built up since the nineteenth century: children continue to be abandoned at the church. Supporting orphanages also continues to appeal outside China: American college students both fundraised and volunteered there. As in the past orphanages are immensely expensive and this one gradually wound down after the priest who founded it left the village. The nursery school was originally established by the village committee, but was refounded as a Montessori school with construction funding and an ongoing subsidy from the church and was then able to attract children from other villages and become a viable going concern. The new primary school is a large white-tiled block for five hundred pupils. The church also runs holiday catechism classes there, which provide safe, cheap childcare as well as religious education and extra tuition in basic schoolwork. There was a long dispute over the monastery buildings, since the army unit occupying them wanted compensation, and the case went as far as the National People's Political Consultative Congress in Beijing before the church was finally successful. Today the buildings are occupied by a small group of young nuns who run summer retreats for village girls from across the plain. Increasing aridity and over-extraction of underground water across the region mean that by the late 1980s the village's water supply was again under strain. The priest provided the money to dig another deep well in the hillside and set up electric pumps to provide water for the parish buildings. At certain times of year this well now provides water for the whole village. The cemetery, which is centered on another impressive Chinese-style building on the side of the hill, replaced a cemetery that had been destroyed during road construction and provides burial space for Catholics from Taiyuan. As such it is a moneymaking venture and the profits support the parish.[25]

All these projects were very much in line with Chinese government expectations of villages. The central government tells village committees to provide basic public services such as school buildings, a water supply, and roads, but it does not provide money for this, instead demanding that the villages fund these services themselves. In Cave Gully there was by this time a village Party committee, but it was undermined by the continuing ban on Catholics joining the Communist Party and the villagers' distrust of anyone who had been an activist in the 1960s. Instead the priest, who was energetic, highly educated, and in control of a significant stream of funding, acted as the village's link to the district government—indeed he was jokingly referred to by his parishioners as the village head. Religious affairs officials were angry when the county education department honored him for funding the new school building, but could do nothing because they were outranked by the officials in the education department. He also dealt with the provincial transport bureau in the negotiations over the route of a new north-south highway through the village, so that the road was built closer to the edge of the hill, preserving both the church buildings and the village's agricultural land.[26]

This position of the priest as the village's point of contact with local government is by no means universal. After this priest left, the priests who followed him had less interest in such matters and the village committee regained some of its power; he himself was unusual in his ability and willingness to undertake this kind of work. However, the situation is also characteristic of the entirely Catholic hill villages. In the plains villages where Catholics are the descendants of certain families, village government is simply the responsibility of the non-Catholics. This also happens in some Catholic hill villages where the village government is entirely undertaken by one or two families who settled in the community after 1949 and never converted. In some of these mixed communities village government is successful and relations are good: in one village, Catholics are said to vote as a block in village elections and the village government provides a Christmas tree and free electricity to the church. In a number of the entirely Catholic villages, however, village government is weak and priests are crucial pivots between the community and the state.[27]

The impact of the priests is especially obvious on the issue of birth control. Here the Chinese state's One Child Policy, which limits family size in the villages to one child or two if the first is a girl and makes heavy use of abortion for family planning, is in obvious conflict with the Vatican's opposition to contraception and abortion. Priests have differed in their response to this conflict. Some priests in the 1980s generated unusually high levels of compliance with the One Child Policy by emphasizing St. Paul's teaching that Christians should accept the existing authorities and obey the law. Not surprisingly in other Catholic villages many families do not abide by the policy, which is in any case widely unpopular. Families of two boys, or a girl and a boy, are common in rural Shanxi, but in the crowds at the great Catholic pilgrimages one also sees little girls with their sisters. In Cave Gully too there are girls with sisters, many families have three or four children, and a few have more. On the whole families simply pay the fines, but from time to time the local government cracks down. One story that circulates is of a priest's response when several women were dragged off to the county lockup for their failure to abide by the birth control laws. When one of the husbands agreed to his wife having an operation (presumably either an abortion or a tubal ligation) the priest refused to admit him to communion. The woman was released, but the others remained in the lockup and the parish priest made the pilgrimage up the mountainside to the shrine of Our Lady of the Seven Sorrows every day in his bare feet to pray for their release. The remaining women came home safely a few days later. The priest was thought to have worked a miracle, and his courage was much admired, because in this case, as in the building projects, local government tends to treat priests as responsible for their villages. The role of priests as pivots between state and community is an unintended effect of the refusal to allow religious believers to join the Communist Party, which makes it hard for some communities to generate an effective village government. It can put priests in difficult situations, but it also undoubtedly adds to their prestige.[28]

Since the seminary reopened, the Catholic villages of Shanxi have produced large numbers of vocations to the priesthood as well as many young women who have become nuns. One reason for this is the religious enthusiasm of the community, growing out of the years of persecution. At the same time the educational opportunities, the perception of a priest as a kind of official, and the relatively high incomes which priests receive for performing rituals are clearly an incentive to young men and their families. When the old priests were first released from prison in the early 1980s some had pensions and they received a small subsidy from the state. However, it soon became obvious that as in the past their main source of income would be payments for masses, especially those masses for the souls in purgatory said every year in November. The new generation of priests also benefited from the money and patronage opportunities that went along with the many building projects. Of course how well they did depended, as it always had, on the wealth of the parish. Nevertheless some priests have very comfortable lifestyles, owning apartments and having cars and drivers to take them to their parishes. Many of the priests, young and old, are very devout and some of them live very simply, but since a simple lifestyle is itself much admired it can in fact result in such priests having even larger and more effective patronage networks as they dispense money through charitable works. Priests provide housing for homeless families, pay children's school fees, and make generous contributions to construction projects. It is also widely believed that they give considerable sums of money to their families. Outside the church, people say that Catholic priests buy and sell religious offices and get rich, while Buddhist monks have relations with women.[29]

Many of the young men who enter the seminary come from villages where other opportunities are extremely limited. The seminary provides them with a good education and although seminarians give up the prospect of marriage and family life they can look forward to a steady job, opportunities for foreign travel, a comfortable lifestyle, semiofficial status, great respect in their communities, and the chance to help their families. Devout parents are often also eager, as they say, to give a son to the church, so it is not surprising that families strongly support sons who show an interest in entering the seminary. Older priests complain that the educational standards expected for young men entering the seminary have dropped since the 1980s, but Taiyuan diocese continues to recruit far more priests than it can employ: of 148 priests ordained between 1985 and 2006, more than half are now working outside the diocese. Many of them are in other parts of Shanxi but there are also priests working across China and abroad. In some cases the priests follow patterns of chain migration as with the seven priests from one mountain village now working in Jiangzhou, or the group who have gone to Jiangxi province in southeast China where one diocese offers full scholarship to Taiyuan seminarians who agree to take up jobs there after graduation. Working as a priest in the impoverished mountain areas of Jiangxi is probably not much easier than many other migrant labor opportunities available in China today, but there are also priests who have gone on to prestigious positions in Shanghai and Beijing.[30]

The power and status of priests and their structural relationship with the state brings advantages to their families but it can also be problematic for the community. As more young priests are ordained they are sent to live in mountain communities where Catholic practice has largely consisted of the traditional chanted prayers, with a priest coming once a year to say mass. The new priests have received an advanced education and many of their ideas are very different from those of the rural communities to whom they are sent. Nor are they always pleased to be there: like the missionaries of earlier generations they tend to prefer positions in the city or in the plains villages. Meanwhile the former leaders feel displaced. Old Duan Runcheng dismisses the young priests as only interested in playing on their computers, not evangelizing. In fact he has a little rhyme about their enthusiasm for building projects:

> They've built a church all red and green,
> But they're ever so cold and they don't go in.
> They've set up a church of reinforced concrete,
> But they've broken the church of the heart and soul.[31]

He complains that when the priests do evangelize they conduct Bible study classes, which frighten the poor and illiterate. Much of Duan's discontent clearly arises from the hierarchy's refusal to provide him with financial support, but the same complaints can be heard from Protestant evangelists in southeast China, which suggests that the underlying issue is the way in which the ordained clergy have regained power since the Cultural Revolution.[32]

The tensions between the older lay leaders and the new clerical hierarchy have obvious similarities with the disputes that took place when the new missionaries arrived after the Opium War. In today's context they interact with ongoing tensions over how much priests should cooperate with a government that is blocking the full integration of the Chinese Catholic church into the bureaucratic structures of the global Catholic church. This question affects the Vatican, the government of the People's Republic of China, and the Chinese church hierarchy, all of whom are still reacting to the structures and events of the early twentieth century, but it is rapidly becoming irrelevant in an increasingly globalized world.

In 2000, on the hundredth anniversary of the Boxer Uprising, Pope John Paul II canonized 120 martyrs who had met their deaths in China. A large group of the new saints had been killed in Shanxi during the Boxer Uprising. Shanxi won this honor because of the materials assembled by Barnaba Nanetti in the desperate interviews that eventually killed him, and his sister Clelia was one of the new saints. The others included Francesco Fogolla (who thought missionaries should be "wise as serpents"), his senior bishop, three other Italian missionaries, and six other missionary nuns. Far more important for the Shanxi Catholics was the fact that five Chinese seminarians and nine men employed by the mission, all of whom died in Taiyuan at the same time as the bishops, were also canonized. They were a miscellaneous group: one of the seminarians was only sixteen and the mission employees ranged from two older men who had trained in the seminary, remained celibate, and worked as administrative assistants, to a young peasant who was the deputy cook. Nevertheless, they were among the first Chinese ever to be recognized as saints by the church and most of them came from families and villages in the Taiyuan area. One of these new saints was the son of a Cave Gully woman and others were from Newtown, Winding Gully, West Willows, and the towns of Qixian and Pingyao. Given the freedom to act, villages and families would undoubtedly have celebrated the promotion of their own people to become saints of the Catholic church. However, the Chinese government took the canonizations as an insult to Chinese nationalism. Catholics in the Taiyuan area were not allowed to celebrate in 2000 and are still not supposed to commemorate these saints. Thus the Vatican praised localization and recognized Chinese people as saints, the Chinese government issued furious statements about imperialism, and the Chinese church hierarchy was inevitably divided.[33]

But all of this is going on in the twenty-first century, with satellite televisions, the Internet, tourism, migration, and many opportunities for Chinese to study abroad. The links these structures create do not go vertically through the clerical hierarchy but horizontally between friends, relatives, and believers on different continents. Today many devout Catholics in Shanxi hang on their walls certificates bearing the pope's congratulation for a long marriage, documents which are available for a small fee to visitors in Rome. Such a certificate is not the result of official links between the church in China and overseas, it merely means that someone visited Europe and thought that such a gift would please them. When Pope John Paul II died in 2005, the news coincided with a visit by the bishop of Taiyuan to Cave Gully. An account of the visit reported that people had been following the pope's sickness on satellite television from Hong Kong and had understood that John Paul had been the great leader predicted by Fatima. In Taiyuan city the cathedral church hung black drapes over the façade in mourning. The authorities found out and ordered that the drapes should be removed, but a woman volunteer working in the cathedral successfully argued that the drapes did not contravene government religious policy because they were a sign of filial piety.[34] Links to the Vatican bring the clergy prestige in a society where connections or travel overseas are important markers of social status,

FIGURE 17. The Holy Family and a prayer card of Jesus of the
Divine Mercy. Photograph by the author.

but the use of filial piety as a justification for mourning the pope suggests
that the official church is bound into global Catholicism at a much
deeper level.

Symbolic of the integration of ordinary people's everyday practice
across the world are a pair of devotional images from a Catholic
household (figure 17). The larger picture shows the Holy Family in a
sentimental nineteenth-century style. People explain that they like such
pictures because the saints look kind and gentle. In the corner of this
picture the owner has stuck a prayer card showing Jesus as Divine
Mercy. This image hung for a while on a huge banner over the main
altar of Taiyuan cathedral, with the words (in English) "Jesus I trust
you," reflecting the Vatican II emphasis on the figure of Jesus, but also
people's engagement in global Catholicism. For this is a Polish cult that
spread across the world as a result of the Polish pope John Paul II.

It shows Jesus as he will appear before the end of the world, as a figure of mercy (alleviating the fears of a terrifying apocalypse that were so powerful in the 1960s).[35] The cult promises blessings to all who look on the miraculous image. Like the seventeenth-century Chinese-style painting of the Virgin Mary (figure 3), this is an image that binds the viewer to a distant original and is in itself powerful.

These connections in Catholic practice across continents are part of the gradual development of the links that bind the Catholics of Cave Gully to the wider church, as travel becomes increasingly easy. Young people who enter the clergy now find themselves linked to global networks that allow them to travel far more broadly than ever before. Talking to local pilgrims at the shrine of Our Lady of the Seven Sorrows one can meet a local priest who has studied in Rome, a young girl whose aunt is a nun studying medicine in Australia, and other families who have used the links provided by clergy working overseas to send young men and women to study and work in the American Midwest or northern Italy. A descendant of the original Duan family, who grew up in Cave Gully then spent several years studying in the United States, has recently been sent out as a missionary to Brazil.

Catholicism is central to the identity of Cave Gully villagers today just as it has been since the eighteenth century and its importance is expressed in the community's rituals as well as their stories.[36] A photograph shows the parish church as the priest was entering to say mass for the Feast of the Assumption in 2009 (figure 18). The grey brick Romanesque church paid for by the missionaries in the 1930s is decorated with banners proclaiming a message that unites the global reach of Catholicism with Chinese national pride:

> Together all peoples celebrate your saving grace and win eternal life.
> We hold fast to our determination to love the Lord and love our
> country.

Earlier that afternoon there had been songs, speeches, and performances by the village children all dressed in matching Sunday school T-shirts and accompanied by amplified music that could be heard across the village. While these were still going on, older people began to enter the church. In the dim light inside, men and women knelt on opposite sides of the aisle as one of the older members of the congregation led them in reciting the rosary and other prayers in their traditional style com-

FIGURE 18. Mass for the feast of the Assumption in 2009. Photograph by the author.

pounded of Buddhist and Gregorian chants and Italian folk melodies. The children lined up to take their places in the front rows. Soon people were packed tight on the narrow benches, but still not everyone could fit. In the courtyard, men stood on the men's side of the building, while young mothers and grandmothers caring for small children gathered on the women's side.

As in the past almost everyone in the village is Catholic. Some young brides are not Catholic when they first arrive, but pressure to be part of the community is strong. A few years ago a conscientious parish priest could boast that there was only one non-Catholic resident in Cave Gully (a divorcee, who would have had to return to her first husband if she had converted). So people take part in festivals like this even if they are not particularly devout. Some of the men hanging around outside chat and young mothers struggle with bored toddlers. But there are also young men home from the seminary for the occasion and among the teenagers gathered at the side door is a heavily made-up girl who wants to be an actress but still goes to evening prayers every day. The one group of people pointedly absent are the few families who became disillusioned with the clergy and joined the so-called underground church.

They refuse to enter the parish church, so this year the underground and official churches had jointly arranged for them to make a pilgrimage to the Church of the Holy Mother for the occasion.

The prayers had been going on for more than two hours when the priest came out of his residence and the procession formed up. Two lines of middle-aged women in matching pink shirts took their places on either side of the church doorway to begin a lively percussion routine with cymbals and big red drums. In the past music groups were the exclusive preserve of men, but social norms have changed and now many parishes have female drum groups. The procession passing through the two lines of cymbal players into the church included a women's brass band in matching army-style shirts and a group of men playing traditional Chinese instruments. With the drums, cymbals, brass band, and Chinese band all playing different music while the congregation sang, the noise was tremendous and strongly reminiscent of the hot and noisy atmosphere so appreciated in Chinese folk religion. At the end of the procession came a large group of children who were going to receive their first communion, the boys wearing red sashes and the girls white veils held on with crowns of fabric roses. Finally there was the priest in his festival vestments. Like most priests, he is a local man, but as he enters the church the chanted prayers in the local dialect end. He leads the mass in standard Chinese and according to modernized rituals now used by the Catholic church across the world.

Predictions for the future of the Catholic church in China tend to be heavily influenced by the ideologies of those who make them. On the one hand are those who look at the many conversions that have taken place since the 1980s and see the inexorable rise of Christianity in China. This is a view shared by many Protestant evangelicals who predict that within a few decades China will become a Christian nation. It is also feared by those Chinese Communist officials who are convinced that it is essential to make strenuous efforts to prevent the expansion of Christianity. On the other hand are those who believe that religion inevitably declines as societies modernize and expect Catholics in China to leave their religion as urbanization increases and old communities fall apart. This view is shared in principle by Chinese officials and with great sincerity by many Western academics. The story of Cave Gully suggests that both of these views are far too sweeping. Catholicism has long been central to the villagers' identity and sense of community. It is surely likely to remain so. The large numbers of conversions to Catholicism that took place in Shanxi in the 1990s and 2000s, on the other hand, were the result of a particular combination of circumstances. As a global religion Christianity naturally appealed at a time of opening up to the outside world, the rise of global linkages, and popular aspirations for modern Westernized lifestyles. But the successful evangelism was also built on the passion generated in Catholic communities by the political oppression that they had suffered in the 1960s and 1970s. This created the commitment that funded and supported the evangelists. It also empowered men and women whose sufferings at that time now make them exceptionally effective preachers. Neither of these two phenomena is likely to continue for many more years. The first generation of lay evangelists are growing old, while the revival of the institutional church is imposing increasing control over them. Like the missionaries who took over in the mid-nineteenth century after an age of expansion, a new generation of clergy looks likely to work towards consolidation and ever closer links with the global church.

Conclusion

In Shanxi today not only do Catholic villagers tell stories of their history, but their teenage children know many of these stories too and gather round to listen, asking questions and evidently fascinated, especially when their elders talk of the events of 1965. Church newsletters publish regular columns on local church history, mostly about the schools, clinics, and other institutions established by the missionaries in the early twentieth century. An astonishingly high proportion of priests are enthusiastic amateur historians and they have accumulated an impressive collection of publications and archives. Much of this book is the result of this collective passion for history, which prompted Shanxi Catholics not only to tell me long and sometimes deeply moving stories, but also to get their friends to hunt out documents in obscure archives in Rome, even to go out to other villages, conduct interviews, and write up the results. Why does their history matter so much to them? Clearly one reason is that the version of their history endorsed by the Chinese state is at once so important in their lives and so deeply in conflict with their own understanding of their past.

The current version of this history is shaped by the Chinese Communist Party, but it has its origins in the perceptions of Qing dynasty officials in the 1860s, who thought that the Catholic villages they saw around them were made up of people converted by the missionaries who had entered China since the Opium War. The missionaries themselves encouraged this idea, and the communal violence of the 1900 Boxer

Uprising made it part of popular consciousness. Then in the early twentieth century it was absorbed into the story of a great national struggle against foreign imperialism, which was later inherited by the Chinese Communist Party. In this story of heroic struggle, Christians found themselves placed on the side of the villains. They were, as the placard Duan Runcheng wore around his neck in Cave Gully in the 1960s said, "running dogs of the imperialists." Today, Catholics are no longer under pressure to renounce their religion (though they still cannot join the Chinese Communist Party without doing so), but this version of history remains pervasive in textbooks and newspapers, on the television, and in the minds of those they meet whenever they go beyond the village.

The Shanxi Catholics' own version of their history is very different. It includes ancestors who converted in the early Qing, Wang Tingrong who went to Rome to protest against missionary domination of the Chinese church, massacres of whole communities by the Boxers, and the many stories of the heroic courage and sometimes the miraculous powers of those who suffered in the campaigns of the 1960s. It is told in opposition to the particular highly romantic form of nationalism widely promoted in school textbooks and television dramas, but it should also make us rethink our own understanding of the history of Christianity in China, which is based on very much the same ideas put forward by late nineteenth-century officials and missionaries. It was the Boxer Uprising as described in missionary reports that prompted Léon Joly's claim that Christianity had failed in China because it was not seen as Chinese. From his arguments has grown a scholarly literature structured around the question of whether or not it is possible to be both Chinese and Christian. This question lies behind many discussions of acculturation, with its suggestion that Christianity can only be successful and authentic as it gradually adapts to local culture. This book has argued, against this framework, that we should instead understand the history of Christianity in China as one in which Christians have over the centuries come to relate increasingly closely to the church as a global institution. The argument has been made by looking at a single Catholic village and its surrounding community over three hundred years. It has been firmly based in the sources but specific to Catholicism and to a small part of one inland northern province. This conclusion turns to consider the implications of this method for a broader understanding of the history of Christianity in China. What might we learn if we were to study other parts of China, and Protestants as well as Catholics, in this way?

If China and the West are not always different, similarities may not be the result of the influence of one culture on another. Christianity, Buddhism, Daoism, and Chinese folk religion are all broad and deep traditions. Over the centuries each has encompassed a wide variety of ideas and practices. It is not surprising that there should be some overlap. Litanies, fasting, paying clergy to perform rituals for the souls of one's ancestors, processions with sacred images, community prayers for rain, and visions and trance states were all part of both Italian Catholicism and Shanxi folk religion. Some nineteenth-century Protestant missionaries saw these similarities and claimed that the Catholics made conversions because of them.[1] Since Protestants at that time generally defined their religious identity against Catholicism this was partly simply a way of saying that Catholics were heathens, but similarities with folk religion also played a strong role in the practices of Protestant converts. The ideas of sin and retribution, struggles against evil forces, supernatural visions and voices, and the hope of immortality were central to early Protestant practice. More recently Chen-yang Kao has described the Pentecostal Protestantism spreading in southeast China since the 1970s as "a form of Christian religious culture carrying minimal distinct beliefs and practices" that enables Christians to denounce other gods as demons and conquer them.[2]

Looking over the long term we see that these similarities between Christianity and Chinese religious practices do not belong to any particular period of time, but are most striking in newly converted groups. Many observers have seen them as evidence of inadequate conversion and beliefs that are not fully Christian, but litanies, fasting, and processions were authentic parts of nineteenth-century Italian Catholicism. As Melissa Inouye has argued, healings, exorcisms, and struggles against demonic forces which are features of much contemporary Chinese Protestantism are also common to contemporary Protestant groups across the world that emphasize literal interpretation of the Bible.[3] Instead of explaining these similarities as signs of inadequate conversion or the result of Christianity gradually adapting to Chinese forms, we should see them as a starting point. Group prayer, fasting, the list of Ten Commandments, and reverence to the Holy Mother of God, all of which are very close to Chinese religious practice, were among the first elements of Catholic Christianity to reach Shanxi. They are still important in Shanxi Catholic practice today, but over the centuries ever increasing contacts with the global church have expanded the range of Catholic practices and ideas. When Catholics in the twentieth century chose to honor Our Lady of Fatima and the Immaculate Heart of Mary, or found help in the idea that they were souls chosen by God to suffer to atone for the sins of others, they were participants in a world of Catholic practice that goes far beyond the elements of the religion similar to Chinese culture.

Reconsidering the theory of acculturation means that we must also reconsider the role of missionaries. Acculturation assumes that missionaries bring in Christianity in its original (foreign) form and then it gradually adapts to the local culture. The role of missionaries is quite clear: they introduce Christianity and their characteristic activity is preaching. We assume that missionaries converted people because that was what they set out to do and when they or their colleagues succeeded they often wrote home describing their achievements. But conversion was not easy and the missionaries were hampered by language and cultural differences as well as by their initial lack of personal networks.

In central Shanxi the main period of Catholic conversion before the 1980s was the early eighteenth century, when there were hardly any missionaries. This fits with Liam Brockey's recent argument that studies of the Jesuit mission have placed too much emphasis on the Jesuit transmission of European scientific and technical knowledge, and that we need to recognize that the primary goal of the mission was evangelism and Christian instruction.[4] However, in this area the Jesuits' contribution was not so much their direct evangelism, but rather their translation of the religion into forms that resonated with Confucianism, and their status at court, which gave their teachings an aura of legitimacy. Because missionaries seldom visited most Catholic communities, the new followers of the Lord of Heaven shaped their own practices in forms that were familiar and acceptable to them, chanting prayers and emphasizing the Ten Commandments and the virtue of filial piety. Since then the majority of Catholics have always inherited their faith rather than converting as adults.

Is this a pattern specific to this part of central Shanxi or might it be more widespread? This study has traced the history of contemporary Catholic villages and combined this with the church's statistical records. Looking at anecdotal missionary reports of conversions and Qing official documents would have produced a much more conventional narrative in which Christianity appears to grow significantly in the late nineteenth century, but clearly both the missionaries and the officials had a personal interest in making these claims. Kang Zhijie's study of a group of Hubei Catholic villages suggests a similar pattern, with the key period of growth being in the early Qing.[5] It seems likely from the sources used in this book that long-term studies of Catholic conversion in Shaanxi, Hebei, and Gansu would produce similar results. The existence of large numbers of Catholic communities dating from the eighteenth century or earlier is also suggested by studies of Catholicism in Sichuan and Fujian.[6] The first Protestant missionaries arrived in China in the nineteenth century and many of them were committed to adult baptism and the idea of conversion as an essential part of the experience of all believers, so their statistics do not distinguish members of Christian families from adult converts. Nevertheless, it is clear that they were slow to build up large congregations. A statistical survey conducted by a Protestant missionary in 1905 concluded that there were just over one million Christians in all of China, the vast majority of whom (84 percent) were Catholics.[7] The great growth in Protestantism was to come later, with Chinese-led denominations in the 1920s and again in the 1980s. At the end of the nineteenth century missionaries were a major political issue in China, but they were not winning large numbers of converts.

Instead of evangelism, which was difficult and often unrewarding for them, most missionaries came to concentrate on institution building and this had important long-term effects. Catholic missionaries in Shanxi ran dioceses, taught in seminaries, and acted as parish priests to the old Catholic villages. After 1900 they did put resources into evangelism and made large numbers of converts, but many of these converts left the church in the 1950s. Early Protestant missionaries who were attempting to build communities from the ground were more likely to evangelize, but by 1911 more than half the Protestant missionaries in China were engaged in education, medicine, or some kind of social work.[8] Schools, hospitals, orphanages, opium refuges, and the diocesan offices allowed missionaries to work in an environment that they controlled and alongside colleagues from their own culture. The type of institutions Catholic and Protestant missionaries chose to establish varied with their different theological emphases and the different cultures of their home countries. Catholics mainly established orphanages and seminaries. They built orphanages because of their belief in infant baptism, but also because they were familiar with the orphanages of southern Europe.[9] Once in existence these orphanages tended to attract the poor, who were most often the ones forced to abandon their children. Children who grew up in the orphanage usually married Catholics and the church required parents who wanted to get their children back to convert, so these institutions drew the poor into the community.

Seminaries, which trained boys for the priesthood, provided important routes to status and power within the Catholic community, but had little appeal to outsiders because of the highly specialized nature of the training. Protestant missionaries, inspired by their belief in Bible reading and influenced by the fact that many of them were not ordained clergy, established schools and clinics. Arriving in the nineteenth century, many of the Protestants settled in China's growing coastal cities where there were good opportunities for those with a Western-style education or training, so these institutions provided important routes to social mobility for converts. Ryan Dunch has argued that while the first generation of Protestant converts in Fujian were often uneducated villagers, their children and grandchildren moved rapidly on to professional jobs in the cities.[10] Protestant missionaries not only came to run some of China's most prestigious hospitals and universities, they also found themselves working full time at such tasks as standardizing the terminology in Chinese chemistry textbooks.[11] These activities cast an aura of Westernization and modernity over the whole Protestant enterprise. They also confirmed the core membership of the Protestant mission churches as urban and middle class, even as the Catholic institutions strengthened the rural nature of the communities they had inherited from the early Qing.

Institutions gave the missionaries power and authority that was dependent on the unequal relationship between China and the major Western powers. This is not to say that the missionary enterprise was inherently imperialist, but rather that the behavior of missionaries was affected by the international context of their time. The free flow of money from Europe that allowed Catholic missionaries in Shanxi to go against their former Chinese patrons was a direct result of the Opium War. Later the foreign powers' extortion of huge reparations for the diocese as part of the Boxer Indemnity made the Catholic missionaries in Shanxi immensely powerful in local society. But this was not a uniform process. Italians, whose country only emerged from division between the European great powers in 1870, tended to be highly defensive about their status. Similar aggressive attitudes by German Catholic missionaries in Shandong have long been known to have played an important role in prompting the murder or suicide of a Chinese official that was one of the flashpoints of the Boxer Uprising.[12] On the other hand most of the Protestant missionaries came either from Britain, which was the dominant imperial power of the time, or America, where their supporters were wealthy enough to provide them with large resources. No Chinese official was likely to ask British missionaries if their country was the same as France, as happened to Francesco Fogolla in Shanxi, and the Americans could rely on their country's wealth to fund impressive institutions that confirmed their own status and skills. With national wealth and military power behind them and an emphasis on their own role as leaders of modernization, Protestant missionaries won respect through their institutions and were probably less likely to express their power directly through violence. The archives of the American Protestant mission in early twentieth-century Shanxi are a mass of minutes of routine meetings and reports of school and hospital activity; it is very hard to imagine any of the participants beating their parishioners in fits of rage.[13]

Nevertheless over the long term, Chinese resistance to missionary power developed in both Catholic and Protestant churches. Chinese Catholic priests demanded promotions and criticized the higher pay of European priests as early as the eighteenth century, but not with great vigor, since the Qing ban on Christianity made it extremely dangerous to be bishop and enabled Chinese Christians to get rid of any Europeans who were unacceptable to them. When the Chinese Catholics lost control of the missionaries sent to them after the Opium War, resistance was immediate and widespread. Wang Tingrong's appeal to Rome was admired well beyond Shanxi, to the consternation of the missionary bishops. Problems in the Protestant churches developed later simply because they did not recruit significant numbers of Chinese clergy until the early twentieth century. Once that happened the disputes over foreign missionary control were similar to those in the Catholic church. Dunch describes tensions over promotion for Chinese pastors in the various Protestant missionary groups in Fujian and the dramatic expansion of the Methodist church, which did promote Chinese clergy.[14] This period also saw the foundation and large-scale growth of independent Chinese denominations of the sort that inspired the Chinese Catholic priests in Taiyuan in 1912. Many of these were strongly influenced by the new Pentecostal movement, which spread from California in the 1900s. Its literal interpretation of the Bible and emphasis on divine inspiration by the Holy Spirit gave new power to ordinary believers; in China, Pentecostal ideas empowered Chinese preachers at the expense of the missionaries. The Chinese-run churches that were formed in this period soon came to be the major source of Protestant church growth both in the early twentieth century and after 1980.[15]

Unequal power relations between China and the West shaped the experiences of Chinese Christians in the nineteenth and early twentieth century, but the effects were complex. The different stories of Cave Gully and Nine Wells villages show how missionary institutions interacted with existing local power structures to the advantage of some and the disadvantage of others. In this case previously wealthy plains villages with a history of long-distance trade lost out in favor of poor hill villages where the missionaries felt more confident of their power. The Cave Gully villagers benefited from missionary investment in their community, which provided job opportunities, increased the size of the community, and gave it an entirely new status and prestige. On the other hand they also struggled with the church over scarce resources and resented the Italian missionaries' support for the Japanese occupation during World War II. The complexity of the relations between Protestant missionaries and Chinese Christians has not been well studied, but continued missionary control of funding in hospitals and other institutions with highly educated Chinese staff seems likely to have provoked very similar tensions. These tensions were then reflected in the divided response in the 1950s to the Communist government's decision to set up national Protestant and Catholic churches that would be Chinese managed and funded. In the Protestant case members of former mission churches proved more willing to enter the new church than members of the independent Chinese churches, while in Shanxi dioceses run by missionaries entered more willingly than those that had been established with Chinese bishops.[16]

Since the 1980s there has been spectacular growth in the number of Chinese Christians, especially Pentecostally influenced Protestant congregations. One of the most common explanations for this is that Christianity has finally adapted to Chinese culture: people are converting to Christianity because it has become culturally Chinese. Without doubt the forms of Christianity to which there has been greatest conversion have much in common with Chinese folk religion, but as we have seen this was the case with conversions in earlier eras as well. The other common explanation is a variation of the idea that people convert to fulfill their needs, in this case for a moral system in the vacuum created by the collapse of communism and the new anxieties of life under a free market.[17] Christian conversion does indeed provide today, as it did in the eighteenth century, a means of creating new supportive communities. But the story of Cave Gully also suggests the crucial role of Maoist campaigns—in this case the Socialist Education Movement and the Cultural Revolution, elsewhere probably also the Great Leap Forward—in creating the context for later evangelism. During these campaigns, heavy government pressure to break the community at a time when the clergy had been imprisoned encouraged ordinary Christians to take on leadership roles. In the absence of clerical control they shaped the church that emerged in the 1980s according to their own needs and expectations, which were well suited to evangelism. Chen-yang Kao has shown a very similar process taking place among Protestants in Fujian, where relatively uneducated Christians preached a form of Christianity with a strong emphasis on prayer and direct divine intervention. Then, as the clerical hierarchy revived, these lay leaders were gradually displaced by a more structured and bureaucratic church.[18] This suggests that although the religious explosion of the 1980s and 1990s was spectacular, it is now beginning to come into conflict with the powerful institutional church that it created.

Taking the whole history of Christianity in China together we can see that ever since the seventeenth century when the first missionaries arrived, there has been a constant tension for Chinese Christians between adapting to Chinese culture and seeking authenticity as members of transnational institutions. Both Chinese culture and global Christianity are diverse and constantly changing. For Shanxi Catholics, ancestral rituals and contributions to temple cults, which have at different times in the past been important markers of identity through which they were excluded from the surrounding society, are seldom important issues today. The stigma that applied to membership in a foreign religion in the early twentieth century has been transformed by the widespread enthusiasm for all things foreign in recent years. At the same time many aspects of global Christianity have changed: Catholics in Europe today take part in a very different set of practices and rituals than they did in the nineteenth century. Being part of a world religion inherently involves a desire to share the ideas and practices of people elsewhere in the world. This does not mean that there is some kind of uniform global Catholicism, but rather that Catholics share in a vast and intensely debated repertoire of ideas and practices. Shanxi Catholics who study in the Philippines, Asia's largest Catholic country, come back eager to introduce everything from new music to left-leaning theologies. This search for authentic membership in a global community is especially strong in the Catholic church, whose members aspire to be part of a single global institution, but it also exists for the official Chinese Protestant church as it seeks international recognition and sends clergy to study abroad. It is weakest in the independent Chinese Protestant groups who claim authenticity in the Pentecostal tradition through Biblical adherence and divine inspiration. In some of these traditions, Chinese believers can see themselves as the center of global salvation history. In the nineteenth-century Taiping Heavenly Kingdom and the group today known as Eastern Lightning, believers draw on Christian scripture and tradition but see salvation as emerging from a Chinese founder.[19] Looking over the long term, the tension between adaptation and the desire to be part of a global religion has been constant. There is no simple progress towards adaptation, nor should we see moments when adaptation is strongest as more authentic forms of Chinese Christianity.

What has changed is not these two desires, which are always present, but rather the political and technological context of world history. When the Jesuit missionaries first arrived in China it was an extraordinarily difficult journey and they could largely control the flow of information between their missions in China and the European church. Over time increasing travel and communications strengthened the pull towards involvement in the bureaucratic structures, practices, ideas, and debates circulating in the rest of the world. This continued even though there was much resistance to the power of foreign missionaries. As the Catholic church has made clear since 1949, resenting missionary control did not mean that Christians wanted to break away from the global church. Chinese-style images of Jesus and the saints were banned in the nineteenth century, but since the 1980s, when the Vatican's support for acculturation has meant that such images are quite acceptable to the clergy, Catholics have continued to buy and put up in their homes very European-looking images.

The opposing pressures for adaptation and global authenticity constantly reshape local practice. In the massive Chinese-style church of Our Lady of the Seven Sorrows on the mountain behind Cave Gully, a group of Catholics who have just completed the Stations of the Cross kneel to chant their prayers in the style used since the seventeenth century. Then someone decides to switch to singing hymns, a practice quite new to the Shanxi Catholic church. A few photocopied hymnals are found at the back of the building and handed out, though in fact most of those present sing from memory. They sing the hymns one after another as they would chant the prayers, and among those they sing is one with the refrain, "In China at five o'clock in the morning the sound of prayers is heard." The composer of this hymn was a young Protestant peasant woman with limited education and no musical training who began composing in the 1990s. The Catholics singing it know her story, not only because her hymns are very popular but because her compositions are believed to come from divine inspiration. The simple repetitive structure clearly draws from modern Western evangelical worship songs, but the melody is in the style of Chinese folk music and the words are highly nationalistic. The singers pray for peace and blessings on China with its "ten thousand rivers and thousand mountains."[20] The devotion to Our Lady of the Seven Sorrows, the modern Chinese-style architecture, the group-chanted prayers, and the modern hymn are all familiar and comfortable to those present. As the stories the villagers tell give the layers of their history, so their religious practice is made of those same layers. Both stories and religious practice belong in the villagers' present-day lives, but in them the long history of their community is revealed.

Notes

ABBREVIATIONS

ACGOFM   Archivio della Curia Generalizia dell'Ordine dei Frati Minori (Rome)

AOPF   Archives de l'Oeuvre de la Propagation de la Foi, Oeuvres Pontificales Missionnaires Centre de Lyon

APF   Archivio Storico della Congregazione per l'Evangelizzazione dei Popoli o "de Propaganda Fide" (Rome)

     SC Cina   Scritture riferite nei congressi, Cina e regni adiacenti, 1800–83

     SC Indie   Scritture riferite nei congressi, Indie orientali e Cina, 1744–99

     SOCP   Scritture Originali della Congregazione Particolare Indie Orientali e Cina, 1721–1856

OFM Bologna   Missione di Yütze (Shan-si, Cina), Provincia di Cristo Re Archivio Provinciale, Frati Minori dell'Emilia Romagna (Bologna)

POSI   Pontificium Opus a Sancta Infantia (Rome)

SBD   Shanxi beijiaoqu dang'an 山西北教區檔案 [Archives of the diocese of Northern Shanxi] (Taiyuan)

SD   Shanxi daxue Zhongguo shehuishi yanjiu zhongxin 山西大學中國社會史研究中心 [Shanxi University Chinese Social History Research Institute], X dadui danweihui tianzhujiao zonghe ziliao he geren dang'an 大隊單位會天主教宗合資料和個人檔案 [X brigade unit committee Catholic general materials and personnel files] (Taiyuan)

INTRODUCTION

1. Joannes Kuo, 1781, APF SOCP 63:754; Leo Cen et al., 22 Oct. 1861, APF SC Cina 19:548; Camillus Ciao, 1 Aug. 1804, APF SOCP 70:313; Josephus Van, 2 June 1873, APF SC Cina 26:89–96; Josephus Van, 9 June 1873, APF SC Cina 25:309–12; Josephus Van, 1 Sept. 1873, APF SC Cina 26:98–104; Josephus Van, 5 Nov. 1873, APF SC Cina 26:106–10.

2. There have been fashions in history writing for both studies of major themes over lengthy periods and for microhistories of incidents and individuals, but these are seldom combined. Some recent exceptions are William T. Rowe, *Crimson Rain: Seven Centuries of Violence in a Chinese County* (Stanford: Stanford University Press, 2007), Joseph W. Esherick, *Ancestral Leaves: A Family Journey through Chinese History* (Berkeley: University of California Press, 2010).

3. Michael Werner and Bénédicte Zimmerman, "Beyond Comparison: Histoire Croisée and the Challenge of Reflexivity," *History and Theory* 45, no. 1 (2006), 30–50.

4. Léon Joly, *Le Christianisme et l'Extrême Orient* (Paris: P. Lethielleux, 1907) and *Le problème des missions: Tribulations d'un vieux chanoine* (Paris: P. Lethielleux, 1908); Jacques Leclercq, *Thunder in the Distance: The Life of Père Lebbe* (New York: Sheed & Ward, 1958), 132.

5. These questions were particularly pertinent for an earlier generation of scholars who looked at the history of Christianity in China in the context of the hostility of the People's Republic of China to the West in the 1960s and 1970s. Paul A. Cohen, *China and Christianity: The Missionary Movement and the Growth of Chinese Anti-Foreignism 1860–1870* (Cambridge: Harvard University Press, 1963), viii–ix; Jacques Gernet, *China and the Christian Impact: A Conflict of Cultures,* trans. Janet Lloyd (Cambridge: Cambridge University Press, 1985; 1st edition, 1982).

6. Robert Antony Orsi, *The Madonna of 115th Street: Faith and Community in Italian Harlem, 1880–1950* (New Haven: Yale University Press, 2002).

7. In the study of Chinese religion this approach began with the work of Erik Zürcher, who wrote on acculturation in both Buddhism and Christianity: Erik Zürcher, *The Buddhist Conquest of China: The Spread and Adaptation of Buddhism in Early Medieval China* (Leiden: E. J. Brill, 1959); Erik Zürcher, "Un 'contrat communal' chrétien de la fin des Ming: Le *Livre d'Admonition* de Han Lin (1641)" in *L'Europe en Chine: Interactions scientifiques, religieuses et culturelles du XVIIᵉ et XVIIIᵉ siècles,* eds. Catherine Jami and Hubert Delahaye (Paris: Collège de France, Institut des hautes études chinoises, 1993), 3–22. Recent scholarship has expanded from Zürcher's focus on texts to include studies of Christian practices and local society: Nicolas Standaert, *The Interweaving of Rituals: Funerals in the Cultural Exchange between China and Europe* (Seattle: University of Washington Press, 2008); Eugenio Menegon, *Ancestors, Virgins, and Friars: Christianity as a Local Religion in Late Imperial China* (Cambridge: Harvard University Asia Center Press, 2009); Zhang Xianqing, *Guanfu, zongzu yu tianzhujiao—17-19 shiji Fuan xiangcun jiaohui de lishi shushi* [State, lineage and Catholicism: A narrative of the history of the church in 17th to 19th century rural Fuan] (Beijing: Zhonghua shuju, 2009). There have also been works that see acculturation as taking place in the nineteenth

and twentieth centuries: Nicole Constable, *Christian Souls and Chinese Spirits: A Hakka Community in Hong Kong* (Berkeley: University of California Press, 1994); Xi Lian, *Redeemed by Fire: The Rise of Popular Christianity in Modern China* (New Haven: Yale University Press, 2010). Inevitably the process of acculturation involves elements of compatibility, but these are usually discussed in the context of the acculturation or localization of Christian practices and belief. A notable execption is Daniel H. Bays, "Christianity and the Chinese Sectarian Tradition," *Ch'ing shih wen-t'i* 4, no 7 (1982), 33–55. Gernet, *China and the Christian Impact*, describes many fascinating similarities but finds them to be superficial.

8. Ian Linden, *Global Catholicism: Diversity and Change since Vatican II* (New York: Columbia University Press, 2009), 239–40.

9. For these events see Nicolas Standaert, ed., *Handbook of Christianity in China*, vol. 1, *635–1800* (Leiden: Brill, 2001), 680–88. In recent years a number of scholars have extended the period of acculturation to include the suppression and the early nineteenth century with an emphasis on similarities with Chinese sectarian religions. See Menegon, *Ancestors, Virgins, and Friars*; Xiaojuan Huang, "Christian Communities and Alternative Devotions in China, 1780–1860" (Phd diss., Princeton University, 2006).

10. For China see Nicolas Standaert, *Yang Tingyun, Confucian and Christian in Late Ming China* (Leiden: E.J. Brill, 1988); Ryan Dunch, *Fuzhou Protestants and the Making of Modern China* (New Haven: Yale University Press, 2001).

11. Joseph Esherick, *The Origins of the Boxer Uprising* (Berkeley: University of California Press, 1987); Paul A. Cohen, *History in Three Keys: The Boxers as Event, Experience and Myth* (New York: Columbia University Press, 1997).

12. Ryan Dunch, "Beyond Cultural Imperialism: Cultural Theory, Christian Missions, and Global Modernity," *History and Theory* 41, no. 3 (2002), 301–25; Jeffrey Cox, *Imperial Fault Lines: Christianity and Colonial Power in India, 1818–1940* (Stanford: Stanford University Press, 2002), 7–19.

13. Joseph Tse-Hei Lee, "Christianity in Contemporary China: An Update," *Journal of Church and State* 49, no. 2 (2007), 277–304; Robert Weller and Sun Yanfei, "The Dynamics of Religious Growth and Change in Contemporary China" in *China Today, China Tomorrow: Domestic Politics, Economy and Society*, ed. Joseph Fewsmith (Lanham: Rowman & Littlefield, 2010); Richard Madsen, *China's Catholics: Tragedy and Hope in an Emerging Civil Society* (Berkeley: University of California Press, 1998); Fenggang Yang, "Lost in the Market, Saved at McDonald's: Conversion to Christianity in Urban China," *Journal for the Scientific Study of Religion* 44, no. 4 (2005), 423–41.

14. Cf. Chen-yang Kao, "The Cultural Revolution and the Post-Missionary Transformation of Protestantism in China" (PhD diss., University of Lancaster, 2009).

15. Jin Ze and Qiu Yonghui, eds., *Zhongguo zongjiao baogao, 2010* [Annual report on China's religions, 2010] (Beijing: Shehui kexue chubanshe, 2010), 98, 191. Figures for numbers of believers are always problematic, and this one is probably too low since it relied on self-reporting in a context where the state is known to be hostile to religion in general and underground religious groups in

particular. However, the official figures for China's total population are also probably too low, so the percentage rate remains a plausible guess though probably at the low end of the spectrum.

16. Pierre Nora, "Between Memory and History: Les lieux de mémoire," *Representations* 26 (1989), 7–24. For the impossibility of what experts in folklore call intertextual transparancy see Charles L. Briggs, "Metadiscursive Practices and Scholarly Authority in Folkloristics," *Journal of American Folklore* 106, no. 422 (1993), 387–434. For another study of Chinese Catholic memories see Wu Fei, *Maimang shang de shengyan—yige xiangcun tianzhujiao qunti zhong de xinyang he shenghuo* [Sacred word above the awn of wheat: Faith and life in a rural Catholic community] (Hong Kong: Daofeng shushe, 2001).

17. Between 2004 and 2011, I conducted approximately ninety interviews in Cave Gully and also in neighboring villages, Taiyuan, Beijing, Rome, and Boston. Some interviews were conducted by telephone and a local person who heard of the questions I was asking kindly conducted several interviews on my behalf. Interviewees included Catholic and non-Catholic villagers, officials, priests, urbanites, and people who have left the area to work elsewhere in China or overseas. Some were illiterate, but others were highly educated and have commented on the manuscript. Because of the political sensitivity of the subject I have cited written sources where possible and have indicated the use of interview material simply with the word "interviews." However, many of my interviewees were in their eighties and some have since died. For these I have given full citations.

CHAPTER 1

1. Guo Chongxi, "Taiyuan tianzhujiao zhuyao tangkou jianjie" [A brief introduction to the main Catholic parishes of Taiyuan], *Taiyuan wenshi ziliao* 15 (1991), 148–64; interviews, including Wu Mingming, Cave Gully, 8 Sept, 2005.

2. The absence of missionaries in the stories predates the Chinese Communist Party. See Barnaba Nanetti, "Sunto di memorie sulle missioni dei due distretti in Pin-iao e Kie Sien (nel San-si) a memoria d'uomo" (manuscript, 1897), OFM Bologna 3:4; Liu Wenbing, *Xugou xianzhi* [Xugou county gazetteer] (Taiyuan: Shanxi renmin chubanshe, 1992; written in the 1930s), 270. For analysis of similar conversion stories from Fujian, see Zhang Xianqing, *Guanfu, zongzu yu tianzhujiao*, 195–241.

3. Zhang Zhengming, *Jinshang xingshuai shi* [A history of the rise and fall of the Shanxi merchants] (Taiyuan: Shanxi guji chubanshe, 1995), 1–56.

4. Nicolas Standaert, *Yang Tingyun, Confucian and Christian in Late Ming China* (Leiden: E. J. Brill, 1988); Liam Matthew Brockey, *Journey to the East: The Jesuit Mission to China, 1579–1724* (Cambridge: Harvard University Press, 2007); Jonathan D. Spence, *The Memory Palace of Matteo Ricci* (New York: Viking Penguin, 1984).

5. An Jiesheng, "Qingdai Shanxi zhongshang fengshang yu jiexiao funü de chuxian" [The custom of emphasizing trade and the appearance of chaste women in Qing dynasty Shanxi] *Qingshi yanjiu* 1 (2001): 27–34.

6. The brothers were Han Lin (Stephanus) and Han Yun (Thomas). The missionary was Giulio Aleni. Fang Hao, *Zhongguo tianzhujiao shi renwu zhuan* [Biographies for the history of the Catholic church in China] (Taizhong: Guangqi chubanshe, 1967), 1:271–73; Huang Yilong, "Ming Qing tianzhujiao zai Shanxi Jiangzhou de fazhan ji qi fantan" [The development of Catholicism in Jiangzhou, Shanxi, during the Ming and Qing dynasties and reactions to it] *Zhongyang yanjiuyuan jindaishi yanjiusuo jikan* 26 (1996), 3–40; Fortunato Margiotti, *Il Cattolicismo nello Shansi dalle origini al 1738* (Roma: Edizioni Sinica Franciscana, 1958), 83–85.

7. L. Carrington Goodrich, ed., *Dictionary of Ming Biography, 1368–1644* (New York: Columbia University Press, 1976), 1332–34; Standaert, *Handbook of Christianity in China*, vol. 1, *635–1800* (Leiden: Brill, 2001), 424–25; Brockey, *Journey to the East*, 68, 80–82; Margiotti, *Il Cattolicismo nello Shansi*, 319–24, 568.

8. Margiotti, *Il Cattolicismo nello Shansi*, 422–29; Standaert, *Handbook of Christianity*, 608–10.

9. Standaert, *Handbook of Christianity*, 424.

10. Alfonso Vagnone, *Jiaoyao jielue* [An introduction to doctrine] (1615), in *Yesuhui Luoma dang'anguan Ming Qing tianzhujiao wenxian* [Chinese Christian texts from the Roman Archives of the Society of Jesus], eds. Nicolas Standaert and Adrian Dudink (Taibei: Lishi xueshe, 2002), 12, 18.

11. Francesco Garretto, 20 Aug. 1736, APF SOCP 40:176.

12. For Buddhist, Daoist, and Catholic commandments see Barend J. Ter Haar, "Buddhist-Inspired Options: Aspects of Lay Religious Life in the Lower Yangzi from 1100 until 1340," *T'oung Pao* 87, no. 1/3 (2001), 92–152; Livia Kohn, *The Taoist Experience: An Anthology* (Albany: State University of New York Press, 1993), 97–98; Albano Biondi, "Aspetti della cultura cattolica posttridentina: Religione e controllo sociale," *Storia d'Italia* 4, *Intellettuali e potere* (1981), 253–302.

13. Margiotti, *Il Cattolicismo nello Shansi*, 594. See also Zürcher, "Un 'contrat communal' chrétien."

14. Shanxi sheng shizhi yanjiuyuan, ed., *Shanxi tongshi* [Shanxi history] (Taiyuan: Shanxi renmin chubanshe, 2001), 5:115–19, 214; Zhongguo renmin daxue lishi xi, Zhongguo di yi lishi dang'anguan, eds., *Qingdai nongmin zhanzheng shi ziliao xuanbian* [Selected historical materials on the peasant wars of the Qing dynasty] (Beijing: Zhongguo renmin daxue chubanshe, 1984), 151–54.

15. *Qingyuan xiangzhi* [Qingyuan township gazetteer] (1882) 8:41–50; *Qingxu xianzhi* [Qingxu county gazetteer] (Taiyuan: Shanxi guji chubanshe, 1999), 583.

16. *Taiyuan xianzhi* [Taiyuan county gazetteer] (1826) 2:3.

17. Cf. Kang Zhijie, *Shangzhu de putaoyuan: Exi Mopanshan tianzhujiao shequ yanjiu* [The Lord's vineyard: Research into the Mopanshan Catholic district in western Hubei] (Taibei: Furen daxue chubanshe, 2006), 14.

18. Giovanni Kuo, 1781, APF SOCP 63:754. See also APF SOCP 64:285; 66:84, 368; 68:252, 70:5.

19. The parishes are taken from Guo Chongxi, "Taiyuan tianzhujiao shilue" [A brief history of Catholicism in Taiyuan] *Taiyuan wenshi ziliao* 17 (1992).

I have added one parish which Guo does not include because it was wiped out by the Boxers in 1900. For the dates see Ioanne Kuo, 1781 and 1782, APF SOCP 63:754 and 64:285; Margiotti, *Il Cattolicismo nello Shansi*, 670.

20. Margiotti, *Il Cattolicismo nello Shansi*, 529–23; APF SOCP 56:14, 61:665, 62:187; APF SC Cina 8:769, 12:23, 18:301, 29:379; Stefano Gitti, *Mons. Gioacchino Salvetti O.F.M. (1769–1843) e la missione dei Francescani in Cina* (Firenze: Studi Francescani, 1958), 144; ACGOFM, Sinae 1, 243; AOPF, E101-1 Chansi indivis 14924, 14929–33, 14939, 14946, 14949–59, 14962–7, E101-2 Chansi Septentrional 1495–80, E136 Chansi Meridional 6, 9, 10; *Acta Ordinis Fratrum Minorum* 15 (1896): 72; 16 (1897): 83; 17 (1898): 84; 18 (1899): 206; 21 (1902): 12; 22 (1903): 21; 23 (1904): 129–31, 362; 24 (1905): 117–19; 25 (1906): 275–76; 26 (1907): 56; 27 (1908): 46–48; 28 (1909): 17–18; 29 (1910): 69–71; 30 (1911): 134–35; 31 (1912): 345; 32 (1913): 47; 33 (1914): 83–84; 34 (1915): 54, 95; 35 (1916): 138; 36 (1917): 31, 47; 37 (1918): 52–53; 38 (1919): 33, 56; 40 (1921): 75, 94; 41 (1922): 20, 277; *Les missions de Chine et du Japon* 1 (1916): 125–29; 2 (1917): 110–13; 3 (1919): 111; 5 (1923): 101–5; 6 (1925): 119–27; 7 (1927): 124–37; 8 (1929): 135–41; 9 (1931): 148–63; 10 (1933): 183–94, 701–3; 11 (1933–34): 212–44; 12 (1934–35): 176–79, 186–99; 15 (1938–39): 143–63; Domenico Gandolfi, "Cenni di Storia del vicariato apostolico di Taiyuanfu Shansi, Cina 1930–1953," *Studi Francescani* 84 (1987): 299–360; Domenico Gandolfi, "Cenni Storici sulla Missione di Yütze (Shansi): 1930–1953," *Studi Francescane* 85 (1988): 121–72. There are no statistics for the period 1800–30, but no other information suggests that the situation during that period was significantly different from the 1790s or 1830s. After 1890, when Shanxi began to be divided into several dioceses, the figures presented are the sum of up to eight other figures. Where one of these is missing, an average of the preceding and subsequent years for that diocese has been used to estimate it. Institutional upheaval also explains the drastic fluctuations in the 1920s and 1930s.

21. Margiotti, *Il Cattolicismo nello Shansi*, 585.

22. Christianus Herdtrich, Annuae Sin. 1673–1677, Archivum Romanum Societatis Iesu, *Jap, Sin.*, 116:265.

23. Margiotti, *Il Cattolicismo nello Shansi*, 116–19.

24. Margiotti, *Il Cattolicismo nello Shansi*, 430–34, 612; Herdtrich, Annuae Sin. 1673–1677, 265v; Brockey, *Journey to the East*, 137; Francesco Garretto, 8 May 1727, APF SOCP 33:456.

25. Untitled Chinese manuscript, APF SOCP 44:441. The quotation is from the *Zhongyong* [The Doctrine of the Mean], 20:7. Translation adapted from James Legge.

26. Ibid., 432.

27. Herdtrich, Annuae Sin. 1673–1677, 260–67; H. Josson and L. Willaert, eds., *Correspondence de Ferdinand Verbiest de la Compagnie de Jésus (1623–1688) Directeur de l'Observatoire de Pékin* (Bruxelles: Palais des Académies, 1938), 337–40; David E. Mungello, *Curious Land: Jesuit Accommodation and the Origins of Sinology* (Stuttgart: Franz Steiner Verlag Wiesbaden GMBH, 1985), 251–59. The original Latin title of the book was *Confucius Sinarum Philosophus* (Paris, 1687).

28. Francesco Garetto, 16 Aug. 1728, APF SOCP 34:231.

29. Nathanael Burger, 20 July 1767, APF SOCP 55:560.

30. For sectarianism and rebellions, see Daniel L. Overmyer, *Folk Buddhist Religion: Dissenting Sects in Late Traditional China* (Cambridge: Harvard University Press, 1976); Barend J. Ter Haar, *The White Lotus Teachings in Chinese Religious History* (Leiden: E. J. Brill, 1992); Susan Naquin, *Millenarian Rebellion in China: The Eight Trigrams Uprising of 1813* (New Haven: Yale University Press, 1976). For similarities with Christianity, see Daniel H. Bays, "Christianity and the Chinese sectarian tradition," *Ch'ing shih wen-t'i* 4, no. 7 (1982): 33–55; Robert E. Entenmann, "Catholics and Society in Eighteenth-century Sichuan" in *Christianity in China from the Eighteenth-Century to the Present*, ed. Daniel H. Bays (Stanford: Stanford University Press, 1996). For more orthodox Buddhist groups see Ter Haar, "Buddhist-Inspired options."

31. Joanne Baptista de Bormio, 21 Dec. 1747, APF SC Indie, 26:228.

32. Zhongguo di yi lishi dang'anguan, ed., *Qing zhongqianqi xiyang tianzhujiao zai Hua huodong dang'an shiliao* [Historical archives relating to the activities of Western Catholics in China in the middle and early Qing] (Beijing: Zhonghua shuju, 2003), 689.

33. Giambatta Cortenova, 29 May 1790, APF SOCP Indie Orientali e Cina 67:496.

34. Zhongguo di yi lishi dang'anguan, ed., *Qing zhongqianqi xiyang tianzhujiao*, 472–76, 1093, 1228; Vagnone, *Jiaoyao jielue*, 1:4a; Gabriele Grioglio, 28 Feb. 1850, APF SC Cina 13:555; Paul Brunner, *L'Euchologe de la mission de Chine: Editio princeps 1628 et développements jusqu'à nos jours* (Münster: Aschendorffsche verlagsbuchhandlung, 1964), 152. The Chinese title of the prayerbook was *Shengjiao rike* (1665).

35. Louis Lecomte, *Un jésuite à Pékin: Nouveaux mémoires sur l'état présent de la Chine 1687–1692* (Paris: Phébus, 1990), 427; Giambatta Cortenova, 1 Sept. 1803, APF SC Cina 2:141; Gabriele Sorda, 1 Aug. 1923, in SBD; Brunner, *L'Euchologe de la mission de Chine*, 157–58. For Buddhist chanting, see Pi-yen Chen, *Chinese Buddhist Monastic Chants* (Middleton, Wisc.: A-R Editions, 2010).

36. Herdtrich, Annuae Sin. 1673–1677, 266v; Margiotti, *Il Cattolicismo nello Shansi*, 513, 539; Guo Chongxi, "Taiyuan tianzhujiao shilue," 189; Menegon, *Ancestors, Virgins, and Friars*, 237–46.

37. Chen, *Chinese Buddhist Monastic Chants*, 8, 32–34; Vincent Goossaert, *The Taoists of Peking, 1800–1949: A Social History of Urban Clerics* (Cambridge: Harvard University Asia Center, 2007), 99–101; Kristofer Schipper, *The Taoist Body* (Berkeley: University of California Press, 1993), 11.

38. Margiotti, *Il Cattolicismo nello Shansi*, 539; Ioanne Baptista de Bormio, 21 Dec. 1747, APF SC Indie 26:228; David Gentilcore, *From Bishop to Witch: The System of the Sacred in Early Modern Terra d'Otranto* (Manchester: Manchester University Press, 1992), 94; Ter Haar, *White Lotus Teachings*, 17–19.

39. The Chinese text is reprinted in Brunner's edition of the 1628 prayer book, Brunner, *L'Euchologe de la mission de Chine*, 281–83. An old copy of the *Gongsi song jing wen* [Public and private prayers] (Shanghai, 1920) in the Zhongguo tianzhujiao lishi ziliao zhongxin [Chinese Catholic history materials center], Taiyuan Shanxi, shows the extent of the use of this litany.

40. Chen, *Chinese Buddhist Monastic Chants*, 7–8; Zhang Jiyu, ed., *Zhonghua Dao cang* [Chinese Daoist collection] (Beijing: Huaxia chubanshe, 2004), 44:50; Goossaert, *Taoists of Peking*, 99.

41. Untitled Chinese prayer book, APF SC Cina 12:690–706; Gabriele Grioglio, 28 Feb. 1850, APF SC Cina 13:552–54.

42. Relatio cuiusdam prodigii, APF SOCP 43:149–53; Eugenio da Bassano, 7 May 1741, APF SOCP 44:385–94. Cf. Nicolas Standaert, "Chinese Christian Visits to the Underworld" in *Conflict and Accommodation in Early Modern East Asia: Essays in Honour of Erik Zürcher*, eds. Leonard Blussé and Harriet T. Zurndorfer (Leiden: E.J. Brill, 1993): 54–70.

43. Alfonso Vagnone, *Shengmu xingshi* [Acts of the Holy Mother] (1798, 1st edition 1631) 3:13; Margiotti, *Il Cattolicismo nello Shansi*, 279–80.

44. Ter Haar, "Buddhist-Inspired Options," 133; Schipper, *Taoist Body*, 134–35.

45. Untitled Chinese manuscript, APF SOCP 44:445; Margiotti, *Il Cattolicismo nello Shansi*, 122, 614. For the history of this debate, see Eric Reinders, *Borrowed Gods and Foreign Bodies: Christian Missionaries Imagine Chinese Religion* (Berkeley: University of California Press, 2004), 146–49.

46. Margiotti, *Il Cattolicismo nello Shansi*, 122.

47. Vagnone, *Shengmu xingshi*, 3:38–39.

48. Berthold Laufer, "The Chinese Madonna in the Field Museum," *The Open Court* 16, no. 1 (1912): 1–5; Pasquale M. D'Elia, *Le origini dell'arte cristiana cinese (1583–1640)* (Roma: Reale Academia d'Italia, 1939), 32–33, 48–49; Kirstin Noreen, "The Icon of Santa Maria Maggiore, Rome: An Image and Its Afterlife," *Renaissance Studies* 19, no. 5 (2005): 660–72; Gu Weimin, *Jidu zongjiao yishu zai Hua fazhanshi* [A History of Christian Arts in China] (Shanghai: Shanghai shudian chubanshe, 2005), 268; Hui-hung Chen, "Encounters in Peoples, Religions and Sciences: Jesuit Visual Culture in Seventeenth Century China" (PhD diss., Brown University, 2004), 63–83. For the iconography of Guanyin see Yü Chün-fang, *Kuan-yin: The Chinese Transformation of Avalokiteśvara* (New York: Columbia University Press, 2001), 129–37, 258–59.

49. Liu Dapeng, *Jinci zhi* [Jinci gazetteer] (Taiyuan: Shanxi renmin chubanshe, 1986); Tracy Miller, *The Divine Nature of Power: Chinese Ritual Architecture at the Sacred Site of Jinci* (Cambridge: Harvard University Asia Center, 2007).

50. Margiotti, *Il Cattolicismo nello Shansi*, 618. Cf. David E. Mungello, *The Spirit and the Flesh in Shandong, 1650–1785* (Lanham: Rowman & Littlefield, 2001), 112–16.

51. Alfonso de Donato, 1843, AOPF E101–1 Chansi indivis 14895.

52. Joanne Baptista de Bormio, 21 Dec. 1747, APF SC Indie 26:226–27.

53. Gu, *Jidu zongjiao yishu zai Hua fazhanshi*, 268–69.

54. Pi-yen Chen, *Chinese Buddhist Monastic Chants*, 36–37, 41; Zhang Xishun and Cheng Lasheng, *Shanxi wenwu jingpin diancang—siguan caisu juan* [Shanxi collected outstanding cultural objects: Colored temple statuary] (Taiyuan: Shanxi renmin chubanshe, 2006), 250.

55. The argument is laid out in Augustine of Hippo, *The City of God*, books 8–9.

56. Joanne Baptista de Bormio, 21 Dec. 1747, APF SC Indie 26:218.

57. *Shengyu guangxun Yongzheng zhijie Wang Youpu jiangjie* [The Sacred Edict with notes by Yongzheng and explanation by Wang Youpu] (1724), 7:13.

58. Giambatta Cortenova, 16 June 1793, APF SOCP 68:673; Francesco Garretto, 16 Aug. 1728, APF SOCP 34:228; Standaert, *Interweaving of Rituals*.

59. Antonio Sacconi, 7 Aug. 1782, APF SOCP 63:744.

60. Francesco Garretto, 8 May 1727, APF SOCP 33:451; Parrenin P. Domenico, *Refutatio querelam Illustrissimi Francisco Maria Ferreris Episcopi Ephestiensis contra R.P. Gallos Societatis Jesu,* Biblioteca Nazionale Centrale di Roma, Fondo Gesuitico 1247:7; Margiotti, *Il Cattolicismo nello Shansi,* 603, 615.

61. Margiotti, *Il Cattolicismo nello Shansi,* 650.

62. Ibid.

63. The Franciscan was Francesco Garretto. Margiotti, *Il Cattolicismo nello Shansi,* 604, 610–13.

64. This was Gabriele da Torino. Margiotti, *Il Cattolicismo nello Shansi,* 471.

65. Stephanus Pauchinus, 1791, APF SOCP 68:248.

66. Filippo Serrati, 16 Sept. 1739, APF SOCP 43:587. The development of lineages has been much less studied for Shanxi than for south China. An argument for the late spread of lineages and their restriction to the gentry is made by Du Zhengzhen, *Cunshe chuantong yu Ming Qing shishen: Shanxi Zezhou xiangtu shehui de zhidu bianqian* [The tradition of the village *she* and Ming Qing gentry: Changes in the structure of rural society in Zezhou, Shanxi] (Shanghai: Shanghai guji chubanshe, 2007), 174–99.

67. Antonio Sacconi, 29 Aug. 1784, APF SOCP 64:561.

68. Gabriele da Torino, 1 Oct. 1738, APF SOCP 42:240; Bernward H. Willeke, ed., "The Report of the Apostolic Visitation of D. Emmanuele Conforti on the Franciscan Missions in Shansi, Shensi and Kansu (1798)," *Archivum Franciscanum Historicum* 84, nos. 1–2 (1991): 212–13.

CHAPTER 2

1. Ioannes Ricci, *Vicariatus Taiyuanfu seu brevis historia antiquae Franciscanae missionis Shansi et Shensi a sua origine ad dies nostros (1700–1928)* (Pekini: Congregationis Missionis, 1929), 60–61.

2. Ibid.

3. Barnaba Nanetti, "Sunto di memorie sulle missioni dei due distretti in Pin-iao e Kie Sien (nel San-si) a memoria d'uomo" (manuscript, 1897), OFM Bologna 3:4, 35–38.

4. Harold Schofield, *Second Annual Report of the Medical Mission at T'ai-yüen-fu, Shansi, North China, in Connection with the China Inland Mission* (Shanghai: American Presbyterian Mission Press, 1883), 25; *Annales de l'Oeuvre de la Sainte Enfance* 20, no. 124 (1868): 305.

5. *The Little Flowers of St Francis with Five Considerations of the Sacred Stigmata,* trans. Leo Sherley-Price (Baltimore: Penguin Books, 1959), 70–73.

6. Antonio Feliciani, 20 Nov. 1859, APF SC Cina 18:530.

7. Stefano Gitti, *Mons. Gioacchino Salvetti O.F.M. (1769–1843) e la missione dei Francescani in Cina* (Firenze: Studi Francescani, 1958), 26; Ricci, *Vicariatus Taiyuanfu,* 55.

8. Interview, Fan family descendant. For Qixian, see Lu Runjie, *Zhaoyu chunqiu* [Qixian annals] (Taiyuan: Shanxi guji chubanshe, 2005), 221–50.

9. The Chinese priest was Stephanus Zhang. Giovacchino Salvetti, 25 Sept. 1811, APF SC Cina 3:859–62; Zhongguo di yi lishi dang'anguan, eds., *Qing zhongqianqi xiyang tianzhujiao zai Hua huodong dang'an shiliao* [Historical archives relating to the activities of Western Catholics in China in the early and mid Qing] (Beijing: Zhonghua shuju, 2003), 901, 915.

10. Bernward H. Willeke, *Imperial Government and Catholic Missions in China during the years 1784–1785* (New York: The Franciscan Institute St. Bonaventure, 1948), 18–48; Luigi Landi, 12 June 1782, APF SC Indie 37:134; Luigi Landi et al., 29 Oct. 1785, APF SC Indie 38:220–21; Luigi Landi, 5 Jan. 1788, APF SOCP 66:86.

11. Gitti, *Mons. Gioacchino Salvetti,* 14–16, 21–24, 151; Zhongguo di yi lishi dang'anguan, eds., *Qing zhongqianqi xiyang tianzhujiao,* 877–79.

12. This missionary was Illuminato Irtelli. Luigi Landi, 8 Oct. 1809, APF SC Cina 3:692.

13. Ibid; Giovacchino Salvetti, 22 Oct. 1833, APF SC Cina 7:627; interview, Winding Gully village.

14. Giovacchino Salvetti, 25 Sept. 1811, APF SC Cina 3:859.

15. Owen Chadwick, *The Popes and European Revolution* (Oxford: Clarendon Press, 1981), 445–534, 598. Francis X. Blouin, *Vatican Archives: An Inventory and Guide to the Historical Documents in the Holy See* (New York: Oxford University Press, 1998), xx–xxi.

16. This priest was Fan Shouyi (Luigi) and the Jesuit was Antonio Provana. Fan's account is reprinted in Fang Hao, *Zhongxi jiaotong shi* [A history of contact between China and the West] (Taibei: Zhongguo wenhua daxue chubanshe, 1983), 855–62. See also Fortunato Margiotti, *Il Cattolicismo nello Shansi dalle origini al 1738* (Roma: Edizioni Sinica Franciscana, 1958), 175, 285.

17. Gianni Criveller, "The Chinese Priests of the College for the Chinese in Naples and the Promotion of the Indigenous Clergy (XVIII-XIX Centuries)" in *Silent Force: Native Converts in the Catholic China Mission,* eds., Rachel Lu Yan and Philip Vanhaelemeersch (Leuven: Ferdinand Verbiest Institute, K.U. Leuven, 2009).

18. Bernward H. Willeke, "The Report of the Apostolic Visitation of D. Emmanuele Conforti on the Franciscan Missions in Shansi, Shensi and Kansu (1798)," *Archivum Franciscanum Historicum* 84, nos. 1–2 (1991): 245, 267; Giambattista Cortenova, 9 Oct. 1803, APF SC Cina 2:584; Emmanuele Conforti, 10 July 1801, APF SOCP 70:22; Giovanni Battista Marchini, 3 Jan. 1807, APF SC Cina 3:285; Ricci, *Vicariatus Taiyuanfu,* 145; Nanetti, "Sunto di memorie," 20–21.

19. Jacobus Vang, 27 April 1816, APF SOCP 73:317; Gitti, *Mons. Gioacchino Salvetti,* 34.

20. Willeke, "The Report of the Apostolic Visitation of D. Emmanuele Conforti," 251–53.

21. Luigi Landi, 19 Oct. 1801, APF SC Cina 1a:671.

22. This was Antonio Sacconi. *Acta Ordinis Fratrum Minorum* 20 (1901): 13; Breve relazione (1785), APF SC Indie 38:246; Luigi Landi, 25 Nov. 1785, APF SOCP 65:563.

23. Camillus Ciao, 8 Oct. 1809, APF SC Cina 3:679.

24. Luigi Landi, 13 Oct. 1802, APF SC Cina 1a:668; Emmanuele Conforti, 12 May 1802, APF SOCP 70:1; Jacobus Ly, 20 Dec. 1801, APF SC Cina 1a:441; Giambattista Cortenova, 9 Oct. 1803, APF SC Cina 2:131; Giovanni Battista Marchini, 31 Jan. 1807, APF SC Cina 3:285–86; Giovanni Battista Marchini, 1807, APF SC Cina 3:539; Giovacchino Salvetti, 25 Oct. 1823, APF SC Cina 5:529; Giovacchino Salvetti, 26 May 1827, APF SC Cina 6:454; Conti della missione di Xan-si, 1846–47, APF SC Cina 12:19.

25. Margiotti, *Il Cattolicismo nello Shansi*, 471–75, 589n66, 601–2, 613; Antonio Sacconi, 7 Aug. 1782, APF SOCP 63:747; Domenico Parrenin, *Refutatio querelam Illustrissimi Francisco Maria Ferreris Episcopi Ephestiensis contra R.P. Gallos Societatis Jesu*, Biblioteca Nazionale Centrale di Roma, Fondo Gesuitico, 198; Nicolas Standaert, *Handbook of Christianity in China*, vol. 1, *635–1800* (Leiden: Brill, 2001), 458–59. For temple committees, see Vincent Goossaert, *The Taoists of Peking, 1800–1949: A Social History of Urban Clerics* (Cambridge: Harvard University Asia Center, 2007), 27; Adam Yuet Chau, *Miraculous Response: Doing Popular Religion in Contemporary China* (Stanford: Stanford University Press, 2006), 51–54.

26. Zhongguo di yi lishi dang'anguan, eds., *Qing zhongqianqi xiyang tianzhujiao*, 469–75. The statement may have been a lie intended to protect the missionary bishop, but even so it suggests the kind of attitudes that were plausible. For the background, see Willeke, *Imperial Government and Catholic Missions*, 27.

27. Giovacchino Salvetti, 20 Oct. 1825, APF SC Cina 6:120. Cf. Eugenio Menegon, *Ancestors, Virgins, and Friars: Christianity as a Local Religion in Late Imperial China* (Cambridge: Harvard University Asia Center Press, 2009), 301–56.

28. Zhongguo di yi lishi dang'anguan, eds., *Qing zhongqianqi xiyang tianzhujiao*, 898.

29. Alfonso de Donato, 30 Oct. 1841, APF SC Cina 10:323; Vitalis Kuo, 24 Dec. 1764, APF SC Indie 30:486; Stephanus Ciang, 15 Oct. 1803, APF SC Cina 2:165; Basilio a Glemona (who worked in Shaanxi), "Brevis methodus confessionis instituendae" in *Francisco Varo's Grammar of the Mandarin Language (1703): An English Translation of "Arte de la lengua Mandarina,"* eds. W. South Coblin and Joseph A. Levi (Amsterdam: John Benjamins Publishing Company, 2000), 221–23. See also Henry Charles Lea, *A History of Auricular Confession and Indulgences in the Latin Church* (Philadelphia: Lea Brothers, 1896), 1:373; Nicolas Standaert and Ad Dudink, eds., *Forgive Us Our Sins: Confession in Late Ming and Early Qing China* (Sankt Augustin: Institut Monumenta Serica, 2006); Cynthia J. Brokaw, *The Ledgers of Merit and Demerit: Social Change and Moral Order in Late Imperial China* (Princeton: Princeton University Press, 1991).

30. Alfonso de Donato, 1843, APF SC Cina 8:99; Menegon, *Ancestors, Virgins, and Friars*, 238–41; Paul Brunner, *L'Euchologe de la mission de Chine:*

Editio princeps 1628 et développements jusqu'à nos jours (Münster: Aschen-dorffsche verlagsbuchhandlung, 1964), 8, 79, 96, 106, 125–28. For Europe, see Louis Châtellier, *The Religion of the Poor: Rural Missions in Europe and the Formation of Modern Catholicism, c. 1500–c. 1800* (Cambridge: Cambridge University Press, 1997), 142; Pietro Zovatto, *Storia della spiritualità italiana* (Roma: Città nuova, 2002), 484; Chadwick, *Popes and European Revolution*, 66–69.

31. Giovacchino Salvetti, 1843, APF SC Cina 10:795; Luigi Landi, 7 March 1806, APF SC Cina 3:109; Luigi Landi, 7 March 1806, APF SC Cina 3:109; Goossaert, *Taoists of Peking*, 47–48, 119–21.

32. Philippe Boutry, *Prêtres et paroisses au pays du Curé d'Ars* (Paris: Les éditions du cerf, 1986), 378–83.

33. The priest was Filippo Huang. Giacomo Di Fiore, *Lettere di missionari dalla Cina (1761–1775): La vita quotidiana nelle missioni attraverso il carteggio di Emiliano Palladini e Filippo Huang con il Collegio dei Cinesi in Napoli* (Napoli: Istituto Universitario Orientale, 1995), 198, 320–22.

34. Giovacchino Salvetti, 28 Oct. 1829, APF SC Cina 7:163. See also Luigi Landi, 8 Oct. 1809, APF SC Cina 3:694; Ricci, *Vicariatus Taiyuanfu*, 151–52.

35. Giovacchino Salvetti, 20 Oct. 1825, APF SC Cina 6:118; Giovacchino Salvetti, 30 Oct. 1834, APF SOCP 76:399; Alfonso De Donato, 1834, APF SC Cina 8:97; Giovacchino Salvetti, 30 Oct. 1834, APF SOCP 76:399; Alfonso De Donato, 2 Dec. 1840, APF SC Cina 9:851; Alfonso De Donato, 1843, APF SC Cina 10:772; Giovacchino Salvetti, 1843, APF SC Cina 10:789; Mungello, *Curious Land*, 249, 307–11. The Book of Changes is the *Yijing*.

36. The missionary who imposed the fine was Emmanuele Conforti. The bishop who tried not to rely on fines was Giambattista Cortenova. Luigi Landi, 13 Oct. 1802, APF SC Cina 1a:668; Indie Orientali Cina Pekino ristretto 1803, APF SOCP 70:111–12; Lea, *History of Auricular Confession*, 1:410–11, 2:59–63, 142–45.

37. Giovacchino Salvetti, 14 Dec. 1816, APF SOCP 72:311; Jacobus Ly, 22 Nov. 1816, APF SOCP 73:315; Zhongguo di yi lishi dang'anguan, eds., *Qing zhongqianqi xiyang tianzhujiao*, 1087, 1093–94, 1097–98. See also J. J. M. De Groot, *Sectarianism and Religious Persecution in China* (1903; repr. Taipei: Ch'eng Wen, 1970), 2:409–86; James Millward, *Eurasian Crossroads: A History of Xinjiang* (New York: Columbia University Press, 2007), 100–1.

38. Alfonso De Donato, 1834, APF SC Cina 8:101; Gitti, *Mons. Gioacchino Salvetti*, 157n15.

39. Jacobus Vang, 9 July 1830, APF SOCP 76:51.

40. Jacobus Vang, March 1827, APF SC Cina 6:479; Jacobus Ly, 9 Dec. 1819, ACGOFM, Missioni 53, Raccolta di lettere degli alunni Cinesi dalla Cina 1753–1883, 179.

41. Giovacchino Salvetti, 14 Dec. 1816, APF SOCP 72:312.

42. Gabriele da Torino, 20 Aug. 1742, APF SOCP 44:460.

43. Di Fiore, *Lettere di missionari dalla Cina*, 219. For Maria Maddalena Sterlich, see Pasquale Palmieri, *I taumaturghi della società: Santi e potere politico nel secolo dei Lumi* (Roma: Viella, 2010), 112–16.

44. Joanna Waley-Cohen, *Exile in Mid-Qing China: Banishment to Xinjiang, 1758–1820* (New Haven: Yale University Press, 1991), 26–32; James A. Millward, *Beyond the Pass: Economy, Ethnicity, and Empire in Qing Central Asia, 1759–1864* (Stanford: Stanford University Press, 1998), 120–21.

45. Jacobus Wang, March 1827, APF SC Cina 6:479. The source is 2 Corinthians 11:25–27.

46. Owen Lattimore, *The Desert Road to Turkestan* (Boston: Little, Brown & Co, 1929), 69–72; Xing Ye and Wang Xinmin, eds., *Lü Meng shang tonglan* [An overview of traveling merchants in Mongolia] (Huhehaote: Neimenggu renmin chubanshe, 2008), 690–706.

47. Zhang Shaomei and Zhang Huajun, "Lun Qingdai Xinjiang Shanxi huiguan" [On Shanxi native place associations in Qing dynasty Xinjiang], *Xinjiang zhiye daxue xuebao* 10, no. 3 (2002): 33–35; Millward, *Beyond the Pass*, 176; Laura J. Newby, *The Empire and the Khanate: A Political History of Qing Relations with Khoqand c. 1760–1860* (Leiden: Brill, 2005), 130.

48. The merchant's name was Qin Lü (Qilong, Peter). Vitalis Kuo, 24 Dec. 1764, APF SC Indie 30:487; Ioannis Kuo, 4 Sept. 1780, APF SOCP 62:703; Zhongguo di yi lishi dang'anguan, eds., *Qing zhongqianqi xiyang tianzhujiao*, 379, 384–85, 469–70. For rhubarb, see Chang Che-chia, "Origins of a Misunderstanding: The Qianlong Emperor's Embargo on Rhubarb Exports to Russia, the Scenario and Its Consequences," *Asian Medicine: Tradition and Modernity* 1, no. 2 (2005); Clifford M. Foust, *Muscovite and Mandarin: Russia's Trade with China and Its Setting, 1727–1805* (Chapel Hill: University of North Carolina Press, 1969), 164–85.

49. Nanetti, "Sunto di memorie," 20–21, 36–37; Willeke, "The Report of the Apostolic Visitation of D. Emmanuele Conforti," 245.

50. Giambatta Cortenova, 12 Aug. 1794, APF SOCP 69:275.

51. Interview, Fan descendant.

52. Newby, *The Empire and the Khanate*, 17.

53. Three of the exiled priests were Simon Liu; Caietanus Xu, who practiced as a doctor; and Philippus Liu, who repaired clocks. The Shanxi merchant had the surname Li. Stephanus Pao and Camillus Ciao, 1 April 1787, APF SOCP 66:79; Simon Lieu et al., 5 Dec. 1787, APF SOCP 66:355; Philippus Lieu, 28 Dec. 1806, APF SC Cina 3:264; Michele Fatica, "L'Istituto Orientali di Napoli come sede di scambio culturale tra Cina e Italia nei secoli XVIII e XIX," *Scritture di Storia* 2 (2001): 85–86; Waley-Cohen, *Exile in Mid-Qing China*, 166–67.

54. Jacobus Ly, 20 Aug. 1818, APF SOCP 74:731. Similar reports reached British India from Chinese Muslims traveling to Mecca: see W.H. Wathen, "Memoir on Chinese Tartary and Khoten," *Journal of the Asiatic Society of Bengal* 4, no. 48 (1835): 653–58.

55. Giuseppe Ciun, 1831, ACGOFM Missioni 53, Raccolta di lettere, 213. The priest who returned from exile was Paulus Van. See also Paulus Van, 29 July 1806, APF SC Cina 3:140–42; Giovacchino Salvetti, 28 Oct. 1822, APF SC Cina 5:381; Giovacchino Salvetti, 14 Dec. 1816, APF SOCP 72:312;

Jacobus Ly, 22 Nov. 1816, APF SOCP 72:316; Giovacchino Salvetti, 28 Oct. 1828, APF SC Cina 6:661. For the Jahangir Rebellion, see Newby, *The Empire and the Khanate*, 95–101.

56. This man was Zhu Tianzhao. Yang Yuchun, 8th of 2nd month 1831, Zhongguo di yi lishi dang'anguan [First Historical Archives], Beijing, Gongzhong zhupi zouzhe, minzu shiwu, 513–11; Zhongguo di yi lishi dang'anguan, eds., *Qing zhong qian qi xiyang tianzhujiao*, 1098.

57. Cf. Jonathan D. Spence, *The Question of Hu* (New York: Knopf, 1988); Giacomo Di Fiore, "Un cinese a Castel Sant'Angelo. La Vicenda di un alunno del Collegio di Matteo Ripa fra trasgressione e reclusione" in *La conoscenza dell'Asia e dell'Africa in Italia nei secoli XVIII e XIX*, eds. Aldo Gallotta and Ugo Marazzi (Napoli: Istituto universitario orientale, 1985), 219–86; Mungello, *The Spirit and the Flesh*, 123–30.

58. This missionary was Vincenzo Frontini. Vincenzo Frontini, 1823, APF SC Cina 5:445, 454, 456; Giovacchino Salvetti, 25 Oct. 1823, APF SC Cina 5:528; Vincenzo Frontini, 25 April 1825, APF SC Cina 6:76–78; Vincenzo Frontini, 1826, APF SC Cina e regni adiacenti 6:198. For Europe, see Craig Harline and Eddy Put, *A Bishop's Tale: Mathias Hovius among His Flock in Seventeenth-Century Flanders* (New Haven: Yale University Press, 2000), 88–91, 132.

59. Giovacchino Salvetti, 20 Oct. 1825, APF SC Cina 6:119–22; Giovacchino Salvetti, 26 May 1827, APF SC Cina 6:452.

60. Giovacchino Salvetti, 20 Oct. 1825, APF SC Cina 6:119.

61. Gitti, *Mons. Gioacchino Salvetti*, 79; Alfonso De Donato, 17 Nov. 1835, APF SC Cina 8:442.

62. Jacobus Wang, 21 Oct. 1835, APF SC Cina 8:430–31. For the Zhaocheng rebellion, see Ma Xisha, "Xiantianjiao yu Cao Shun shijian shimo" [The Teaching of Former Heaven and the events of the Cao Shun incident], *Qingshi yanjiu tongxun* 1 (1988).

63. Ricci, *Vicariatus Taiyuanfu*, 63, 155; Giovacchino Salvetti, 10 Dec. 1838, APF SC Cina 9:210.

64. Jacobus Vang, 22 Oct. 1837, APF SC Cina 8:742; Traductio epistolo christianorum Xansi et Xensi, 1841, APF SC Cina 10:198; Alfonso De Donato, AOPF E101 Chansi indivis 14895.

65. The charismatic missionary was Giuseppe Rizzolati. Alfonso De Donato, AOPF E101 Chansi indivis 14894; Giovacchino Salvetti, 30 Oct. 1834, APF SC Cina 8:36; Alfonso De Donato, 1834, APF SC Cina 8:97.

66. Ricci, *Vicariatus Taiyuanfu*, 61–62.

67. Alfonso De Donato, 1834, APF SC Cina 8:97–98; Alfonso De Donato, APF SC Cina 10:772.

68. Alfonso De Donato, 1834, APF SC Cina 8:101 and passim. See also Alfonso De Donato, 1834, APF SOCP 76:586.

69. Nanetti, "Sunto di memorie," 49.

70. The young missionary was Alfonso De Donato. Alfonso De Donato, 1834, APF SC Cina 8:97.

71. Alfonso De Donato, 1834, APF SC Cina 8:105.

72. Letter from Ugolino Villeret, *Oriente Serafico* 4 (1892): 376.

CHAPTER 3

1. Interview, Wu Mingming, 8 Sept. 2005; Barnaba Nanetti, "Sunto di memorie sulle missioni dei due distretti in Pin-iao e Kie Sien (nel San-si) a memoria d'uomo" (manuscript, 1897), OFM Bologna 3:4, 7; *Fenyang jiaoqu shi, 1926–1996* [Fenyang diocese history, 1926–1996] (Tianzhujiao Fenyang jiaoqu, 1996), 29; Qin Geping, *Taiyuan jiaoqu jianshi* [A simple history of Taiyuan diocese] (Tianzhujiao Taiyuan jiaoqu, 2008), 356.

2. *Fenyang jiaoqu shi,* 29; Letter from Francesco Fogolla, *Oriente Serafico* 8 (1896): 440; Giovacchino Salvetti, 1843, APF SC Cina 10:797. For the wealth of priests, see Gabriele Grioglio, 3 April 1844, APF SC Cina 11:402–3; Josephus Vam, 25 Jan. 1839, APF SC Cina 9:323; Giovacchino Salvetti, 10 Dec. 1838, APF SC Cina 9:211; Bartolomeo Sandrini, 22 Sept. 1852, APF SC Cina 14:1156.

3. Gabriele Grioglio, 12 June 1845, APF SC Cina 11:775; Kenneth Scott Latourette, *A History of Christian Missions in China* (London: Society for Promoting Christian Knowledge, 1929), 228–30.

4. Gabriele Grioglio, 4 June 1845, AOPF E101 Chansi indivis 14898; AOPF E101-2 Chansi Septentrional 14916; Domenico Cannetti, 19 Sept, 1858, POSI C432 Shansi; Antonio Feliciani, 14 Jan. 1865, POSI C432 Shansi; Conti della missione di Xan-si 1846–7, APF SC Cina 12:19; Henrietta Harrison, "'A Penny for the Little Chinese': The French Holy Childhood Association in China, 1843–1951," *American Historical Review* 113, no. 1 (2008): 72–92.

5. Gabriele Grioglio, 21 Oct. 1857, AOPF E101-1 Chansi indivis, 14906. See also Gabriele Grioglio, 22 Oct. 1857, APF SC Cina 17:530.

6. Catalogo dei sacramenti amministrati nel San-si, 1858, APF SC Cina 18:302; Interviews conducted by Liu Anrong, Cave Gully, 2005.

7. Letter from Gabriele Grioglio, *Annales de l'Oeuvre de la Sainte Enfance* 4, no. 24 (1852): 52–53; Antonio Feliciani, Compte-rendu de exposés du Xansi 1862–1863, POSI C432 Shansi; Antonio Feliciani, 14 Jan. 1865, POSI C432 Shansi. The two little boys cost 17,967 cash per year and the orphanage building cost 1,183,988 cash. For adopted daughters-in-law see Margery Wolf, *Women and the Family in Rural Taiwan* (Stanford: Stanford University Press, 1972), 171–90. This practice was also common in Shanxi.

8. Antonio Feliciani, 14 Jan. 1865, and Luigi Moccagatta, 6 Oct. 1875, POSI C432 Shansi. For women in medical lineages see Charlotte Furth, *A Flourishing Yin: Gender in China's Medical History, 960–1665* (Berkeley: University of California Press, 1999), 284–95. For France, see Ralph Gibson, *A Social History of French Catholicism 1789–1914* (London: Routledge, 1989), 104–27, 231, 248–49.

9. Gabriele Grioglio, 20 Dec. 1849, APF SC Cina 19:599.

10. These ideas are known as ultramontanism and reached their peak at the First Vatican Council in 1870.

11. Gabriele Grioglio, 18 May 1847, APF SC Cina 13:107. The sermons were those of Emmanuele Conforti. For Europe, see Pietro Zovatto, *Storia della spiritualità italiana* (Roma: Città nuova, 2002), 508–12.

12. Gabriele Grioglio, *Shengjiao daoli yuexuan* [Selected truths of the holy religion] (Taiyuan: Tianzhutang yinshuguan, 1916; 1st ed. 1851), 32; Domenico

Cannetti, 24 June 1848, APF SC Cina 12:941; Gabriele Grioglio, 20 Dec. 1849, APF SC Cina 19:599; Gabriele Grioglio, 20 Oct. 1851, APF SC Cina 14:548; Gabriele Grioglio, 20 Aug. 1852, APF SC Cina 14:1052; Domenico Cannetti and Prospero Falcetti, 6 Sept. 1857, APF SC Cina 17:408.

13. Gabriele Grioglio, 1 Oct. 1852, APF SC Cina 14:1199; Domenico Cannetti and Prospero Falcetti, 6 Sept. 1857, APF SC Cina 17:408; Nanetti, "Sunto di memorie," 37, 97. For Shanxi banks, see Zhang Zhengming, *Jinshang xingshuai shi* [A history of the rise and fall of the Shanxi merchants] (Taiyuan: Shanxi guji chubanshe, 1995), 111–20. For Chinese interest rates, see David Faure, *The Rural Economy of Pre-Liberation China: Trade Expansion and Peasant Livelihood in Jiangsu and Guangdong, 1870–1937* (Hong Kong: Oxford University Press, 1989), 80–81; Qu Jiluan, *Guangdong zhi diandangye* [The Guangdong pawnshop trade] (Guangzhou: Guoli Zhongshan daxue jingji diaocha chu, 1934), 42–48. For changing Catholic doctrine on usury, see Paola Vismara, *Questioni di interesse: La Chiesa e il denaro in età moderna* (Milano: Bruno Mondadori, 2009), 135–36.

14. Nova statua vicariatus apostolici Xan-si, 1853, APF SC Cina 16: 1003–29.

15. Gabriele Grioglio, 28 Feb. 1850, APF SC Cina 13:552; Gabriele Grioglio, 1860, AOPF E136 Chansi Meridional 16 .

16. Domenico Cannetti and Prospero Falcetti, 6 Sept. 1857, APF SC Cina 17:408; Gabriele Grioglio, 14 July 1858, APF SC Cina 17:976; Domenico Cannetti, 7 April 1859, APF SC Cina 18:170.

17. Gabriele Grioglio, 28 Feb. 1850, APF SC Cina 13:552. See also Giovanni Ricci, *Le avventure di un missionario in Cina: Memorie di Mons. Luigi Moccagatta, O.F.M. Vescovo Titolare di Zenopoli e Vicario Apostolico del San-Si* (Modena: Tip. Pontificia ed Arcivescovile dell'Immacolata Concezione, 1909), 27–29.

18. Gabriele Grioglio, ed., *Tong gong jing* [Common prayer] (Taiyuan: Mingyuan tang yinshuguan, 1915; 1st ed. 1845), 2; Paul Brunner, *L'Euchologe de la mission de Chine: Editio princeps 1628 et développements jusqu'à nos jours* (Münster: Aschendorffsche verlagsbuchhandlung, 1964), 152–54.

19. Feng Baolü et al., 1848, APF SC Cina 13:332–34. Cf. David E. Mungello, "The Return of the Jesuits to China in 1841 and the Chinese Christian Backlash," *Sino-Western Cultural Relations Journal* 27 (2005): 9–46.

20. Giovanni Battista Mong, 27 Nov. 1855, APF SC Cina 16:416. For the Chinese College, see *Poliorama Pittoresco* 5 (1840–41): 253–55 and 6 (1841–42): 270; Nicola Nicolini, *L'Istituto Orientale di Napoli: Origine e statuti* (Roma: Edizioni universitarie, 1942), 15–25, 37; Michele Fatica, "L'Istituto Orientali di Napoli," 87–88; and Michele Fatica, "Per una mostra bibliografica ed iconografica su Matteo Ripa, il Collegio dei Cinesi e il Real Collegio Asiatico (1682–1888)," and Tiziana Ianello, "Il Collegio dei Cinesi durante il decennio francese (1806–15)" in *La missione Cattolica in Cina tra i secoli XVIII–XIX: Matteo Ripa e il Collegio dei Cinesi: Atti del Colloquio Internazionale Napoli, 11–12 febbraio 1997*, eds. Michele Fatica and Francesco D'Arelli (Napoli: Istituto universitario orientale, 1999). For the clergy of the Kingdom of Naples, see Angelomichele De Spirito, "La formazione del clero meridionale nelle regole dei

primi seminari" in *Studi di storia sociale e religiosa: Scritti in onore di Gabriele de Rosa*, ed. Antonio Cestaro (Napoli: Ferraro, 1980).

21. Notizie sul Collegio Cinese di Napoli, APF SOCP 76:486.

22. There were eight recorded accusations of sexual misconduct against priests who worked in Shanxi for the period before 1900: three against foreign missionaries (two in the eighteenth century which were extremely serious and combined with suggestions of insanity, and one in the nineteenth century), and five against Chinese priests trained in Naples. No accusation was recorded against a priest trained entirely in Shanxi. APF SOCP 44:219, 419; 45:324–25; APF SC Cina 3:140, 16:999, 19:549; Giacomo Di Fiore, *Lettere di missionari dalla Cina (1761–1775): La vita quotidiana nelle missioni attraverso il carteggio di Emiliano Palladini e Filippo Huang con il Collegio dei Cinesi in Napoli* (Napoli: Istituto Universitario Orientale, 1995), 169–70, 201.

23. Antonio Cestaro, *Le diocesi di Conza e di Campagna nell'età della restaurazione* (Roma: Edizioni di storia e letteratura, 1971); Romeo De Maio, *Società e vita religiosa a Napoli nell'età moderna (1656–1799)* (Napoli: Edizioni scientifiche italiane, 1971), 96–115, 346–50; Adriana Valerio, "Donna e celibato ecclesiastico: Le concubine del clero" in *Donne e religione a Napoli secoli XVI–XVIII*, eds. Giuseppe Galasso and Adriana Valerio (Milano: FrancoAngeli, 2001). In English, see Michael P. Carroll, "Religion, 'Ricettizie,' and the Immunity of Southern Italy to the Reformation," *Journal of the Scientific Study of Religion* 31, no. 3 (1992): 247–60; John A. Davis, *Naples and Napoleon: Southern Italy and the European Revolutions (1780–1860)* (Oxford: Oxford University Press, 2006), 249–51.

24. Ianello, "Il Collegio dei Cinesi," 274–76; Fatica, "Per una mostra bibliografica," 25, 29.

25. Renato Composto, "Fermento sociali nel clero siciliano prima dell'unificazione," *Studi storici* 5, no. 2 (1964): 263–79; Paul Ginsborg, *Daniele Manin and the Venetian Revolution of 1848–49* (Cambridge: Cambridge University Press, 1979), 165; Jonathan Sperber, *The European Revolutions, 1848–1851* (Cambridge: Cambridge University Press, 1994), 172.

26. Gabriele Grioglio, 25 Sept. 1850, APF SC Cina 14:468.

27. Giuseppe Vam, 21 Oct. 1856, APF SC Cina 16:910.

28. Josephus Wang, 1858, APF SC Cina 17:175–78; Domenico Cannetti, 9 Aug. 1858, APF SC Cina 17:1034–41.

29. Valerio Icardi, 6 Aug. 1858, APF SC Cina 17:1028; Giuseppe Vam, 21 Oct. 1856, APF SC Cina 16:910–12.

30. Josephus Wang, 14 Dec. 1858, APF SC Cina 17:1180.

31. Giuseppe Vam, 21 Oct. 1856, APF SC Cina e regni adicenti 16:912; Valerio Icardi, 1858, APF SC Cina 17:1029. For the lack of interest in conversions, see also Xiaojuan Huang, "Christian Communities and Alternative Devotions in China 1780–1860" (PhD diss., Princeton University, 2006), 149.

32. Gabriele Grioglio, 20 May 1852, APF SC Cina 14:1076.

33. Nanetti, "Sunto di memorie," 6.

34. Domenico Cannetti, 9 Aug. 1858, APF SC Cina 17:1035; Leo Cen et al., 22 Oct. 1861, APF SC Cina 19:548; Shanxi sheng zuipu deng, 14th of 6th month 1862, APF SC Cina 20:517.

35. Domenico Cannetti, 8 Sept. 1857, APF SC Cina 17:421–27.

36. Domenico Cannetti and Prospero Falcetti, 6 Sept. 1857, APF SC Cina 17:407–25.

37. Gabriele Grioglio, 14 July 1858, APF SC Cina 17:976. For reserved cases, see Henry Charles Lea, *A History of Auricular Confession and Indulgences in the Latin Church* (Philadelphia: Lea Brothers & Co., 1896), 1:318–37.

38. Gabriele Grioglio, 14 July 1858, APF SC Cina 17:977; Domenico Cannetti and Prospero Falcetti, 6 Sept. 1857, APF SC Cina 17:407. See also An Jiesheng, "Qingdai Shanxi zhongshang fengshang yu jiexiao funü de chuxian" [The custom of emphasizing trade and the appearance of chaste women in Qing dynasty Shanxi], *Qingshi yanjiu* 1 (2001): 27–34.

39. Domenico Cannetti and Prospero Falcetti, 6 Sept, 1857, APF SC Cina 17:423–24; Leo Cen et al., 22 Oct. 1861, APF SC Cina 19:547.

40. Domenico Cannetti and Prospero Falcetti, 6 Sept. 1857, APF SC Cina 17:405.

41. D.L. Ambrosi, 25 April 1860, APF SC Cina 18:726. See also Annibale Fantoni, 15 Dec. 1856, APF SC Cina 16:1071; Domenico Cannetti, 7 April 1859, APF SC Cina 18:166; Gabriele Grioglio, 11 Sept. 1859, APF SC Cina 18:533; Giovanni Ricci, *Barbarie e trionfi: Ossia le vittime illustri del San-si in Cina nella persecuzione del 1900* (Firenze: Tipografia Barbèra, 1910), 711.

42. Gabriele Grioglio, 6 June 1861, APF SC Cina 18:1092; Zhongguo Shanxi tong sheng jiao you, 19 Sept. 1861, APF SC Cina 19:395; *Acta Ordinis Fratrum Minorum* 10 (1891): 32.

43. Kenneth Scott Latourette, *A History of Christian Missions in China* (London: Society for Promoting Christian Knowledge, 1929), 274–75.

44. Shanxi sheng zuipu deng, 14th of 6th month 1862, APF SC Cina 20:517; Zhongyang yanjiuyuan jindaishi yanjiusuo, ed., *Jiaowu jiaoan dang* [Archives of religious affairs and cases](Taibei: Zhongyang yanjiuyuan jindaishi yanjiusuo, 1974), 1:688. The equality that Cannetti claimed was not in fact in any treaty negotiated at this time. For the texts of the treaties, see William Frederick Mayers, ed., *Treaties between the Empire of China and Foreign Powers, together with Regulations for the Conduct of Foreign Trade* (Shanghai: J.B. Tootal, 1877), 11–20, 59–71.

45. Zhongyang yanjiuyuan jindaishi yanjiusuo, ed., *Jiaowu jiaoan dang,* 1:713; Matthaeus Li and Petrus Ciao, 2 Feb. 1862, APF SC Cina 19:544.

46. The governor was Ying Gui. Zhongyang yanjiuyuan jindaishi yanjiusuo, ed., *Jiaowu jiaoan dang,* 1:687.

47. Zhongyang yanjiuyuan jindaishi yanjiusuo, ed., *Jiaowu jiaoan dang,* 1:721–22; Fortunato Margiotti, *Il Cattolicismo nello Shansi dalle origini al 1738* (Roma: Edizioni Sinica Franciscana, 1958), 244. For temple festivals, see Roger R. Thompson, "Twilight of the Gods in the Chinese Countryside: Christians, Confucians, and the Modernising State, 1861–1911" in *Christianity in China from the Eighteenth Century to the Present,* ed. Daniel H. Bays (Stanford: Stanford University Press, 1996): 53–72; David Johnson, *Spectacle and Sacrifice: The Ritual Foundations of Village Life in North China* (Cambridge: Harvard University Asia Center, 2009), 13–15, 177–337.

48. Leo Cen et al., 22 Oct. 1861, APF SC Cina 19:550. See also Luigi Moccagatta, 30 Sept. 1862, APF SC Cina 19:1074.

49. Leo Cen et al., 22 Oct. 1861, APF SC Cina 19:552.

50. Domenico Cannetti, 22 Feb. 1862, APF SC Cina 19:726; Luigi Moccagatta, 30 Sept. 1862, APF SC Cina 19:1075; Luigi Moccagatta, 20 Oct. 1867, APF SC Cina 19:230; Josephus Van, 1 Sept. 1873, APF SC Cina 26:100; Ricci, *Avventure,* 180–88.

51. Petrus Ciao, 24 Sept. 1862, APF SC Cina 19:1150. See also Josephus Van, 1 Sept. 1873, APF SC Cina 26:100; Jacques Leclercq, *Thunder in the Distance: The Life of Père Lebbe,* trans. George Lamb (New York: Sheed & Ward, 1958), 54–58.

52. Relazio dell'origine, APF SC Cina 22:578; Relazio dell'origine, 1870, ACGOFM Sinae 1:240; Luigi Moccagatta, 22 June 1866, AOPF E136 Chansi meridional 29; Paolo Carnevale, 1 Oct. 1869, AOPF E101 Chansi 14921.

53. Letter from Paolo Carnevale, *Annales de L'Oeuvre de la Sainte Enfance* 25, no. 158 (1874): 174–75; Luigi Moccagatta, 23 April 1873, APF SC Cina 25:596–97; *The Tientsin Massacre, being documents published in the Shanghai Evening Courier, From June 16th to Sept. 10th, 1870, with an introductory narrative* (Shanghai: A.H. de Carvalho, 1870).

54. Josephus Van, 2 June 1873, APF SC Cina 26:93–96; Ricci, *Barbarie e trionfi,* 289.

55. Wang Ruose, "Cai cha ge" [Tea picking song], Pontificio Istituto Missioni Estere (Rome), Kaifeng, Henan, 1605.

56. Josephus Van, 9 June 1873, APF SC Cina 25:309.

57. Josephus Van, 16 Aug. 1873, APF SC Cina 26:86.

58. Josephus Van, 12 Sept. 1873, APF SC Cina 26:104; Franciscus Li, 20 Oct. 1857, APF SC Cina 17:510. Wang Tingrong asked for seven hundred thousand to eight hundred thousand cash, while Franciscus Li said he could live on sixty thousand to seventy thousand cash.

59. Gabriele Grioglio, 3 April 1844, APF SC Cina 11:402; Josephus Van, 22 June 1874, APF SC Cina 26:76.

60. Josephus Van, 20 Aug. 1873, APF SC Cina 26:82; Paolo Carnevale, 4 Jan. 1874, APF SC Cina 25:835; Luigi Moccagatta, 29 April 1875, APF SC Cina 26:119.

61. Wang Ruose, "Cai cha ge."

62. Gregorio Grassi, 15 Nov. 1882, APF SC Cina 29:377–78; Inscriptions from Heshangjie and Honggou churches reproduced in Guo Quanzhi, "Shanxi tianzhujiao gaishu" [An outline of Catholicism in Shanxi] (manuscript, 2007), 6; Guo Chongxi, "Taiyuan tianzhujiao zhuyao tangkou jianjie" [A brief introduction to the main Catholic parishes of Taiyuan], *Taiyuan wenshi ziliao* 15 (1991): 159.

63. APF Acta 242 (1874): 328.

64. Zhongguo Shanxi tong sheng jiaoyou, 19th of 9th month, APF SC Cina 19:395.

CHAPTER 4

1. Interview, Wu Mingming, Cave Gully, 8 Sept. 2005.

2. In 1907 Barnaba Nanetti gathered details of 1,953 people who had been martyred. This did not include those who renounced their faith but were killed

nevertheless. He also did not include the very large numbers who were killed in northern Shanxi (Datong, Suiyuan) because he died before he completed the task. His work was published by Giovanni Ricci, "Acta Martyrum Sinensium anno 1900 in Provincia San-si occisorum historice collecta ex ore testium singulis locis ubi Martyres occubuere. Relatio ex-officio ex parte Ordinis Fratrum Minorum," *Acta Ordinis Fratrum Minorum* 30 (1911); 32 (1913); and "Acta Martyrum Sinensium Vicariatus Apostolici Shansi Meridionalis anno 1900 pro fide Catholica interfectorum," *Acta Ordinis Fratrum Minorum* 33 (1914). Nanetti's total is not dissimilar to the 1,686 Christian deaths recorded by Chinese officials for the same districts: see Zhongyang yanjiuyuan jindaishi yanjiusuo, ed., *Jiaowu jiaoan dang* (Taibei: Zhongyang yanjiuyuan jindaishi yanjiusuo, 1974) 7:496–507. For some villages, Nanetti's figures can also be compared with inscriptions put up immediately after the uprising, e.g. "Shanxi sheng gengzi nian jiaonan qianhou jishi" [A record of the events before and after the 1900 persecution in Shanxi province] in *Yihetuan* [The Boxers], ed. Jian Bozan et al. (Shanghai: Shenzhou guoguang she, 1951), 517–19. For the 159 Protestant missionaries and family members killed, see E. H. Edwards, *Fire and Sword in Shansi: The Story of the Martyrdom of Foreigners and Chinese Christians* (Edinburgh: Oliphant Anderson & Ferrier, 1903), 14–16.

3. Joseph W. Esherick, *Origins of the Boxer Uprising* (Berkeley: University of California Press, 1987); Paul A. Cohen, *History in Three Keys: The Boxers as Event, Experience and Myth* (New York: Columbia University Press, 1997).

4. For Europe, see Jacques Le Goff, *The Birth of Purgatory,* trans. Arthur Goldhammer (Chicago: University of Chicago Press, 1984), 289–332; Henry Charles Lea, *A History of Auricular Confession and Indulgences in the Latin Church* (Philadelphia: Lea Brothers & Co., 1896), 3:296–371; Michel Vovelle, *Les âmes du purgatoire ou le travail du deuil* (Paris: Gallimard, 1996), 254–61; Stefano De Matteis and Marino Nicola, *Antropologia delle anime in pena: Il resto della storia: Un culto del Purgatorio* (Lecce: Argo, 1997), 21, 42. For China, see Vincent Goossaert, *The Taoists of Peking, 1800–1949: A Social History of Urban Clerics* (Cambridge: Harvard University Asia Center, 2007), 249–55, 333–36; Barend J. Ter Haar, "Buddhist-Inspired Options: Aspects of Lay Religious Life in the Lower Yangzi from 1100 until 1340," *T'oung Pao 87,* no. 1/3 (2001): 113–22; Stephen F. Teiser, *The Scripture of the Ten Kings and the Making of Purgatory in Medieval Chinese Buddhism* (Honolulu: Hawaii University Press, 1994); Robert P. Weller, *Resistance, Chaos and Control in China: Taiping Rebels, Taiwanese Ghosts and Tiananmen* (Seattle: University of Washington Press, 1994), 130–31.

5. Francesco Vitali, *Month of the Souls in Purgatory Containing Devotions for Each Day in November,* trans. M. Comerford (Dublin: G. P. Warren, 1871), 154–56; for its popularity, see Pietro Zovatto, *Storia della spiritualità italiana* (Roma: Città nuova, 2002), 515–16; Tian Wendu, *Lianyu shengyue* [The holy month of purgatory] (Shanxi beiqin, 1921; 1st ed., 1880), 7–8.

6. For Italians in China, see Giuliano Bertuccioli and Federico Masini, *Italia e Cina* (Roma-Bari: Laterza, 1996); Gianni La Bella, "Pius X" in *The Catholic Church and the Chinese World: Between Colonialism and Evangelisation 1840–1911,* eds. Agostino Giovagnoli and Elisa Giunipero (Roma: Urbaniana

University, 2005): 51–68; Maurizio Marinelli, "The Genesis of the Italian Concession in Tianjin: A Combination of Wishful Thinking and Realpolitik," *Journal of Modern Italian Studies* 15, no. 4 (2010): 536–56.

7. The governor was Cen Chunxuan. Gugong bowuyuan Ming Qing dang'an bu, ed., *Yihetuan dang'an shiliao* (Beijing: Zhonghua shuju, 1959), 1233.

8. Zhongyang yanjiuyuan jindaishi yanjiusuo, ed., *Jiaowu jiaoan dang* (Taibei: Zhongyang yanjiuyuan jindaishi yanjiusuo, 1974), 4:330–31; interview, Ren family descendant; Wu Jianjie, *Zhang Zhidong nianpu changbian* [Zhang Zhidong chronological biography draft edition] (Shanghai: Shanghai jiaotong daxue chubanshe, 2009), 1:72–77.

9. The exact sum distributed was 219,991 French francs. Timothy Richard, *Forty-Five Years in China* (London: T. Fisher Unwin, 1916), 125–42; Luigi Moccagatta, 13 Sept. 1879, APF SC Cina 27:1257; Luigi Moccagatta, 25 March 1878, ACGOFM Sinae 2:465–67. For the new expenditure on evangelism, see diocesan budgets in AOPF E101 Chansi 14939, 14951, 14954. For the famine, see Kathryn Edgerton-Tarpley, *Tears from Iron: Cultural Reponses to Famine in Nineteenth-Century China* (Berkeley: University of California Press, 2008).

10. APF SC Cina 9:876, 12:23, 18:301, 29:379; Giovanni Ricci, *Vicariatus Taiyuanfu seu brevis historia antiquae Franciscanae missionis Shansi et Shensi a sua origine ad dies nostros (1700–1928)* (Pekini: Congregationis Missionis, 1929), 102; ACGOFM Sinae 1:243; AOPF E136 Chansi Meridional 6, 9; AOPF E101 Chansi 14924, 14929–33, 14939, 14946, 14949–59, 14962; AOPF E101-2 Chansi Septentrional 14964–80. *Acta Ordinis Fratrum Minorum* 5 (1886): 129; 15 (1896): 71–72; 16 (1897): 83; 17 (1898): 84; 18 (1899): 206; 21 (1902): 12; 22 (1903): 21; 23 (1904): 129–31; 24 (1905): 117–19; 25 (1906): 275–76; 26 (1907): 56; 27 (1908): 46–48; 28 (1909): 17–18; 29 (1910): 69–71; 30 (1911): 134–35; 31 (1912): 345; 32 (1913): 47; 33 (1914): 83–84; 34 (1915): 54, 95; 35 (1916): 138; 36 (1917): 31, 47; 37 (1918): 52–53; 38 (1919): 33, 56; 40 (1921): 75, 94; 41 (1922): 20, 276–77. *Missions de Chine* 1 (1916): 129; 2 (1917): 113; 3 (1919): 103, 111; 5 (1923): 101–4; 6 (1925): 115–27; 7 (1927): 128–37; 8 (1929): 130–41; 9 (1931): 148–63; 10 (1933): 183–94, 701–3; 11 (1933–34): 212–44; 12 (1934–35): 176–79, 186–99; 15 (1938–39): 143–63. Domenico Gandolfi, "Cenni di storia del vicariato apostolico di Taiyuanfu Shansi, Cina 1930–1953," *Studi Francescani* 84 (1987). See also notes on figure 2. The data for North Shanxi in 1897 appears to be erroneous and has been omitted.

11. Ricci, *Barbarie e trionfi*, 124; Luigi Moccagatta, 25 Sept. 1885, POSI C432 Shansi; Letter from Pacifico Nascetti, *Oriente Serafico* 5 (1893): 317.

12. Edwards, *Fire and Sword in Shansi*, 47; AOPF E101-2 Chansi Septentrional 14979; *Acta Ordinis Fratrum Minorum* 18 (1899): 206.

13. Wang Wangde, *Nongmin zheng tan* [Straight talk from a farmer] (Taiyuan, 1862–91), 8.

14. Ibid., 1.

15. Ibid., 4.

16. Tian Wendu, *Zhenli jingyan shi* [Truths respectfully addressed to the age] (Taiyuan: Mingyuan tang, 1917; 1st edition, 1888), 7.

17. Ibid., 90.

18. Ibid., 136.

19. *Acta Ordinis Fratrum Minorum* 18 (1899): 205; AOPF E101–2 Chansi Septentrional 14977; Edwards, *Fire and Sword in Shansi*, 14–16.

20. The governor was Hu Pin. Zhongyang yanjiuyuan jindaishi yanjiusuo, ed., *Jiaowu jiaoan dang*, 6:740; Letter from Hugolin Villeret, *Oriente Serafico* 2, no. 7 (1890): 217; Ricci, *Barbarie e trionfi*, 258; Guo Chongxi, "Taiyuan tianzhujiao shilue" [A brief history of Catholicism in Taiyuan], *Taiyuan wenshi ziliao* 17 (1992): 154.

21. Ricci, *Barbarie e trionfi*, 162–63; Gregorio Grassi, 1891, ACGOFM Sinae 8:312; Barnaba Nanetti, 19 Sept. 1893, ACGOFM Sinae 9:243–44.

22. Gregorio Grassi 21, May 1891, ACGOFM Sinae 8:315–16. See also Giovanni Ricci, *Il Fratello di una Martire: Memorie del P. Barnaba da Cologna, O.F.M. Missionario Apostolico in Cina* (Torino: P. Celanza, 1912), 9–12, 139, 183; Barnaba Nanetti, 19 Sept. 1893, ACGOFM Sinae 9:244; Francesco Saccani, 18 Aug. 1893, ACGOFM Sinae 9:248; Francesco Saccani, Oct. 1898, OFM Bologna 1, Lettere di missionari 33.

23. Letter from Barnaba Nanetti, *Oriente Serafico* 10 (1898): 21; Joannis Hofman, Feb. 1902, ACGOFM Sinae 12:553; Francesco Albertini, 30 Aug. 1896, ACGOFM Sinae 10:247.

24. Barnaba d'Alsazia, "L'Infanzia in Cina," *Oriente Serafico* 4 (1892): 400.

25. Léon de Kerval, *Le R.P. Hugolin de Doullens ou la vie d'un Frère Mineur missionnaire en Chine au XIXᵉ siècle* (Rome: Francisc. Miss., 1902), 215–21.

26. Barnabé d'Alsace, 9 April 1891, POSI C436 Shensi meridional; Luigi Moccagatta, 1 Oct. 1883, POSI C432 Shansi; *Yasongda zouguo de lu, qianbei fuwu, Yasongda xingshi ji xubian* [The path Assunta trod—humble service. The Deeds of Assunta and a supplement] (Taiyuan, 2005), 56. See also Henrietta Harrison, "'A Penny for the Little Chinese' : The French Holy Childhood Association in China, 1843–1951," *American Historical Review* 113, no. 1 (2008).

27. Letter from Barnaba Nanetti, *Missioni Francescane* 6, no. 5 (1895): 267.

28. Letter from Francesco Fogolla, *Oriente Serafico* 8 (1896): 439.

29. Ricci, *Barbarie e trionfi*, 416–17.

30. The Naples-trained priest was Meng Changde. Franciscus Ly, 30 Jan. 1851, APF SC Cina 14:215; Barnaba Nanetti, 10 July 1895, ACGOFM Sinae 10:197.

31. Ricci, "Acta martyrum Sinensium anno 1900 in Provincia San-si occisorum." The total number of marriages recorded is 180.

32. For the term *christianitas*, see Xiaojuan Huang, 141–42.

33. Kerval, *Hugolin de Doullens*, 221–25. For the priest, Stanislaus Chen, see Hugolin Villeret, 24 Sept. 1888, POSI C432 Chan-Si.

34. Letter from Barnaba Nanetti, *Oriente Serafico* 8 (1896): 378. See also Nanetti, "Sunto di memorie sulle missioni dei due distretti in Pin-iao e Kie Sien (nel San-si) a memoria d'uomo" (manuscript, 1897), Archivio della Provincia Osservante di Bologna, poi del SS, Redentore, Bologna, Missione di Yütze (Shan-si, Cina), 41.

35. Léon de Kerval, *Deux Martyrs Francais de l'ordre des frères mineurs le R.P. Théodoric Balat et le Fr. André Bauer massacrés en Chine le 9 Juillet 1900*

Aperçus biographiques (Rome and Paris: Lemière, 1914), 158–62; Kerval, *Hugolin de Doullens*, 161.

36. OFM Bologna 2.16 Miscellanea. The attribution to this particular famine is uncertain. See also Jeffrey Snyder-Reinke, *Dry Spells: State Rainmaking and Local Governance in Late Imperial China* (Cambridge: Harvard University Asia Center, 2009).

37. For the pilgrimage, see Kerval, *Hugolin de Doullens*, 134–57. See also Fortunato Margiotti, *Il Cattolicismo nello Shansi dalle origini al 1738* (Roma: Edizioni Sinica Franciscana, 1958), 299; Gabriele Grioglio, 1860, AOPF E136 Chansi Meridional, 16.

38. For Dragon Kings and other local rain rituals, see Liu Dapeng, *Jinci zhi* [Jinci gazetteer], eds. Mu Xiang, Lü Wenxing (Taiyuan: Shanxi renmin chubanshe, 1986), 194, 734–35, 1256–57, 1277–78; Liu Dapeng, *Tuixiangzhai riji* [Diary from the chamber to which one retires to ponder], ed. Qiao Zhiqiang (Taiyuan: Shanxi renmin chubanshe, 1980), 143–44; *Taiyuan shi nanjiaoqu zhi* [Taiyuan city southern suburban district gazetteer] (Beijing: Sanlian shudian, 1994), 843. See also Prasenjit Duara, *Culture, Power and the State: Rural North China, 1900–1942* (Stanford: Stanford University Press, 1988), 31–35. The Catholic reference is from an interview with a Cold Springs Road resident.

39. Kerval, *Hugolin de Doullens*, 84–85, 122. For another case of local participation in Catholic prayers at the shrine, see Paolo Carnevale, 4 Oct. 1867, AOPF E101 Chansi 14919. For firearms in Italy, see Antonio Cestaro, *Le diocesi di Conza e di Campagna nell'età della restaurazione* (Roma: Edizioni di storia e letteratura, 1971), 81; Carlo Levi, *Christ Stopped at Eboli*, trans. Frances Frenaye (Harmondsworth: Penguin Books, 1982), 116. For temples and disputes in China, see David K. Jordan, *Gods, Ghosts, and Ancestors: The Folk Religion of a Taiwanese Village* (Berkeley: University of California Press, 1972), 42–53.

40. Duara, 118–57; David Johnson, *Spectacle and Sacrifice: The Ritual Foundations of Village Life in North China* (Cambridge: Harvard University Asia Center, 2009); Zhao Shiyu, *Kuanghuan yu richang—Ming Qing yilai de miaohui yu minjian shehui* [Carnivals in daily life: Temple fairs and local society since the Ming and Qing] (Beijing: Sanlian, 2002).

41. Petr. Vinc. De Tartre, 19 Nov. 1720, Archivium Romanum Societatis Iesu, *Jap. Sin.* 182:351; Margiotti, *Il Cattolicismo nello Shansi*, 444; Antonio Sacconi, 7 Aug. 1782, APF SOCP 63:745; Alfonso De Donato, 1842, AOPF E101-1 Chansi indivis 14894. See also Margiotti, *Il Cattolicismo nello Shansi*, 248; Nathanael Burger, 20 July 1767, APF SOCP 55:560.

42. Zhongyang yanjiuyuan jindaishi yanjiusuo, ed., *Jiaowu jiaoan dang* 4:320.

43. Ricci, *Fratello di una Martire*, 52–53.

44. Liu Dapeng, "Qianyuan suoji" in *Yihetuan zai Shanxi diqu shiliao* [Local historical materials on the Boxers in Shanxi], ed. Qiao Zhiqiang (Taiyuan: Shanxi renmin chubanshe, 1980), 28; Ricci, *Barbarie e trionfi*, 579–80; "Shanxi sheng gengzi nian jiaonan qianhou jishi" [A record of the events before and after the 1900 persecution in Shanxi province], in *Yihetuan* [The Boxers], ed. Jian Bozan, vol. 1 (Shanghai: Shenzhou guoguan she, 1951), 497; Shi Rongchang, "Gengzi ganshi shi" [Poems in response to 1900], *Jindaishi ziliao* 11, no. 4 (1956): 160.

45. Liu Dapeng, "Qianyuan suoji," 35–36; Liu Dapeng, *Jinci zhi,* 1049; Ricci, "Acta Martyrum Sinensium anno 1900 in Provincia San-si occisorum," 32:196; Gugong bowuyuan Ming Qing dang'an bu, ed., *Yihetuan dang'an shiliao,* 294, 313.

46. Edoardo Manini, *Episodi della Rivoluzione Cinese, 1900* (Parma: Rossi Ubaldi, 1901), 31–37.

47. Liu Dapeng, "Qianyuan suoji," 30, 34–35, 39–40; Manini, *Episodi della Rivoluzione Cinese,* 56, 62.

48. Ricci, "Acta martyrum Sinensium anno 1900 in Provincia San-si occisorum," 30:367, 31:108; Manini, *Episodi della Rivoluzione Cinese,* 57–69; Ricci, *Barbarie e trionfi,* 711; Liu Dapeng, "Qianyuan suoji," 39.

49. The missionary who survived in Cave Gully was Michele Chiapetta. Manini, *Episodi della Rivoluzione Cinese,* 67–74; Ricci, "Acta martyrum Sinensium anno 1900 in Provincia San-si occisorum" 30:279.

50. Ricci, *Barbarie e trionfi,* 711–5; Liu Dapeng, "Tuixiangzhai riji" [Diary from the chamber to which one retires to ponder] (manuscript, Shanxi Provincial Library), 10th of 3rd month 1901; "Shanxi sheng gengzi nian jiaonan," 521.

51. Liu Dapeng, *Jinci zhi,* 1048; Liu Dapeng, "Qianyuan suoji," 47–48; Manini, *Episodi della Rivoluzione Cinese,* 65–66.

52. Liu Wenbing, *Xugou xianzhi* (Taiyuan: Shanxi renmin chubanshe, 1992), 285; Liu Dapeng, *Jinci zhi,* 1048; Liu Dapeng, "Qianyuan suoji," 48; Manini, *Episodi della Rivoluzione Cinese,* 60–63.

53. Liu Dapeng, *Jinci zhi,* 1048; Liu Dapeng, "Qianyuan suoji," 39, 48–49; Ricci, *Barbarie e trionfi,* 770–71; Letter from Michele Chiapetta, *Oriente Serafico* 13 (1901): 86–94; Manini, *Episodi della Rivoluzione Cinese,* 64; Letter from Barnaba Nanetti, "Diguozhuyi esha Shanxi Yihetuan de zuizheng" [Proof of the guilt of imperialism in smothering the Shanxi Boxers] trans. Zhang Maoxian, *Shanxi wenshi ziliao* 2 (1962): 31; Lu Runjie, "Shanxi yihetuan yundong" [The Boxer movement in Shanxi] in *Jindai de Shanxi* [Modern Shanxi] ed. Jiang Di (Taiyuan: Shanxi renmin chubanshe, 1988), 384.

54. Zhongyang yanjiuyuan jindaishi yanjiusuo, ed., *Jiaowu jiaoan dang,* 7:496–510.

55. Ricci, "Acta martyrum Sinensium anno 1900 in Provincia San-si occisorum," 31:186.

56. Ricci, "Acta martyrum Sinensium anno 1900 in Provincia San-si occisorum"; Ricci, "Acta Martyrum Sinensium Vicariatus Shansi Merdionalis." This figure may have some bias as young children were not thought capable of apostatizing.

57. Ricci, "Acta martyrum Sinensium anno 1900 in Provincia San-si occisorum," 32:192; Liu Dapeng, *Tuixiangzhai riji,* 99.

58. Liu Dapeng, *Tuixiangzhai riji,* 89–90; Liu Dapeng, "Tuixiangzhai riji" (manuscript, Shanxi Provincial Library), 11th of the 3rd month 1901; Letter from Barnaba Nanetti, "Diguozhuyi esha," 3:131.

59. "Shanxi sheng gengzi nian jiaonan," 1:517.

60. "Shanxi sheng gengzi nian jiaonan," 1:521.

61. Liu Dapeng, "Tuixiangzhai riji" [Diary from the chamber to which one retires to ponder] *Jindaishi ziliao Yihetuan shiliao* [Modern history materials Boxer historical materials] (Beijing: Zhongguo shehui kexue chubanshe, 1982), 2:819.

CHAPTER 5

1. Interviews with Cave Gully residents and other local people.

2. Liu Dapeng, *Jinci zhi* [Jinci gazetteer], eds. Mu Xiang and Lü Wenxing (Taiyuan: Shanxi renmin chubanshe, 1986), 1120, 1455; Taiyuan xishan kuangwuju, ed., *Xishan meikuang shi* [A history of coal mining in the Western Hills] (1961), 50–51.

3. Letter from Barnaba Nanetti, "Diguozhuyi esha Shanxi Yihetuan de zuizheng" [Proof of the guilt of imperialism in smothering the Shanxi Boxers], trans. Zhang Maoxian, *Shanxi wenshi ziliao* 2–3 (1962); *North China Herald*, 4 Sept. 1901, 442.

4. Letter from Domenico Agostinelli, *Oriente Serafico* 13 (1901): 664.

5. *Xinxuan shengjiao duilian* [New selection of Catholic couplets] (Lu'an, 1904), 19. See also Ruth Harris, *Lourdes: Body and Spirit in a Secular Age* (Harmondsworth: Penguin, 1999), 1–8, 289–95.

6. Enzo Tramontani, *Tai-yuan: L'ora del sogno: Maria Chiara Nanetti nella Cina dei martiri* (Bologna: Editrice missionaria italiana, 2000), 33; Giovanni Ricci, *Il Fratello di una Martire: Memorie del P. Barnaba da Cologna, O.F.M. Missionario Apostolico in Cina* (Torino: P. Celanza, 1912), 173–75.

7. Zhongguo di yi lishi dang'anguan, Fujian shifan daxue lishixi, eds., *Qingmo jiaoan* [Late Qing religious cases] (Beijing: Zhonghua shuju, 1996), 3:547, 831. Much of the secondary literature confuses Nanetti's failed negotiations with the final deal. A careful narrative can be found in Lu Runjie, "Shanxi yihetuan yundong" [The Boxer movement in Shanxi], in *Jindai de Shanxi* [Modern Shanxi], ed. Jiang Di (Taiyuan: Shanxi renmin chubanshe, 1988), 413–22.

8. Liu Dapeng, "Qianyuan suoji," in *Yihetuan zai Shanxi diqu shiliao* [Local historical materials on the Boxers in Shanxi], ed. Qiao Zhiqiang (Taiyuan: Shanxi renmin chubanshe, 1980), 55; Fu Andao, 22 Sept. 1904, SBD. A notable exception is the Li family of Taiyuan, who received one thousand taels: see "Diguozhuyi esha Shanxi Yihetuan," 3:104. For Protestants, see "Native indemnity disbursed in Shansi Mission in 1901," Papers of the American Board of Commissioners of Foreign Missions, Shansi 5, Shansi Mission 1900–1909, Documents etc.

9. Nicola Cerasa, *Breve Storia della Missione di Taiyuan Shansi* (Roma: Provincia Romana dei Frati Minori, 1998), 177, 285; Guo Chongxi, "Taiyuan tianzhujiao shilue," [A brief history of Catholicism in Taiyuan], *Taiyuan wenshi ziliao* 17 (1992): 241; *Shanxi tongzhi* [Shanxi gazetteer] (Beijing: Zhonghua shuju, 1997), 46:370, 422; Giornale dal 1° Giugno 1910 al 31 Agosto 1912, manuscript, Zhongguo tianzhujiao lishi ziliao zhongxin, Taiyuan (a daybook recording payments made and received by the diocese); *Zongjiao gongzuo xuanchuan cailiao* [Propaganda materials for religious work] (Zhonggong Taiyuan shiwei siqing zongjiao bangongshi, 1966), 1:10; Song Jianxun, "Bazhan tianchan er san shi" [Two or three cases of seizing land and property], ed. Taiyuanshi tianzhujiao aiguohui, *Wenshi ziliao* 1 (1964): 68–69; Paul Lesourd, *Histoire générale de l'Oeuvre Pontificale de la Sainte-Enfance depuis un siècle* (Paris: Centre Catholique International de Documentation e de Statistiques, 1947), 69–71; AOPF E-135 Chansi Septentrional 1. For exchange rates, see

Liang-lin Hsiao, *China's Foreign Trade Statistics, 1864–1949* (Cambridge: Harvard University Press, 1974), 191–92.

10. Ugolino Arcari, 13 April 1913, OFM Bologna 1:3.

11. Agapito Fiorentini, 20 Sept. 1918, POSI C433 Shansi Septentrional; *Acta Ordinis Fratrum Minorum* 38 (1919): 33–34.

12. Wang Chongli, 13 Aug. 1908, SBD; Eugenio Massi, 22 Aug. 1903, SBD; Martino Antonelli, 26 June 1913, SBD.

13. Martino Antonelli, undated letter beginning "Mando a Tsin-yuen-fou il latore della presente," SBD; Gabriele Sorda, 24 Dec. 1925, SBD.

14. Tito Mostarda, 10 June 1908, SBD. See also his letter of 18 Oct. 1908, SBD.

15. Alfonso De Donato, 1834, APF SC Cina 8:98; Benvenuto Marrotta, undated letter beginning "Qui in Pu li," SBD; Chen Guodi, 2 Aug. 1921, SBD.

16. Interview, Wu Mingming, 8 Sept. 2005.

17. Martino Antonelli, 7 Feb. 1906, SBD. See also his letter of 20 Nov. 1904, SBD.

18. Eugenio Pilotti, 10 June 1743, APF SOCP 45:324–25; Nova statua vicariatus apostolicus Xan-si 1853, APF SC Cina 16:1010.

19. See also Han Yaozong, "Cong Lei Jingshi kan chuanjiaoshi" [Ugolino Arcari as an example of a missionary], ed. Taiyuanshi tianzhujiao aiguohui, *Wenshi ziliao* 1 (1964): 47.

20. Francesco Fazzini, 31 July 1912 (speaking of Domenico Agostinelli) and 4 March 1916, SBD; Wang Qindian, 15 Dec. 1924, SBD; Basilio Pucello, 12 April 1912, SBD.

21. Ricci, *Fratello di una Martire*, 195–212; Barnaba Nanetti, *Copia di un memoriale*, APF Nuova serie 503 (1911): 421.

22. *Les missions de la Chine* 10 (1933); *Acta Ordinis Fratrum Minorum* 25 (1906): 276–77; 26 (1907): 56–57. I have not included missionary nuns. The 1770s saw the arrival of several groups of Naples-trained Chinese priests at a time when the Qing made it very hard for Europeans to reach Shanxi.

23. The places of origin are known because the Franciscans often used them instead of surnames. For Pofi, see Nicola Cerasa, *Gioioso Centenario: Biografia di Mons. Luca Domenico Capozi* (Pofi: Umberto Capozi e Giuseppe Leonardi, 1999), 20–23.

24. Jacques Leclercq, *Thunder in the Distance: The Life of Père Lebbe*, trans. George Lamb (New York: Sheed & Ward, 1958), 54–58; Léopold Levaux, *Le Père Lebbe: Apôtre de la Chine moderne (1877–1940)* (Bruxelles: Éditions universitaires, 1948), 136–49. The newspaper was *Yishi bao* [Social welfare].

25. Giornale dal 1° Giugno 1910, 25 Feb. 1911, Sept. 1911; letter from Antonius Maria Fu, *Acta Ordinis Fratrum Minorum* 17 (1898): 114.

26. Eugenio Massi, 3 July 1904, SBD.

27. Chen Guodi (Luigi), 3 July 1905, SBD. See also Eugenio Massi, 4 Dec. 1907 and 4 Sept. 1909, SBD; Joannis Hofman, Feb. 1902, ACGOFM Sinae 12:553; Alfredo Berta, *Mons. Eugenio Massi o.f.m. Vescovo e Vicario Apostolico di Taiyuanfu, Sianfu e Hankow (Cina) (1875–1944)* (Ancona: Biblioteca Francescana, 1955), 26–31.

28. Du Bingtian, 4 April 1932, SBD. See also Tianzhujiao Fenyang jiaoqu, ed., *Fenyang jiaoqu shi, 1926–1996* [Fenyang diocese history] (1996), 49.

29. Eugenio Massi, 6 Dec. 1908, SBD; Ioannis Hofman, Feb. 1902, ACGOFM Sinae 12:550.

30. The missionary who worked in Bolivia was Francesco Zocconali. Domenico Gandolfi, "Cenni di storia del vicariato apostolico di Taiyuanfu Shansi, Cina 1930–1953," *Studi Francescani* 84 (1987): 316; interview, Han Yaozong (priest, born 1921), 26 July 2007.

31. Francesco Fazzini, 26 Feb. 1912, SBD.

32. Francesco Fazzini, 11 Dec. 1912, SBD.

33. Eligio Ferretti, 6 Nov. 1913, SBD; Gao Buqing, 3 Dec. 1921 and 19 Feb. 1922, SBD.

34. Fu Bingyi, 17 April 1914, SBD; Chen Guodi, 14 April 1914, SBD.

35. Domenico Gandolfi, "Cenni Storici sulla Missione di Yütze (Shansi): 1930–1953," *Studi Francescane* 85 (1988): 128 (re: Mario Balboni); Basilio Pucello, 15 Dec. 1933, SBD.

36. Contract made by Ren Wutao, 20th of the 8th month 1910, Geliaogcou cun cunweihui dang'anju [Geliaogou village village party committee archive office], Baochihui [Orphanage]. See also Sun Zhanyuan, 3 Oct. 1913, SBD; Fu Bingyi, 20 April 1903, SBD; Wang Chongde, 2 March 1921, SBD.

37. Liu Anrong, *Shanxi tianzhujiao shi yanjiu* [Historical research on Catholicism in Shanxi] (Taiyuan: Beiyue wenyi chubanshe, 2011). See also Bernardino Larghetti, 19 Dec. 1914, SBD.

38. Ermengildo Focaccia, 27 Sept. 1914 and 12 Nov. 1914, SBD.

39. Cerasa, *Gioioso Centenario*, 42–43; Michele Chiapetta, 7 Jan. 1916, SBD; Ren Wenhuan, 1 Oct. 1923, SBD; Theodosius Maestri, "Apparition of a Martyr Bishop to Pagans," *Franciscans in China* 7 (1924): 156; Letter from Luca Capozi, *Acta Ordinis Fratrum Minorum* 54 (1935): 313; Gandolfi, "Cenni di storia del vicariato apostolico di Taiyuanfu," 306.

40. Michele Chiapetta, 7 Jan. 1916, SBD; Liu Anrong, *Shanxi tianzhujiao shi yanjiu*.

41. Wang Mingqin, 11 April 1923, SBD; Basilio Pucello, 4 Feb. 1905, SBD; Eugenio Massi, 28 Aug. 1904, SBD; Michele Chiapetta, 27 Dec. 1903 and 8 Feb. 1905, SBD; interviews with Cave Gully residents conducted by Liu Anrong in 2005.

42. Martino Antonelli, 19 Jan. 1912, SBD; Giornale dal 1° Giugno 1910, Dec. 1911; Jiaoyou shenghuo bianjibu, ed., *Tianzhujiao Changzhi jiaoqu jianshi* [A brief history of Changzhi Catholic diocese] (1997), 77; Letter from Agapito Fiorentini, *Acta Ordinis Fratrum Minorum* 28 (1909): 19.

43. *Shanxi tongzhi*, 46:389; Guo Chongxi, "Taiyuan tianzhujiao shilue," 231–33; Guo Quanzhi, "Shanxi tianzhujiao gaishu" [An outline of Catholicism in Shanxi] (manuscript, 2007), 68–69, 77–78; Chen Guodi, 12 Nov. 1913, SBD. See also Henrietta Harrison, "Rethinking Missionaries and Medicine in China: The Miracles of Assunta Pallotta, 1905–2005," *Journal of Asian Studies* 71, no. 1 (2012): 127–48.

44. Du Gantang, 9 June 1913, SBD. See also Sun Zhanyuan, 30 Dec. 1912, SBD.

45. Martino Antonelli, 10 July 1913, and undated letter beginning "Il cristiano di Sciao-i," SBD.

46. Martino Antonelli, undated letter beginning "Occludo una lettera del P. Mon—G.B.," SBD; *Shanxi tongzhi*, 46:480; Xi Lian, *Redeemed by Fire: The Rise of Popular Christianity in Modern China* (New Haven: Yale University Press, 2010), 53; Wei Yisa, *Zhen Yesuhui chuangli sanshi zhounian jinian zhuankan* [Special commemorative issue on the 30th anniversary of the founding of the True Jesus Church] (Nanjing: Zhen Yesuhui, 1948), C18, M10; Joannes Ricci, 1 Jan. 1914, Archives Vincent Lebbe, Société des Auxiliaires des Missions, Bruxelles, A6.1, 4, www.vincentlebbe.net.

47. Michele Chiapetta, 25 Feb. 1913, SBD; Francesco Fazzini, 11 Dec. 1912, SBD; Eugenio Massi, 20 Dec. 1907, SBD.

48. Innocenzo Pentonzoli, 9 April 1912 and 5 June 1912, SBD.

49. Ugolino Arcari, 28 Feb. 1913, SBD; Paul Zhang, undated letter no. 7, SBD.

50. Chang Jiala, 22nd of 6th month 1912, Michele Chiapetta file, SBD.

51. Michele Chiapetta, 26 March 1912, SBD.

52. Francesco Fazzini, 9 March 1912, SBD; Du Yongqing, 10 April 1906, SBD; Eugenio Mostarda, 30 Nov. 1923, SBD; Paul Zhang, 6 March 1905, SBD; Fu Bingyi, 13 April 1907, SBD; Chen Guodi, 6 April 1905, SBD.

53. Francesco Fazzini, 20 Jan. 1914, undated letter beginning "Gia i lavoranti sono partiti," SBD; *Yasongda zouguo de lu, qianbei fuwu, Yasongda xingshi ji xubian* [The path Assunta trod—humble service. The deeds of Assunta and a supplement] (Taiyuan, 2005), 46; Léon de Kerval, *Le R.P. Hugolin de Doullens ou la vie d'un Frère Mineur missionnaire en Chine au XIXe siècle* (Rome: Francisc. Miss., 1902), 82.

54. Interviews with Cave Gully residents; Michele Chiapetta, 11 March 1913, SBD; Francesco Fazzini, 2 Dec. 1914, SBD.

55. The missionaries who terraced the hillside and supplied water were Valerio Icardi and Barnaba d'Alsazia. Alfonso De Donato, 1834, APF SC Cina 8:109; Giacomo Di Fiore, *Lettere di missionari dalla Cina (1761–1775): La vita quotidiana nelle missioni attraverso il carteggio di Emiliano Palladini e Filippo Huang con il Collegio dei Cinesi in Napoli* (Napoli: Istituto Universitario Orientale, 1995), 259; Elia Facchini, 4 Jan. 1892, OFM Bologna 1:11; Letter from Barnaba Nanetti, *Oriente Serafico* 7 (1895): 214–16.

56. Francesco Fazzini, 12 Aug. 1914, SBD; Ermengildo Focaccia, 29 Aug. 1924, SBD; interviews with Cave Gully residents.

57. Innocenzo Petonzoli, 23 March 1912, SBD; Francesco Fazzini, 12 and 16 Feb. 1913, 16 and 20 Jan. 1914, 22 June 1914, 23 and 29 July 1914, SBD.

58. Francesco Fazzini, 23 June 1915 and 2 July 1915, SBD; Wang Chongli, 1 July 1915, SBD; Sun Zhanyuan, 6 and 25 July 1915, SBD.

59. Joannes Ricci, 11 July 1914, Archives Vincent Lebbe; Giovanni Ricci, 2 Feb. 1916, OFM Bologna 1:32; Yan Fu, "Diguozhuyi chuanjiaoshi zhengduo quanli de choutai" [The ugly scene of imperialist missionaries struggling for power], ed. Taiyuanshi tianzhujiao aiguohui, *Wenshi ziliao* (1964): 2:54.

60. *Missions de Chine* 8 (1929): 136; Tianzhujiao Fenyang jiaoqu, ed., *Fenyang jiaoqu shi*, 8; Ermengildo Focaccia, 23 April 1929, SBD; *Shanxi tongzhi*, 46:378, 422.

61. The missionary was Eligio Ferretti and the superior was Ermengildo Focaccia. Gandolfi, "Cenni storici sulla missione di Yütze," 123; Ugolino Arcari, 17 July 1912, OFM Bologna 1:3; Daniele Lorenzini, 14 July 1922, SBD; Basilio Pucello, 15 July 1923, SBD; Teodosio Lombardi, *Un Grande Ideale: Monsignor Ermengildo Focaccia O.F.M. Vescovo di Yütze in Cina* (Bologna: Edizioni Antoniano, 1968), 56.

62. Zhang Anduoni and Tian Wendu, *Shengmu qiku* [The Seven Sorrows of the Mother of God] (Shanxi: Mingyuan tang, 1878). See also Paul Brunner, *L'Euchologe de la mission de Chine: Editio princeps 1628 et développements jusqu'à nos jours* (Münster: Aschendorffsche verlagsbuchhandlung, 1964), 106; Michael P. Carroll, *Veiled Threats: The Logic of Popular Catholicism in Italy* (Baltimore: Johns Hopkins University Press, 1996), 92–98.

63. Bernardino Larghetti, 24 Aug. 1912, SBD; l'Abbé Durosel, *La Madone de Campocavallo ou recit de N.-D. des Sept Douleurs a Campocavallo des guérisons, conversions et faveurs diverses attribuées a son intercession, avec un appendice sur le sanctuaire de N.-D. de Lorette* (Abbeville: C. Paillart, 1896).

64. Interviews with Cave Gully residents; Sun Zhanyuan, 27 June 1916, SBD.

65. Guo Chongxi, "Taiyuan tianzhujiao shilue," 158–60; Guo Chongxi, "Taiyuan tianzhujiao zhuyao tangkou jianjie" [A brief introduction to the main Catholic parishes of Taiyuan], *Taiyuan wenshi ziliao* 15 (1991): 156.

66. Interview with former orphan; Bernardo Stacchini, *Ombre rosse sulla Cina* (Bologna: Abes, 1956), 8; Teodosio Maestri, 4 Sept. 1931, SBD; Guo Chongxi, "Mei Deli de diguozhuyi xiang" [The imperialist face of Teodosio Maestri], ed. Taiyuanshi tianzhujiao aiguohui, *Wenshi ziliao* 1 (1964): 32, 36; Han Yaozong, "Cong Lei Jingshi kan chuanjiaoshi," 46; Lombardi, *Un Grande Ideale*, 194. See also J. F. Pollard, "Fascism and Catholicism" in *The Oxford Handbook of Fascism*, ed. R. J. B. Bosworth (Oxford: Oxford University Press, 2009): 166–84; Anthony L. Cardoza, *Agrarian Elites and Italian Fascism: The Province of Bologna 1901–1926* (Princeton: Princeton University Press, 1982).

67. Gandolfi, "Cenni storici," 135–37; Lombardi, *Un Grande Ideale*, 214–17; Zhao Peicheng et al., *Xinzhou diqu zongjiao zhi* [Xinzhou district religion gazetteer] (Taiyuan: Shanxi renmin chubanshe, 1993), 291–92; Michele Chiapetta, 14 Nov. 1937, SBD; Xing Huamin, "Li Lujia zai Taiyuan jiaoqu de huodong diandi" [The activities of Luca Capozi in Taiyuan diocese], ed. Taiyuanshi tianzhujiao aiguohui, *Wenshi ziliao* 2 (1964): 21.

68. Yan Fu, "Diguozhuyifenzi An Shigao de yidian shishi" [Some historical facts about the imperialist Elia Carosi], ed. Taiyuanshi tianzhujiao aiguohui, *Wenshi ziliao* 1 (1964): 61–62; Vincent Lebbe, 28 Feb. 1931, 13 March 1937, 1 Feb. 1938, Archives Vincent Lebbe; Leclerq, *Thunder in the Distance*, 278, 291–302, 321; Levaux, *Le Père Lebbe*, 388–89.

CHAPTER 6

1. Interviews with Cave Gully residents and other local people.

2. Edgar Haering, 31 Oct. 1946, POSI C440 Shohchow; Su Ruoyi, *Zhongguo jindai jiaonan shiliao (1948–1957)* [Historical materials on China's

modern religious persecution (1948–1957)] (Taibei: Furen daxue chubanshe, 2000), p. 53–23–4; *China Missionary* 1, no. 4 (1948): 488; Chen Yongfa, "Neizhan: Mao Zedong he tudi geming: Cuowu panduan haishi zhengzhi moulue" [Civil war: Mao Zedong and the land revolution: Error of judgement or political strategy] *Dalu zazhi* 92, nos. 1–3 (1996).

3. The bishop was Luca Capozi. Guo Chongxi, "Fan Li Lujia douzheng de qianqianhouhou" [The struggle against Luca Capozi from beginning to end], ed. Taiyuan tianzhujiao aiguohui, *Wenshi ziliao* 2 (1964): 2–17. There was a similar campaign in Yuci diocese, see Domenico Gandolfi, "Cenni Storici sulla Missione di Yütze (Shansi): 1930–1953," *Studi Francescane* 85 (1988): 152–53.

4. The Belgian was Raymond de Jaegher. Luca Capozi, "Relazione dell'arcivescovo di Taiyuan alla Sacra Congregazione di Propaganda 1 luglio 1950—30 giugno 1953" in *Gioioso Centenario: Biografia di Mons. Luca Domenico Capozi*, ed. Nicola Cerasa (Pofi: Umberto Capozi e Giuseppe Leonardi, 1999), 202. See also Raymond J. de Jaegher and Irene Corbally Kuhn, *The Enemy Within: An Eyewitness Account of the Communist Conquest of China* (New York: Doubleday, 1952).

5. Nicola Cerasa, *Breve Storia della Missione di Taiyuan Shansi* (Roma: Provincia Romana dei Frati Minori, 1998), 187; *Shanxi ribao* [Shanxi daily news], 25 March 1951, 1 and 12 Aug. 1951, 1; Paul P. Mariani, *Church Militant: Bishop Kung and Catholic Resistance in Communist China* (Cambridge: Harvard University Press, 2011), 47–50.

6. Cerasa, *Breve storia*, 150–51, 198, 204, 223; Gandolfi, "Cenni storici sulla Missione di Yütze," 154–55; *Shanxi ribao*, 20 June 1951, 3 and 8 July 1951, 1; Interview. See also William Hinton, *Shenfan* (New York: Random House, 1983), 531.

7. The new Chinese bishop of Taiyuan was Hao Nai. The missionary in Cave Gully was Mario Balboni. Capozi, "Relazione dell'arcivescovo," 180–234; Guo Quanzhi, "Shanxi tianzhujiao gaishu" [An outline of Catholicism in Shanxi] (manuscript, 2007), 52–54; *Yasongda zouguo de lu, qianbei fuwu, Yasongda xingshi ji xubian* [The path Assunta trod—humble service. The deeds of Assunta and a supplement] (Taiyuan, 2005), 96; interviews.

8. Only two Taiyuan diocese priests did not subscribe to the new church: Wang Chongli, who had been Bishop Capozi's secretary and was elderly and sick, and Zhang Xin (later bishop of Taiyuan), who was studying in Beijing. Li Dehua became bishop after the arrest of Hao Nai in 1955 and was consecrated in Beijing in 1962. Cerasa, *Breve storia*, 254–56; Guo Chongxi, "Fan Li Lujia douzheng," 27; Cerasa, *Gioioso centenario*, 135.

9. For Protestants, see Philip L. Wickeri, *Reconstructing Christianity in China: K. H. Ting and the Chinese Church* (Maryknoll: Orbis Books, 2007), 36–42, 97–106; Xi Lian, *Redeemed by Fire: The Rise of Popular Christianity in Modern China* (New Haven: Yale University Press, 2010), 198. Catholic Liberation Theology is a later development: see Ian Linden, *Global Catholicism: Diversity and Change since Vatican II* (New York: Columbia University Press, 2009), 169.

10. Cerasa, *Breve storia*, 247. See also Sandra L. Zimdars-Swartz, *Encountering Mary from La Salette to Medjugorje* (Princeton: Princeton University

Press, 1991), 67–73, 90–91, 190–218; Una M. Cadegan, "The Queen of Peace in the Shadow of War: Fatima and U.S. Catholic Anticommunism," *U.S. Catholic Historian* 22, no. 4 (2004): 1–15.

11. Capozi, "Relazione dell'arcivescovo," 216; Mariani, *Church Militant,* 21; interviews.

12. Zhonggong Taiyuan shiwei siqing zongjiao bangongshi, ed., *Zongjiao gongzuo xuanchuan cailiao* [Propaganda materials for religious work] (1966), 10:10–12, 13:5; *Shanxi ribao,* 12 Aug. 1951, 1; Bernardo Stacchini, *Ombre Rosse sulla Cina* (Bologna: Abes editrice, 1956), 24–27.

13. Li Ye, "Zai difang dang'an zhong faxian lishi—Jinzhong xin qu tugai yundong zhong de qunzhong dongyuan" [Discovering history in local archives: Mass mobilisation during the Land Reform movement in the new districts of central Shanxi] *Shanxi dang'an,* no. 3 (2008): 49–51. See also Huang Daoxuan, "192–194 niandai Zhongguo dongnan diqude tudi zhanyou—jiantan dizhu nongmin yu tudi geming" [Land tenure in southeast China 1920s–1940s: A combined discussion of landlords, peasants and the land revolution] *Lishi yanjiu,* no. 1 (2005): 34–53.

14. Interviews with Wu Mingming, 30 July 2007, and other Cave Gully residents.

15. Stacchini, *Ombre Rosse,* 20; interviews. See also William Hinton, *Fanshen: A Documentary of Revolution in a Chinese Village* (New York: Vintage Books, 1966) and his later study *Shenfan* (New York: Random House, 1983).

16. Tianzhujiao Fenyang jiaoqu, ed., *Fenyang jiaoqu shi, 1926–1996* [Fenyang diocese history] (1996), 35; Song Jianxun, "Xinzhou diqu tianzhujiao fazhan gaikuang" [An outline of the development of Catholicism in Xinzhou district] (manuscript), 27–29; Guo Quanzhi, "Shanxi tianzhujiao gaishu," 94–97.

17. Cave Gully's parish priest was Wang Shiwei. Li Jiantang from Cave Gully (later bishop of Taiyuan) was ordained in 1956. Qin Geping, *Taiyuan jiaoqu jianshi* [A simple history of Taiyuan diocese] (Tianzhujiao Taiyuan jiaoqu, 2008), 38; Guo Quanzhi, "Shanxi tianzhujiao gaishu," 5, 8; Guo Chongxi, "Taiyuan tianzhujiao shilue" [A brief history of Catholicism in Taiyuan], *Taiyuan wenshi ziliao* 17 (1992): 174; Zhonggong Taiyuan shiwei siqing zongjiao bangongshi, ed., *Zongjiao gongzuo xuanchuan cailiao,* 11:5, 13:9; *Shanxi tongzhi* [Shanxi gazetteer] (Beijing: Zhonghua shuju, 1997), 46:405; Capozi, "Relazione dell'arcivescovo," 186; interviews with Wu Mingming, Cave Gully, 8 Sept. 2005 30 July 2007, and with other Cave Gully residents; Chang Libing, "Cong yishi dao saoluan—dui 1965 nian Qingxu xian H cun tianzhujiaotu de zhengzhi shiying zhi yanjiu" [From ritual to riot: Research on the Catholics' adaptation to government in H village, Qingxu county, 1965] (Paper presented at Zhongguo shehuishi huiyi, 2008), 6.

18. For the Socialist Education Movement, see Richard Baum and Frederick C. Teiwes, *Ssu-ch'ing: The Socialist Education Movement of 1962–1966* (Berkeley: Center for Chinese Studies, 1968); Zhang Letian, *Gaobie lixiang: Renmin gongshe zhidu yanjiu* [Farewell to ideals: Research into the people's commune system] (Shanghai: Shiji chubanshe, 2005), 107–53. For Shanxi, see Zhongguo Guomindang zhongyang weiyuanhui, ed., *Shanxi sheng de duoquan*

douzheng [The struggle for power in Shanxi province] (Taibei, 1967); Meng Yonghua, "Shanxi nongcun 'Siqing' yundong shuping" [An evaluation of the 'Four Cleans' movement in Shanxi villages], *Dangshi yanjiu yu jiaoxue*, no. 4 (2007): 50–56.

19. *Zongjiao gongzuo tongxun* [Religious work report], 18 Jan. 1964, 6–13.
20. *Zongjiao gongzuo tongxun*, 3 Sept. 1964, 3.
21. *Zongjiao gongzuo tongxun*, 13 Feb. 1965, 10.
22. *Acta Ordinis Fratrum Minorum* 62 (1943): 13–17.
23. Zhonggong Taiyuan shiwei siqing zongjiao bangongshi, ed., *Zongjiao gongzuo xuanchuan cailiao*, 13:10–11.
24. *Shanxi tongzhi*, 46:423; Qin Geping, *Taiyuan jiaoqu jianshi*, 362–63.
25. Chang Libing, "Cong yishi dao saoluan," 4–5; Tanbai cailiao, 6 Feb. 1966, and Buchong cailiao, 5 Oct. 1965, SD. In order to preserve the anonymity of the subjects of these personnel files I have ommitted both personal names and the name of the village concerned (which is not Cave Gully).
26. Interviews. Unless otherwise noted all interviews from this point on are with participants or onlookers.
27. *Shanxi tongzhi*, 46:423–24; Qin Geping, *Taiyuan jiaoqu jianshi*, 365–66; Ziwo jiancha, 3 May 1970, SD; Tanbai jianju cailiao kapian, 2 June 1966, SD; Huiyi lu Tianzhujiao jiaodai wenti, 23 Sept. 1965, SD Zonghe; Zhonggong Taiyuan shiwei siqing zongjiao bangongshi, ed., *Zongjiao gongzuo xuanchuan cailiao*, 2:11; interviews.
28. Jibuqingming zai sanyue jian, 4 Oct. 1965, SD; Geren jiancha, 7 May 1965, SD; interviews.
29. Zhonggong Taiyuan shiwei siqing zongjiao bangongshi, ed., *Zongjiao gongzuo xuanchuan cailiao*, 11:2; *Zongjiao gongzuo tongxun*, 28 Dec. 1965, 12; Di yi ci tianzhujiaotu X jiaodai tianzhujiao fangeming naoshi zaoyao, 14 Nov. 1965, SD; interviews.
30. *Zongjiao gongzuo tongxun*, 28 Dec. 1965, 12; Geren jiancha, 7 May 1965, SD; interview. See also Paolo Apolito, *Apparitions of the Madonna at Oliveto Citra: Local Visions and Cosmic Drama*, trans. William A. Christian Jr. (University Park: Pennsylvania State University Press, 1998).
31. *Zongjiao gongzuo tongxun*, 28 Dec. 1965, 13. See also Tianzhujiao xunlianban xueyuan jiefa kapian, 2 March 1966, SD; Di yi ci tianzhujiao X jiaodai tianzhujiao fangeming naoshi zaoyao, 14 Nov. 1965, SD; Jiancha cailiao, n.d., SD; Zaijia fanren jianju hefa dengjibiao, 20 Aug. 1965, SD; Jianju cailiao, 28 Aug. 1965, SD.
32. *Zongjiao gongzuo tongxun*, 28 Dec. 1965, 12; X de tanbai jiaodai cailiao, 18 April 1965, SD; Guanyu X dadui tianzhujiaotu X cailiao zhengli, 30 July 1965, SD Zonghe; interviews. See also William A. Christian Jr., *Visionaries: The Spanish Republic and the Reign of Christ* (Berkeley: University of California Press, 1996); Kristofer Schipper, *The Taoist Body*, trans. Karen C. Duval (Berkeley: University of California Press, 1993), 45–54; Liu Dapeng, "Qianyuan suoji," in *Yihetuan zai Shanxi diqu shiliao* [Local historical materials on the Boxers in Shanxi], ed. Qiao Zhiqiang (Taiyuan: Shanxi renmin chubanshe, 1980), 27–28.
33. Guanyu tianzhujiao sancha huiyi, 22 Sept. 1965, SD Zonghe; Guanyu X dadui tianzhujiaotu X cailiao zhengli, 30 July 1965, SD Zonghe; Jiancha

cailiao, n.d., SD; Zicong tianzhujiao naoshile, circa 22 Sept. 1965, SD Zonghe; Jiancha jiaodao, 13 Sept. 1966, SD; Fangeming jiaotu X di er ci jiancha tianzhujiao huodong shishi, 15 Nov. 1965, SD.

34. Zhonggong Taiyuan shiwei siqing zongjiao bangongshi, ed., *Zongjiao gongzuo xuanchuan*, 14:8; interview.

35. Zhonggong Taiyuan shiwei siqing zongjiao bangongshi, ed., *Zongjiao gongzuo xuanchuan cailiao*, 2:11; *Zongjiao gongzuo tongxun*, 28 Dec. 1965, 23; Qingli jieji duiwu geren lülibiao, 1970, SD; Jiaodai, 15 April 1970, SD; Jiancha shu, 1 Oct. 1965, SD; Dahui jilu, 29 Sept. 1965, SD Zonghe; Qin Geping, *Taiyuan jiaoqu jianshi*, 366; interviews.

36. Zhonggong Taiyuan shiwei siqing zongjiao bangongshi, ed., *Zongjiao gongzuo xuanchuan cailiao*, 4:1; Jiancha ren wu juexin, n.d., SD; Zicong zhe, 5 Oct. 1965, SD; Michel de la Sainte Trinité, *The Whole Truth about Fatima*, vol. 3, *The Third Secret (1942–1960)*, trans. John Collorafi (Buffalo: Immaculate Heart Publications, 1990), 642–52; William A. Christian Jr., "Religious Apparitions and the Cold War in Southern Europe" in *Religion, Power and Protest in Local Communities: The Northern Shore of the Mediterranean*, ed. Eric R. Wolf (Berlin: Mouton, 1984).

37. Zhonggong Taiyuan shiwei siqing zongjiao bangongshi, ed., *Zongjiao gongzuo xuanchuan cailiao*, 8:1; *Zongjiao gongzuo tongxun*, 28 Dec. 1965, 15; Buchong cailiao, 5 Oct. [1965], SD; Tanbai jiaodai, n.d, SD Zonghe; interview.

38. Zhonggong Taiyuan shiwei siqing zongjiao bangongshi, ed., *Zongjiao gongzuo xuanchuan cailiao*, 14:8.

39. *Zongjiao gongzuo tongxun*, 28 Dec. 1965, 15; X tanbai jiaodai, SD Zonghe; Zicong tianzhujiao naoshile, SD Zonghe.

40. Jianju cailiao, 28 Aug. 1965, SD; Fangeming jiaotu X di er ci jiancha tianzhujiao huodong shishi, 15 Nov. 1965, SD; *Zongjiao gongzuo tongxun*, 28 Dec. 1965, 12; interview.

41. Zhonggong Taiyuan shiwei siqing zongjiao bangongshi, ed., *Zongjiao gongzuo xuanchuan*, 2:11; *Zongjiao gongzuo tongxun*, 28 Dec. 1965, 12; Tanbai cailiao, 6 Feb. 1966, SD; Jiancha jiaodai, 13 Sept. 1966, SD; Geren jiancha, 22 Sept. 1966, SD; Chang Libing, "Cong yishi dao saoluan"; interviews.

42. *Zongjiao gongzuo tongxun*, 28 Dec. 1965, 12; interviews.

43. Duan Runcheng, *Wode xinyang licheng* [My faith journey] (2005), 5.

44. Cerasa, *Breve storia*, 249; *Shanxi tongzhi*, 46:417, 424; Qin Geping, *Taiyuan jiaoqu jianshi*, 367; interviews.

45. Interviews. See also Zongjiao gongzuo tongxun, 28 Dec. 1965, 13; Jiancha jiaodai, 24 Sept. 1965, SD.

46. *Zongjiao gongzuo tongxun*, 27 Nov. 1965, 2 and 28 Dec. 1965, 13; *Kongsu: Shi shei haisile wo ma?* [Accusation: Who killed my mother?] (Taiyuan, c. 1966), 9; X tanbai jiaodai, SD Zonghe; interviews. See also Jibuqingming zai sanyue jian, 4 Oct. 1965, SD; Zi cong sanyue naoshi, 5 Oct. 1965, SD.

47. Zhonggong Taiyuan shiwei siqing zongjiao bangongshi, ed., *Zongjiao gongzuo xuanchuan cailiao*, 9:1.

48. *Zongjiao gongzuo tongxun*, 28 Dec, 1965, 23, 25; Tianzhu Jidu jiao diaocha duixiang dengjibiao, 1966, SD.

49. Guo Jifen, *Fangjihuishi Guo Jifen shenfu jiniance* [Memorial volume for Franciscan Father Guo Jifen] (Taiyuan, 2003), 15; Qin Geping, *Taiyuan jiaoqu jianshi*, 363–68; interviews. For the early Cultural Revolution in Shanxi, see *Shanxi tongshi* 10:405–87; *Shanxi sheng de duoquan douzheng*.

50. Juexin shu, 7 Sept. 1966, SD.

51. Tuijiaoshu, 10 Sept. 1966, SD.

52. Interviews.

53. Duan Runcheng, *Wode xinyang licheng*, 6–7; Qin Geping, *Taiyuan jiaoqu jianshi*, 363; interviews.

54. *Zongjiao gongzuo tongxun*, 27 Nov. 1965, 3 and 28 Dec. 1965, 15.

55. *Shanxi tongzhi*, 46:396; Qin Geping, *Taiyuan jiaoqu jianshi*, 368–69.

56. *Shanxi tongshi*, 10:488–514; *Shanxi ribao*, 27 Feb. 1970, 1; interviews.

57. Shanxi sheng Jinzhong diqu zhongji renmin fayuan zai shen xingshi panjue shu 80:27 [Shanxi province Jinzhong district mid-level people's court review of capital case 80:27], 1980.

58. Duan Runcheng, *Wode xinyang licheng*, 7–9.

59. *Shanxi tongzhi*, 46:405–9; Guo Quanzhi, "Shanxi tianzhujiao gaishu," 19; Guo Chongxi, "Taiyuan tianzhujiao shilue," 184–222; Jiaoyou shenghuo bianjibu, ed., *Tianzhujiao Changzhi jiaoqu jianshi*, 71–206; Tianzhujiao Fenyang jiaoqu, ed., *Fenyang jiaoqu shi, 1926–1996*, 32–42.

60. Beijing daxue zhexuexi zongjiaoxue zhuanye 84 ji fu Shanxi sheng shehui diaocha zu, ed., *Shehui zhuyi chuji jieduan zongjiao zhuangkuang diaocha baogao xuanji* [Selections from the report of investigation on religion during the primary stage of socialism] (Beijing daxue zhexuexi Makesi zhuyi zongjiao jiaoxue jiaoyanshi, 1987), 3:73; *Liuhe xingxing* [Stars of Liuhe], 15 July 2007.

61. Duan Runcheng, *Wode xinyang licheng*, 7; interviews.

62. Duan Runcheng, *Wode xinyang licheng*, 1–2. See also Robert A. Orsi, *Between Heaven and Earth: The Religious Worlds People Make and the Scholars Who Study them* (Princeton: Princeton University Press, 2005), 110–45.

63. Interview.

64. Interviews, Wu Mingming Cave Gully, 30 July 2007 and others; Yang Xiaolin, "Jinci quan liuliang shuaijian fenxi" [An analysis of the decline in the flow rates of the Jinci spring], *Shanxi shuili*, no. 6 (2005) .

CHAPTER 7

1. Interviews.

2. Duan Runcheng, *Wode xinyang licheng* [My faith journey] (2005), 9; Guo Jifen, *Fangjihuishi Guo Jifen shenfu jiniance* [Memorial volume for Franciscan Father Guo Jifen] (Taiyuan, 2003), 17; *Liwu yu jianzheng—Han Yaozong shenfu jinduo jingangqing jiniance* [Gift and testimony: Commemorative volume for the golden anniversary of Fr Han Yaozong's ordination] (Taiyuan, 2006), 87; Interviews, Wu Mingming, Cave Gully, 30 July 2007 and others.

3. Guo Jifen, *Fangjihuishi Guo Jifen*, 19–22; Guo Chongxi, "Taiyuan tianzhujiao shilue"; Beijing daxue zhexuexi zongjiaoxue zhuanye 84 ji fu Shanxi sheng shehui diaocha zu, ed., *Shehui zhuyi chuji jieduan zongjiao zhuangkuang*

diaocha [Selections from the report of investigation on religion during the primary stage of socialism] (Beijing daxue zhexuexi Makesi zhuyi zongjiao jiaoxue jiaoyanshi, 1987), 72. For the context, see Central Committee of the Chinese Communist Party, "The Basic Viewpoint and Policy on the Religious Question during our Country's Socialist Period. Document no. 19 (March 31, 1982)," *Chinese Law and Government* 33, no. 2 (2000); Taiyuan shi tongjiu, ed., *Taiyuan "liu wu" jianshe chengjiu 1981–1985* [Taiyuan's construction achievements for the sixth five-year plan, 1981–1985] (Taiyuan: Zhongguo tongji chubanshe, 1987), 223.

4. Beijing daxue zhexuexi zongjiaoxue zhuanye 84 ji fu Shanxi sheng shehui diaocha zu, ed., *Shehui zhuyi chuji jieduan zongjiao zhuangkuang diaocha*, 78; interviews.

5. Interviews.

6. Guo Quanzhi, "Shanxi tianzhujiao gaishu" [An outline of Catholicism in Shanxi] (manuscript, 2007), 19; *Banquanshan shengmutang jianjie* [Introduction to the Banquanshan church of Our Lady] (Taiyuan jiaoqu, 2000); Guo Chongxi, "Taiyuan tianzhujiao zhuyao tangkou jianjie" [A brief introduction to the main Catholic parishes of Taiyuan], *Taiyuan wenshi ziliao* 15 (1991): 158; "St Mary's Church near Taiyuan rebuilt," *Tripod* 42 (1987), 31–33.

7. Interview.

8. Beatrice Leung and William T. Liu, *The Chinese Catholic Church in Conflict 1949–2001* (Boca Raton: Universal Publishers, 2004), 145–46; *Repression in China since June 4, 1989* (Asia Watch, 1990), 96; interviews. For the underground church elsewhere, see Paul P. Mariani, *Church Militant: Bishop Kung and Catholic Resistance in Communist China* (Cambridge: Harvard University Press, 2011), 176–78; Wu Fei, *Maimang shang de shengyan: Yige xiangcun tianzhujiao qunti zhong de xinyang he shenghuo* [Sacred word above the awn of wheat: Faith and life in a rural Catholic community] (Hong Kong: Daofeng shushe, 2001), 321–34.

9. Benedict XVI, "Letter to the Bishops, Priests, Consecrated Persons and the Lay Faithful in the People's Republic of China," 27 May 2007, Papal Encyclicals Online, www.papalencyclicals.net.

10. Domenico Gandolfi, "Cenni di storia del vicariato apostolico di Taiyuanfu Shansi, Cina 1930–1953," *Studi Francescani* 84 (1987): 340–41; interviews.

11. Beijing daxue zhexuexi zongjiaoxue zhuanye 84 ji fu Shanxi sheng shehui diaocha zu, ed., *Shehui zhuyi chuji jieduan zongjiao zhuangkuang diaocha*, 148; interviews. Cf. Wu Fei, *Maimang shang de shengyan*, 130.

12. Duan Runcheng, *Chuanjiao shisinian—jingyan tihui huilu* [Fourteen years of evangelism: Collected experiences and knowledge] (Dongergou, 2007), 11, 16. This text is a revised edition of his *Wode xinyang licheng* (2005).

13. Duan Runcheng, *Wode xinyang licheng*; interview. Cf. Wu Fei, *Maimang shang de shengyan*, 35, 141.

14. Duan Runcheng, *Wode xinyang licheng*.

15. Duan Runcheng, *Wode xinyang licheng*, 17.

16. Duan Runcheng, *Wode xinyang licheng*, 23; Duan Runcheng, *Chuanjiao shisinian*, 14.

246 | Notes to Pages 181–191

17. Duan Runcheng, *Wode xinyang licheng*, 9, 11.

18. Duan Runcheng, *Wode xinyang licheng*, 14 (this is his own wording of the Bible passage). See also pages 10–12, 28.

19. Duan Runcheng, *Wode xinyang licheng*, 26; Duan Runcheng, *Chuanjiao shisinian*. Cf. Chen-yang Kao, "The Cultural Revolution and the Emergence of Pentecostal-style Protestantism in China," *Journal of Contemporary Religion* 24, no. 2 (2009); Wu Fei, *Maimang shang de shengyan*, 135.

20. The new bishop was Zhang Xin. Nicola Cerasa, *Breve Storia della Missione di Taiyuan Shansi* (Roma: Provincia Romana dei Frati Minori, 1998), 252; Beijing daxue zhexuexi zongjiaoxue zhuanye 84 ji fu Shanxi sheng shehui diaocha zu ed., *Shehuizhuyi chuji jieduan zongjiao zhuangkuang diaocha*, 67–69; *Times* (London), 24 Dec. 2005, 29; Beatrice Leung, "Communist Party–Vatican Interplay over the Training of Church Leaders in China," *Journal for the Scientific Study of Religion* 40, no. 4 (2001): 666.

21. Interview.

22. *Liuu yu jianzheng*, 89–91; interviews. See also Wu Fei, *Maimang shang de shengyan*, 90, 94–98; John W. O'Malley, *What Happened at Vatican II* (Cambridge: Harvard University Press, 2008).

23. Interviews, Wu Mingming Cave Gully, 30 July 2007 and others.

24. Interviews. Cf. Gareth Fisher, "The Spiritual Land Rush: Merit and Morality in New Chinese Buddhist Temple Construction," *Journal of Asian Studies* 67, no. 1 (2008): 143–70.

25. Wu Gaoshou and Wang Jie, "Guanyu Dongergou cun xinjiao cunminde zhongji guanhuai de diaocha baogao" [Report on an investigation into Dongergou village religious believers' ultimate concerns], *Shijie zongjiao yanjiu*, no. 2 (2006) : 130–34; *Yasongda zouguo de lu, qianbei fuwu, Yasongda xingshi ji xubian* [The path Assunta trod—humble service. The deeds of Assunta and a supplement] (Taiyuan, 2005), 120–21; Shanxi zhengwu ducha [Shanxi government affairs supervision], 9 Sept. 2004, Shanxi sheng renmin zhengfu, www. shanxigov.cn, accessed 28 May 2008 but no longer available online; interviews.

26. Interviews; Lily L. Tsai, *Accountability without Democracy: Solidary Groups and Public Goods Provision in Rural China* (Cambridge: Cambridge University Press, 2007).

27. Interviews with state employees as well as Catholics.

28. Guo Quanzhi, 14, 22; Beijing daxue zhexuexi zongjiaoxue zhuanye 84 ji fu Shanxi sheng shehui diaocha zu, ed., *Shehuizhuyi chuji jieduan zongjiao zhuangkuang diaocha*, 76–78; interview, Wu Mingming, Cave Gully, 30 July 2007.

29. Beijing daxue zhexuexi zongjiaoxue zhuanye 84 ji fu Shanxi sheng shehui diaocha zu, ed., *Shehuizhuyi chuji jieduan zongjiao zhuangkuang diaocha*, 74, 94; interviews. Of course there are also occasional sex scandals in the church, as in a story of a young priest who ran off with a woman, but there is less gossip about these. For Buddhist financial scandals, see Fisher, "Spiritual Land Rush."

30. Beijing daxue zhexuexi zongjiaoxue zhuanye 84 ji fu Shanxi sheng shehui diaocha zu, ed., *Shehuizhuyi chuji jieduan zongjiao zhuangkuang diaocha*, 69, 147; Qin Geping, *Taiyuan jiaoqu jianshi* [A simple history of Taiyuan diocese] (Tianzhujiao Taiyuan jiaoqu, 2008), 54–96; interviews.

31. Interview, Duan Runcheng, 5 Aug. 2009.

32. Chen-yang Kao, "Cultural Revolution," 84.

33. *Acta Ordinis Fratrum Minorum* 30 (1911): 280–84 and 62 (1943): 13–15; "Agostino Zhao Rong (1815) and 119 Companions, Martyrs in China (1648–1930), 1 October 2000," The Holy See, www.vatican.va; Guo Chongxi, "Taiyuan tianzhujiao shilue," 246; Cipriano Silvestri, *La Testimonia del Sangue: Biografie dei Beati Cinesi uccisi il 7, 8, e 9 iuglio 1900* (Roma: Don Luigi Guanella, 1943), 369–88; *Renmin ribao* [People's Daily], 3 Oct. 2000, 1.

34. *Yasongda zouguo de lu*, 139–41.

35. Ivan Gaskell, "*Jesus Christ as the Divine Mercy* by Eugenius Kazimirowski: The Most Influential Polish Painting of the Twentieth Century?" *Ars: Journal of the Institute of Art History of Slovak Academy of Sciences* 42, no. 1 (2009): 81–93.

36. Cf. Xiao-qing Wang, "How Has a Chinese village Remained Catholic? Catholicism and Local Culture in a Northern Chinese Village," *Journal of Contemporary China* 15, no. 49 (2006): 687–704; Wu Fei, *Maimang shang de shengyan.*

CONCLUSION

1. Eric Reinders, *Borrowed Gods and Foreign Bodies: Christian Missionaries Imagine Chinese Religion* (Berkeley: University of California Press, 2004), 110–11.

2. Chen-yang Kao, "The Cultural Revolution and the Post-Missionary Transformation of Protestantism in China" (PhD diss., University of Lancaster, 2009), 162. See also Ryan Dunch, *Fuzhou Protestants and the Making of Modern China* (New Haven: Yale University Press, 2001), 2–15.

3. Melissa Wei-Tsing Inouye, "Miraculous Mundane: The True Jesus Church and Chinese Christianity in the Twentieth Century" (PhD diss., Harvard University, 2010).

4. Liam Matthew Brockey, *Journey to the East: The Jesuit Mission to China, 1579–1724* (Cambridge: Harvard University Press, 2007).

5. Kang Zhijie, *Shangzhu de putaoyuan: Exi Mopanshan tianzhujiao shequ yanjiu* [The Lord's vineyard: Research into the Mopanshan Catholic district in western Hubei] (Taibei: Furen daxue chubanshe, 2006).

6. Robert E. Entenmann, "Catholics and Society in Eighteenth-century Sichuan," in *Christianity in China from the Eighteenth-Century to the Present*, ed. Daniel H. Bays (Stanford: Stanford University Press, 1996), 8–23; Eugenio Menegon, *Ancestors, Virgins, and Friars: Christianity as a Local Religion in Late Imperial China* (Cambridge: Harvard University Asia Center Press, 2009).

7. Donald MacGillivray, *A Century of Protestant Missions in China (1807–1907) Being the Centenary Conference Historical Volume* (Shanghai: American Presbyterian Mission Press, 1907), 674–77. The figures are 950,058 Catholics and 178,251 Protestants.

8. Xi Lian, *The Conversion of Missionaries: Liberalism in American Protestant Missions in China, 1907–1932* (University Park: Pennsylvania State University Press, 1997), 29.

9. Henrietta Harrison, "'A Penny for the Little Chinese' : The French Holy Childhood Association in China, 1843–1951," *American Historical Review* 113, no. 1 (2008): 72–92.

10. Dunch, *Fuzhou Protestants*, 32–47.

11. Benjamin A. Elman, *On Their Own Terms: Science in China, 1550–1900* (Cambridge: Harvard University Press, 2005), 365.

12. Joseph W. Esherick, *The Origins of the Boxer Uprising* (Berkeley: University of California Press, 1987), 123–35.

13. Archives of the American Board of the Commissioners of Foreign Missions, North China Mission, Harvard University, Cambridge, MA.

14. Dunch, *Fuzhou Protestants*, 17–24.

15. Xi Lian, *Redeemed by Fire: The Rise of Popular Christianity in Modern China* (New Haven: Yale University Press, 2010).

16. This statement is impressionistic, but see Joseph Tse-Hei Lee, "Watchman Nee and the Little Flock Movement in Maoist China," *Church History* 74, no. 1 (2005): 68–96; Philip L. Wickeri, *Reconstructing Christianity in China: K.H. Ting and the Chinese Church* (Maryknoll: Orbis Books, 2007); Lian, *Redeemed by Fire*, 197–202.

17. Joseph Tse-hei Lee, "Christianity in Contemporary China: An Update," *Journal of Church and State* 49 (2007); Fenggang Yang, "Lost in the Market, Saved at McDonald's: Conversion to Christianity in Urban China," *Journal for the Scientific Study of Religion* 44, no. 4 (2005): 423–41; Lian, *Redeemed by Fire*, 2, 230–32.

18. Chen-yang Kao,"The Cultural Revolution and the Emergence of Pentecostal-style Protestantism in China," *Journal of Contemporary Religion* 24, no. 2 (2009): 171–88.

19. Lee, "Christianity in Contemporary China," 298; Lian, *Redeemed by Fire*, 226–29; Thomas H. Reilly, *The Taiping Heavenly Kingdom: Rebellion and the Blasphemy of Empire* (Seattle: University of Washington Press, 2004).

20. *Jianan shige* [Canaan hymns], Zhongguo zaochen de wudianzhong, http://cclw.net/resources/Cannan/Cannan.htm. John Yasuda brought this hymn to my attention in his Harvard University senior thesis.

Glossary

Both missionaries and Chinese Christians used multiple names and did not spell them consistently. Place names and their transliterations also vary and have changed through time. This glossary gives variations to help the reader identify the people and places in other secondary literature and in the primary sources.

Arcari, Ugolino	雷警世
beijiao	背教
Cannetti, Domenico d'Assisi	梁多明
Cave Gully, Dongergou (Tun ol cou, Tun-ol-cho, Tunalko, Ton-ol-keo, T'oung-eul-kéou, Toungeulkeou, Tungerhkow)	洞兒溝
Chen Guodi (Luigi Tcheng, Aloysius Tch'en, Tch'eng, Cen)	陳國砥
Cipparone, Antonio (Ciperone)	任重仁
Cold Springs Road, Liangquandao (Lean-tciuen-tao)	梁泉道 (now Liuhe, 六合)
Dashengkui	大盛魁
Dongmuzhuang	東穆莊
Duan	段
Duan Gun (Pietro)	段滾 (九章)
Duan Runcheng	段潤成
Duan Tianhe	段天和
Duan Wanhe	段萬和

Fan	范
Fazzini, Francesco	法濟尼
Fen	汾
Ferretti, Eligio	艾士杰
Focaccia, Ermengildo	福濟才
Fogolla, Francesco a Monteregio	富格辣
Four Fragrances	四香
Gao Anna (Ko-Anna, Kao Anna, Cao Anna)	高亞納
gong	公
Grioglio, Gabriele da Moretta	杜嘉畢阨爾
Guandi	關帝
Guanyin (Avalokitesvara)	觀音
Hanlin	翰林
Han Qingxiang	韓清香
Herdtrich, Christian	恩理格 (性涵)
huai jiao	壞教
huizhang	會長
Jiangzhou	絳州 (now Xinjiang, 新絳)
jiaodai	交代 (or 交待)
jie	戒
Jinci	晉祠
jingtian	敬天
Kulun (now Ulaan Bataar)	庫倫
Landi, Luigi da Signa	路類思
Lebbe, Vincent	雷鳴遠
lianyuhun	煉獄魂
Li Zhenxiang	李珍香
Li Zibiao (Jacobus, Giacomo Ly)	李自標
Massi, Eugenio	希賢
Mazu	媽祖
Moccagatta, Luigi da Castellazzo	江類思
Nanetti, Barnaba da Cologna	安懷珍
Newtown, Xinli	新立
Nine Springs, Jiuji (Cieu cia tzun, Kieu-kia-cung, K'iu-ci tseung)	九汲
Pingyao	平遙
Qingyuan (Cin-iuen)	清源 (now Qingxu, 清徐)

Qin Zhanyu (Agatha)	秦占玉
Qixian	祁縣
Red Gully, Honggou (Houn-Kéou-Tzen)	紅溝
Ricci, Giovanni	林茂才
Ricci, Matteo	利瑪竇
Rudiya guo ren	茹地亞國人
Saccani, Francesco da Pedrignon	范方濟
Salvetti, Giovacchino (Gioacchino)	艾若雅敬
Sandy Gully, Shagou (Sa-kéou)	沙溝
sha	殺
Shangdi	上帝
shen	神
Shengmu	聖母
Shengmujun	聖母軍
Song zi niangniang	送子娘娘
Taiping	太平
Taiyuan	太原
Tian (a Catholic family)	田
Tian (Heaven)	天
Tian Fenglan (Bonaventura)	田豐蘭（文都）
Tian laoye	天老爺
Tian Meixiang	田梅香
Tianzhu	天主
Upper Mines, Yaozishang (Yaotzetsoun)	窯子上 (now Yaoshang, 堯尚)
Vagnone (Vagnoni), Alfonso	高一志 (則聖)，王豐肅
Vanzolini, Domenico	李文全
Ventura, Patrizio	溫儉讓
Villeret, Hugolin de Doullens	武奧林
wai qian	外遷
Wang Jacobus (Giacomo Wang)	王雅格
Wang Tingrong (Josephus, Giuseppe, Vam, Van)	王廷荣 (若瑟)
wan you zhenyuan	萬有真源
Weituo (Skanda)	韋馱
West Willows, Xiliulin (Lieou-lin-tsoan, Liu-lien-tzon, Lieu-kia-tchouang)	西柳林
Winding Gully, Geliaogou (Koleaokow, Ké-léao-kéou, Ke-leo-kow)	圪潦溝
Wu	吳

Wu Family Cliff, Wujiaya	吳家溰
xiang	香
Xiantianjiao	先天教
Yawu Maliya manbei elajiya zhe	亞物瑪利亞滿被額辣濟亞者
Yili	伊犁
Youtai ren	猶太人
Yuci (Yütze)	榆次
Zai tian wo deng fu zhe	在天我等父者
Zhang Zhidong	張之洞
Zhao Yuqian (Petrus, Pierre, Ciao, Chao, Tciao, Tchao)	趙毓謙
Zheng Fentao	鄭粉桃

Bibliography

Acta Ordinis Fratrum Minorum. 1882–1954.

An Jiesheng 安介生. "Qingdai Shanxi zhongshang fengshang yu jiexiao funü de chuxian" 清代山西重商風商與節孝婦女的出現 [The custom of emphasizing trade and the appearance of chaste women in Qing dynasty Shanxi]. *Qingshi yanjiu* 清史研究 1 (2001): 27–34.

Annales de l'Oeuvre de la Sainte Enfance. 1846–1909.

Apolito, Paolo. *Apparitions of the Madonna at Oliveto Citra: Local Visions and Cosmic Drama.* University Park: Pennsylvania State University Press, 1998. Translated by William A. Christian, Jr.

Archives de l'Oeuvre de la Propagation de la Foi, Oeuvres Pontificales Missionnaires Centre de Lyon (AOPF).

Archives of the American Board of the Commissioners of Foreign Missions. Harvard University. Cambridge, MA.

Archives Vincent Lebbe. Société des Auxiliaires des Missions, Bruxelles. www.vincentlebbe.net.

Archivio della Curia Generalizia dell'Ordine dei Frati Minori, Rome (ACGOFM).

Archivio Provinciale, Provincia di Cristo Re, Frati Minori dell'Emilia Romagna, Bologna (OFM Bologna).

Archivio Storico della Congregazione per l'Evangelizzazione dei Popoli o "de Propaganda Fide," Rome (APF).

Banquanshan shengmutang jianjie 阪泉山聖母堂簡 [Introduction to the Banquanshan church of Our Lady]. Taiyuan jiaoqu, 2000.

Baum, Richard, and Frederick C. Teiwes. *Ssu-ch'ing: The Socialist Education Movement of 1962–1966.* Berkeley: Center for Chinese Studies, 1968.

Bays, Daniel H. "Christianity and the Chinese Sectarian Tradition." *Ch'ing shih wen-t'i* 4, no. 7 (1982): 33–55.

Beijing daxue zhexuexi zongjiaoxue zhuanye 84 ji fu Shanxi sheng shehui dia-ocha zu 北京大學哲學系宗教學專業84級赴山西省社會調查組, editors. *She-hui zhuyi chuji jieduan zongjiao zhuangkuang diaocha baogao xuanji* 社會主義初級階段宗教狀況調查報告選集 [Selections from the report of investi-gation on religion during the primary stage of socialism]. Beijing daxue zhexuexi Makesi zhuyi zongjiao jiaoxue jiaoyanshi, 1987.

Benedict XVI. Letter to the Bishops, Priests, Consecrated Persons and the Lay Faithful in the People's Republic of China, 27 May 2007. Papal Encyclicals Online, www.papalencyclicals.net.

Berta, Alfredo. *Mons. Eugenio Massi o.f.m. Vescovo e Vicario Apostolico di Taiyuanfu, Sianfu e Hankow (Cina) (1875–1944)*. Ancona: Biblioteca Fran-cescana, 1955.

Bertuccioli, Guiliano, and Federico Masini. *Italia e Cina*. Roma-Bari: Laterza, 1996.

Biondi, Albano. "Aspetti della cultura cattolica post-tridentina: Religione e controllo sociale." *Storia d'Italia 4 Intelletuali e potere* (1981), 253–302.

Blouin, Francis X. *Vatican Archives: An Inventory and Guide to Historical Documents in the Holy See*. New York: Oxford University Press, 1998.

Boutry, Philippe. *Prêtres et paroisses au pays du Curé d'Ars*. Paris: Les éditions du cerf, 1986.

Briggs, Charles L. "Metadiscursive practices and scholarly authority in folklor-istics." *Journal of American Folklore* 106, no. 422 (1993), 387–434.

Brockey, Liam Matthew. *Journey to the East: The Jesuit Mission to China, 1579–1724*. Cambridge: Harvard University Press, 2007.

Brokaw, Cynthia J. *The Ledgers of Merit and Demerit: Social Change and Moral Order in Late Imperial China*. Princeton: Princeton University Press, 1991.

Brunner, Paul. *L'Euchologe de la mission de Chine: Editio princeps 1628 et développements jusqu'à nos jours*. Münster: Aschendorffsche verlagsbuch-handlung, 1964.

Cadegan, Una M. "The Queen of Peace in the Shadow of War: Fatima and U.S. Catholic Anticommunism," *U.S. Catholic Historian* 22, no. 4 (2004): 1–15.

Capozi, Luca. "Relazione dell'arcivescovo di Taiyuan alla Sacra Congregazione di Propaganda 1 luglio 1950–30 giugno 1953." In *Gioioso Centenario: Bio-grafia di Mons. Luca Domenico Capozi*, edited by Nicola Cerasa. Pofi: Umberto Capozi e Giuseppe Leonardi, 1999.

Cardoza, Anthony L. *Agrarian Elites and Italian Fascism: The Province of Bologna 1901–1926*. Princeton: Princeton University Press, 1982.

Carrington, Goodrich L., editor. *Dictionary of Ming Biography, 1368–1644*. New York: Columbia University Press, 1976.

Carroll, Michael P. "Religion, 'Ricettizie,' and the Immunity of Southern Italy to the Reformation." *Journal of the Scientific Study of Religion* 31, no. 3 (1992): 247–60.

———. *Veiled Threats: The Logic of Popular Catholicism in Italy*. Baltimore: Johns Hopkins University Press, 1996.

Central Committee of the Chinese Communist Party. "The Basic Viewpoint and Policy on the Religious Question during our Country's Socialist Period, Document 19 (March 31, 1982)." *Chinese Law and Government* 33, no. 2 (2000): 17–34.

Cerasa, Nicola. *Breve Storia della Missione di Taiyuan Shansi.* Roma: Provincia Romana dei Frati Minori, 1998.

———. *Gioioso Centenario: Biografia di Mons. Luca Domenico Capozi.* Pofi: Umberto Capozi e Giuseppe Leonardi, 1999.

Cestaro, Antonio. *Le diocesi di Conza e di Campagna nell'età della restaurazione.* Roma: Edizioni di storia e letteratura, 1971.

Chadwick, Owen. *The Popes and European Revolution.* Oxford: Clarendon Press, 1981.

Chang Che-chia. "Origins of a Misunderstanding: The Qianlong Emperor's Embargo on Rhubarb Exports to Russia, the Scenario and its Consequences." *Asian Medicine: Tradition and Modernity* 1, no. 2 (2005): 335–54.

Chang Libing 常利兵. "Cong yishi dao saoluan—dui 1965 nian Qingxu xian H cun tianzhujiaotu de zhengzhi shiying zhi yanjiu" 從儀式到騷亂—對1965 年清徐縣 H 村天主教徒的政治適應之研究 [From ritual to riot: Research on the Catholics' adaptation to government in H village, Qingxu county, 1965]. Paper presented at Zhongguo shehuishi huiyi 中國社會史會議, 2008.

Châtellier, Louis. *The Religion of the Poor: Rural Missions in Europe and the Formation of Modern Catholicism, c. 1500–c. 1800.* Cambridge: Cambridge University Press, 1997. Translated by Brian Pearce.

Chau, Adam Yuet. *Miraculous Response: Doing Popular Religion in Contemporary China.* Stanford: Stanford University Press, 2006.

Chen, Hui-hung. "Encounters in Peoples, Religions and Sciences: Jesuit Visual Culture in Seventeenth Century China." PhD thesis, Brown University, 2004.

Chen, Pi-yen. *Chinese Buddhist Monastic Chants.* Middleton, WI: A-R Editions, 2010.

Chen Yongfa 陳永發. "Neizhan: Mao Zedong he tudi geming: Cuowo panduan haishi zhengzhi moulüe" 內戰：毛澤東和土地革命：錯誤判斷還是政治謀略 [Civil War: Mao Zedong and the land revolution: An error of judgement or a political strategy]. *Dalu zazhi* 大陸雜誌 92, no. 1 (1996): 9–19; no. 2 (1996): 41–48; no. 3 (1996): 11–29.

Christian, William A., Jr. "Religious Apparitions and the Cold War in Southern Europe." In *Religion, Power and Protest in Local Communities: The Northern Shore of the Mediterranean,* edited by Eric R. Wolf. Berlin: Mouton, 1984.

———. *Visionaries: The Spanish Republic and the Reign of Christ.* Berkeley: University of California Press, 1996.

Coblin, W. South, and Joseph A. Levi, editors. *Francisco Varo's Grammar of the Mandarin Language (1703): An English Translation of 'Arte de la lengua Mandarina.'* Amsterdam: John Benjamins Publishing Company, 2000.

Cohen, Paul A. *China and Christianity: The Missionary Movement and the Growth of Chinese Anti-Foreignism.* Cambridge: Harvard University Press, 1963.

———. *History in Three Keys: The Boxers as Event, Experience and Myth.* New York: Columbia University Press, 1997.

Composto, Renato. "Fermento sociali nel clero siciliano prima dell'unificazione." *Studi storici* 5, no. 2 (1964): 263–79.

Constable, Nicole. *Christian Souls and Chinese Spirits: A Hakka Community in Hong Kong.* Berkeley: University of California Press, 1994.

Cox, Jeffrey. *Imperial Fault Lines: Christianity and Colonial Power in India, 1818–1940.* Stanford: Stanford University Press, 2002.

Criveller, Gianni. "The Chinese Priests of the College for the Chinese in Naples and the Promotion of the Indigenous Clergy (XVIII-XIX Centuries)." In *Silent Force: Native Converts in the Catholic China Mission,* edited by Rachel Lu Yan and Philip Vanhaelemeersch. Leuven: Ferdinand Verbiest Institute, K.U. Leuven, 2009.

Davis, John A. *Naples and Napoleon: Southern Italy and the European Revolutions (1780–1860).* Oxford: Oxford University Press, 2006.

De Groot, J.J.M. *Sectarianism and Religious Persecution in China.* Taipei: Ch'eng Wen, 1970. 1st ed., 1903.

De Jaegher, Raymond J., and Irene Corbally Kuhn. *The Enemy Within: An Eyewitness Account of the Communist Conquest of China.* New York: Doubleday, 1952.

D'Elia, Pasquale M. *Le origini dell'arte cristiana cinese (1583–1640).* Roma: Reale Academia d'Italia, 1939.

De Maio, Romeo. *Società e vita religiosa a Napoli nell'età moderna (1656–1799).* Napoli: Edizioni scientifiche italiane, 1971.

De Matteis, Stefano, and Marino Nicola. *Antropologia delle anime in pena: Il resto della storia: Un culto del Purgatorio.* Lecce: Argo, 1997.

De Spirito, Angelomichele. "La formazione del clero meridionale nelle regole dei primi seminari." In *Studi di Storia Sociale e Religiosa: Scritti in onore di Gabriele de Rosa,* edited by Antonio Cestaro. Napoli: Ferraro, 1980.

Di Fiore, Giacomo. "Un cinese a Castel Sant'Angelo: La vicenda di un alunno del Collegio di Matteo Ripa fra trasgressione e reclusione." In *La conoscenza dell'Asia e dell'Africa in Italia nei secoli XVIII e XIX,* edited by Aldo Gallotta and Ugo Marazzi, 219–86. Napoli: Istituto Universitario Orientale, 1985.

———. *Lettere di missionari dalla Cina (1761–1775): La vita quotidiana nelle missioni attraverso il carteggio di Emiliano Palladini e Filippo Huang con il Collegio dei Cinesi in Napoli.* Napoli: Istituto Universitario Orientale, 1995.

"Diguozhuyi esha Shanxi Yihetuan de zuizheng" 帝國主義扼殺山西議和團的罪證 [Proof of the guilt of imperialism in smothering the Shanxi Boxers]. *Shanxi wenshi ziliao* 山西文史資料 2–3 (1962). Translated by Zhang Maoxian 張茂先.

Duan Runcheng 段潤成. Wode xinyang licheng 我的信仰里程 [My faith journey]. 2005.

———. *Chuanjiao shisinian—jingyan tihui huilu* 傳教十四年—經驗體會薈萃 [Fourteen years of evangelism: Collected experiences and knowledge]. Dongergou, 2007.

Duara, Prasenjit. *Culture, Power and the State: Rural North China, 1900–1942.* Stanford: Stanford University Press, 1988.

Dunch, Ryan. *Fuzhou Protestants and the Making of Modern China.* New Haven: Yale University Press, 2001.

———. "Beyond Cultural Imperialism: Cultural Theory, Christian Missions, and Global Modernity." *History and Theory* 41 (Oct. 2002): 301–25.

Durosel, l'Abbé. *La Madone de Campocavallo ou recit de N.-D. des Sept Douleurs a Campocavallo des guérisons, conversions et faveurs diverses attribuées a son intercession, avec un appendice sur le sanctuaire de N.-D. de Lorette*. Abbeville: C. Paillart, 1896.

Du Zhengzhen 杜正貞. *Cunshe chuantong yu Ming Qing shishen—Shanxi Zezhou xiangtu shehui de zhidu bianqian* 村社傳統與明清士紳—山西澤州鄉土社會的制度變遷 [The tradition of the village *she* and Ming Qing gentry: Changes in the structure of rural society in Zezhou, Shanxi]. Shanghai: Shanghai guji chubanshe, 2007.

Edgerton-Tarpley, Kathryn. *Tears from Iron: Cultural Reponses to Famine in Nineteenth-Century China*. Berkeley: University of California Press, 2008.

Edwards, E.H. *Fire and Sword in Shansi: The Story of the Martyrdom of Foreigners and Chinese Christians*. Edinburgh: Oliphant Anderson & Ferrier, 1903.

Elman, Benjamin A. *On Their Own Terms: Science in China, 1550–1900*. Cambridge: Harvard University Press, 2005.

Entenmann, Robert E. "Catholics and Society in Eighteenth-century Sichuan." In *Christianity in China from the Eighteenth-Century to the Present*, edited by Daniel H. Bays. Stanford: Stanford University Press, 1996.

Esherick, Joseph W. *The Origins of the Boxer Uprising*. Berkeley: University of California Press, 1987.

———. *Ancestral Leaves: A Family Journey through Chinese History*. Berkeley: University of California Press, 2010.

Fang Hao 方豪. *Zhongguo tianzhujiao shi renwu zhuan* 中國天主教史人物傳 [Biographies for the history of the Catholic church in China]. Taizhong: Guangqi chubanshe, 1967.

———. *Zhongxi jiaotong shi* 中西交通史 [A history of contact between China and the West]. Taibei: Zhongguo wenhua daxue chubanshe, 1983. 1st ed., 1953.

Fatica, Michele. " Per una mostra bibliografica ed iconografica su Matteo Ripa, il Collegio dei Cinesi e il Real Collegio Asiatico (1682–1888)." In *La missione Cattolica in Cina tra i secoli XVIII-XIX: Matteo Ripa e il Collegio dei Cinesi: Atti del Colloquio Internazionale Napoli, 11–12 febbraio 1997*, edited by Michele Fatica and Francesco D'Arelli. Napoli: Istituto universitario orientale, 1999.

———. "L'Istituto Orientali di Napoli come sede di scambio culturale tra Cina e Italia nei secoli XVIII e XIX." *Scritture di Storia* 2 (2001): 83–93.

Faure, David. *The Rural Economy of Pre-Liberation China: Trade Expansion and Peasant Livelihood in Jiangsu and Guangdong, 1870 to 1937*. Hong Kong: Oxford University Press, 1989.

Fisher, Gareth. "The Spiritual Land Rush: Merit and Morality in New Chinese Buddhist Temple Construction." *Journal of Asian Studies* 67, no. 1 (2008): 143–70.

Foust, Clifford M. *Muscovite and Mandarin: Russia's Trade with China and Its Setting, 1727–1805*. Chapel Hill: University of North Carolina Press, 1969.

Furth, Charlotte. *A Flourishing Yin: Gender in China's Medical History, 960–1665*. Berkeley: University of California Press, 1999.

Gandolfi, Domenico. "Cenni di storia del vicariato apostolico di Taiyuanfu Shansi, Cina 1930–1953." *Studi Francescani* 84 (1987): 299–360.

———. "Cenni storici sulla Missione di Yütze (Shansi): 1930–1953." *Studi Francescane* 85 (1988): 121–72.

Gaskell, Ivan. "*Jesus Christ as the Divine Mercy* by Eugenius Kazimirowski. The Most Influential Polish Painting of the Twentieth Century?" *Ars: Journal of the Institute of Art History of Slovak Academy of Sciences* 42, no. 1 (2009): 81–93.

Geliaogcou cun cunweihui dang'anju 圪潦溝村村委會檔案局 [Geliaogou Village Village Party Committee Archive Office]. Baochihui 保赤會 [Orphanage]. 1902–1944.

Gentilcore, David. *From Bishop to Witch: The System of the Sacred in Early Modern Terra d'Otranto.* Manchester: Manchester University Press, 1992.

Gernet, Jacques. *China and the Christian Impact: A Conflict of Cultures.* Cambridge: Cambridge University Press, 1985. Translated by Janet Lloyd.

Gibson, Ralph. *A Social History of French Catholicism 1789–1914.* London: Routledge, 1989.

Ginsborg, Paul. *Daniele Manin and the Venetian Revolution of 1848–49.* Cambridge: Cambridge University Press, 1979.

Giornale dal 1° Giugno 1910 al 31 Agosto 1912. Zhongguo tianzhujiao lishi ziliao zhongxin 中國天主教歷史資料中心 [China Catholic History Materials Center], Taiyuan.

Gitti, Stefano. *Mons. Gioacchino Salvetti O.F.M. (1769–1843) e la missione dei Francescani in Cina.* Firenze: Studi Francescani, 1958.

Gongsi song jingwen 公私誦經文 [Public and private prayers]. Shanghai, 1920.

Goossaert, Vincent. *The Taoists of Peking, 1800–1949: A Social History of Urban Clerics.* Cambridge, MA: Harvard University Asia Center, 2007.

Grioglio, Gabriele 杜嘉畢阤爾. *Shengjiao daoli yuexuan* 聖教道理約選 [Selected truths of the Holy Religion]. Taiyuan: Mingyuantang, 1916. 1st ed., 1851.

Gugong bowuyuan Ming Qing dang'an bu 故宮博物院明清檔案部, editors. *Yihetuan dang'an shiliao* 義和團檔案史料 [Archival documents on the Boxers]. Beijing: Zhonghua shuju, 1959.

Guo Chongxi 郭崇禧. "Mei Deli de diguozhuyi xiang" 梅德立的帝國主義相 [The imperialist face of Teodosio Maestri]. *Wenshi ziliao* 文史資料 2 (1964), edited by Taiyuanshi tianzhujiao aiguohui 太原市天主教愛國會.

———. "Fan Li Lujia douzheng de qianqianhouhou" 反李路加鬥爭的前前後後 [The struggle against Luca Capozi from beginning to end]. *Wenshi ziliao* 文史資料 2 (1964), edited by Taiyuanshi tianzhujiao aiguohui 太原市天主教愛國會.

———. "Taiyuan tianzhujiao zhuyao tangkou jianjie" 太原天主教主要堂口簡介 [A brief introduction to the main Catholic parishes of Taiyuan]. *Taiyuan wenshi ziliao* 太原文史資料 15 (1991): 148–64.

———. "Taiyuan tianzhujiao shilue" 太原天主教史略 [A brief history of Catholicism in Taiyuan]. *Taiyuan wenshi ziliao* 太原文史資料 17 (1992): 145–254.

Guo Jifen 郭繼汾. *Fangjihuishi Guo Jifen shenfu jiniance* 方濟會士郭繼汾神父紀念冊 [Memorial volume for Franciscan Father Guo Jifen]. Taiyuan, 2003.

Guo Quanzhi 郭全智. "Shanxi tianzhujiao gaishu" 山西天主教概述 [An outline of Catholicism in Shanxi]. Manuscript, 2007.

Gu Weimin 顧衛民. *Jidu zongjiao yishu zai Hua fazhanshi* 基督宗教藝術在華發展史 [A History of Christian Arts in China]. Shanghai: Shanghai shudian chubanshe, 2005.

Han Yaozong 韓耀宗. "Cong Lei Jingshi kan chuanjiaoshi" 從雷警世看傳教士 [Ugolino Arcari as an example of a missionary]. *Wenshi ziliao* 文史資料 I (1964): 44–52, edited by Taiyuanshi tianzhujiao aiguohui 太原市天主教愛國會.

Harline, Craig, and Eddy Put. *A Bishop's Tale: Mathias Hovius among His Flock in Seventeenth-Century Flanders*. New Haven: Yale University Press, 2000.

Harris, Ruth. *Lourdes: Body and Spirit in a Secular Age*. Harmondsworth: Penguin, 1999.

Harrison, Henrietta. "'A Penny for the Little Chinese': The French Holy Childhood Association in China, 1843–1951." *American Historical Review* 113, no. 1 (2008): 72–92.

———. "Rethinking Missionaries and Medicine in China: The Miracles of Assunta Pallotta, 1905–2005." *Journal of Asian Studies* 71, no. 1 (2012): 127–48.

Herdtrich, Christianus. Annuae Sin. 1673–1677. Archivum Romanum Societatis Iesu. *Jap, Sin.* 116:260–67.

Hinton, William. *Fanshen: A Documentary of Revolution in a Chinese Village*. New York: Vintage Books, 1966.

———. *Shenfan*. New York: Random House, 1983.

Hsiao, Liang-lin. *China's Foreign Trade Statistics, 1864–1949*. Cambridge: Harvard University Press, 1974.

Huang, Xiaojuan. "Christian Communities and Alternative Devotions in China, 1780–1860." PhD thesis, Princeton University, 2006.

Huang Daoxuan 黃道炫. "192–194 niandai Zhongguo dongnan diqu de tudi zhanyou—jiantan dizhu nongmin yu tudi geming" 一九二——九四年代中國東南地區的土地占有—兼談地主農民與土地革命 [Land ownership in southeast China 1920s-1940s: A joint discussion of landlords, peasants and the land revolution]. 歷史研究 *Lishi yanjiu*, no. 1 (2005): 34–53.

Huang Yilong 黃一農. "Ming Qing tianzhujiao zai Shanxi Jiangzhou de fazhan ji qi fantan" 明清天主教在山西絳州的發展及其反彈 [The development of Catholicism in Jiangzhou, Shanxi, during the Ming and Qing dynasties and reactions to it]. *Zhongyang yanjiuyuan jindaishi yanjiusuo jikan* 中央研究院近代史研究所集刊 26 (1996): 3–40.

Ianello, Tiziana. "Il Collegio dei Cinesi durante il decennio francese (1806–15)." In *La missione Cattolica in Cina tra i secoli XVIII-XIX: Matteo Ripa e il Collegio dei Cinesi: Atti del Colloquio Internazionale Napoli, 11–12 febbraio 1997*, edited by Michele Fatica and Francesco D'Arelli. Napoli, 1999.

Inouye, Melissa Wei-Tsing. "Miraculous Mundane: The True Jesus Church and Chinese Christianity in the Twentieth Century." PhD thesis, Harvard University, 2010.

Jia'nan shige 迦南詩歌 [Canaan hymns], http://cclw.net/resources/Cannan/Cannan.htm.

Jiaoyou shenghuo bianjibu 〈教友生活〉編輯部, editors. *Tianzhujiao Changzhi jiaoqu jianshi* 天主教長治教區簡史 [A brief history of Changzhi Catholic diocese]. 1997.

Jin Ze 金澤 and Qiu Yonghui 邱永輝, editors. *Zhongguo zongjiao baogao, 2010* 中國宗教報告 [Annual report on China's religions, 2010]. Beijing: Shehui kexue chubanshe, 2010.

Johnson, David. *Spectacle and Sacrifice: The Ritual Foundations of Village Life in North China*. Cambridge: Harvard University Asia Center, 2009.

Joly, Léon. *Le Christianisme et l'Extrême Orient*. Paris: P. Lethielleux, 1907.

———. *Le problème des missions: Tribulations d'un vieux chanoine*. Paris: P. Lethielleux, 1908.

Jordan, David K. *Gods, Ghosts, and Ancestors: The Folk Religion of a Taiwanese Village*. Berkeley: University of California Press, 1972.

Josson, H., and L. Willaert, editors. *Correspondence de Ferdinand Verbiest de la Compagnie de Jésus (1623–1688) Directeur de l'Observatoire de Pékin*. Bruxelles: Palais des Académies, 1938.

Kang Zhijie 康志傑. *Shangzhu de putaoyuan—Exi Mopanshan tianzhujiao shequ yanjiu* 上主的葡萄園—鄂西磨盤山天主教社區研究 [The Lord's vineyard: Research into the Mopanshan Catholic district in western Hubei]. Taibei: Furen daxue chubanshe, 2006.

Kao, Chen-yang. "The Cultural Revolution and the Post-Missionary Transformation of Protestantism in China." PhD thesis, University of Lancaster, 2009.

———. "The Cultural Revolution and the Emergence of Pentecostal-style Protestantism in China." *Journal of Contemporary Religion* 24, no. 2 (2009): 171–88.

Kerval, Léon de. *Le R.P. Hugolin de Doullens ou la vie d'un Frère Mineur missionnaire en Chine au XIXe siècle*. Rome: Francisc. Miss., 1902.

———. *Deux Martyrs Francais de l'ordre des Frères Mineurs, le R.P. Théodoric Balat et le Fr. André Bauer massacrés en Chine le 9 Juillet 1900, aperçus biographiques*. 3rd ed. Paris: Lemière, 1914.

Kohn, Livia. *The Taoist Experience: An Anthology*. Albany: State University of New York Press, 1993.

Kongsu—shi shei haisile wo ma? 控訴—是誰害死了我媽? [Accusation: Who killed my mother?]. Taiyuan, c. 1965.

La Bella, Gianni. "Pius X." In *The Catholic Church and the Chinese World: Between Colonialism and Evangelism 1840–1911*, edited by Agostino Giovagnoli and Elisa Guinipero. Roma: Urbaniana University Press, 2005.

Latourette, Kenneth Scott. *A History of Christian Missions in China*. London: Society for Promoting Christian Knowledge, 1929.

Laufer, Berthold. "The Chinese Madonna in the Field Museum." *The Open Court* 16, no. 1 (1912): 1–6.

Lea, Henry Charles. *A History of Auricular Confession and Indulgences in the Latin Church*. Philadelphia: Lea Brothers & Co., 1896.

Leclercq, Jacques. *Thunder in the Distance: The Life of Père Lebbe*. New York: Sheed & Ward, 1958. Translated by George Lamb.

Lecomte, Louis. *Un jésuite à Pékin: Nouveaux mémoires sur l'état présent de la Chine 1687–1692*. Paris: Phébus, 1990.

Lee, Joseph Tse-Hei. "Watchman Nee and the Little Flock Movement in Maoist China." *Church History* 74, no. 1 (2005): 68–96.

———. "Christianity in Contemporary China: An Update." *Journal of Church and State* 49 (2007): 277–304.

Le Goff, Jacques. *The Birth of Purgatory*. Chicago: University of Chicago Press, 1984. Translated by Arthur Goldhammer.

Lesourd, Paul. *Histoire générale de l'Oeuvre Pontificale de la Sainte-Enfance depuis un siècle*. Paris: Centre Catholique International de Documentation e de Statistiques, 1947.

Leung, Beatrice. "Communist Party–Vatican Interplay over the Training of Church Leaders in China." *Journal for the Scientific Study of Religion* 40, no. 4 (2001): 657–73.

Levaux, Léopold. *Le Père Lebbe: Apôtre de la Chine moderne (1877–1940)*. Bruxelles: Éditions universitaires, 1948.

Levi, Carlo. *Christ Stopped at Eboli*. Harmondsworth: Penguin Books, 1982. Translated by Frances Frenaye.

Lian, Xi. *The Conversion of Missionaries: Liberalism in American Protestant Missions in China, 1907–1932*. University Park: Pennsylvania State University Press, 1997.

———. *Redeemed by Fire: The Rise of Popular Christianity in Modern China*. New Haven: Yale University Press, 2010.

Linden, Ian. *Global Catholicism: Diversity and Change since Vatican II*. New York: Columbia University Press, 2009.

The Little Flowers of St Francis with Five Considerations of the Sacred Stigmata. Baltimore: Penguin Books, 1959. Translated by Leo Sherley-Price.

Liu Anrong 劉安榮. *Shanxi tianzhujiao shi yanjiu* 山西天主教史研究 [Historical research on Catholicism in Shanxi]. Taiyuan: Beiyue wenyi chubanshe, 2011.

Liu Dapeng 劉大鵬. "Tuixiangzhai riji" 退想齋日記 [Diary from the chamber to which one retires to ponder]. Manuscript, Shanxi Provincial Library 山西省圖書館.

———. *Tuixiangzhai riji* 退想齋日記 [Diary of the chamber to which one retires to ponder]. Taiyuan: Shanxi renmin chubanshe, 1980. Edited by Qiao Zhiqiang 喬志強.

———. "Qianyuan suoji" 潛園瑣記. In *Yihetuan zai Shanxi diqu shiliao* 義和團在山西地區史料 [Local historical materials on the Boxers in Shanxi], edited by Qiao Zhiqiang 喬志強. Taiyuan: Shanxi renmin chubanshe, 1980, 26–75.

———. "Tuixiangzhai riji" 退想齋日記 [Diary from the chamber to which one retires to ponder]. *Jindaishi ziliao Yihetuan shiliao* 近代史資料義和團史料 [Modern history materials Boxer historical materials]. Vol 2. Beijing: Zhongguo shehui kexue chubanshe, 1982.

———. *Jinci zhi* 晉祠志 [Jinci gazetteer], edited by Mu Xiang 慕湘 and Lü Wenxing 呂文幸. Taiyuan: Shanxi renmin chubanshe, 1986.

Liuhe xingxing 六合星星 [Stars of Liuhe], 2007.

Liu Wenbing 劉文炳. *Xugou xianzhi* 徐溝縣志 [Xugou county gazetteer]. Taiyuan: Shanxi renmin chubanshe, 1992.

Liwu yu jianzheng—Han Yaozong shenfu jinduo jingangqing jiniance 禮物與見證—韓耀宗神父進鐸金剛慶紀念冊 [Gift and testimony: Commemorative volume for the golden anniversary of Fr Han Yaozong's ordination]. Taiyuan, 2006.

Li Ye 李曄. "Zai difang dang'an zhong faxian lishi—Jinzhong xin qu tugai yundong zhong de qunzhong dongyuan" 在地方檔案中發現歷史—晉中新區土改運動中的群眾動員 [Discovering history in local archives: Mass mobilisation during the Land Reform movement in the new districts of central Shanxi]. *Shanxi dang'an* 山西檔案 3 (2008): 49–51.

Lombardi, Teodosio. *Un Grande Ideale: Monsignor Ermengildo Focaccia O.F.M. Vescovo di Yütze in Cina*. Bologna: Edizioni Antoniano, 1968.

Lu Runjie 盧潤杰. "Shanxi yihetuan yundong" 山西議和團運動 [The Boxer movement in Shanxi]. In *Jindai de Shanxi* 近代的山西 [Modern Shanxi], edited by Jiang Di 江地. Taiyuan: Shanxi renmin chubanshe, 1988.

———. *Zhaoyu chunqiu* 昭餘春秋 [Qixian annals]. Taiyuan: Shanxi guji chubanshe, 2005.

MacGillivray, Donald. *A Century of Protestant Missions in China (1807–1907) being the Centenary Conference Historical Volume*. Shanghai: American Presbyterian Mission Press, 1907.

Madsen, Richard. *China's Catholics: Tragedy and Hope in an Emerging Civil Society*. Berkeley: University of California Press, 1998.

Maestri, Theodosius. "Apparition of a Martyr Bishop to Pagans." *Franciscans in China* 7 (1924).

Manini, Edoardo. *Episodi della Rivoluzione Cinese, 1900*. Parma: Rossi Ubaldi, 1901.

Margiotti, Fortunato. *Il Cattolicismo nello Shansi dalle origini al 1738*. Roma: Edizioni Sinica Franciscana, 1958.

Mariani, Paul P. *Church Militant: Bishop Kung and Catholic Resistance in Communist China*. Cambridge: Harvard University Press, 2011.

Marinelli, Maurizio. "The Genesis of the Italian Concession in Tianjin: A Combination of Wishful Thinking and Realpolitik." *Journal of Modern Italian Studies* 15, no. 4 (2010): 536–56.

Ma Xisha 馬西沙. "Xiantianjiao yu Cao Shun shijian shimo" 先天教與曹順事件始末 [The Teaching of Former Heaven and the events of the Cao Shun incident]. *Qingshi yanjiu tongxun* 清史研究通訊 1 (1988).

Mayers, William Frederick, editor. *Treaties between the Empire of China and Foreign Powers, together with Regulations for the Conduct of Foreign Trade*. Shanghai: J.B. Tootal, 1877.

Menegon, Eugenio. *Ancestors, Virgins, and Friars: Christianity as a Local Religion in Late Imperial China*. Cambridge: Harvard University Asia Center Press, 2009.

Meng Yonghua 孟永華. "Shanxi nongcun Siqing yundong shuping" 山西農村四清運動述評 [An evaluation of the Four Cleans movement in Shanxi villages]. *Dangshi yanjiu yu jiaoxue* 党史研究與教學, no. 4 (2007): 50–56.

Michel de la Sainte Trinité. *The Whole Truth about Fatima*. Vol. 3. *The Third Secret (1942–1960)* Buffalo: Immaculate Heart Publications, 1990. Translated by John Collorafi.

Miller, Tracy. *The Divine Nature of Power: Chinese Ritual Architecture at the Sacred Site of Jinci*. Cambridge: Harvard University Press, 2007.

Millward, James A. *Beyond the Pass: Economy, Ethnicity, and Empire in Qing Central Asia, 1759–1864*. Stanford: Stanford University Press, 1998.

———. *Eurasian Crossroads: A History of Xinjiang*. New York: Columbia University Press, 2007.

Le Missioni Francescane in Palestina ed in altre Regioni della Terra (Firenze), 1891–95.

Les Missions de Chine et du Japon. Pekin: Imprimerie des Lazaristes, 1916–39.

Mungello, David E. *Curious Land: Jesuit Accommodation and the Origins of Sinology*. Stuttgart: Franz Steiner Verlag Wiesbaden GMBH, 1985.

———. *The Spirit and the Flesh in Shandong, 1650–1785*. Lanham: Rowman & Littlefield, 2001.

———. "The Return of the Jesuits to China in 1841 and the Chinese Christian Backlash." *Sino-Western Cultural Relations Journal* 27 (2005): 9–46.

Nanetti, Bárnaba. "Sunto di memorie sulle missioni dei due distretti in Pin-iao e Kie Sien (nel San-si) a memoria d'uomo." Manuscript, 1897. Archivio della Provincia Osservante di Bologna, poi del SS. Redentore, Bologna. Missione di Yütze (Shan-si, Cina) 3:4.

Naquin, Susan. *Millenarian Rebellion in China: The Eight Trigrams Uprising of 1813*. New Haven: Yale University Press, 1976.

Newby, Laura J. *The Empire and the Khanate: A Political History of Qing Relations with Khoqand c. 1760–1860*. Leiden: Brill, 2005.

Nicolini, Nicola. *L'Istituto Orientale di Napoli: Origine e statuti*. Roma: Edizioni universitarie, 1942.

Nora, Pierre. "Between Memory and History: Les Lieux de Mémoire" *Representations* 26 (1989): 7–24.

Noreen, Kirstin. "The Icon of Santa Maria Maggiore, Rome: An image and Its Afterlife." *Renaissance Studies* 19, no. 5 (2005): 660–72.

O'Malley, John W. *What Happened at Vatican II*. Cambridge: Harvard University Press, 2008.

L'Oriente Serafico. 1889–1906.

Orsi, Robert A. *The Madonna of 115th Street: Faith and Community in Italian Harlem, 1850–1950*. New Haven: Yale University Press, 2002.

———. *Between Heaven and Earth: The Religious Worlds People Make and the Scholars who Study Them*. Princeton: Princeton University Press, 2005.

Overmyer, Daniel L. *Folk Buddhist Religion: Dissenting Sects in Late Traditional China*. Cambridge: Harvard University Press, 1976.

Palmieri, Pasquale. *I taumaturghi della società: Santi e potere politico nel secolo dei Lumi*. Roma: Viella, 2010.

Papers of the American Board of Commissioners of Foreign Missions. Houghton Library, Cambridge, MA.

Parrenin, Domenico. "Refutatio querelam Illustrissimi Francisco Maria Ferreris Episcopi Ephestiensis contra R.P. Gallos Societatis Jesu." Biblioteca Nazionale Centrale di Roma. Fondo Gesuitico 1247:7.

Poliorama pittoresco. 1841–42.

Pollard, J. F. "Fascism and Catholicism." In *The Oxford Handbook of Fascism*, edited by R. J. B. Bosworth. Oxford: Oxford University Press, 2009.

Pontificium Opus a Sancta Infantia (Rome) (POSI).

Qin Geping 秦格平. *Taiyuan jiaoqu jianshi* 太原教區簡史 [A simple history of Taiyuan diocese]. Tianzhujiao Taiyuan jiaoqu, 2008.

Qingxu xianzhi 清徐縣志 [Qingxu county gazetteer]. Taiyuan: Shanxi guji chubanshe, 1999.

Qingyuan xiangzhi 清源鄉志 [Qingyuan township gazetteer]. 1882.

Qu Jiluan 區季鸞. *Guangdong zhi diandangye* 廣東之典當業 [The Guangdong pawnshop trade]. Guangzhou: Guoli Zhongshan daxue jingji diaocha chu, 1934.

Reilly, Thomas H. *The Taiping Heavenly Kingdom: Rebellion and the Blasphemy of Empire*. Seattle: University of Washington Press, 2004.

Reinders, Eric. *Borrowed Gods and Foreign Bodies: Christian Missionaries Imagine Chinese Religion*. Berkeley: University of California Press, 2004.

Renmin ribao 人民日報 [People's Daily]. 2000.

Ricci, Giovanni (Ioannes). *Le avventure di un missionario in Cina: Memorie di Mons. Luigi Moccagatta, O.F.M. Vescovo Titolare di Zenopoli e Vicario Apostolico del San-Si*. Modena: Tip. Pontificia ed Arcivescovile dell'Immacolata Concezione, 1909.

———. *Barbarie e trionfi ossia le vittime illustri del San-si in Cina nella persecuzione del 1900*. Firenze: Tipografia Barbèra, 1910.

———. "Acta Martyrum Sinensium anno 1900 in Provincia San-si occisorum historice collecta ex ore testium singulis locis ubi Martyres occubuere: Relatio ex-officio ex parte Ordinis Fratrum Minorum." *Acta Ordinis Fratrum Minorum* 30–32 (1911–13).

———. *Il Fratello di una Martire: Memorie del P. Barnaba da Cologna, O.F.M. Missionario Apostolico in Cina*. Torino: P. Celanza, 1912.

———. "Acta Martyrum Sinensium Vicariatus Apostolici Shansi Meridionalis anno 1900 pro fide Catholica interfectorum." *Acta Ordinis Fratrum Minorum* 33–34 (1914–15).

———. *Vicariatus Taiyuanfu seu brevis historia antiquae Franciscanae missionis Shansi et Shensi a sua origine ad dies nostros (1700–1928)*. Pekini: Congregationis Missionis, 1929.

Rowe, William T. *Crimson Rain: Seven Centuries of Violence in a Chinese County*. Stanford: Stanford University Press, 2007.

Schipper, Kristofer. *The Taoist Body*. Berkeley: University of California Press, 1993. Translated by Karen C. Duval.

Schofield, Harold. *Second Annual Report of the Medical Mission at T'ai-yüen-fu, Shansi, North China, in Connection with the China Inland Mission*. Shanghai: American Presbyterian Mission Press, 1883.

Shanxi beijiaoqu dang'an 山西北教區檔案 [Archives of the diocese of Northern Shanxi], Taiyuan (SBD).

Shanxi daxue Zhongguo shehuishi yanjiu zhongxin 山西大學中國社會史研究中心 [Shanxi University Chinese Social History Research Institute], X dadui danweihui tianzhujiao zonghe ziliao he geren dang'an □□大隊單位會天主

教宗合資料和個人檔案 [X brigade unit committee Catholic general materials and personnel files], Taiyuan (SD).

Shanxi ribao 山西日報 [Shanxi daily news]. 1949–52.

"Shanxi sheng gengzi nian jiaonan qianhou jishi" 山西省庚子年教難前後記事 [A record of the events before and after the 1900 persecution in Shanxi province]. In *Yihetuan* 義和團 [The Boxers], edited by Jian Bozan 翦伯贊 et al. Vol. 1. Shanghai: Shenzhou guoguan she, 1951.

Shanxi sheng shizhi yanjiuyuan 山西省史志研究院, editors. *Shanxi tongshi* 山西通史 [Shanxi history]. Taiyuan: Shanxi renmin chubanshe, 2001.

Shanxi tongzhi 山西通志 [Shanxi gazetteer]. Beijing: Zhonghua shuju, 1997.

Shengyu guangxun Yongzheng zhijie Wang Youpu jiangjie 聖諭廣訓雍正直解王又樸講解 [The Sacred Edict with notes by Yongzheng and explanation by Wang Youpu]. 1724.

Shi Rongchang 石榮昶. "Gengzi ganshi shi" 庚子感事詩 [Poems in response to 1900]. *Jindaishi ziliao* 近代史資料 11, no. 4 (1956).

Silvestri, Cipriano. *La testimonia del sangue: Biografie dei Beati Cinesi uccisi il 7, 8, e 9 iuglio 1900*. Roma: Don Luigi Guanella, 1943.

Song Jianxun 宋建勳. "Bazhan tianchan er san shi" 霸占田產二, 三事 [Two or three cases of seizing land and property] *Wenshi ziliao* 文史資料 1 (1964). Edited by Taiyuanshi tianzhujiao aiguohui 太原市天主教愛國會.

———. "Tianzhujiao zai Xinzhou dongnan bu fazhan qingkuang" 天主教在忻州東南部發展情況 [The circumstances of the development of Catholicism in the southeastern part of Xinzhou]. Manuscript.

———. "Xinzhou diqu tianzhujiao fazhan gaikuang" 忻州地區天主教發展概況 [An outline of the development of Catholicism in Xinzhou district]. Manuscript.

Spence, Jonathan D. *The Memory Palace of Matteo Ricci*. New York: Viking Penguin, 1984.

———. *The Question of Hu*. New York: Knopf, 1988.

Sperber, Jonathan. *The European Revolutions, 1848–1851*. Cambridge: Cambridge University Press, 1994.

Stacchini, Bernardo. *Ombre rosse sulla Cina*. Bologna: Abes editrice, 1956.

Standaert, Nicolas. *Yang Tingyun, Confucian and Christian in Late Ming China*. Leiden: E. J. Brill, 1988.

———. "Chinese Christian Visits to the Underworld." In *Conflict and Accommodation in Early Modern East Asia: Essays in Honour of Erik Zürcher*, edited by Leonard Blussé and Harriet T. Zurndorfer, 54–70. Leiden: E.J. Brill, 1993.

———, editor. *Handbook of Christianity in China*. Vol. 1, *635–1800*. Leiden: Brill, 2001.

———. *The Interweaving of Rituals: Funerals in the Cultural Exchange between China and Europe*. Seattle: University of Washington Press, 2008.

Standaert, Nicolas, and Ad Dudink, editors. *Forgive Us Our Sins: Confession in Late Ming and Early Qing China*. Sankt Augustin: Institut Monumenta Serica, 2006.

Su Ruoyi 蘇若裔. *Zhongguo jindai jiaonan shiliao (1948–1957)* 中國近代教難史料 [Historical materials on China's modern religious persecution (1948–1957)]. Taibei: Furen daxue chubanshe, 2000.

Taiyuan shi nanjiaoqu zhi 太原市南郊區志 [Taiyuan city south suburban district gazetteer]. Beijing: Shanlian shudian, 1994.

Taiyuanshi tongjiju 太原市統計局, editors. *Taiyuan "liuwu" jianshe chengjiu* 太原" 六五" 建設成就 [Taiyuan's construction achievements for the sixth five-year plan] Taiyuan: Zhongguo tongji chubanshe, 1987.

Taiyuan xian zhi 太原縣志 [Taiyuan county gazetteer]. 1826.

Taiyuan xishan kuangwuju 太原西山礦務局, editors. *Xishan meikuang shi* 西山煤礦史 [A history of coal mining in the Western Hills], 1961.

Teiser, Stephen F. *The Scripture of the Ten Kings and the Making of Purgatory in Medieval Chinese Buddhism.* Honolulu: Hawaii University Press, 1994.

Ter Haar, Barend J. *The White Lotus Teachings in Chinese Religious History.* Leiden: E. J. Brill, 1992.

———. "Buddhist-Inspired Options: Aspects of Lay Religious Life in the Lower Yangzi from 1100 until 1340." *T'oung Pao* 87, nos. 1/3 (2001), 92–152.

Thompson, Roger R. "Twilight of the Gods in the Chinese Countryside: Christians, Confucians, and the Modernising State, 1861–1911." In *Christianity in China from the Eighteenth Century to the Present,* edited by Daniel H. Bays. Stanford: Stanford University Press, 1996.

Tian Wendu 田文都. *Lianyu shengyue* 煉獄聖月 [The holy month of purgatory]. Shanxi beiqin, 1921. 1st ed., 1880.

———. *Zhenli jingyan shi* 真理敬言世 [Truths respectfully addressed to the age]. Taiyuan: Mingyuan tang, 1917. 1st ed., 1888.

Tianzhujiao Fenyang jiaoqu 天主教汾陽教區, editor. *Fenyang jiaoqu shi, 1926–1996* 汾陽教區史 [Fenyang diocese history, 1926–1996], 1996.

Tramontani, Enzo. *Tai-yuan: L'ora del sogno: Maria Chiara Nanetti nella Cina dei martiri.* Bologna: Editrice missionaria italiana, 2000.

Tsai, Lily. *Accountability without Democracy: Solidary Groups and Public Goods Provision in Rural China.* Cambridge: Cambridge University Press, 2007.

Vagnone, Alfonso 高一志. *Jiaoyao jielue* 教要解略 [An introduction to doctrine], 1615. Reprinted in *Yesuhui Luoma dang'anguan Ming Qing tianzhujiao wenxian* 耶穌會羅馬檔案館明清天主教文獻 [Chinese Christian texts from the Roman Archives of the Society of Jesus], edited by Nicolas Standaert and Adrian Dudink. Taibei: Lishi xueshe, 2002.

———. *Shengmu xingshi* 聖母行史 [Acts of the Holy Mother]. 1798. 1st ed., 1631.

Valerio, Adriana. "Donna e celibato ecclesiastico: Le concubine del clero." In *Donne e religione a Napoli secoli XVI–XVIII,* edited by Giuseppe Galasso and Adriana Valerio. Milano: FrancoAngeli, 2001.

Vismara, Paola. *Questioni di interesse: La Chiesa e il denaro in età moderna.* Milano: Bruno Mondadori, 2009.

Vitali, Francesco. *Month of the Souls in Purgatory Containing Devotions for each Day in November.* Dublin: G. P. Warren, 1871. Translated by M. Comerford.

Vovelle, Michel. *Les âmes du purgatoire ou le travail du deuil.* Paris: Gallimard, 1996.

Waley-Cohen, Joanna. *Exile in Mid-Qing China: Banishment to Xinjiang 1758–1820.* New Haven: Yale University Press, 1991.

Wang, Xiao-qing. "How Has a Chinese Village Remained Catholic? Catholicism and Local Culture in a Northern Chinese Village." *Journal of Contemporary China* 15, no. 49 (2006): 687–704.

Wang Ruose 王若瑟. "Cai cha ge" 採茶歌 [Tea picking song]. Pontificio Istituto Missioni Estere (Rome). Kaifeng, Henan, 1605.

Wang Wangde 王望德. *Nongmin zheng tan* 農民正談 [Straight talk from a farmer]. Taiyuan, 1862–91.

Wathen, W. H. "Memoir on Chinese Tartary and Khoten." *Journal of the Asiatic Society of Bengal* 4, no. 48 (1835): 653–64.

Wei Yisa 魏以撒. *Zhen Yesuhui chuangli sanshi zhounian jinian zhuankan* 真耶穌會創立三十週年紀念專刊 [Special commemorative issue on the 30th anniversary of the founding of the True Jesus Church]. Nanjing: Zhen Yesuhui, 1948.

Weller, Robert P. *Resistance, Chaos and Control in China: Taiping Rebels, Taiwanese Ghosts and Tiananmen.* Seattle: University of Washington Press, 1994.

Weller, Robert P., and Sun Yanfei. "The Dynamics of Religious Growth and Change in Contemporary China" In *China Today, China Tomorrow: Domestic Politics, Economy and Society,* edited by Joseph Fewsmith. Lanham: Rowman & Littlefield, 2010.

Werner, Michael, and Bénédicte Zimmerman. "Beyond Comparison: Histoire Croisée and the Challenge of Reflexivity." *History and Theory* 45, no. 1 (2006): 30–50.

Wickeri, Philip L. *Reconstructing Christianity in China: K. H. Ting and the Chinese Church.* Maryknoll: Orbis Books, 2007.

Willeke, Bernward H. *Imperial Government and Catholic Missions in China during the years 1784–1785.* New York: The Franciscan Institute St. Bonaventure, 1948.

———, editor. "The Report of the Apostolic Visitation of D. Emmanuele Conforti on the Franciscan Missions in Shansi, Shensi and Kansu (1798)." *Archivum Franciscanum Historicum* 84, nos. 1–2 (1991).

———. "Franciscan Theological Education in China" in *Historiography of the Chinese Catholic Church: Nineteenth and Twentieth Centuries,* edited by Jeroom Heyndrickx. K.U. Leuven: Ferdinand Verbiest Foundation, 1994.

Wolf, Margery. *Women and the Family in Rural Taiwan.* Stanford: Stanford University Press, 1972.

Wu Fei 吳飛. *Maimang shang de shengyan—yige xiangcun tianzhujiao qunti zhong de xinyang he shenghuo* 麥芒上的聖言——一個鄉村天主教群體中的信仰和生活 [Sacred word above the awn of wheat: Faith and life in a rural Catholic community]. Hong Kong: Daofeng shushe, 2001.

Wu Gaoshou 吳高壽 and Wang Jie 王潔. "Guanyu Dongergou cun xinjiao cunminde zhongji guanhuai de diaocha baogao" 關與洞兒溝村信教村民的終極關懷的調查報告 [Report on an investigation into Dongergou village religious believers' ultimate concerns]. *Shijie zongjiao yanjiu* 世界宗教研究, no. 2 (2006): 130–34.

Wu Jianjie 吳劍杰. *Zhang Zhidong nianpu changbian* 張之洞年譜長編[Zhang Zhidong chronological biography draft edition]. Shanghai: Shanghai jiaotong daxue chubanshe, 2009.

Xing Huamin 邢化民. "Li Lujia zai Taiyuan jiaoqu de huodong diandi" 李路加在太原教區的活動點滴 [The activities of Luca Capozi in Taiyuan diocese]. *Wenshi ziliao* 2 (1964): 18–23, edited by Taiyuanshi tianzhujiao aiguohui.

Xing Ye 邢野 and Wang Xinmin 王新民, editors. *Lü Meng shang tonglan* 旅蒙商通覽 [An overview of travelling merchants in Mongolia]. Huhehaote: Neimenggu renmin chubanshe, 2008.

Xinxuan shengjiao duilian 新选圣教对联 [New selection of Catholic couplets]. Lu'an, 1904.

Yan Fu 閻福. "Diguozhuyifenzi An Shigao de yidian shishi" 帝國主義分子安世高的一點歷史事實 [Some historical facts about the imperialist Elia Carosi]. *Wenshi ziliao* 1 (1964): 60–62, edited by Taiyuanshi tianzhujiao aiguohui.

———. "Diguozhuyi chuanjiaoshi zhengduo quanli de choutai" 帝國主義傳教士爭奪權利的丑態 [The ugly scene of imperialist missionaries struggling for power]. *Wenshi ziliao* 文史資料 2 (1964): 48–52, edited by Taiyuanshi tianzhujiao aiguohui 太原市天主教愛國會.

Yang Fenggang. "Lost in the Market, Saved at McDonald's: Conversion to Christianity in Urban China." *Journal for the Scientific Study of Religion* 44, no. 4 (2005): 423–41.

Yang Xiaolin 楊銷林. "Jinci quan liuliang shuaijian fenxi" 晉祠泉流量衰減分析 [An analysis of the decline in the flow rates of the Jinci spring]. *Shanxi shuili* 山西水利, no. 6 (2005).

Yang Yuchun 楊遇春. Letter, 8th of 2nd month 1831. Zhongguo di yi lishi dang'anguan 中國第一歷史檔案館 [First Historical Archives], Beijing. Gongzhong zhupi zouzhe 宮中朱批奏摺, minzu shiwu 民族事務, 513–11.

Yasongda zouguo de lu, qianbei fuwu, Yasongda xingshi ji xubian 亞松達走過的路, 謙卑服務, 亞松達行實及續編 [The path Assunta trod—humble service. The deeds of Assunta and a supplement]. Taiyuan, 2005.

Yü Chün-fang. *Kuan-yin: The Chinese Transformation of Avalokiteśvara*. New York: Columbia University Press, 2001.

Zhang Anduoni 張安多尼 and Tian Wendu 田文都. *Shengmu qiku* 聖母七苦 [The Seven Sorrows of the Mother of God]. Shanxi: Mingyuan tang, 1878.

Zhang Jiyu 張繼禹, editor. *Zhonghua Dao cang* 中華到藏 [Chinese Daoist collection]. Beijing: Huaxia chubanshe, 2004.

Zhang Letian 張樂天. *Gaobie lixiang—Renmin gongshe zhidu yanjiu* 告別理想—人民公社制度研究 [Farewell to ideals: Research into the people's commune system]. Shanghai: Shiji chubanshe, 2005.

Zhang Shaomei 張韶梅 and Zhang Huajun 張華軍. "Lun Qingdai Xinjiang Shanxi huiguan" 論清代新疆山西會館 [On Shanxi native place associations in Qing dynasty Xinjiang]. *Xinjiang zhiye daxue xuebao* 新疆職業大學學報 10, no. 3 (2002): 33–35.

Zhang Xianqing 張先清. *Guanfu, zongzu yu tianzhujiao—17–19 shiji Fuan xiangcun jiaohui de lishi xushi* 官府, 宗族與天主教—17–19 世紀福安鄉村教會的歷史敘事 [State, lineage and Catholicism: A narrative of the history of the church in seventeenth- to nineteenth-century rural Fuan]. Beijing: Zhonghua shuju, 2009.

Zhang Xishun 張希舜 and Cheng Lasheng 程臘生. *Shanxi wenwu jingpin diancang: Siguan caisu juan* 山西文物精品典藏. 寺觀彩塑卷 [Shanxi collected outstanding cultural objects: Colored temple statuary]. Taiyuan: Shanxi renmin chubanshe, 2006.

Zhang Zhengming 張正明. *Jinshang xingshuai shi* 晉商興衰史 [A history of the rise and fall of the Shanxi merchants]. Taiyuan: Shanxi guji chubanshe, 1995.

Zhao Peicheng 趙培成, et al. *Xinzhou diqu zongjiao zhi* 忻州地區宗教志 [Xinzhou district religion gazetteer]. Taiyuan: Shanxi renmin chubanshe, 1993.

Zhao Shiyu 趙世瑜. *Kuanghuan yu richang—Ming Qing yilai de miaohui yu minjian shehui* 狂歡與日常—明清以來的廟會與民間社會 [Carnivals in daily life: Temple fairs and local society since the Ming and Qing]. Beijing: Sanlian, 2002.

Zhonggong Taiyuan shiwei siqing zongjiao bangongshi 中共太原市委四清宗教辦公室, editors. *Zongjiao gongzuo xuanchuan cailiao* 宗教工作宣傳材料 [Propaganda materials for religious work]. 1966.

Zhongguo di yi lishi dang'anguan 中國第一歷史檔案館, editors. *Qing zhongqianqi xiyang tianzhujiao zai Hua huodong dang'an shiliao* 清中前期西洋天主教在華活動檔案史料 [Historical archives relating to the activities of Western Catholics in China in the early and mid Qing]. Beijing: Zhonghua shuju, 2003.

Zhongguo di yi lishi dang'anguan 中國第一歷史檔案館 and Fujian shifan daxue lishixi 福建師範大學歷史系, editors. *Qingmo jiaoan* 清末教案 [Late Qing religious cases]. Beijing: Zhonghua shuju, 1996.

Zhongguo guomindang zhongyang weiyuanhui 中國國民黨中央委員會, editors. *Shanxi sheng de duoquan douzheng* 山西省的奪權鬥爭 [The struggle for power in Shanxi province]. Taibei, 1967.

Zhongguo renmin daxue lishi xi 中國人民大學歷史系 and Zhongguo di yi lishi dang'anguan 中國第一歷史檔案館, editors. *Qingdai nongmin zhanzheng shi ziliao xuanbian* 清代農民戰爭史資料選編 [Selected historical materials on the peasant wars of the Qing dynasty]. Beijing: Zhongguo renmin daxue chubanshe, 1984.

Zongjiao gongzuo tongxun 宗教工作通訊 [Religious work report], 1964–65.

Zhongyang yanjiuyuan jindaishi yanjiusuo 中央研究院近代史研究所, editors. *Jiaowu jiaoan dang* 教務教案檔 [Archives of religious affairs and cases]. Taibei: Zhongyang yanjiuyuan jindaishi yanjiusuo, 1974.

Zovatto, Pietro. *Storia della spiritualità italiana*. Roma: Città nuova, 2002.

Zürcher, Erik. *The Buddhist Conquest of China: The Spread and Adaptation of Buddhism in Medieval China*. Leiden: E. J. Brill, 1959.

———. "Un 'contrat communal' chrétien de la fin des Ming: Le *Livre d'Admonition* de Han Lin (1641)." In *L'Europe en Chine: Interactions scientifiques, religieuses et culturelles du XVIIᵉ et XVIIIᵉ siecles*, edited by Catherine Jami and Hubert Delahaye. Paris: Collège de France, Institut des hautes études chinoises, 1993, 3–22.

Index